Interactions II

Interactions II

A Cognitive Approach to Beginning Chinese

Jennifer Li-chia Liu   **Margaret Mian Yan**
劉力嘉   嚴棉

Illustrations by Chee Cheong Kung

Indiana University Press
Bloomington and Indianapolis

This book is a publication of

INDIANA UNIVERSITY PRESS
601 North Morton Street
Bloomington, IN 47404-3797 USA

http://www.indiana.edu/~iupress

Telephone orders 800-842-6796
Fax orders 812-855-7931
Orders by email iuporder@indiana.edu

The paper used in this publication meets the minimum
requirements of American National Standard for Information
Science—Permanence of Paper for Printed Library
Materials, ANSI Z39.48-1984.

MANUFACTURED IN THE UNITED STATES OF AMERICA

Cataloging information is available from the Library of Congress.

By Margaret Mian Yan and Jennifer Li-chia Liu
ISBN 0-253-21122-0 paperback (Interactions I)
ISBN 0-253-21202-2 paperback (Interactions I: Workbook)

By Jennifer Li-chia Liu and Margaret Mian Yan
ISBN 0-253-21123-9 paperback (Interactions II)
ISBN 0-253-21203-0 paperback (Interactions II: Workbook)
ISBN 0-253-21201-4 paperback (Interactions I & II: Teacher's Manual)

1 2 3 4 5 02 01 00 99 98

Contents

Preface   ix

Acknowledgments   xiii

A Note to Students   xv

Abbreviations   xix

Conventions   xx

Cast of Characters   xxi

Lesson		Page
14. How Was Your Winter Break?	寒假過得怎麼樣？	1
15. This Apartment Must Be Very Expensive, Right?	這個房子一定很貴吧！	29
16. Are You Used to Living Here?	你們住得還習慣嗎？	61
17. Have You Finished Taking a Bath?	你洗好澡了沒有？	91
18. Have You Ever Heard Chinese Music?	你聽過中國音樂嗎？	117
19. Which Team Won?	哪一隊贏了？	147
20. Do You Have a Fever?	你有沒有發燒？	177
21. Do You Want to Send It Regular or Express Mail?	你要寄平郵還是快信？	205
22. What Happened to My Car?	我的車怎麼不見了？	241
23. Any Plans for the Summer?	你們暑假打算做什麼？	269

Appendixes   303

1. Review of Lessons 14-18 and 19-23   304

2. Supplementary Characters (SC41-80)   318

3. Radicals   323

4. Characters with Two or More Readings   338

5. Bibliography   339

Indexes for All Lessons   341

1. Vocabulary
   By Pinyin   342
   By English   372

2. Characters
   By Pinyin   410
   By Stroke Number   416

3. Sentence Patterns   423

4. Measure Words   429

目 錄

L	Communication	Grammar	Characters Introduced
14.	Asking about a person's routine activities Asking about Christmas gift giving	The post-verbal preposition 在 Question words as indefinites The verb 給 一...就...construction Durative time expressions Verbs with extent complements The co-verb 跟	弟 常 候 第 腦 姐 身 平 動 久 鞋 媽 全 如 信 原 果 用 房
15.	Talking about a house Asking about options of payment Asking for a favor	把 construction Verbs with directional complements Place words The particle ...的話 The particle 吧 知道 vs. 認識	念 樓 邊 死 百 知 吵 空 累 付 道 進 旁 站 收 搬 左 右 把 現
16.	Giving directions Asking and giving information about an address Expressing congratulations Making a comparison	A對B有影響 / B受A的影響 又...又...construction 往 X V expression A 管 B 叫 X The usage of 幫(忙) The usage of 夠 The usage of SV 得很 把...給... construction	又 街 習 影 響 路 慣 管 容 往 受 幫 易 住 孩 夠 怕 謝 王 花
17.	Complaining Talking about one's physical appearance Talking about a person's temperament	什麼都...,就是... construction 可...,要不然... construction The conditional usage of 才 A 對 B 有意思/ 有興趣 The adverbial phrase 快/ 慢一點兒 The causative markers 害、弄 為什麼 and 因為...所以...	直 等 急 然 害 晚 慢 當 向 覺 雖 更 內 睡 思 洗 定 意 臉 澡
18.	Giving compliments Expressing modesty Making plans for the weekend	連...都... construction A 對 B 有研究 A 給 B 寄 O 來/去 More resultative verb compounds Vivid reduplicates	考 唱 新 歌 樂 研 究 音 亮 心 客 其 漂 專 氣 連 忘 實 記 尤

19.	Talking about the TV schedule Talking about sports Accepting or refusing an invitation	再過..., 就... construction Comparison of two events Comparison of two performances A 不如 B... construction The co-verb 跟 Winning prizes and awards The difference between 跟、和、也	視 贏 賽 低 發 手 輸 停 變 必 員 夜 練 拉 該 隊 昨 教 難 應
20.	Describing health problems Showing concern and giving advice	The co-verbs 叫 and 讓 The usage of 約 The preposition 從 The interrogative adverb 多 A 對 B 過敏 The adverb 只是 More on the co-verb 給 The usage of 打噴嚏 難受 vs. 難過	疼 服 法 紅 題 病 舒 藥 睛 倒 風 涼 醫 眼 屋 吹 熱 約 讓 同
21.	Expressing and correcting opinions Requesting something Giving alternative suggestions Inviting someone to come along Talking about the past Showing appreciation to a friend	The adverb 正 The co-verb 用 不但..., 而且/並且...construction Expressions of distance Comparison of distance The co-verb/verb 帶 The co-verb/verb 替	些 票 掛 機 碰 擔 郵 帶 飛 共 提 封 拿 離 馬 存 寄 替 遠 場
22.	Questioning what has happened Indicating and reacting to something wrong Giving and reacting to advice	The usage of 借 一邊兒... 一邊兒... construction The passive marker 被 The adverb 從來 The movable adverb 難道 The reduplicated adverbs 偏偏、明明	位 句 輕 辦 陪 單 改 腿 照 被 借 許 張 萬 非 求 剛 緊 千 總
23.	Talking about school Talking about future plans Showing agreement and disagreement Expressing and reacting to conjecture Stating and reacting to concerns	先...然後...construction More on 才 and 就 The Chinese concept of location VO 對 X 有幫助 The complement 不得了 The successive aspect 下去 The differences between 的、地、得	告 末 底 費 算 報 週 暑 旅 驗 本 言 息 留 經 附 語 休 妹 已

Preface

Interactions I and *II* are intended for many different kinds of beginners, who may have very diverse interests and backgrounds in pursuing Chinese as a foreign language and varying degrees of exposure to the Chinese language and culture. Whether they are real beginners or advanced beginners who are strong in one or two language skills but lack others, they will find these two learner-centered textbooks accommodating, motivating, and thought-provoking.

I. Rationales and Instructional Design

We share a number of convictions that have motivated us since we first contemplated writing a beginning Chinese textbook. First, we believe in the cognitive approach to the design of language instruction. We are convinced that effective teaching of Chinese should go beyond simply providing language stimuli and linguistic information. By focusing on students' thought processes more than on rote practice, we believe language education can promote deeper, more active and meaningful learning. Thus we seek to design a textbook that enables learners to constructively *interact* with the language. For example, we explicate grammar by offering not just linguistic rules but also conceptual principles that relate to students' existing world knowledge. We advance character memorization by providing students with writing practice of meaningful compounds, sentences, or paragraphs rather than copying characters hundreds of times over. We supply real words and compounds instead of senseless syllables to help students practice pronunciation.

Second, we believe that the process of second-language acquisition can be enhanced if learners are given a central role in language instruction. This belief is based on the tenet that language input is best delivered from the perspective of the learner rather than that of the teacher. Therefore throughout the books we attempt to cover expressions and usages that are relevant and applicable to students' lives. The lesson topics revolve around the typical events occurring in a college setting over a year. Four personas that most learners of Chinese will run into and can identify with were created—a Chinese from mainland China, another from Taiwan, a non-Chinese American, and a Chinese American.

Third, we believe that learners of Chinese should acquire natural, appropriate, and contextualized language rather than simple textbook artifacts. Students should be exposed to not only the language structure but also its dynamic use in various sociocultural contexts. We weigh the significance of "appropriateness" over that of "standard" and present Chinese in variant forms (traditional vs. simplified characters) and usages (mainland China vs. Taiwan). Guided by the criteria of naturalness and frequency of use rather than the consideration of difficulty, we develop communication-driven rather than grammar-centered texts. Although some difficult yet common high-frequency linguistic structures have to be introduced early, we remedy the problem with a recycling strategy—complicated grammatical points are reintroduced in later chapters.

Fourth, we believe that language instruction should recognize each student as an individual with various needs and learning styles. Some learners seek to practice their literacy skills, whereas others desire aural-oral practice. Some are slow-paced, while others embrace challenges. Some prefer textual presentation, but others relate well to visuals. In the textbooks we address the diversity of learners with a balanced and multimodal treatment of the four language skills. We highlight the essential information while providing additional challenges in different styles, such as explanatory notes, diagrams, tables, and graphics.

Fifth, we contend that the dimension of culture is inseparable from language instruction. Therefore we have included in each lesson important cultural information (values, attitudes, behaviors) that can enlighten learners and help them develop a deeper understanding of the Chinese people and society.

Sixth, we believe that maximum learning effects can be achieved by studying not only hard but also smart. Throughout the textbooks we provide many tools, such as conventions and icons, to help students focus on key information; different groupings of lesson vocabulary, cross-references, and indexes to facilitate review and preview of vocabulary and grammar; and illuminating graphics and thought-provoking illustrations to maintain learning interest as well as promote character recognition and retention.

II. Organization of the Text
Introductory Chapters
The books begin with three introductory lessons that offer both conceptual and learning tools for the study of Chinese. Lesson 1 gives an overview of the Chinese languages and highlights their common characteristics and major differences. Lesson 2 introduces the components of the Chinese sound system (e.g., tones, initials, and finals) and discusses related linguistic phenomena (e.g., tone sandhi, stress and intonation, and dialectal differences). Useful classroom expressions are included as well. Lesson 3 examines important concepts related to the Chinese writing system. The topics included are stroke types, stroke order, six principles of character formation, transformation of writing styles, simplification of Chinese characters, Chinese radicals, and the use of dictionaries.

Core Lessons
Following the three introductory chapters are twenty core lessons, with 4 to 13 in *Interactions I* and 14 to 23 in *Interactions II*. These chapters cover topics of everyday life and situations in which functional language is introduced naturally. Lesson 4 deals with the notion of time and introduces usages related to numbers and dates. Lesson 5 focuses on a discussion of class schedules and reinforces time usages introduced earlier. Lesson 6 further discusses school work, with particular attention to conversation openers and closure. Shopping for school materials, expressing quantities, and using monetary terms are the focus of Lesson 7. Lessons 8 through 11 talk about meeting new friends, making phone calls, dining in a restaurant, and going to a movie. Major communicative functions are introduced and key concepts and usage are recycled. Lesson 12 centers on weather and clothing and Lesson 13 on holidays.

With the start of the spring semester, Lesson 14 discusses winter break. Lesson 15, about looking for a new apartment and moving in, introduces the concept of movement and relevant usages. Lesson 16, with its topic of going to a party, brings in expressions for giving directions and making comparisons. Lesson 17 highlights daily life usages and introduces terms about a person's temperament and personality. Lessons 18 through 20 revolve around the topics of music, sports, and health, respectively. Lesson 21 has its scenes set in a post office and a bank. Lesson 22, with its topic of driving, introduces the form and function of the passive voice in Chinese. As the semester draws to its end, Lesson 23 discusses various summer plans.

Each core lesson begins with a humorous illustration that provides an attention grabber to the chapter and stimulates learners to contemplate its contents. Then comes the Dialogue, which motivates learning through the natural use of language in diverse settings. The Dialogue is intended to provide comprehensible input and exposure to natural language. Its essential communicative functions are captured in the succeeding section, the Mini-Dialogue, which can be used for memorization and as a model for the student's own skit writing and performances. In the Vocabulary, Characters, and Grammar sections that follow the Mini-Dialogue, target language uses and structures are explained with diagrams, examples, notes, and visuals. Although we put stress on providing interesting and effective devices to intrigue learners, we equally value the teaching of language structures per se. Only by firmly grasping sentence structures can one perform in a functional way. Thus in the Grammar sections, aside from conceptual principles, we incorporate contrastive analyses of Chinese and English into the explanations of structures in order to help students see the differences from various perspectives. Each lesson ends with a section of Cultural Notes that aims to provide students with Chinese do's and don'ts so that they will be able to interact appropriately with native Chinese and can gain cross-cultural awareness.

Appendixes
Five appendixes are included in each book. The first one presents review lessons which summarize major grammatical points introduced in the core lessons. The second appendix lists supplementary characters (SC) that may be of interest to students who need more reading-writing practice. It also provides additional challenges for advanced beginners. The third appendix provides a list of radicals arranged by number of strokes. The fourth appendix presents a table on characters with two or more readings. The last one supplies a bibliography of sources used in the textbooks and refers students to other important resources.

Indexes
Each book concludes with four useful indexes: (1) lesson vocabulary, (2) lesson characters, (3) sentence patterns, and (4) measure words.

By designing and writing textbooks like these, we do not claim that we have discovered a solution to all the instructional challenges that many of us deal with on a daily basis. We only attempt to tackle some of the teaching and learning issues from a new perspective and hope to share insights that have come along over the years. We hope these books will inspire many more persons to come forth and help us march into a new era with pedagogical innovations and imagination.

The Authors

Acknowledgments

This textbook project was launched by Margaret M. Yan in 1986, after it was determined that Chinese language students needed a set of good, up-to-date basic textbooks. Originally entitled "Active Chinese," it was started with a review of all available materials concerning Chinese language teaching, including textbooks, workbooks, video tapes, and computer software. The literature survey was supported by a grant from the College of Arts and Sciences of Indiana University and resulted in the precursor of our book, the introductory chapters and two conversational lessons of the "Active Chinese." In 1995, Yan invited Jennifer L. C. Liu to join her in compiling the texts, now entitled *Interactions I and II: A Cognitive Approach to Beginning Chinese*.

A project of this scope cannot succeed without institutional support and the help of many people. We would like to thank the College of Arts and Sciences of Indiana University for funding the preliminary literature review in 1986. Their support made it possible for the later collaborative work *Interactions I and II* to receive further funding for the partial editorial service and the cartoon illustrations in 1995. Special gratitude goes to Professor John Hou for his willingness to work with the drafts of these books at the 1996 Chinese School of the East Asian Summer Language Institute (EASLI) at Indiana University, as well as for his many valuable comments and suggestions. Thanks must also be extended to his students and teaching assistants as well as students and teaching assistants of 1996-97, 1997-98 First-year Chinese classes at IU who gave feedback that prompted us to perfect our books.

We would also like to thank Kenneth Goodall, Ruth I. Meserve, Virginia Harper Ho, William Moriarty, and Chih-kwang Sung for their editorial help, Chun-fang Bettina Hahn for her typing of the song Jasmine Flower, Kai-ping Hsu for writing the stroke orders of radicals, John Hollingsworth for his cartographic service, and Chang Kuang-yuan for his calligraphy of the bronze, oracle bone, and seal scripts. We thank Chee Cheong Kung for his willingness to take on the project of illustrations and to share his talents with us. His artwork has enriched our books. Thanks to Lung-sheng Sung for taking pictures for us in Taiwan and collecting relevant materials.

Jennifer Liu is especially grateful to Prof. James Chan for his inspiration during the development of this project, his excellent technical support and advice, his many comments on book layout and instructional design, as well as his generous critique of the pedagogical principles employed. She also thanks him for the wonderful electronic resources provided, which has made the creation of visuals and modification of clipart images possible. The clip arts used are from Corel Gallery by Corel Corporation (1994), ClipArt Library by Softkey International Corporation (1994), and Art Explosion 125,000 by Nova Development Corporation (1966).

Margaret Yan would like to express her sincere thanks to her mentor, the late Professor Yuen Ren Chao, of Cornell University, whose teaching and work on Chinese grammar and sound system have provided the basis and much of the inspiration for a major part of the second chapter and many grammatical points throughout the books as well as for the art of Chinese language instruction. Her hearty gratitude also goes to James H-Y. Tai for his brilliant invention of Temporal Sequence Principle (1989), which inspired her to propose the From Whole to Part Principle and the Principle of Simultaneous Existence (1993) and to apply these three conceptual principles in explaining many grammatical points in these books. If there are any errors or inadequacies in the grammar, Yan alone should be blamed for them.

Finally but not least, the patience and assistance of John Gallman, the Director of the Indiana University Press, and his staff is much appreciated.

A Note to Students

The following list captures a few essential qualities or attributes that we have found in many of our students who are successful in acquiring Chinese as a foreign language. Though everyone has his/her own unique learning style, we hope you can make the most of this beginning Chinese course with an effort to:

1. **Be active and adventurous**

   Interactions I and *II* provide you with many resources and tools. However, you cannot benefit from the rich linguistic input or the learning environment we provide unless you are actively engaged in the learning process. By "active" we mean that you have to put in cognitive efforts to organize, connect, sort, construct, or de-construct knowledge for yourself rather than relying on rote memorization of fixed rules or information supplied. As a beginner, you may be intimidated by the amount of knowledge you have to absorb or the level of skill you need to attain. You may sometimes feel like a total fool when you speak up in class. However, as long as you are willing to venture out to explore this new language and culture and use it whenever you can (e.g., greeting your classmates in Chinese, writing a note to your teacher in pinyin, etc.), you will find yourself picking up the language in good time. As long as you are not afraid of making mistakes and are willing to take initiatives to test your own hypothesis, perhaps hundreds of times, you can master Chinese some day.

   As the subtitle of our books suggests, the cognitive aspect of language learning is emphasized. We do not want you to learn the language through passive reception and memorization of presented information and rules. There are, actually, many roads leading to the success of learning Chinese if you put in your own creative efforts and take on the challenge from many different angles and perspectives. We as textbook writers can design a wonderful stage and prepare intricate props for you to act upon; however, we cannot be the lead actors and actresses that all of you are in your study and your life.

2. **Be creative and playful**

   On the same note, you need to be creative with the learning tasks at hand so that you will not fall into the trap of thinking repetition alone will make magic. This is especially true with character learning. Although the traditional way of practicing writing in China is to copy characters as many times as possible, we want to encourage you to be different. Our experience tells us that you will learn and recall characters better if you can invent your own tricks and stories that facilitate character memorization. To illustrate our points, we have provided visual mnemonics throughout the books that may help register or anchor the image of a character in your mind. Remember that you are not studying the etymology of characters, though the knowledge of a character's history may deepen your understanding of the written language. You certainly do not have to be bound by the question of how each character originated. Your concern should be on how each character means or looks to you. Thus you should take your own notes and apply characters in a meaningful context.

In addition to being as creative as possible in all of your learning tasks, you need to be playful. We have found that a lighthearted attitude will ease any embarrassment you may bring upon yourself when you start practicing tones. A sense of humor will also help you through many frustrations that are part of your everyday life when you study Chinese. Certainly, the language is difficult, but you do not have to make it harder than it needs to be. If you can make things fun and relevant to you, we are sure you will be able to handle and even enjoy the many challenges that come with the study of Chinese. On this note, we encourage you to use the lesson dialogues and mini-dialogues as models, write your own skits, and role-play them in front of your class from time to time. If possible, you should also create a macro context for your study of Chinese, i.e., find a conversation partner, a pen pal, or a Chinese friend to make your study more meaningful and interesting.

3. Be patient and realistic

By attempting to study a language as "foreign" or "difficult" as Chinese, you already possess an essential quality to be successful with your study—courage. However, there is another mindset that may contribute to your acquisition of the language: patience. This is particularly true with the study of characters if you have never been exposed to a nonalphabetic writing system before. As adult learners, you may understand and learn various grammatical structures quickly. Yet it is very unlikely that you can acquire many Chinese characters in a short time. In fact, the acquisition of characters will be painfully slow at the initial stage. You need to be patient and set a realistic goal for yourself. Your reading and writing competence probably won't progress at the same rate as your aural-oral skill. However, you should not avoid or delay the task of reading and writing and be content with your proficiency in listening and speaking.

In our books, we advocate the integrated practice of four language skills because we believe that all skills reinforce each other and because literacy skills are highly valued and respected in Chinese society. However, we also understand that the written language puts an enormous burden on students. Therefore we highlight twenty characters in each lesson to help you focus your study. We also enrich the vocabulary section with many useful and relevant lexical items so that you have enough words to communicate aural-orally in Chinese. If you prioritize the learning tasks and do not expect to "cram," over time you will acquire a base on which you can rapidly build and refine important skills in the future.

4. Be disciplined and flexible

The study of Chinese will test not only your patience but also your perseverance. You may be patient and realistic in terms of the goals you set for yourself. However, you also need to be disciplined in terms of the approach you take to studying the language. Using the study of characters as an example, if you want to learn twenty characters over five days, you have to study four per day; better still, you need to build a system of review for yourself. Without a disciplined approach, you will find yourself spending much time ineffectively and not making the most of your study. Passion and enthusiasm may get you started in your study of Chinese; however, it takes discipline to get you to the level of proficiency you desire.

You need to be aware that discipline does not imply that you have to be rigid. Rather, we encourage you to be flexible, especially in arranging your study schedule. Instead of spending three straight hours studying Chinese, it may be more effective for you to practice the language for shorter periods two or three times per day, making use of the odd hours that many of us find when we wait for a bus or a class, when we take an afternoon break, when we retire in the evening, etc.

5. Be tolerant and receptive

To be able to study Chinese well, it is also crucial for you to be tolerant of and receptive to differences, be they linguistic or cultural. You may feel disoriented or confused at the beginning, given the amount of differences between your native language and Chinese. And it is more than natural that you resort to your own culture and use it as a frame of reference to understand and interpret Chinese ways. Eventually you want to see things in the light of Chinese people and to obtain an insider's perspective. In this regard, our cultural notes may offer some assistance. You will certainly add many more notes of your own as you make contact with Chinese people and their culture.

It is important that you be tolerant not only of differences but also of ambiguities. In other words, it is best for you to study a lexical item or a grammatical structure in its context and to accept the fuzziness that sometimes comes with it. We have seen students who are so concerned with every single detail at each step of their study that their general comprehension suffers because of their hair-splitting efforts. If you can analyze the Chinese language system, that is fine. Yet it will prove to be far more productive if you learn to take in chunk of information rather than isolated details. The more you study Chinese, the better you will understand the significance of contextual cues, which play an important role in the use of this language.

6. **Be resourceful and responsive**

We can offer only a few general suggestions to guide your study of Chinese and provide only a limited number of exercises to help reinforce and consolidate your skills and understanding. You need to be resourceful and responsive to the questions and problems that emerge during your study of Chinese. You need to apply different learning strategies to various tasks and to identify or invent options and means to apply, internalize, and acquire this new language.

Abbreviations

Adj	Adjective	形容詞	xíngróngcí
Adv	Adverb	副詞	fùcí
Asp	Aspect Suffix	體貌詞尾	tǐmàocíwěi
AuxV	Auxiliary Verb	助動詞	zhùdòngcí
Comp	Complement	補語	bǔyǔ
Conj	Conjunction	連詞	liáncí
CV	Co-verb	輔動詞	fǔdòngcí
Dem	Demonstrative	指示詞	zhǐshìcí
Det	Determinative	定詞	dìngcí
EV	Equative Verb	對等動詞	duìděngdòngcí
Inter	Interjection	嘆詞	tàncí
IE	Idiomatic Expression	成語/習慣用語	chéngyǔ/xíguàn yòngyǔ
Loc	Localizer	方位詞	fāngwèicí
M	Measure Word	量詞	liàngcí
MA	Movable Adverb	可移副詞	kěyí fùcí
MTA	Movable Time Adverb	可移時間副詞	kěyí shíjiān fùcí
N	Noun	名詞	míngcí
Neg	Negative	否定詞	fǒudìngcí
No	Number	數詞	shùcí
NP	Noun Phrase	名詞	míngcí
O	Object	名詞詞組	míngcí cízǔ
O_d/O_i	Direct/indirect Object	直接/間接賓語	zhíjiē/jiānjiē bīnyǔ
Part	Particle	語助詞	yǔzhùcí
Place	Place Word	地方詞	dìfāngcí
Poss	Possesive	所有格	suǒyǒugé
PP	Prepositional Phrase	介詞詞組	jiècícízǔ
Pref	Prefix	詞頭	cítóu
P(rep)	Preposition	介詞	jiècí
Prog	Progressive Suffix	進行式詞尾	jìnxíngshì cíwěi
Pron	Pronoun	代名詞	dàimíngci
QW	Question Word	疑問詞	yíwèncí
QP	Question Particle	疑問語助詞	yíwèn yǔzhùcí
RE	Resultative Verb Ending	結果動詞補語	jiéguǒ dòngcí búyǔ
RV	Resultative Verb	結果動詞	jiéguǒ dòngcí
S	Subject	主詞	zhǔcí
SN	Surname	姓	xìng
Suf	Suffix	詞尾	cíwěi
SV	Stative Verb	靜態動詞	jìngtài dòngcí
TW	Time Word	時間詞	shíjiāncí
V	Verb	動詞	dòngcí
VO	Verb-Object Compound	動賓複詞	dòngbīn fùcí

Conventions

◎	This icon marks two subsections of Vocabulary in each lesson —one groups new words by their order of appearance in the main dialogue and the other by their grammatical categories.
✚	This icon introduces the subsection Supplementary Vocabulary in each lesson.
*	This symbol, in front of entries in the Vocabulary and Characters sections, calls the learner's attention to lexical items not used in the main dialogues but relevant to those used and possibly of interest for further study.
Ⓐ	This icon points out the first Grammar subsection, Major Sentence Patterns.
Ⓑ	This icon points out the second Grammar subsection, Usage of Common Phrases.
Ⓒ	This icon points out the third Grammar subsection, Reentry, the review of some major sentence patterns.
💡	This icon marks essential information and concise explanations for grammatical points.
↻	This icon indicates cross-references to grammatical points.
✗	This icon calls attention to commonly made errors or incorrect sentence formation.
👥	This icon, pointing to various mini-dialogues, highlights the major communication functions in each lesson.
今 jīn now 4 人 (person)	character the pronunciation of the character the meaning of the character the stroke number of the character radical the meaning of the radical

Cast of Characters
人物表 Rénwùbiǎo

高德中

高德中	David Gore (Gāo Dézhōng)	
美國人	Měiguórén	American
研究生	Yánjiūshēng	Graduate student
專業：比較文學	Zhuānyè: bǐjiǎo wénxué	Major: Comparative Literature
年紀：二十七歲	Niánjì: èrshíqī suì	Age: 27
性別：男	Xìngbié: nán	Sex: male
個性：穩重、老實	Gèxìng: wěnzhòng, lǎoshí	Personality: focused
愛好：讀書、看電影	Aìhào: dúshū, kàn diànyǐng	Hobbies: studying, watching movies

李明

李明	Lǐ Míng	
中國人（大陸）	Zhōngguórén	Chinese (from the mainland)
大學生（大三）	Dàxuéshēng (dà sān)	Undergraduate (junior)
專業：商學	Zhuānyè: shāngxué	Major: Business
年紀：二十二歲	Niánjì: èrshí'èr suì	Age: 22
性別：男	Xìngbié: nán	Sex: male
個性：外向、好動	Gèxìng: wàixiàng, hàodòng	Personality: outgoing
愛好：旅行、拍照、美食	Aìhào: lǚxíng, pāizhào, měishí	Hobbies: traveling, photography, food

林美英

林美英	Lín Měiyīng	
華裔美國人	Huáyì Měiguórén	Chinese American
大學生（大二）	Dàxuéshēng (dà'èr)	Undergraduate (sophomore)
專業：音樂	Zhuānyè: yīnyuè	Major: Music
年紀：二十歲	Niánjì: èrshí suì	Age: 20
性別：女	Xìngbié: nǚ	Sex: female
個性：外向、活潑	Gèxìng: wàixiàng, huópō	Personality: outgoing, active
愛好：唱歌、跳舞、運動	Aìhào: chànggē, tiàowǔ, yùndòng	Hobbies: singing, dancing, exercising

王華

王華	Wáng Huá	
中國人（台灣）	Zhōngguórén (Táiwān)	Chinese (from Taiwan)
大學生（大一）	Dàxuéshēng (dà'yī)	Undergraduate (freshman)
專業：電腦	Zhuānyè: diànnǎo	Major: Computer Science
年紀：十九歲	Niánjì: shíjiǔ suì	Age: 19
性別：女	Xìngbié: nǚ	Sex: female
個性：內向、文靜	Gèxìng: nèixiàng, wénjìng	Personality: reserved
愛好：看電視、球賽	Aìhào: kàn diànshì, qiúsài	Hobbies: watching TV, playing sports

第十四課　寒假過得怎麼樣？

對話	2 頁
小對話	9 頁
生詞	10 頁
漢字	15 頁
語法	21 頁
文化點滴	28 頁

對話

〔寒假剛過，小李在街上蹼到小林和小王。〕

小李：嘿！好久不見！

小林：好久不見！寒假過
　　　得怎麼樣？有沒有
　　　上哪兒去玩兒？

小李：哪兒也都沒去，待
　　　在宿舍裏。天天睡
　　　懶覺真好！利用假
　　　期正好給我父母寫信，免得他們擔心。

小王：可不是嗎？一開學就寫不了了。上個學期我有時候忙起來
　　　，一個月才打一次電話回家。

小李：長途電話太貴了。電話裏也說不了什麼。如果有時間，還
　　　是寫信好。寒假的時候，你也待在這兒嗎？怎麼我沒看見
　　　你呢？

小王：我到美國朋友家過耶誕節了。他們真有意思，一家人在一
　　　塊兒，不是吃東西，就是看電視。

小林：那不是正合你的「胃口」嗎？

小王：才不呢！他們還帶我到山上去滑雪，好玩兒極了！那是我第一次看見雪。可是才滑了一個小時的雪，我就全身酸痛，累得走不動了。

小林：你看，平常整天對著電腦、電視，動一下就不行了。明天跟我上體育館去吧！

小王：你剛回來，不要立刻給我「機會教育」。說說你自己的寒假吧！

小林：我們全家人：爸爸、媽媽、大姐、小弟和我都在一塊兒過耶誕節。我收到四份兒禮物：一個雷射唱盤、一條牛仔褲、一件毛衣和一雙球鞋。

小王：難怪你要去體育館鍛練了。原來是有了新鞋。

小林：你那麼喜歡看籃球、說籃球，「光說不練」怎麼行？

小李：好了！好了！兩位小姐，別吵了。我看你們不是要上哪兒去嗎？

小王：我們打算搬到校外去，正想去看房子呢！

对话

〔寒假刚过，小李在街上碰到小林和小王。〕

小李：嘿！好久不见！

小林：好久不见！寒假过得怎么样？有没有上哪儿去玩儿？

小李：哪儿也都没去，待在宿舍里。天天睡懒觉真好！利用假期正好给我父母写信，免得他们担心。

小王：可不是吗？一开学就写不了了。上个学期我有时候忙起来，一个月才打一次电话回家。

小李：长途电话太贵了。电话里也说不了什么。如果有时间，还是写信好。寒假的时候，你也待在这儿吗？怎么我没看见你呢？

小王：我到美国朋友家过耶诞节了。他们真有意思，一家人在一块儿，不是吃东西，就是看电视。

小林：那不是正合你的「胃口」吗？

小王：才不呢！他们还带我到山上去滑雪，好玩儿极了！那是我第一次看见雪。可是才滑了一个小时的雪，我就全身酸痛，累得走不动了。

小林：你看，平常整天对着电脑、电视，动一下就不行了。明天跟我上体育馆去吧！

小王：你刚回来，不要立刻给我「机会教育」。说说你自己的寒假吧！

小林：我们全家人：爸爸、妈妈、大姐、小弟和我都在一块儿过耶诞节。我收到四份儿礼物：一个雷射唱盘、一条牛仔裤、一件毛衣和一双球鞋。

小王：难怪你要去体育馆锻炼了。原来是有了新鞋。

小林：你那么喜欢看篮球、说篮球，「光说不练」怎么行？

小李：好了！好了！两位小姐，别吵了。我看你们不是要上哪儿去吗？

小王：我们打算搬到校外去，正想去看房子呢！

My questions:

Duìhuà

(Hánjià gāng guò. Xiǎo Lǐ zài jiē .shàng pèng.dào Xiǎo Lín hé Xiǎo Wáng.)

Xiǎo Lǐ: Hèi! Hǎo jiǔ bú jiàn.

Xiǎo Lín: Hǎo jiǔ bú jiàn! Hánjià guò.de zěn.meyàng? Yǒu
              méi.yǒu shàng nǎr qù wánr?

Xiǎo Lǐ: Nǎr yě dōu méi qù, dāi zài sùshè .lǐ. Tiāntiān
              shuǐlǎnjiào zhēn hǎo. Lìyòng jiàqī zhènghǎo gěi wǒ
              fùmǔ xiěxìn, miǎn.de tā.men dānxīn.

Xiǎo Wáng: Kě bú.shì .ma? Yì kāixué jiù xiě.buliǎo .le. Shàng .ge
              xuéqī wǒ yǒushí.hòu máng.qǐ.lái yí .ge yuè cái
              dǎ yí cì diànhuà huíjiā.

Xiǎo Lǐ::   Chángtú diànhuà tài guì .le. Diànhuà .lǐ yě shuō.buliǎo shén.me.
              Rúguǒ yǒushíjiān hái.shì xiěxìn hǎo. Hánjià .de shí.hòu, nǐ yě dāi zài
              zhèr .ma? Zěn.me wǒ méi kàn.jiàn nǐ .ne?

Xiǎo Wáng: Wǒ dào Měi.guó péng.yǒu jiā guò Yēdànjié .le. Tā.men zhēn
              yǒuyì.si. Yì jiā rén zài yíkuàir, bú.shì chī dōng.xī, jiù.shì kàn diànshì.

Xiǎo Lín: Nà bú.shì zhèng hé nǐ .de "wèikǒu" .ma?

Xiǎo Wáng: Cái bù .ne! Tā.men hái dài wǒ dào shān .shàng qù huáxuě, hǎowánr jí
              .le! Nà shì wǒ dìyí cì kàn.jiàn xuě. Kě.shì cái huá .le yí .ge xiǎoshí
              .de xuě, wǒ jiù quánshēn suāntòng, lèi .de zǒu.budòng .le.

Xiǎo Lín: Nǐ kàn, píngcháng zhěngtiān duì.zhe diànnǎo diànshì, dòng.yíxià jiù bù
              xíng .le. Míng.tiān gēn wǒ shàng tǐyùguǎn qù .ba!

Xiǎo Wáng: Nǐ gāng huí.lái, bú yào lìkè gěi wǒ "jīhuì jiàoyù." Shuō.shuō nǐ zìjǐ .de
              hánjià .ba!

Xiǎo Lín: Wǒ.men quán jiā rén: bà.bà, mā.mā, dàjiě, xiǎodì, hé wǒ dōu zài yíkuàir
              guò Yēdànjié. Wǒ shōu.dào sì fènr lǐwù: yí .ge léishè chàngpán, yì tiáo
              niúzǎikù, yí jiàn máoyī, hé yì shuāng qiúxié.

Xiǎo Wáng: Nánguài nǐ yào qù tǐyùguǎn duàn.liàn .le. Yuánlái shì yǒu .le xīnxié.

Xiǎo Lín: Nǐ nà.me xǐ.huān kàn lánqiú, shuō lánqiú, "guāng shuō bú liàn" zěn.me
              xíng?

Xiǎo Lǐ: Hǎo.le, hǎo.le. Liǎng wèi xiǎo.jiě, bié chǎo .le. Wǒ
              kàn nǐ.men bú.shì yào shàng nǎr qù .ma?

Xiǎo Wáng: Wǒ.men dǎsuàn bān.dào xiàowài qù, zhèng xiǎng qù
              kàn fáng.zi .ne!

Dialogue

(Just after winter break, Xiǎo Lǐ runs into Xiǎo Lín and Xiǎo Wáng on the street.)

Xiǎo Lǐ:　　Hey! Long time no see!

Xiǎo Lín:　　Long time no see! How was your winter break? Did you go anywhere for fun?

Xiǎo Lǐ:　　I didn't go anywhere. I stayed in the dorm. It's really nice to get up late every day. I took advantage of the break to write to my parents, so that they wouldn't be worried.

Xiǎo Wáng:　　Isn't that so? Once school starts, you cannot write. Last semester sometimes I was so busy that I called home only once a month.

Xiǎo Lǐ:　　Long-distance calls are too expensive. You can't talk about much on the phone. If you have time, it's better to write letters. During the break, did you stay here, too? How come I didn't see you?

Xiǎo Wáng:　　I went to my American friends' place to spend Christmas. They were really interesting. The whole family got together; if they weren't eating, they were watching TV.

Xiǎo Lín:　　Isn't that what you wanted?

Xiǎo Wáng:　　No! They also took me to a mountain to ski. It was a lot of fun. That was the first time I saw snow. Yet after skiing for just an hour, I was sore all over. I was so tired that I couldn't walk.

Xiǎo Lín:　　See! You are always in front of the computer or TV all day long. You can't even do a little exercise. Come with me to the gym tomorrow.

Xiǎo Wáng:　　You just came back. Don't give me an "on-the-spot lecture." Tell me about your winter break.

Xiǎo Lín:　　Our whole family, father, mother, big sister, younger brother, and I all got together for Christmas. I got four gifts: one laser disc, one pair of jeans, one sweater, and a pair of tennis shoes.

Xiǎo Wáng:　　No wonder you want to go to the gym to work out. It's because you have a new pair of shoes.

Xiǎo Lín: You like to watch and talk about basketball so much, how could you just "talk and not play"?

Xiǎo Lǐ: All right, all right. Don't quarrel, ladies. I thought you were going to go somewhere, weren't you?

Xiǎo Wáng: We plan to move off campus, (so) we just want to look at houses!

Mini-Dialogue
小對話 Xiǎoduìhuà

Asking about a person's routine activities

1. A: 你寒假裏做了些什麼了呢？

   Nǐ hánjià .lǐ zuò .le xiē shén.me .le .ne?

   What did you do during the winter break?

   B: 每天早上睡懶覺，下午看看書，晚上寫寫信。

   Měitiān zǎo.shàng shuìlǎnjiào, xià.wǔ kàn.kàn shū, wǎn.shàng xiě.xiě xìn.

   I slept late every morning, read books in the afternoon, and wrote letters in the evening.

2. A: 你每天都做些什麼呢？

   Nǐ měitiān dōu zuò xiē shén.me .ne?

   What do you do everyday?

   B: 我平常每天早上上課，下午打電腦或者上體育館鍛練，晚上就看電視。

   Wǒ píngcháng měitiān zǎo.shàng shàngkè, xià.wǔ dǎ diànnǎo huò.zhě shàng tǐyùguǎn duàn.liàn, wǎn.shàng jiù kàn diànshì.

   I usually go to class in the morning, work on the computer or go to the gym to do exercise in the afternoon, then watch TV in the evening.

Asking about Christmas gift giving

1. A: 今年聖誕節你要送給你爸爸媽媽什麼禮物呢？

   Jīn.nián Shèngdànjié nǐ yào sòng gěi nǐ bà.bà mā.mā shén.me lǐwù .ne?

   What gifts are you going to give to your parents this Christmas?

   B: 今年我要送給我爸爸一雙球鞋，送媽媽一件毛衣。

   Jīn.nián wǒ yào sòng gěi wǒ bà.bà yì shuāng qiúxié, sòng mā.mā yí jiàn máoyī.

   I am going to give my father a pair of sneakers (and) my mother a sweater.

Vocabulary
生詞 Shēngcí

◎ **By Order of Appearance**

寒假		hánjià	N	[cold-holiday] winter vacation
好久不見		hǎo jiǔ bú jiàn	IE	[good-long time-no-see] (= 很久不見) I haven't seen ... for a long time
* 多久		duójiǔ	QW	[much-long] how long
玩		wán	V	to play
待		dāi	V	to stay
睡懶覺	睡懒觉	shuìlǎnjiào	VO	[sleep-lazy-sleep] to get up late
* 睡覺	睡觉	shuìjiào	VO	[sleep-sleep] to sleep
假期		jiàqī	N	[holiday-period] holiday, vacation
寫信	写信	xiěxìn	VO	[write-letter] to write a letter
免得		miǎn.de	V	[avoid-Part] to avoid, so as not to…
擔心	担心	dānxīn	V	[to shoulder-heart] to worry
一…就…		yī…jiù…	Conj	[one-then] as soon as
寫不了	写不了	xiě.buliǎo	RV	[write-not-finish] (to be) unable to write
有時候	有时候	yǒushí.hòu	Adv	[have-time] sometimes
-起來	-起来	-.qǐ.lái	RE	[-rise-come] to start (an action)
長途	长途	chángtú	N	[long-road] long distance
說不了	说不了	shuō.buliǎo	RV	[say-not-finish] (to be) unable to say
如果		rúguǒ	Conj	[as-result] if (= 要是)
看見	看见	kàn.jiàn	V	[see-see] to see, catch sight of
耶誕節	耶诞节	Yēdànjié	N	[Jesus-birth-festival] Christmas (M: 個)
* 聖誕節	圣诞节	Shèngdànjié	N	[Saint-birth-festival] Christmas (M: 個) (=耶誕節)
一家人		yì jiā rén	N	[family-people] the whole family
合		hé	V	to suit, fit
才不呢		cái bù .ne	IE	no!
呢		.ne	Part	particle for sarcastic retort
帶	带	dài	V	to bring along; to carry; to lead; to train
山		shān	N	mountain (M: 座 zuò)
滑雪		huáxuě	VO	[slip-snow] to ski
好玩兒	好玩儿	hǎowánr	SV	[good-play] (to be) fun
雪		xuě	N	snow
全		quán	Adj	complete, whole

酸痛		suāntòng	SV	[sour-pain] (to be) sore, (muscle) ache
走不動	走不动	zǒu.budòng	RV	[walk-not-move] (to be) too tired to walk
平常		píngcháng	Adv/ SV	ordinarily, usually, (to be) ordinary, (to be) usual
整天		zhěngtiān	N	[entire-day] all day long
對著	对着	duì.zhe	V	[face to-Prog] (to be) facing
跟...去/來	跟...去/来	gēn...qù/lái	PP	[follow...go/come] to follow...to (there/here)
體育館	体育馆	tǐyùguǎn	N	[body-education-hall] gym (M: 個) (=健身房)
剛	刚	gāng	Adv	just a moment ago
立刻		lìkè	Adv	[stand-quarter-time] immediately
機會教育	机会教育	jīhuì jiàoyù	N	[opportunity-education] on-the-spot lecture
姐姐		jiě.jiě	N	[older sister-older sister] older sister
弟弟		dì.dì	N	[younger brother-younger brother] younger brother
收到		shōu.dào	RV	[receive-arrive] to receive
* 送(給)	送(给)	sòng(gěi)	V	[send-give] to present as a gift
份兒	份儿	fēnr	M	measure word for gifts and newspapers
禮物	礼物	lǐwù	N	[ritual-thing] gift, present (M: 個)
雷射唱盤	雷射唱盘	léishè chàngpán	N	[thunder-shot-sing-saucer] laser disc (M: 個)
牛仔褲	牛仔裤	niúzǎikù	N	[cow-child-pants] jeans (M: 條)
球鞋		qiúxié	N	[ball-shoes] athletic shoes, sneakers (M: 雙/隻)
難怪	难怪	nánguài	Adv	[difficult-blame] no wonder
那麼	那么	nà.me	Adv	so (as that)
光		guāng	Adv	just
小姐		xiǎo.jiě	N	[small-elder sister] miss, young lady
吵(架)		chǎo(jià)	V(O)	to argue
打算		dǎsuàn	V/N	to plan, a plan
搬到		bān.dào	V	to move to
* 搬		bān	V	to move
校外		xiàowài	N	[school-outside] off campus
房子		fáng.zi	N	[house-Suf] house (M: 所/個)

◎ By Grammatical Categories

Nouns/Pronouns

寒假		hánjià	N	[cold-holiday] winter vacation
假期		jiàqī	N	[holiday-period] holiday, vacation
耶誕節	耶诞节	Yēdànjié	N	[Jesus-birth-festival] Christmas (M: 個)
* 聖誕節	圣诞节	Shèngdànjié	N	[Saint-birth-festival] Christmas (M: 個) (=耶誕節)
長途	长途	chángtú	N	[long-road] long distance
整天		zhěngtiān	N	[entire-day] all day long
一家人		yì jiā rén	N	[family-people] the whole family
姐姐		jiě.jiě	N	[older sister-older sister] older sister
弟弟		dì.dì	N	[younger brother-younger brother] younger brother
小姐		xiǎo.jiě	N	[small-elder sister] miss, young lady
禮物	礼物	lǐwù	N	[ritual-thing] gift, present (M: 個)
雷射唱盤	雷射唱盘	léishè chàngpán	N	[thunder-shot-sing-saucer] laser disc (M: 個)
牛仔褲	牛仔裤	niúzǎikù	N	[cow-child-pants] jeans (M: 條)
球鞋		qiúxié	N	[ball-shoes] athletic shoes, sneakers (M: 雙 / 隻)
山		shān	N	mountain (M: 座 zuò)
雪		xuě	N	snow
體育館	体育馆	tǐyùguǎn	N	[body-education-hall] gym (M: 個) (=健身房)
房子		fáng.zi	N	[house-Suf] house (M: 所/個)
校外		xiàowài	N	[school-outside] off campus
機會教育	机会教育	jīhuì jiàoyù	N	[opportunity-education] on-the-spot lecture

Measure Words

份兒	份儿	fènr	M	measure word for gifts and newspapers

Verbs/Stative Verbs/Adjectives

玩		wán	V	to play
待		dāi	V	to stay
合		hé	V	to suit, fit
帶	带	dài	V	to bring along; to carry; to lead; to train
免得		miǎn.de	V	[avoid-Part] to avoid, so as not to…
擔心	担心	dānxīn	V	[to shoulder-heart] to worry

看見	看见	kàn.jiàn	V	[see-see] to see, catch sight of
對著	对着	duì.zhe	V	[face to-Prog] (to be) facing
打算		dǎsuàn	V/N	to plan, a plan
搬到		bān.dào	V	to move to
* 搬		bān	V	to move
睡懶覺	睡懒觉	shuìlǎnjiào	VO	[sleep-lazy-sleep] to get up late
* 睡覺	睡觉	shuìjiào	VO	[sleep-sleep] to sleep
寫信	写信	xiěxìn	VO	[write-letter] to write a letter
滑雪		huáxuě	VO	[slip-snow] to ski
吵(架)		chǎo(jià)	V(O)	to argue
* 送(給)	送(给)	sòng(gěi)	V	[send-give] to present as a gift
收到		shōu.dào	RV	[receive-arrive] to receive
寫不了	写不了	xiě.buliǎo	RV	[write-not-finish] (to be) unable to write
說不了	说不了	shuō.buliǎo	RV	[say-not-finish] (to be) unable to say
走不動	走不动	zǒu.budòng	RV	[walk-not-move] (to be) too tired to walk
-起來	-起来	-.qǐ.lái	RE	[-rise-come] to start (an action)
好玩兒	好玩儿	hǎowánr	SV	[good-play] (to be) fun
酸痛		suāntòng	SV	[sour-pain] (to be) sore, (muscle) ache
全		quán	Adj	complete, whole
跟…去/來	跟…去/来	gēn…qù/lái	PP	[follow…go/come] to follow…to (there/here)

Adverbs

有時候	有时候	yǒushí.hòu	Adv	[have-time] sometimes
平常		píngcháng	Adv/SV	ordinarily, usually, (to be) ordinary, (to be) usual
難怪	难怪	nánguài	Adv	[difficult-blame] no wonder
那麼	那么	nà.me	Adv	so (as that)
立刻		lìkè	Adv	[stand-quarter-time] immediately
剛	刚	gāng	Adv	just a moment ago
光		guāng	Adv	just

Conjunctions

一…就 …		yī…jiù…	Conj	[one-then] as soon as
如果		rúguǒ	Conj	[as-result] if (=要是)

Particles

| 呢 | .ne | Part | particle for sarcastic retort |

Question Words

| * 多久 | duójiǔ | QW | [much-long] how long |

Idiomatic Expressions

| 好久不見 | hǎo jiǔ bú jiàn | IE | [good-long time-no-see] (=很久不見) I haven't seen … for a long time |
| 才不呢 | cái bù .ne | IE | no! |

✚ Supplementary Vocabulary

1. Odds and Ends

| 國際 | 国际 | guójì | Adj | [country-border] international |
| 國內 | 国内 | guónèi | Adj | [country-inside] domestic |

2. American Holidays

暑假		shǔjià	N	[summer-holiday] summer vacation
春假		chūnjià	N	[spring-holiday] spring vacation
節日	节日	jiérì	N	[festival-day] festival
情人節	情人节	Qíngrénjié	N	[affection-person-festival] Valentine's Day
愚人節	愚人节	Yúrénjié	N	[fool-person-festival] April Fool's Day
國慶	国庆	Guóqìng	N	[country-celebrate] the National Day
復活節	复活节	Fùhuójié	N	[restore-live-festival] Easter
萬聖節	万圣节	Wànshèngjié	N	[ten thousand-saints-festival] Halloween

3. Religion

耶穌		Yēsū	N	[Part-revive] Jesus
基督		Jīdū	N	[foundation-supervise] Christ
神		Shén	N	God
上帝		Shàngdì	N	[above-emperor] God
聖母		Shèngmǔ	N	[saint-mother] the Holy Mother

Characters
漢字 Hànzì

爸	媽	姐	弟
全	身	平	常
如	果	動	腦
信	用	久	候
原	房	鞋	第

爸

bà
dad   父
8   (father)

爸爸   bà.bà   father

A: 你**爸爸**是中學老師嗎？
B: 不是，他在大學教書。

媽

mā
mom   女
13   (female)

媽媽   mā.mā   mother

A: 你家有幾個人？
B: 三個，爸爸、**媽媽**，還有我。

姐

jiě
elder sister   女
8   (female)

姐姐   jiě.jiě   elder sister
小姐   xiǎo.jiě   Miss, young lady
*大姐   dàjiě   eldest sister
*二姐   èrjiě   second eldest sister

A: 你今天打算做什麼？
B: 我要給我**姐姐**寫信。

弟

dì
younger brother
           弓
7   (a bow)

弟弟   dì.dì   younger brother
*大弟   dàdì   eldest younger brother
*二弟   èrdì   second eldest younger
                         brother
*小弟   xiǎodì   youngest brother

A: 你有**弟弟**沒有？
B: 沒有，我們家就我、爸爸、媽媽三個
   人。

繁簡對照：	其他漢字：	✎ **My notes:**
媽妈	妹 L23 *哥 SC41	

全

quán
perfect, entire
入
6　　(to enter)

全身	quánshēn	all over the body
*全國	quánguó	the whole nation
*全班	quánbān	the whole class
*全世界	quánshìjiè	the whole world

A: 我**全身**酸疼。
B: 誰叫你平常不鍛練？

身

shēn
body
身
7　　(body)

身上	shēn.shàng	on the body; on the lap

A: 你**身上**有沒有錢，能不能借我二十塊？
B: 我只有十塊。

平

píng
flat, ordinary 干
5　　(to offend,
　　　　a stem)

平常	píngcháng	ordinarily, commonly
*公平	gōngpíng	(to be) fair
*水平	shuǐpíng	level

A: 你現在能不能看中文報？
B: 還不能，我才學了一年的中文，**水平**不夠高。

常

cháng
common, often
巾
8　　(towel)

*常常	chángcháng	often
*非常	fēicháng	extremely

A: 你**平常**每天看多久的電視？
B: 我**平常**每天看兩個小時的電視。

繁簡對照：	其他漢字：	**My notes:**

如果　　　　rúguǒ　　　　　　if

如

rú
if, as if,
supposing　女
6　　(female)

A: 你今天**如果**有時間的話，應該去看看
　　小王，聽說他不舒服。
B: 我今天没空兒，明天才有時間。

*水果　　　shuǐguǒ　　　　　fruit

果

guǒ
fruit, result,
outcome　木
8　　(tree)

A: **如果**你有錢的話，你打算做什麼？
B: 我要搬到校外住，請一個中國廚子，
　　天天做中國飯給我吃。

走不動　　zǒu.budòng　　　(to be) too tired to walk
*動手　　dòngshǒu　　　　to start work
*動身　　dòngshēn　　　　to go on a journey

動

dòng
to move, act,
change　力
11　　(power)

A: 你怎麼了？
B: 我昨天滑了一整天的雪，現在累得**走
不動**了。

電腦　　　diànnǎo　　　　　computer
*腦子　　nǎo.zi　　　　　　brain

腦

nǎo
brain　　月
9　　(flesh)

A: 你整天對著**電腦**，難怪沒有時間鍛煉。
B: 才不呢！我每天都上體育館。

繁簡對照：	其他漢字：	✎ **My notes:**
動动 腦脑	*運 SC42 *肚 SC43 頭 L12	

信

xìn
to believe; letter
亻
9 (person)

寫信	xiěxìn	to write letters
*寄信	jìxìn	to send letters
*信封	xìnfēng	envelope
*信紙	xìnzhǐ	letter paper

A: 你寒假過得怎麼樣?
B: 還不錯,我待在宿舍裏,給家人朋友**寫寫信**。

用

yòng
to use
用
5 (to use)

利用	lìyòng	to utilize, to use
*有用	yǒuyòng	useful
*沒用	méiyòng	useless
*好用	hǎoyòng	easy to use

A: 下星期就是小王的生日了,你禮物買好了沒有?
B: 還沒有,我想**利用**這個週末出去看看。

久

jiǔ
for a long time,
long
丿
3

多久	duójiǔ	how long
好久不見	hǎo jiǔ bú jiàn	I haven't seen you for a long time
*好久	hǎo jiǔ	very long

A: 你**多久**沒給爸爸媽媽寫信了?
B: 三個月吧!

候

hòu
to wait, to
expect
亻
10 (person)

| *時候 | shí.hòu | time |
| *什麼時候 | shén.me shí.hòu | what time? when? |

A: 我們**什麼時候**放春假?
B: 期中考以後吧。

繁簡對照:	其他漢字:	✎ **My notes:**
	*雨 SC44 *雪 SC45	

原

原來	yuánlái	originally
*原因	yuányīn	cause, reason
*原文	yuánwén	original text

yuán
original, former
厂
10

A: 我剛買了一雙球鞋。
B: 難怪你要去鍛煉了，**原來**是有了新鞋。

房

房子	fáng.zi	house
*房間	fángjiān	room
*房東	fángdōng	landlord, landlady

fáng
house, building,
room   戶
8   (door)

A: 你們上哪兒去？
B: 我們打算搬到校外住，正要去看**房子**。

鞋

球鞋	qiúxié	sneakers
*鞋子	xié.zi	shoes
*皮鞋	píxié	leather shoes

xié
shoe   革
15   (leather)

A: **那雙鞋**怎麼樣？
B: 看起來不錯，可是穿起來不太舒服。

第

第一	dìyī	first
第二	dì'èr	second
第三	dìsān	third

dì
ordinal prefix
竹
11   (bamboo)

A: 你們這個星期上**第幾課**？
B: 我們這個星期上**第十四課**。

繁簡對照：	其他漢字：	✎ **My notes:**
	屋 L20	
	*雙 SC46	

Grammar
語法 yǔfǎ

Ⓐ Major Sentence Patterns 主要句型 zhǔyào jùxíng

1. The post-verbal preposition 在

Structure	Gloss
S (不)(要/想/喜歡) V₁ 在 Place (V₂O₂)	S (AuxV) V₁ at Place (V₂ O₂)

1. 寒假的時候他想待在哪兒？

   Hánjià .de shí.hòu tā xiǎng dāi zài nǎr?
   Where does he want to stay during the winter break?

   寒假的時候他想待在宿舍裏。

   Hánjià .de shí.hòu tā xiǎng dāi zài sùshè .li.
   He would like to stay in the dorm during the winter break.

2. 你以後想住在什麼地方？

   Nǐ yǐhòu xiǎng zhù zài shén.me dì.fāng?
   Where do you want to live in the future?

   我以後想住在西部。

   Wǒ yǐhòu xiǎng zhù zài xībù.
   I would like to live on the West Coast in the future.

3. 你要坐在哪兒看他滑雪？

   Nǐ yào zuò zài nǎr kàn tā huáxuě?
   Where would you like to sit to watch him ski?

   我要坐在山上看他滑雪，不要坐在這兒看他滑雪。

   Wǒ yào zuò zài shān .shàng kàn tā huáxuě, bú yào zuò zài zhèr kàn tā huáxuě.
   I would like to sit on the mountain to watch him ski; (I) don't want to sit here to watch him ski.

4. 他喜歡躺在哪兒看電視？

   Tā xǐ.huān tǎng zài nǎr kàn diànshì?
   Where does he like to lie down to watch TV?

   他喜歡躺在沙發上看電視。

   Tā xǐ.huān tǎng zài shāfā .shàng kàn diànshì.
   He likes to lie down on the sofa to watch TV.

5. 他喜歡趴在哪兒睡覺？

   Tā xǐ.huān pā zài nǎr shuìjiào?
   Where does he like to lie down to sleep?

   他喜歡趴在桌上睡覺。

   Tā xǐ.huān pā zài zhuō .shàng shuìjiào.

He likes to lie down on the desk to sleep.

6.   你喜歡坐在什麼地方看書？

Nǐ xǐ.huān zuò zài shén.me dì.fāng kànshū?
Where do you like to sit down to read?

我喜歡坐在地上看書。

Wǒ xǐ.huān zuò zài dì .shàng kànshū.
I like to sit on the floor to read.

When the prepositional phrase [在 Place] follows a verb that takes a location as an object, [在 Place] denotes the location of the result of an action.

See L7–A2, L8–A4, L9–A3, L11–B2 for more on 在.

2.   Question words as indefinites

Structure					Gloss
S 哪兒/什麼地方	都			去過了	S has been everywhere
S 哪兒/什麼地方	都/也 不/沒		去		S doesn't/didn't go anywhere
S 什麼 N		都 AuxV	V		S AuxV V everything
S 什麼 N		都		V 過了	S has V-ed everything
S 什麼(N)	都/也 不/沒		V		S doesn't/didn't V O (at all)

1.   寒假你到哪兒去了？

Hánjià nǐ dào nǎr qù .le?
Where did you go during the winter break?

寒假我哪兒也沒去。

Hánjià wǒ nǎr yě méi qù.
I didn't go to anywhere during the winter break.

2.   他今天要做什麼？

Tā jīn.tiān yào zuò shén.me?
What does he want to do today?

他今天很累，什麼(事)都不想做。

Tā jīn.tiān hěn lèi, shén.me (shì) dōu bù xiǎng zuò.
He is very tired today; (he) doesn't want to do anything.

3.   小林要買什麼東西？

Xiǎo Lín yào mǎi shén.me dōng.xī?
What does Xiao Lin want to buy?

小林什麼東西都要買。

Xiǎo Lín shén.me dōng.xī dōu yào mǎi.
Xiao Lin wants to buy everything.

In an affirmative sentence, when the question words (or interrogatives) 誰, 什麼, and 哪兒 are followed by 都 or 也 plus a verb, they function as indefinites and denote inclusiveness. In a negative sentence, they also function as indefinites but denote exclusiveness.

See L11–A6, L17–A1 for more on question words used as inclusives and exclusives.

3. The verb 給

Function	Structure	Gloss
main verb	S (沒/不) 給 O_i O_d	S give O_i O_d
preposition — indirect object marker	S (沒/不) V O_d 給 O_i	S VO to O_i
co-verb/preposition — beneficial marker	S (沒/不) 給 O_i V O_d	S VO_d for O_i

1. 你媽媽給了你多少錢？

Nǐ mā.mā gěi .le nǐ duō.shǎo qián?
How much money did your mother give you?

我媽媽給了我十塊錢。

Wǒ mā.mā gěi .le wǒ shí kuài qián.
My mother gave me ten dollars.

我媽媽沒給我十塊錢，她只給了我五塊錢。

Wǒ mā.mā méi gěi wǒ shí kuài qián, tā zhǐ gěi .le wǒ wǔ kuài qián.
My mother didn't give me ten dollars; she gave me only five dollars.

2. 你姐姐給了你什麼東西？

Nǐ jiě.jiě gěi .le nǐ shén.me dōng.xī?
What did your older sister give you?

她給了我一雙球鞋，她沒給我牛仔褲。

Tā gěi .le wǒ yì shuāng qiúxié, tā méi gěi wǒ niúzǎikù.
She gave me a pair of sneakers; she didn't give me (any) jeans.

The meaning of 給 depends on its position and function in the sentence. When 給 serves as a main verb, it means "to give," and the negative marker 沒/不 precedes it, as in examples 1 and 2.

3. 小王明天要寫信給誰？

Xiǎo Wáng míng.tiān yào xiěxìn gěi shéi?
To whom will Xiao Wang write a letter tomorrow?

小王明天要寫信給他父母。

Xiǎo Wáng míng.tiān yào xiěxìn gěi tā fùmǔ.
Xiao Wang will write a letter to his parents tomorrow.

4. 你送禮物給你父母了嗎？

Nǐ sòng lǐwù gěi nǐ fùmǔ .le .ma?
Did you give the gifts to your parents?

我沒送禮物給我父母。

Wǒ méi sòng lǐwù gěi wǒ fùmǔ.
I didn't give the gifts to my parents.

When 給 occurs post-verbally and functions as a preposition, it means "to," and the negative marker 沒/不 must precede the main verb, as in examples 3 and 4.

5. 誰要給你打英文信？

Shéi yào gěi nǐ dǎ Yīngwén xìn?
Who will type the English letter for you?

小高要給我打英文信。

Xiǎo Gāo yào gěi wǒ dǎ Yīngwén xìn.
Xiao Gao will type the English letter for me.

6. 是不是小林要給你做飯，你要給她寫中文信？

Shì .bu.shì Xiǎo Lín yào gěi nǐ zuòfàn, nǐ yào gěi tā xiě Zhōngwén xìn?
Is it true that Xiao Lin will cook for you (and) you will write a Chinese letter for her?

不，小林不要給我做飯，我也不要給她寫中文信。

Bù, Xiǎo Lín bú yào gěi wǒ zuòfàn, wǒ yě bú yào gěi tā xiě Zhōngwén xìn.
No, Xiao Lin won't cook for me (and) I won't write a Chinese letter for her either.

When 給 occurs pre-verbally and functions as a beneficial marker, it means "for," and the negative marker 沒/不 precedes it, as in examples 5 and 6.

See L9–A1, L18–A3, L22–A1 for more on 給.

4. 一 ... 就 ... construction

Structure	Gloss
S 一 V$_1$O$_1$,(S) 就 V$_2$ O$_2$...	As soon as S V$_1$O$_1$,(S) V$_2$ O$_2$...

1. 小王一過完耶誕節就要到哪兒去？

Xiǎo Wáng yí guòwán Yēdànjié jiù yào dào nǎr qù?
As soon as Christmas is over, where will Xiao Wang go?

小王一過完耶誕節就要回學校去。

Xiǎo Wáng yí guòwán Yēdànjié jiù yào huí xuéxiào qù.

As soon as Christmas is over, Xiao Wang will return to school.

2. 他一放寒假就去做什麼？

Tā yí fàng hánjià jiù qù zuò shén.me?

As soon as winter vacation started, what did he do?

他一放寒假就去看女朋友。

Tā yí fàng hánjià jiù qù kàn nǚpéng.yǒu.

As soon as winter vacation started, he went to see his girlfriend.

3. 小王一看電視，小林就說什麼？

Xiǎo Wáng yí kàn diànshì, Xiǎo Lín jiù shuō shén.me?

As soon as Xiao Wang starts watching TV, what does Xiao Lin say?

小王一看電視，小林就說：「別看電視了，咱們上體育館去吧！」

Xiǎo Wáng yí kàn diànshì, Xiǎo Lín jiù shuō: "Bié kàn diànshì .le! Zá.men shàng tǐyùguǎn qù .ba!"

As soon as Xiao Wang starts watching TV, Xiao Lin says, "Don't watch TV! Let's go to the gym!"

一…, (S) 就 'as soon as/once…, then…' is a pair of words that serves as a conjunction to bind two clauses together to form a complex sentence. If the subject of the two clauses is the same, then you can omit the second one. If the subjects are different, then the second subject (S₂) must precede 就, because 就 is an adverb that can occur only in front of a verb.

5. Durative time expressions

Structure	Gloss
S (VO) V 了 Time-Spent (了)	S did (has done) V O for Time-Spent
S V 了/過 Time-Spent (的) O	S did/has done V O for Time-Spent
S (AuxV) V Time-Spent (的) O	S (will/shall) V O for Time-Spent
S Time-Spent 沒/不 V O	S won't/didn't V O for Time-Spent

1. 他看電視看了多久？／
他看了多久的電視？

Tā kàn diànshì kàn .le duójiǔ?/
Tā kàn .le duójiǔ .de diànshì?
How long did he watch TV?

他看電視看了一整天。／

Tā kàn diànshì kàn .le yì zhěngtiān./

他看了一整天的電視。

Tā kàn .le yì zhěngtiān .de diànshì.
He watched TV for all day.

2. 我每天應該做多久的運動？

Wǒ měitiān yīnggāi zuò duójiǔ .de
yùndòng?
How many hours of exercise do I have to
do every day?

你每天應該做兩個小時的運動。

Nǐ měitiān yīnggāi zuò liǎng .ge xiǎoshí
.de yùndòng.
You should do two hours of exercise
every day.

3. 你已經幾天沒睡覺了？

Nǐ yǐ.jīng jǐ tiān méi shuìjiào .le?
How long has it been since you have
gotten any sleep?

最近功課很忙，我已經三天沒
睡覺了。

Zuìjìn gōngkè hěn máng, wǒ yǐ.jīng sān
tiān méi shuìjiào .le.
Lately, I have been very busy (with my
homework); I haven't slept for three days.

In an affirmative sentence, the durative time expression *follows* the verb. In a negative
sentence, the durative time expression must *precede* the negative adverb 不、沒.

See L10–A4, L11–A2.2 for more on 過.

6. Verbs with extent complements

Structure	Gloss
S(VO) V 得 怎麼樣？	After Ving O, what happened to S?
S(VO) V 得 Comp	After Ving O, S was so... that...

1. 你們滑雪滑得怎麼樣？

Nǐ.men huáxuě huá.de zěn.meyàng?
What happened to you after skiing?

我們滑雪滑得全身酸痛。

Wǒ.men huáxuě huá.de quánshēn
suāntòng.
After skiing we were sore all over.

2. 小王才滑了一小時的雪就累得
怎麼樣了？

Xiǎo Wáng cái huá .le yì xiǎoshí .de xuě
jiù lèi.de zěn.meyàng .le?
After skiing for just an hour, what
happened to Xiao Wang?

小王才滑了一小時的雪就累得
走不動了。

Xiǎo Wáng cái huá .le yì xiǎoshí .de xuě
jiù lèi.de zǒu.budòng .le.
After skiing for just an hour, Xiao Wang
was so tired that she couldn't walk.

💡 The word order of a sentence that consists of a verb with an extent complement follows the Temporal Sequence Principle: the subject must first initiate the action and keep doing it until he/she reaches the extent of the state. The verb precedes the extent complement.

🔄 See L9–A6, L10–A1, L11–A3 for more on complement marker 得.

7. The co-verb 跟

Structure	Gloss
A (AuxV)　　跟 B　VO	A (AuxV)　VO with B
A (不/沒/別) 跟 B　VO	A (Neg)　　VO with B

1.　你寒假跟誰去滑雪了？

Nǐ hánjià gēn shéi qù huáxuě .le?
Who went skiing with you during the winter vacation?

我寒假跟朋友去滑雪了。

Wǒ hánjià gēn péng.yǒu qù huáxuě .le.
I went skiing with my friends during the winter vacation.

2.　你的中文是跟誰學的啊？

Nǐ .de Zhōngwén shì gēn shéi xué .de a?
Who taught you Chinese?

我的中文是跟王老師學的，不
是跟李老師學的。

Wǒ .de Zhōngwén shì gēn Wáng lǎoshī xué
.de, bú.shì gēn Lǐ lǎoshī xué .de.
I learned Chinese with Teacher Wang,
not with Teacher Li.

3.　我跟他學打網球，怎麼樣？

Wǒ gēn tā xué dǎ wǎngqiú, zěn.meyàng?
How about me learning to play tennis
from him?

他網球打得不好，你別跟他學。

Tā wǎngqiú dǎ .de bù hǎo, nǐ bié gēn tā xué.
He doesn't play tennis well. Don't learn
from him!

💡 When 跟 occurs with another verb in a verbal expression, it functions as a co-verb, which is always translated as the preposition "with" in English. In a sentence that includes the co-verb 跟, the auxiliary verb or negative adverb 不/沒/別 should precede 跟.

🔄 See L5–A2.3, L19–B2 for more on 跟.

Cultural Notes
文化點滴 wénhuà diǎndī

1. The Chinese people have been greatly influenced by the Confucian concept of filial piety (孝順 xiàoshùn) for over twenty-five hundred years. Supporting one's parents is one of the most important deeds of filial piety. In the old days, in order to show filial piety for their parents, people wouldn't travel far from home if their parents were still alive (父母在，不遠遊 fùmǔ zài, bù yuǎn yóu). But nowadays, studying abroad has become an important step in moving up the social ladder in a young person's life. Instead of staying at home with parents, people now go abroad to study. Nevertheless, they try to write or call their parents frequently to show filial piety and love.

2. In Chinese society, precedence must be maintained between seniors and juniors (長幼有序 zhǎngyòu yǒu xù). This social rule applies to family members, colleagues, and schoolmates. Thus at home, younger siblings cannot address their older siblings by name; they must address them by appropriate kinship terms according to their birth order; for example, 大哥 dàgē 'eledest brother, ' 大姐 dàjiě 'eldest sister,' 二哥 èrgē 'second older brother,' 二姐 èrjiě 'second older sister,' 三哥 sāngē 'third older brother,' 三姐 sānjiě 'third older sister,' and so on. But one's younger siblings can be addressed using either the given names or kinship terms.

3. In China and Taiwan, young people have adopted the Western practice of celebrating Christmas by sending greeting cards and holding dances, but usually they don't buy Christmas presents for each other, whereas American Chinese do follow this gift-giving custom.

4. In classical Chinese, most nouns and verbs are monosyllabic. But owing to historical sound changes and other factors, the Chinese language has evolved more and more homonyms, and to avoid ambiguity, the Chinese people have coined more and more disyllabic or polysyllabic words. For example, 朋 péng and 友 yǒu both mean "friend," but in modern Chinese you cannot say 他是我的朋 Tā shì wǒ.de péng or 他是我的友 Tā shì wǒ.de yǒu to mean "He is my friend." Instead, you should say 他是我的朋友 Tā shì wǒ.de péng.yǒu. The usage of monosyllabic words is more restrictive. For example, the verb 練 liàn means "to practice," and the compound verb 練習 liànxí also means "to practice." But in the idiomatic expression 光說不練 guāng shuō bú liàn 'talk but not play,' you cannot say 光說不練習.

第十五課 這個房子一定很貴吧？

對話	30 頁
小對話	38 頁
生詞	40 頁
漢字	45 頁
語法	51 頁
文化點滴	59 頁

對話

〔小王、小林在大學路上找房子。〕

小林：　　這間公寓應該就是了。（看著「吉屋出租」的廣告）

小王：　　看起來還不錯
　　　　　，旁邊兒有游泳
　　　　　池、網球場、洗
　　　　　衣房，附近也有
　　　　　公車站，很方
　　　　　便。

小林：　　不知道裏邊兒怎
　　　　　麼樣？（敲管理員的門）

管理員：兩位是來看房子的吧！

小林：　　我們剛才打過電話來問，你說有空房。

管理員：沒錯，請跟我來。（帶林、王上二樓）

小王：　　嗯，有廚房、洗澡間，兩房一廳，比宿舍大多了。一定
　　　　　很貴吧！

管理員：一個月四百五，包水電。如果要的話，得先給定金兩百
　　　　　，另外的兩百五搬進來以後再付。

小林：　　我們沒有現金，開支票可以嗎？我也有信用卡。

管理員：支票可以，我們不收信用卡。你們是印大的學生吧！

小王：　　對，我們都在印大念書。宿舍太吵，飯又不好，所以才
　　　　　想搬出來，過過「新生活」。

管理員：這兒很安靜，你們一定會喜歡的。樓下的房客也是印大的學生。

　　　　　　　（三天以後，林、王搬了進去）

小林：　王華！你幫我把書搬上來行嗎？那箱書太重了，我搬不動。

小王：　好吧！我來，（把書搬上來）放在哪兒？客廳還是你的房間？

小林：　先放在客廳好了。等（一）會兒我整理好了，再放到書架上去。

小王：　你看這張畫兒掛在哪兒好呢？我們的電視應該擺在哪兒呢？

小林：　把電視放在牆邊兒吧！畫兒掛在左邊兒的牆上吧！這樣，我們一進門就看得見中國山水。右邊兒再掛張咱們的照片。

小王：　歇會兒吧！你快把我累死了！

对话

（小王、小林在大学路上找房子。）

小林：　这间公寓应该就是了。（看着「吉屋出租」的广告）

小王：　看起来还不错，旁边儿有游泳池、网球场、洗衣房，附近也有公车站，很方便。

小林：　不知道里边儿怎么样？（敲管理员的门）

管理员：两位是来看房子的吧！

小林：　我们刚才打过电话来问，你说有空房。

管理员：没错，请跟我来。（带林、王上二楼）

小王：　嗯，有厨房、洗澡间，两房一厅，比宿舍大多了。一定很贵吧！

管理员：一个月四百五，包水电。如果要的话，得先给定金两百，另外的两百五搬进来以后再付。

小林：　我们没有现金，开支票可以吗？我也有信用卡。

管理员：支票可以，我们不收信用卡。你们是印大的学生吧！

小王：　对，我们都在印大念书。宿舍太吵，饭又不好，所以才想搬出来，过过「新生活」。

管理员：这儿很安静，你们一定会喜欢的。楼下的房客也是印大的学生。

（三天以后，林、王搬了进去）

小林：　王华！你帮我把书搬上来行吗？那箱书太重了，我搬不动。

小王：　好吧！我来，（把书搬上来）放在哪儿？客厅还是你的
　　　　房间？

小林：　先放在客厅好了。等（一）会儿我整理好了，再放到书
　　　　架上去。

小王：　你看这张画儿挂在哪儿好呢？我们的电视应该摆在哪儿
　　　　呢？

小林：　把电视放在墙边儿吧！画儿挂在左边儿的墙上吧！这样
　　　　，我们一进门就看得见中国山水。右边儿再挂张咱们的
　　　　照片。

小王：　歇会儿吧！你快把我累死了！

My questions:

Duìhuà

(Xiǎo Wáng, Xiǎo Lín zài Dàxué lù .shàng zhǎo fáng.zi.)

Xiǎo Lín: Zhè jiān gōngyù yīnggāi jiù.shì .le. (Kàn.zhe "jíwū chūzū" .de
                guǎnggào.)

Xiǎo Wáng: Kàn.qǐ.lái hái búcuò. Páng.biānr yǒu yóuyǒngchí, wǎngqiúchǎng,
                xǐyīfáng. Fùjìn yě yǒu gōngchēzhàn, hěn fāng.biàn.

Xiǎo Lín: Bù zhī.dào lǐ.biānr zěn.meyàng? (Qiāo guǎnlǐyuán .de mén.)

Guǎnlǐyuán: Liǎng wèi shì lái kàn fáng.zi .de .ba!

Xiǎo Lín: Wǒ.men gāngcái dǎ.guò diànhuà lái wèn, nǐ shuō yǒu kōngfáng.

Guǎnlǐyuán: Méicuò, qǐng gēn wǒ lái. (Dài Lín, Wáng shàng èrlóu.)

Xiǎo Wáng: .En, yǒu chúfáng, xǐzǎojiān, liǎng fáng yì tīng, bǐ sùshè dà duō .le.
                Yídìng hěn guì .ba!

Guǎnlǐyuán: Yí .ge yuè sìbǎiwǔ, bāo shuǐdiàn. Rúguǒ yào .de huà, děi xiān gěi
                dìngjīn liǎngbǎi, lìngwài .de liǎngbǎiwǔ bānjìn.lái yǐhòu zài fù.

Xiǎo Lín: Wǒ.men méi.yǒu xiànjīn, kāi zhīpiào kě.yǐ .ma? Wǒ yě yǒu
                xìnyòngkǎ.

Guǎnlǐyuán: Zhīpiào kě.yǐ. Wǒ.men bù shōu xìnyòngkǎ. Nǐ.men shì Yìndà .de
                xué.shēng .ma?

Xiǎo Wáng: Duì! Wǒ.men dōu zài Yìndà niànshū. Sùshè tài chǎo,
                fàn yòu bù hǎo, suǒ.yǐ cái xiǎng bānchū.lái, guò.guò
                "xīn shēng.huó."

Guǎnlǐyuán: Zhèr hěn ānjìng. Nǐ.men yídìng huì xǐ.huān .de. Lóu.xià .de
                fángkè yě shì Yìndà .de xué.shēng.

(Sāntiān yǐhòu, Lín hé Wáng bān .le jìn.qù.)

Xiǎo Lín: Wáng Huá, nǐ bāng wǒ bǎ shū bān.shàng.lái xíng .ma? Nà xiāng shū tài zhòng .le. Wǒ bān.budòng.

Xiǎo Wáng: Hǎo .ba! Wǒ lái. (Bǎ shū bān.shàng.lái) Fàng zài nǎr? Kètīng hái.shì nǐ .de fángjiān?

Xiǎo Lín: Xiān fàng zài kètīng hǎo.le. Děng (yì)huǐr wǒ zhěng.lǐhǎo .le, zài fàng.dào shūjià .shàng .qù.

Xiǎo Wáng: Nǐ kàn zhè zhāng huàr guà zài nǎr hǎo .ne? Wǒ.men .de diànshì yīnggāi bǎi zài nǎr .ne?

Xiǎo Lín: Bǎ diànshì fàng zài qiáng.biānr .ba! Huàr guà zài zuǒ.biānr .de qiáng .shàng .ba! Zhèyàng, wǒ.men yí jìnmén jiù kàn.dejiàn Zhōng.guó shānshuǐ. Yòu.biānr zài guà zhāng zán.men .de zhàopiàn.

Xiǎo Wáng: Xiē huǐr .ba! Nǐ kuài bǎ wǒ lèi.sǐ .le!

Dialogue

(Xiǎo Wáng and Xiǎo Lín are looking for houses on College Road.)

Xiǎo Lín: This apartment should be the one. (Looking at the "house for rent" sign.)

Xiǎo Wáng: It looks fine. There is also a swimming pool, a tennis court, and a laundry room next to it. There is also a bus stop nearby. It's very convenient.

Xiǎo Lín: I wonder what it's like inside. (Knocking at the manager's door)

Manager: I suppose you two are coming to see the apartment?

Xiǎo Lín: We just called and asked. You told us that you have an apartment available.

Manager: That's right. Please come with me. (Taking Lín and Wáng upstairs.)

Xiǎo Wáng: Hmm, there is a kitchen, a bathroom, two bedrooms and a living room, much bigger than the room in the dorm. I guess it must be very expensive.

Manager: Four hundred and fifty per month, including utilities. If you want this one, you have to give me two hundred dollars to hold the apartment for you. The other two hundred and fifty can be paid when you move in.

Xiǎo Lín: We don't have cash. Could we write a check? I also have a credit card.

Manager: A check is fine. We don't take credit cards. You must be students at IU.

Xiǎo Wáng: Yes, we both study at IU. The dorm is too noisy and the food is bad, so we want to move out and start a "new life."

Manager: It is quiet here. You will definitely like it. The tenants downstairs are also students at IU.

(After three days, Lín and Wáng move in.)

Xiǎo Lín: Wáng Huá! Could you help me bring the books upstairs? That box of books is too heavy. I cannot move it.

Xiǎo Wáng: O.K.! Let me try. (Moving the books upstairs.) Where should I put this? In the living room or in your bedroom?

Xiǎo Lín: Put it in the living room first. I will put the books on the bookshelves after I sort them out.

Xiǎo Wáng: Look, where should we hang this painting? Where should we put our TV?

Xiǎo Lín: Put the TV near the wall! Hang the painting on the left wall. That way, we will be able to see the Chinese landscape right after we enter the door. On the right wall hang up a picture of ours.

Xiǎo Wáng: Take a break! You are going to wear me out.

Mini-Dialogue
小對話 Xiǎoduìhuà

Talking about a house

1. A: 這個房子看起來不錯，很
        方便。公車站就在旁邊兒。

Zhè .ge fáng.zi kàn.qǐ.lái búcuò, hěn
fāng.biàn .de yàng.zi. Gōngchē zhàn
jiù zài páng.biānr.
This house looks good. It's very
convenient. The bus stop is nearby.

    B: 裏邊兒也不錯。有廚房、
        洗澡間，三房一廳。

Lǐ.biānr yě búcuò. Yǒu chúfáng,
xǐzǎojiān, sān fáng yì tīng.
The inside of the house is good, too.
There is a kitchen, a bathroom, three
bedrooms, and a living room.

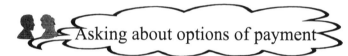
Asking about options of payment

1. A: 我們身上沒有帶現金，你
        們收不收信用卡？

Wǒ.men shēn.shàng méi.yǒu dài xiànjīn,
nǐ.men shōu .bushōu xìnyòngkǎ?
We don't have cash with us. Do you
take credit cards?

    B: 信用卡可以，個人支票更
        好。

Xìnyòngkǎ kě.yǐ, gèrén zhīpiào gèng
hǎo.
Credit cards are fine. Personal checks
are even better.

 Asking for a favor

1. A: 你幫我把書搬上來，好嗎？

Nǐ bāng wǒ bǎ shū bān.shàng.lái, hǎo .ma?

Could you help me move the books upstairs?

   B: 好啊！要不要連電腦也一起拿上來？

Hǎo .a! Yào .búyào lián diànnǎo yě yìqǐ ná.shàng.lái?

O.K.! Do you want me to take the computer upstairs, too?

   A: 不必了。

Búbì .le.

It's not necessary.

2. A: 你幫我把這本書還了，好不好？

Nǐ bāng wǒ bǎ zhèi běn shū huán .le, hǎo .buhǎo?

Could you help me return this book?

   B: 好啊！可是我明天才去圖書館。

Hǎo a! Kě.shì wǒ míng.tiān cái qù túshūguǎn.

O.K.! But I won't go to the library till tomorrow.

   A: 沒關係，這本書後天到期。

Méiguān.xī, zhèi běn shū hòu.tiān dàoqī.

No problem. This book is due the day after tomorrow.

Vocabulary
生詞 Shēngcí

◎ **By Order of Appearance**

一定		yídìng	Adv	[one-settle] certainly, definitely (=肯定)
公寓		gōngyù	N	[public-residence] apartment (M:間)
旁邊兒	旁边儿	páng.biānr	Loc	[side-side-Suf] side
* 邊兒	边儿	biānr	Loc	[side-Suf] side, border (suffix)
游泳池		yóuyǒngchí	N	[swim-swim-pond] swimming pool (M: 個)
網球場	网球场	wǎngqiúchǎng	N	[net-ball-field] tennis court (M: 個)
洗衣房		xǐyīfáng	N	[wash-clothes-room] laundry room (M:間)
附近		fùjìn	N	[attach-near] nearby
站		zhàn	N	station
知道		zhī.dào	V	[know-way] to know
吧		.ba	Part	particle for conjecture or supposition
空房		kōngfáng	N	[empty-room] vacant room (M:間)
* 間	间	jiān	M	[the space between] measure word for rooms and buildings
* 房間	房间	fángjiān	N	[room-interval] room (M:間)
* 屋子		wū.zi	N	[room-Suf] room (M:間) (=房間)
廚房		chúfáng	N	[kitchen-room] kitchen (M:間)
洗澡間	洗澡间	xǐzǎojiān	N	[wash-bath-interval] bathroom (M:間)
* 客廳	客厅	kètīng	N	[guest-hall] living room (M:間)
* 飯廳	饭厅	fàntīng	N	[meal-hall] dining room (M:間)
包		bāo	V	to include, to wrap
水電	水电	shuǐdiàn	N	[water-electricity] utilities charge
定金		dìngjīn	N	[settle-gold] down payment, deposit
* 押金		yājīn	N	[pledge-gold] deposit
另外		lìngwài	Adv	[other-outside] another, other, besides
進	进	jìn	V	to enter
付		fù	V	to pay (a bill)
現金	现金	xiànjīn	N	[now-gold] cash
支票		zhīpiào	N	[support-ticket] check (M:張 zhāng)
信用卡		xìnyòngkǎ	N	[believe-use-card] credit card (M:張)
印大		Yìndà	N	[seal-big] IU (Indiana University)
吵		chǎo	SV	(to be) noisy
生活		shēng.huó	N	[live-live] life
安靜	安静	ānjìng	SV	[peace-quiet] (to be) quiet

樓下	楼下	lóu.xià	N	[story building-below] downstairs
* 樓上	楼上	lóu.shàng	N	[story building-above] upstairs
房客		fángkè	N	[room-guest] tenant
* 房東	房东	fángdōng	N	[room-east] landlord, landlady
* 租		zū	V	to rent
把		bǎ	CV	[hold/handle] executive/disposal construction marker
箱子		xiāng.zi	N	[suitcase-Suf] suitcase, box (M: 個/ 隻)
放		fàng	V	to put
一會兒	一会儿	yìhuǐr	Adv/ N	[one-meet-Suf] a little while, a moment
整理		zhěng.lǐ	V	[tidy-arrange] to put in order, to tidy up
* 打掃	打扫	dǎsǎo	V	[hit-sweep] to clean up
書架	书架	shūjià	N	[book-frame] bookcase (M:個)
畫兒	画儿	huàr	N	[paint-Suf] painting (M:張)
* 山水畫	山水画	shānshuǐhuà	N	[mountain-water-paint] landscape painting (M:張)
掛	挂	guà	V	to hang up
擺	摆	bǎi	V	to place, to spread out
* 拿		ná	V	to take, to bring (something)
牆	墙	qiáng	N	wall
左邊兒	左边儿	zuǒ.biānr	Loc	[left-side-Suf] left side
右邊兒	右边儿	yòu.biānr	Loc	[right-side-Suf] right side
* 前邊兒	前边儿	qián.biānr	Loc	[front-side-Suf] front (= 前頭)
* 後邊兒	后边儿	hòu.biānr	Loc	[back-side-Suf] behind (= 後頭)
* 上邊兒	上边儿	shàng.biānr	Loc	[above-side-Suf] on top of, above (=上頭)
* 下邊兒	下边儿	xià.biānr	Loc	[below-side-Suf] underneath, below (=下頭)
這樣	这样	zhèyàng	Adv	this way, so (as this), such
* 那樣	那样	nàyàng	Adv	that way, so (as that)
照片		zhàopiàn	N	[reflect-piece] picture, photo (M:張)
* 相片		xiàngpiàn	N	[image-piece] picture, photo (M:張) (=照片)
歇		xiē	V	to rest (=休息)
累死		lèi.sǐ	RV	[tired-die] (to be) very tired

◎ By Grammatical Categories

Nouns/Pronouns

	公寓		gōngyù	N	[public-residence] apartment (M:間)
	游泳池		yóuyǒngchí	N	[swim-swim-pond] swimming pool (M:個)
	網球場	网球场	wǎngqiúchǎng	N	[net-ball-field] tennis court (M:個)
	洗衣房		xǐyīfáng	N	[wash-clothes-room] laundry room (M:間)
	空房		kōngfáng	N	[empty-room] vacant room (M:間)
*	房間	房间	fángjiān	N	[room-interval] room (M:間)
*	屋子		wū.zi	N	[room-Suf] room (M:間) (=房間)
*	客廳	客厅	kètīng	N	[guest-hall] living room (M:間)
*	飯廳	饭厅	fàntīng	N	[meal-hall] dining room (M:間)
	廚房		chúfáng	N	[kitchen-room] kitchen (M:間)
	洗澡間	洗澡间	xǐzǎojiān	N	[wash-bath-interval] bathroom (M:間)
	牆	墙	qiáng	N	wall
	站		zhàn	N	station
	附近		fùjìn	N	[attach-near] nearby
	樓下	楼下	lóu.xià	N	[story building-below] downstairs
*	樓上	楼上	lóu.shàng	N	[story building-above] upstairs
	生活		shēng.huó	N	[live-live] life
	房客		fángkè	N	[room-guest] tenant
*	房東	房东	fángdōng	N	[room-east] landlord, landlady
	水電	水电	shuǐdiàn	N	[water-electricity] utilities charge
	定金		dìngjīn	N	[settle-gold] down payment, deposit
*	押金		yājīn	N	[pledge-gold] deposit
	現金	现金	xiànjīn	N	[now-gold] cash
	支票		zhīpiào	N	[support-ticket] check (M:張 zhāng)
	信用卡		xìnyòngkǎ	N	[believe-use-card] credit card (M:張)
	箱子		xiāng.zi	N	[suitcase-Suf] suitcase, box (M:個/隻)
	書架	书架	shūjià	N	[book-frame] bookcase (M:個)
	畫兒	画儿	huàr	N	[paint-Suf] painting (M:張)
*	山水畫	山水画	shānshuǐhuà	N	[mountain-water-paint] landscape painting (M:張)
	照片		zhàopiàn	N	[reflect-piece] picture, photo (M:張)
*	相片		xiàngpiàn	N	[image-piece] picture, photo (M:張) (=照片)
	印大		Yìndà	N	[seal-big] IU (Indiana University)

Measure Words

*	間	间	jiān	M	[the space between] measure word for rooms and buildings

Verbs/Stative Verbs/Adjectives

	進	进	jìn	V	to enter
*	租		zū	V	to rent
	包		bāo	V	to include, to wrap
	付		fù	V	to pay (a bill)
	放		fàng	V	to put
	掛	挂	guà	V	to hang up
	擺	摆	bǎi	V	to place, to spread out
*	拿		ná	V	to take, to bring (something)
	歇		xiē	V	to rest (=休息)
	整理		zhěng.lǐ	V	[tidy-arrange] to put in order, to tidy up
*	打掃	打扫	dǎsǎo	V	[hit-sweep] to clean up
	知道		zhī.dào	V	[know-way] to know
	累死		lèi.sǐ	RV	[tired-die] (to be) very tired
	吵		chǎo	SV	(to be) noisy
	安靜	安静	ānjìng	SV	[peace-quiet] (to be) quiet
	把		bǎ	CV	[hold/handle] executive/disposal construction marker

Adverbs

	一定		yídìng	Adv	[one-settle] certainly, definitely (=肯定)
	一會兒	一会儿	yìhuǐr	Adv/N	[one-meet-Suf] a little while, a moment
	另外		lìngwài	Adv	[other-outside] another, other, besides
	這樣	这样	zhèyàng	Adv	this way, so (as this), such
*	那樣	那样	nàyàng	Adv	that way, so (as that)

Particles

| | 吧 | | .ba | Part | particle for conjecture or supposition |

Localizers

*	邊兒	边儿	biānr	Loc	[side-Suf] side, border (suffix)
	旁邊兒	旁边儿	páng.biānr	Loc	[side-side-Suf] side
	左邊兒	左边儿	zuǒ.biānr	Loc	[left-side-Suf] left side
	右邊兒	右边儿	yòu.biānr	Loc	[right-side-Suf] right side
*	前邊兒	前边儿	qián.biānr	Loc	[front-side-Suf] front (= 前頭)
*	後邊兒	后边儿	hòu.biānr	Loc	[back-side-Suf] behind (= 後頭)
*	上邊兒	上边儿	shàng.biānr	Loc	[above-side-Suf] on top of, above (=上頭)
*	下邊兒	下边儿	xià.biānr	Loc	[below-side-Suf] underneath, below (=下頭)

✚ Supplementary Vocabulary

1. Odds and Ends

搬家		bānjiā	V	[move-home] to move (one's) home
出租		chūzū	V	[go out-rent] (to be) for rent
租		zū	V	to rent
出售		chūshòu	V	[go out-sell] (to be) for sale
吉屋		jíwū	N	[lucky-house] lucky house
廣告	广告	guǎnggào	N	[broad-tell] advertisement
畫家	画家	huàjiā	N	[paint-expert] artist, painter
國畫	国画	guóhuà	N	[country-paint] Chinese painting
西洋畫	西洋画	xīyánghuà	N	[west-ocean-paint] Western painting

2. Things in the House

家具/傢俱	家具	jiājù	N	[home-tool/furniture-tool] furniture (M: 套 tào)
臥房/臥室	臥房/臥室	wòfáng/wòshì	N	[lie down-room] bedroom (M: 間)
床單	床单	chuángdān	N	[bed-single] bed sheets (M: 張)
床罩		chuángzhào	N	[bed-cover] bedspread (M: 個)
枕頭	枕头	zhěn.tóu	N	[pillow-head] pillow (M: 個)
檯燈	檯灯	táidēng	N	[table-lamp] desk lamp (M: 盞 zhǎn)
燈泡	灯泡	dēngpào	N	[lamp-bubble] light bulb (M: 個)
爐子	炉子	lú.zi	N	[stove-Suf] stove (M: 個)
微波爐	微波炉	wēibōlú	N	[tiny-wave-stove] microwave
冰箱		bīngxiāng	N	[ice-chest] refrigerator (M: 個)
洗碗機	洗碗机	xǐwǎnjī	N	[wash-bowl-machine] dishwasher (M: 個)
洗衣機	洗衣机	xǐyījī	N	[wash-clothes-machine] washer
烘乾機	烘乾机	hōnggānjī	N	[dry near a fire-dry-machine] dryer
盤子	盘子	pán.zi	N	[plate-Suf] plates, saucers (M: 個)
碗		wǎn	N	bowl (M: 個/隻)
筷子		kuài.zi	N	[chopstick-Suf] chopsticks (M: 雙/隻)
調羹	调羹	tiáogēng	N	[stir-soup] spoon (M: 把)
茶匙		cháchí	N	[tea-spoon] teaspoon (M: 把)
湯匙	汤匙	tāngchí	N	[soup-spoon] soup spoon (M: 把)
刀子		dāo.zi	N	[knife-Suf] knife (M: 把)
叉子		chā.zi	N	[fork-Suf] fork (M: 個/隻)
杯子		bēi.zi	N	[cup-Suf] cup, mug (M: 個)
茶壺	茶壶	cháhú	N	[tea-kettle] tea kettle (M: 個)
茶杯		chábēi	N	[tea-cup] tea cup (M: 個)
咖啡壺	咖啡壶	kāfēihú	N	[coffee-kettle] coffee pot (M: 個)

Characters
漢字 Hànzì

知	道	吵	念
搬	進	空	樓
左	右	旁	邊
把	站	累	死
現	收	付	百

知道   zhī.dào   to know

知

zhī
to know   矢
8   (dart)

A: 你**知道**小高把你的書都搬走了嗎？
B: 我**不知道**。

道

dào
way, to say   辶
13

A: 你**知道**我們上邊兒住的是什麼人嗎？
B: **不知道**，我想一定不是什麼好人。

吵

吵死了   chǎo.sǐ.le   (to be) very noisy
*吵架   chǎojià   to quarrel

chǎo
to quarrel   口
7   (mouth)

A: 這附近**吵不吵**？
B: **不太吵**，沒有什麼車。

念

念書   niànshū   to study

niàn
to read out loud,
to think of   心
8   (heart)

A: 你們是哪兒的學生？
B: 我們都在印大**念書**。

繁簡對照：	其他漢字：	✎ **My notes:**
	*認 SC47 *識 SC48	

搬

| 搬到 | bān.dào | to move to (a place) |
| *搬家 | bānjiā | to move |

bān
to move 扌
13 (hand)

A: 你什麼時候**搬家**？
B: 下個月。

進

| *進來 | jìn.lái | to come in |
| *請進 | qǐngjìn | please come in |

jìn
enter 辶
13

A: 你幫我把這些東西**搬進來**，行不行？
B: 沒問題。

空

有空兒	yǒu kòngr	to have free time
沒空兒	méi kòngr	to be busy
空房	kōngfáng	vacant room
*空間	kōngjiān	space

kòng, kōng
unoccupied
time, space 穴
8 (a cave)

A: 你中午**有沒有空兒**？
B: 有，什麼事？

樓

樓下	lóu.xià	downstairs
*樓上	lóu.shàng	upstairs
*二樓	èrlóu	second floor
*大樓	dàlóu	building

lóu
a building of
two or more
stories 木
15 (wood)

A: 你喜歡住**樓上**還是**樓下**？
B: 我喜歡**樓上**，**樓上**比較安靜。

| 繁簡對照： | 其他漢字： | ✎ **My notes:** |
| 進 进
樓 楼 | 出 L9
*牆 SC49 | |

左

zuǒ
left   工
5   (labor)

左邊兒   zuǒ.biānr   left side
*左手   zuǒshǒu   left hand

A: 你把咱們的照片掛在**左邊兒**的牆上吧！
B: 掛右邊兒不好嗎？。

右

yòu
right   口
5   (mouth)

右邊兒   yòu.biānr   right side
*右手   yòushǒu   right hand

A: 這兒有沒有洗衣房？
B: 有，就在游泳池的**右邊兒**。

旁

páng
side   方
10   (square)

旁邊兒   páng.biānr   side

A: 那個房子怎麼樣？
B: 不錯，很方便，**旁邊兒**就是公車站。

邊

biān
side, suffix in
place words 辶
19

左邊兒   zuǒ.biānr   left side
右邊兒   yòu.biānr   right side
*前邊兒   qián.biānr   front
*後邊兒   hòu.biānr   behind

A: 我們的電視應該擺在哪兒呢？
B: 放在**牆邊兒**吧！

繁簡對照：	其他漢字：	✎ **My notes:**
邊边	前 L9 後 L9	

把

bǎ
M for things
with handles 扌
7   (hand)

A: 你功課做完了沒有？
B: 我早就**把**功課做完了。

站

zhàn
to stand   立
10   (to stand)

公車站	gōngchēzhàn	bus stop
*火車站	huǒchēzhàn	train station
*站住	zhànzhù	to stop

A: 這附近有沒有公車到學校？
B: 有，前邊兒就有個**公車站**。

累

lèi
(to be) tired 系
11

累死   lèi.sǐ   (to be) very tired

A: 今天**真累**！
B: 你做了什麼這麼**累**？

死

sǐ
to die   歹
6   (bad)

| *餓死 | è.sǐ | (to be) very hungry |
| *忙死 | máng.sǐ | (to be) very busy |

A: 我快**累死了**！
B: 你坐下來，歇一會兒吧！

繁簡對照：	其他漢字：	✎ **My notes:**
	坐 L7 *活 SC50	

現金   xiànjīn   cash
*現在   xiànzài   now

現

xiàn
now, to appear
王
11   (jade)

A: 我身上沒有**現金**，只有支票。
B: 開支票也行。

收

shōu
to receive,
accept   夂
6   (tap)

收到   shōu.dào   to receive
*收信   shōuxìn   to receive letters

A: 你們**收不收**信用卡？
B: **收**，我們也**收**個人支票。

付

fù
to pay, hand
over to   亻
5   (person)

付錢   fùqián   to pay money
*付稅   fùshuì   to pay taxes

A: 我們這個月的**房錢**還沒**付**。
B: 是嗎？我已經沒錢了。

百

一百   yì bǎi   one hundred
*百貨公司   bǎihuò gōngsī   department store

bǎi
a hundred   白
6   (white)

A: 這兒一個月要付多少？
B: 一個月**四百五**。

繁簡對照：	其他漢字：	✎ **My notes:**
現现	千 L22 萬 L22	

Grammar
語法 yǔfǎ

Ⓐ Major Sentence Patterns 主要句型 zhǔyào jùxíng

1. 把 construction

Structure	Gloss
S (沒/不/別) 把 O V complement	S (doesn't/didn't) do... to O

1. 你把那些書搬到哪兒去了?

   Nǐ bǎ nèixiē shū bān.dào nǎr qù .le?
   Where did you move those books to?

   我把那些書搬到樓上去了。

   Wǒ bǎ nèixiē shū bān.dào lóu.shàng qù .le.
   I have moved those books upstairs.

2. 他昨天有沒有把支票給你?/
   他昨天把支票給了你沒有?

   Tā zuó.tiān yǒu .méi.yǒu bǎ zhīpiào gěi nǐ?/ Tā zuó.tiān bǎ zhīpiào gěi .le nǐ méi.yǒu?
   Did he give you the check yesterday?

   他昨天把支票給了我了。

   Tā zuó.tiān bǎ zhīpiào gěi .le wǒ .le.
   He gave me the check yesterday.

   他昨天沒(有)把支票給我。

   Tā zuó.tiān méi(.yǒu) bǎ zhīpiào gěi wǒ.
   He didn't give me the check yesterday.

3. (請你)別把那張畫兒掛在牆上。

   (Qǐng nǐ) bié bǎ nèi zhāng huàr guà zài qiáng .shàng.
   (Please) don't hang that picture on the wall.

4. 請你把窗戶打開,把門關上。

   Qǐng nǐ bǎ chuāng.hù dǎ.kāi, bǎ mén guān.shàng.
   Please open the window and close the door.

5. 誰把我的隨身聽拿走了?

   Shéi bǎ wǒ .de suíshēntīng ná.zǒu .le?
   Who took my Walkman?

   小王把你的隨身聽拿走了。

   Xiǎo Wáng bǎ nǐ .de suíshēntīng ná.zǒu .le.
   Xiao Wang took your Walkman.

6. 你要我搬書,還要我搬電視,
   你快把我累死了!

   Nǐ yào wǒ bān shū, hái yào wǒ bān diànshì, nǐ kuài bǎ wǒ lèi.sǐ .le.
   You want me to move the books, you want me to move the TV set; you're killing me!

7. 老師給我們很多功課，把我們忙死了！

Lǎoshī gěi wǒ.men hěn duō gōngkè, bǎ wǒ.men máng.sǐ .le.
The teacher gave us a lot of homework, (which) is killing us!

The lexical meaning of 把 bǎ is "to take hold of, to grasp." But in modern Chinese, 把 bǎ is used basically as a grammatical function word. A bǎ construction (把字句 bǎzìjù) frequently occurs with the verbs listed in the tables 2.1 and 2.2. The construction usually implies that (1) the actor can execute an action on the object, as in examples 1-5, or (2) some event causes the object to be in a certain state, as in examples 6 and 7.
The word order of the 把 construction follows the Temporal Sequence Principle. The subject or event (S) must first "grasp or cause (把)" the object (O), then execute the action (V), and then the action results in a certain state (complement).

Note: The negative adverb 沒/不/別 of a 把 construction must precede 把.

See L16–C1, L22–A1 for more on 把.

2. Verbs with directional complements

2.1 Verbs with single directional complements

Motion/Action Verb	Directional Complement	Gloss
搬 bān	來 /去	to move here/there
拿 ná	來 /去	to bring over here/there
走 zǒu	來 /去	to walk over here/there
跑 pǎo	來 /去	to run over here/there
上 shàng	來 /去	to go up here/there
下 xià	來 /去	to go down here/there
進 jìn	來 /去	to enter here/there

1. 他是什麼時候搬來這兒的？

Tā shì shén.me shí.hou bān.lái zhèr .de?
When did he move here?

他是上個月搬來這兒的。

Tā shì shàng .ge yuè bān.lái zhèr .de.
He moved here last month.

2. 我們可以進去客廳坐嗎？

Wǒ.men kě.yǐ jìn.qù kètīng zuò .ma?
Can we go into the living room to sit down?

請進去客廳坐吧！

Qǐng jìn.qù kètīng zuò .ba!
Please go into the living room to sit down.

The motion or action verbs listed above can combine with a directional complement to form a verb compound. When a verb combines with the directional complement 來 'to come,' it always denotes that the motion or action is toward where the speaker is located; when a verb combines with the directional complement 去 'to go,' it always denotes motion or action away from where the speaker is located.

2.2 Verbs with double directional complements

Motion/Action Verb	Double Directional Complement	Gloss
搬 bān	進來/進去	to move over here/there
放 fàng	進來/進去	to put over here/there
拿 ná	進來/進去	to bring...in/out
拿 ná	上去/下來	to bring...up/down
走 zǒu	進來/進去	to walk into/out
跑 pǎo	進來/進去	to run into/out

1. 他把書搬到哪兒去了？

   Tā bǎ shū bān.dào nǎr qù .le?
   Where did he move the books?

   他把書搬進去了。

   Tā bǎ shū bānjìn.qù .le.
   He moved the books inside.

2. 你要我把畫兒放在哪兒？

   Nǐ yào wǒ bǎ huàr fàng zài nǎr?
   Where do you want me to put this painting?

   請你把畫兒拿上來。

   Qǐng nǐ bǎ huàr náshàng.lái.
   Please bring the painting up here.

Action Verb	Double Directional Complement	Gloss
穿 chuān	上去	to wear, to put on (clothes)
脫 tuō	下來	to take (clothes) off
戴 dài	上去	to put (jewelry, hat, glasses) on
拿 ná	下來	to take (jewelry, hat, glasses) off

3. 他把外套穿上去了嗎？

   Tā bǎ wàitào chuān.shàng.qù .le .ma?
   Has he put on his overcoat?

   他已經把外套穿上去了。

   Tā yǐ.jīng bǎ wàitào chuān.shàng.qù .le.
   He has put on his overcoat.

4. 他爲什麼把毛衣脫下來呢？

   Tā wèishén.me bǎ máoyī tuō.xià.lái .ne?
   Why did he take the sweater off?

因爲天氣太熱了。

Yīn.wèi tiān.qì tài rè .le.
Because (it is) too warm.

Action Verb	Double Directional Complement	Gloss
寫 xiě	下 來	to write/take (notes) down
記 jì	下 來	to write/record...down

5. 你們把這些生詞寫下來了嗎？

Nǐ.men bǎ zhèixiē shēngcí xiě.xià.lái .le .ma?
Did you take down these new words?

我們還没把那些生詞寫下來。

Wǒ.men hái méi bǎ nèixiē shēngcí xiě.xià.lái.
We haven't taken down those new words.

6. 你把什麼東西記下來了？

Nǐ bǎ shén.me dōng.xī jì.xià.lái .le?
What did you write down?

我把房東的電話號碼記下來了。

Wǒ bǎ fángdōng .de diànhuà hàomǎ jì.xià.lái .le.
I wrote down the landlord's telephone number.

Some motion or action verbs can combine with double directional complements to form verbal compounds or idioms.

2.3 Resultative verbs with directional complements

	Structure		Gloss
Actual form	回來/ 回去	huí.lái/ huí.qù	to come/go back
	進來/ 進去	jìn.lái/ jìn.qù	to come/go in
	上來/ 上去	shàng.lái/ shàng.qù	to come/go up
Positive potential form	回得來/ 回得去	huí.de.lái/ huí.de.qù	can come/go back
	進得來/ 進得去	jìn.de.lái/ jìn.de.qù	can come/go in
	上得來/ 上得去	shàng.de.lái/ shàng.de.qù	can come/go up
Negative potential form	回不來/ 回不去	huí.bu.lái/ huí.bu.qù	cannot come/go back
	進不來/ 進不去	jìn.bu.lái/ jìn.bu.qù	cannot come/go in
	上不來/ 上不去	shàng.bu.lái/ shàng.bu.qù	cannot come/go up

1. 你明天回得來嗎？

Nǐ míng.tiān huí.de.lái .ma?
Can you come back tomorrow?

明天我很忙，大概回不去。

Míng.tiān wǒ hěn máng dàgài huí.bu.qù.
I will be very busy tomorrow, (I) probably will be unable to come back.

2. 五十樓你上得去嗎？

Wǔshí lóu nǐ shàng.de.qù .ma?
Can you go up to the fiftieth floor?

五十樓太高了，我上不去。

Wǔshí lóu tài gāo .le, wǒ shàng.bú.qù.
The fiftieth floor is too high; I cannot go up (there).

See L7–A6, L9–A6, L15–A2.3, L18–A4 for more on resultative verbs.

See L9–A6, L10–A1, L11–A3, L14–A6, L18–A4, L23–C1.5 for more on complement marker 得.

3. Place words

Whole 》 Part		Gloss
X	旁邊兒	side of X/next to X
X	左邊兒	left side of X/to the left of X
X	右邊兒	right side of X/to the right of X
X	前邊兒/前頭兒/前面	front side of X/in front of X
X	後邊兒/後頭兒/後面	back side of X/behind X
X	上(邊兒)/上(頭兒)/上面	upper side of X/on top of X
X	下(邊兒)/下(頭兒)/下面	lower side of X/underneath of X

1. 你們宿舍旁邊兒有沒有公車站？

Nǐ.men sùshè páng.biānr yǒu .méiyǒu gōngchēzhàn?
Is there a bus stop near your dormitory?

我們宿舍旁邊兒有公車站。

Wǒ.men sùshè páng.biānr yǒu gōngchēzhàn.
There is a bus stop near our dormitory.

2. 請問，洗手間在哪兒？

Qǐngwèn, xǐshǒujiān zài nǎr?
May I ask, where is the restroom?

洗手間就在客廳的右邊兒。

Xǐshǒujiān jiù zài kètīng .de yòu.biānr.
The restroom is next to the living room, down the hall on the right.

3. 請問，你要我把書放在樓上還是樓下？

Qǐngwèn, nǐ yào wǒ bǎ shū fàng zài lóu.shàng hái.shì lóu.xià?
May I ask, do you want me to put the books upstairs or downstairs?

請你把書放在樓下。

Qǐng nǐ bǎ shū fàng zài lóu.xià.
Please put the books downstairs.

The word order of place words with localizers follows the From Whole to Part Principle. When one refers to a side location of X, X as a whole is used as a reference point, whereas any side of X is a part of X. Thus X precedes the side of X. This word order is just the opposite of its English counterpart.

See L4–A1, L15–A3, L23–B2 for more on From Whole to Part Principle.

B Usage of Common Phrases 詞組用法 cízǔ yòngfǎ

1. The particle ... 的話

Structure	Gloss
(如果/要是) S V (O) 的話	If S V (O)

1.   (如果) 我要租的話，要先給定
     金多少錢？

(Rúguǒ) wǒ yào zū .de huà, yào xiān gěi dìngjīn duō.shǎo qián?
(If) I would like to rent (it), how much (would I have to) pay in advance for the deposit?

(如果) 你要租的話，可以先給定
金兩百塊錢。

(Rúguǒ) nǐ yào zū .de huà, kě.yǐ xiān gěi dìngjīn liǎng bǎi kuài qián.
(If) you would like to rent (it), (you) may pay two hundred dollars in advance for the deposit.

2.   (要是) 你有錢的話，你要做什
     麼？

(Yào.shì) nǐ yǒu qián .de huà, nǐ yào zuò shén.me?
(If) you had money, what would you do?

(要是) 我有錢的話，我要到中國
去學中文。

(Yào.shì) wǒ yǒu qián .de huà, wǒ yào dào Zhōng.guó qù xué Zhōngwén.
(If) I had money, I would go to China to study Chinese.

... 的話 'in case or in the event' is a compound particle that follows an adjectival clause to form a supposition. The adjectival clause may be preceded by the conjunction 要是 yàoshì or 如果 rúguǒ 'if.'

2. The particle 吧

Structure	Gloss
S... 吧？	S... , I suppose/I guess

1. 你們是來看房子的吧？

   Nǐ.men shì lái kàn fáng.zi .de .ba?
   You came here to see the house, I suppose?

   對了，我們是來看房子的。

   Duì.le, wǒ.men shì lái kàn fáng.zi .de.
   Yes, we came to see the house.

2. 這兒有公車站吧？

   Zhèr yǒu gōngchēzhàn .ba?
   There is a bus stop here, I suppose?

   不，這兒沒有公車站。

   Bù, zhèr méi.yǒu gōngchēzhàn.
   No, there is no bus stop here.

3. 這箱書太重了，你搬不動吧？

   Zhèi xiāng shū tài zhòng .le, nǐ
   bān.budòng .ba?
   This box of books is too heavy. I guess
   you can't move it.

   這箱書不太重，我搬得動。

   Zhèi xiāng shū bú tài zhòng, wǒ bān.dedòng.
   This box of books is not very heavy. I
   can move it.

Besides functioning as a particle for agreement, the sentence particle 吧 denotes "conjecture or supposition," as shown in examples 1-3. In this case, the intonation of the sentence is softer and slightly lower.

See L7–B5, L10–B1, L13–B2 for more on 吧.

3. 知道 vs. 認識

Structure	Gloss
S₁ 知道 [S₂ (Neg) V O]	S₁ knows (that)...
S₁ 不知道 [S₂ V-not-V O]	S₁ doesn't know [(if)...]
S₁ 不知道 [QW Question] (information/fact/matter)	S₁ doesn't know [QW Question]

1. 你知道那間公寓包水電嗎？

   Nǐ zhī.dào nèi jiān gōngyù bāo shuǐdiàn
   .ma?
   Do you know if the apartment rent
   includes the utilities?

我不知道那間公寓包不包水電。   Wǒ bù zhī.dào nèi jiān gōngyù bāo .bu bāo shuǐdiàn.
I don't know if the apartment rent includes the utilities.

2. 你知道他們收不收信用卡？   Nǐ zhī.dào tā.men shōu .bushōu xìnyòngkǎ?
Do you know if they accept credit cards?

我知道他們不收信用卡。   Wǒ zhī.dào tā.men bù shōu xìnyòngkǎ.
I know they don't accept credit cards.

3. 你知道他叫什麼名字嗎？   Nǐ zhī.dào tā jiào shén.me míng.zi .ma?
Do you know what his name is?

我不知道他叫什麼名字。   Wǒ bù zhī.dào tā jiào shén.me míng.zi.
I don't know what his name is.

知道 is a transitive verb that means "to know." It takes a clause as an object. But the object clause must concern information, fact, or matter, not a person. For a sentence with negative form 不知道, the object clause should be a choice-type (A-not-A) question or a question-word question.

Structure	Gloss
S (不) 認識 O (person/character/word)	S (doesn't) know (the person) S (doesn't) recognize/comprehend (the character/word)

4. 你認識王先生嗎？   Nǐ rèn.shì Wáng xiān.shēng .ma?
Do you know Mr. Wang?

我不認識王先生，我認識王太太。   Wǒ bú rèn.shì Wáng xiān.shēng, Wǒ rèn.shì Wáng tài.tài.
I don't know Mr. Wang, (but) I know Mrs. Wang.

5. 你認不認識這個字？   Nǐ rèn .burèn.shì zhèi .ge zì?
Do you know this character?

我不認識這個字，這個字我還沒學過。   Wǒ bú rèn.shì zhèi .ge zì, zhèi .ge zì wǒ hái méi xué.guò.
I don't know this character. I haven't learned this character yet.

認識 is a transitive verb that means "to know, to recognize, to comprehend." Its object can only be a person or 字 character/word.

Cultural Notes
文化點滴 wénhuà diǎndī

1. Chinese always try to avoid using words that are homophonous with ill omens or bad things. Thus when people have a house for sale or for rent, they usually use the expression 吉屋出售 jíwū chūshòu 'lucky house for sale' or 吉屋出租 jíwū chūzū 'lucky house for rent' rather than 空屋出售 kōngwū chūshòu 'empty house for sale' or 空屋出租 kōngwū chūzū 'empty house for rent.' That is because 空 kōng also stands for 虧空 kuī.kōng 'to be in the red.'

吉屋自售

2909 S. Archer大街共兩層,樓面店鋪
,二樓居室,三大房,一客廳,全地
下室,車房後院As is 廉售7萬8千,
可議價,經紀請勿電,誠者電請電

312-842-1503

2. After moving to a new (and better) house, Chinese invite relatives and friends to have a banquet or 吃湯圓 chī tāngyuán 'to eat sweet-rice balls'

to celebrate 喬遷之喜 qiáo qiān zhī xǐ '[the happiness of moving into a new house] house-warming party.' 圓 yuán means "round," but it symbolizes "perfection" because a circle is an unbroken line. Guests who come to express their congratulations bring gifts for household use.

3. In terms of a Chinese house, there is a difference between 房 fáng 'bedroom' and 廳 tīng 'living or dining room.' Traditionally, 洗澡間 xǐzǎojiān 'bathroom where people take baths' and 廁所 cèsuǒ 'lavatory where the toilet is located' are separate rooms in a Chinese house, and they are not called 房 fáng, which can refer only to "bedrooms." A typical Chinese advertisement for a house/apartment for sale or rent says #房#廳, 廚廁俱全 # fáng # tīng, chú cè jù quán 'no. of bedrooms, living room/dining room, with kitchen and restroom.'

4. In both China and Taiwan, only businessmen use checks. Ordinary people use cash all the time, and most working people get their salary or wages in cash. Nowadays in Taiwan, salaries from civil service or schools can be deposited directly into the bank accounts of the employees.

對話	62 頁
小對話	69 頁
生詞	71 頁
漢字	75 頁
語法	81 頁
文化點滴	88 頁

第十六課　你們住得還習慣嗎？

對話

〔小高、小李去參加林美英、王華辦的晚會。〕

小高：（開車）是大學路吧！

小李：對，再往前走，過了第三街，往右轉就是大學路。

小高：她們的地址是多少號？

小李：三二九號。過了這個紅綠燈就得往右轉。嗯，再往前開一
　　　點兒，對了！對了！就是這兒。（下車拿東西）

小高：你帶了什麼？

小李：兩打汽水兒，夠不夠？你呢？巧克力糖還是花兒？

小高：當然是花兒！你沒聽說最近她們倆都在減肥嗎？

小李：肯定是球迷受了舞迷的影響。上次我還聽見美英叫王華跟
　　　她一塊兒去鍛練呢！（按鈴）

小林：小高、小李，這兒
　　　不難找吧！

小高：容易得很。恭喜你
　　　們搬了新家。住得
　　　還習慣吧？（給花）

小林：（接花）謝謝！剛
　　　開始的幾天不大習
　　　慣，現在好多了。
　　　這兒沒有宿舍那麼

熱鬧。所以找你們來慶祝一下。

小李：真是應該慶祝慶祝。後天就是中國新年了。

小高：在美國怎麼過中國年呢？

小王：後天晚上中國同學會要舉辦一個新年晚會，你可以去參加。我也會去幫他們的忙。

小李：（四處看）這兒比宿舍舒服多了。這麼大，夠六個人住了！

小林：是住了「一家六口」！看！這是我們的「家人」。（指一缸魚和一隻貓）

小李：你們真有意思。又養魚又養貓，不怕貓餓了(貓)把那三條魚給吃了嗎？

小王：不會的，這隻貓跟我一樣「光看不練」。

小林：所以我們管他叫「王子」。（摸摸貓）他好像「孔子」、「老子」一樣，是這屋子裏的哲學家。

小高：我看是王華的孩子吧！

对话

〔小高、小李去参加林美英、王华办的晚会。〕

小高：（开车）是大学路吧！

小李：对，再往前走，过了第三街，往右转就是大学路。

小高：她们的地址是多少号？

小李：三二九号。过了这个红绿灯就得往右转。嗯，再往前开一点儿，对了！对了！就是这儿。（下车拿东西）

小高：你带了什么？

小李：两打汽水儿，够不够？你呢？巧克力糖还是花儿？

小高：当然是花儿！你没听说最近她们俩都在减肥吗？

小李：肯定是球迷受了舞迷的影响。上次我还听见美英叫王华跟她一块儿去锻练呢！（按铃）

小林：小高、小李，这儿不难找吧！

小高：容易得很。恭喜你们搬了新家。住得还习惯吧？（给花）

小林：（接花）谢谢！刚开始的几天不大习惯，现在好多了。这儿没有宿舍那么热闹。所以找你们来庆祝一下。

小李：真是应该庆祝庆祝。后天就是中国新年了。

小高：在美国怎么过中国年呢？

小王：后天晚上中国同学会要举办一个新年晚会，你可以去参加。我也会去帮他们的忙。

小李：（四处看）这儿比宿舍舒服多了。这么大，够六个人住了！

小林：是住了「一家六口」！看！这是我们的「家人」。（ 指一
　　　缸鱼和一隻猫 ）

小李：你们真有意思。又养鱼又养猫，不怕猫饿了(猫)把那三条
　　　鱼给吃了吗 ？

小王：不会的，这隻猫跟我一样「光看不练」。

小林：所以我们管他叫「王子」。（ 摸摸猫 ）他好象「孔子」、
　　　「老子」一样，是这屋子里的哲学家。

小高：我看是王华的孩子吧！

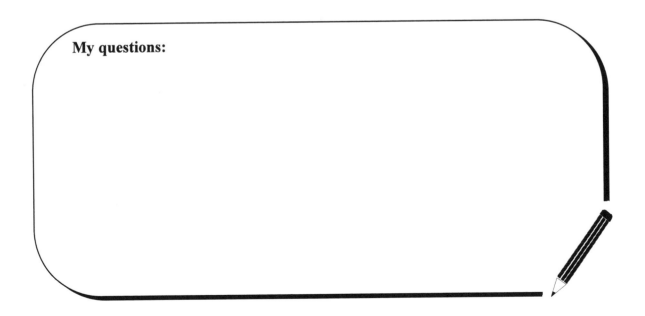

My questions:

Duìhuà

(Xiǎo Gāo, Xiǎo Lǐ qù cānjiā Lín Měiyīng, Wáng Huá bàn .de wǎnhuì.)

Xiǎo Gāo: (Kāichē) Shì Dàxué lù .ba!

Xiǎo Lǐ: Duì, zài wàng qián zǒu, guò .le dìsān jiē, wàng yòu zhuǎn
             jiù.shì Dàxué lù.

Xiǎo Gāo: Tā.men .de dìzhǐ shì duō.shǎo hào?

Xiǎo Lǐ: Sān'èrjiǔ hào. Guò .le zhè .ge hónglǜdēng jiù děi wàng yòu
             zhuǎn. En, zài wàng qián kāi yì.diǎnr. Duì.le, duì.le, jiù.shì
             zhèr. (Xiàchē ná dōng.xī)

Xiǎo Gāo: Nǐ dài .le shén.me?

Xiǎo Lǐ: Liǎng dǎ qìshuǐr, gòu .bugòu? Nǐ .ne? Qiǎokèlì
             táng hái.shì huār?

Xiǎo Gāo: Dāngrán shì huār! Nǐ méi tīngshuō zuìjìn tā.men liǎ dōu
             zài jiǎnféi .ma?

Xiǎo Lǐ: Kěndìng shì qiúmí shòu .le wǔmí .de yǐngxiǎng. Shàng.cì wǒ
             hái tīng.jiàn Měiyīng jiào Wáng Huá gēn tā yíkuàir qù duàn.liàn
             .ne! (Àn líng)

Xiǎo Lín: Xiǎo Gāo, Xiǎo Lǐ, zhèr bù nán zhǎo .ba?

Xiǎo Gāo: Róng.yì .de hěn. Gōngxǐ nǐ.men bān .le xīnjiā. Zhù .de hái
             xíguàn .ba? (Gěi huār)

Xiǎo Lín: (Jiē huār) Xiè.xie! Gāng kāishǐ .de jǐ tiān bú dà xíguàn, xiànzài
             hǎo duō .le. Zhèr méi.yǒu sùshè nà.me rè.nào, suǒ.yǐ zhǎo
             nǐ.men lái qìngzhù.yíxià.

Xiǎo Lǐ: Zhēn shì yīnggāi qìngzhù qìngzhù, hòu.tiān jiù.shì Zhōng.guó
             xīnnián .le.

Xiǎo Gāo: Zài Měi.guó zěn.me guò Zhōng.guó nián .ne?

Xiǎo Wáng: Hòu.tiān wǎn.shàng Zhōng.guó tóngxuéhuì yào jǔ bàn
             yí .ge xīnnián wǎnhuì, nǐ kě.yǐ qù cānjiā. Wǒ yě huì qù
             bāng tā.men .de máng.

Xiǎo Lǐ: (Sìchù kàn) Zhèr bǐ sùshè shū.fú duō .le. Zhè.me dà, gòu liù
                .ge rén zhù .le.

Xiǎo Lín: Shì zhù .le "yì jiā liù kǒu." Kàn! Zhè shì wǒ.men .de
                "jiārén." (Zhǐ yì gāng yú hé yì zhī māo.)

Xiǎo Lǐ: Nǐ.men zhēn yǒuyì.si. Yòu yǎng yú, yòu yǎng māo, bú pà
                māo è .le (māo) bǎ nèi sān tiáo yú gěi chī .le .ma?

Xiǎo Wáng: Bú huì .de. Zhèi zhī māo gēn wǒ yíyàng, "guāng kàn bú liàn."

Xiǎo Lín: Suǒ.yǐ wǒ.men guǎn tā jiào "wángzǐ." (Mō.mō māo) Tā
                hǎo.xiàng "Kǒngzǐ," "Lǎozǐ" yíyàng, shì zhè wū.zi lǐ .de
                zhéxuéjiā.

Xiǎo Gāo: Wǒ kàn shì Wáng Huá .de "hái.zi" .ba!

Dialogue

(Xiǎo Gāo and Xiǎo Lǐ leave to attend the party held by Lín Měiyīng and Wáng Huá.)

Xiǎo Gāo: (Driving) Is this College Road?

Xiǎo Lǐ: Yes, go farther. After you pass Third Street, turn right and that is College Road.

Xiǎo Gāo: What's the number of their address?

Xiǎo Lǐ: Three-twenty-nine. After this stoplight, you have to turn right. Hmm, go a little farther ahead. Yes, yes, it's here. (Getting out of the car and taking something.)

Xiǎo Gāo: What did you bring?

Xiǎo Lǐ: Four six packs of soda. Is that enough? How about you? Did you bring chocolate or flowers?

Xiǎo Gāo: Flowers, of course. Didn't you hear that they have been on a diet recently?

Xiǎo Lǐ: I am sure the sports fan has been influenced by the dance fan. Last time I heard that Měiyīng had asked Wáng Huá to go with her to work out. (Ringing the bell.)

Xiǎo Lín: Xiǎo Lǐ, Xiǎo Gāo, this place isn't difficult to find, is it?

Xiǎo Gāo: Very easy. Congratulations on moving to a new place. Have you gotten used to staying here? (Giving her the flowers.)

Xiǎo Lín: (Taking the flowers:) Thanks! The first few days we were not used to this place. Now it's much better. Here it is not as exciting as in the dorm. That's why we asked you guys to come over and have a celebration.

Xiǎo Lǐ: We really should celebrate. The day after tomorrow is Chinese New Year.

Xiǎo Gāo: How do you celebrate Chinese New Year in the United States?

Xiǎo Wáng: The day after tomorrow the Chinese Student Association is going to hold a New Year's party in the evening. You can attend it. I'll also go and help them.

Xiǎo Lǐ: (Looking around:) This place is much more comfortable than the dorm. It's so big. It can accommodate six people.

Xiǎo Lín: Yes, we do have six family members. Look! This is our "family" (pointing at a bowl of fish and a cat).

Xiǎo Lǐ: You are really interesting. You keep fish and a cat. Aren't you afraid that the cat will eat up those three fish once he gets hungry?

Xiǎo Wáng: No, he won't. This cat is just like me, "just looking, not touching."

Xiǎo Lín: So we call him "Prince." (Stroking the cat) He is like "Kǒngzǐ" and "Lǎozǐ." He is the philosopher in this house.

Xiǎo Gāo: I think he is Wáng Huá's "child"!

Mini-Dialogue
小對話 Xiǎoduìhuà

 Giving directions

1. A: 請問，大學路三二九號在哪兒？

   Qǐngwèn, Dàxué lù sān'èrjiǔ hào zài nǎr?

   May I ask, where is 329 College Road?

   B: 就在前邊兒。過了那個紅綠燈，左轉就到了。

   Jiù zài qián.biānr. Guò .le nà .ge hónglǜdēng, zuǒ zhuǎn jiù dào .le.

   It's just ahead. After that stoplight, turn left and you will be there.

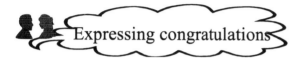

Asking and giving information about an address

1.　A:　你的地址是…？

　　　　　　　　　　　　　　　　Nǐ .de dìzhǐ shì...?
　　　　　　　　　　　　　　　　Your address is...?

　　B:　大學路，三八九號。

　　　　　　　　　　　　　　　　Dàxué lù, sānbājiǔ hào.
　　　　　　　　　　　　　　　　389 College Road.

Expressing congratulations

1.　A:　恭喜你搬了新家。

　　　　　　　　　　　　　　　　Gōngxǐ nǐ bān .le xīnjiā.
　　　　　　　　　　　　　　　　Congratuations on moving to a new
　　　　　　　　　　　　　　　　place.

　　B:　謝謝！地方不大，有時間
　　　　過來坐坐。

　　　　　　　　　　　　　　　　Xiè.xie! Dì.fāng bú dà, yǒu shíjiān
　　　　　　　　　　　　　　　　guò.lái zuò.zuò.
　　　　　　　　　　　　　　　　Thanks! My place is not very big, but
　　　　　　　　　　　　　　　　(please) come over sometime.

Making a comparison

1.　A:　這兒比宿舍大多了，一定
　　　　很舒服。

　　　　　　　　　　　　　　　　Zhèr bǐ sùshè dà duō .le, yídìng hěn
　　　　　　　　　　　　　　　　shū.fú.
　　　　　　　　　　　　　　　　This place is much bigger than the
　　　　　　　　　　　　　　　　dorm. It must be very comfortable.

　　B:　哪裏。就多了客廳和廚房
　　　　，臥室跟宿舍的一樣大，
　　　　洗澡間小了些。

　　　　　　　　　　　　　　　　Nǎ.lǐ. Jiù duō .le kètīng hé chúfáng,
　　　　　　　　　　　　　　　　wòshì gēn sùshè .de yíyàng dà,
　　　　　　　　　　　　　　　　xǐzǎojiān xiǎo .le xiē.
　　　　　　　　　　　　　　　　Not necessarily. We have a living
　　　　　　　　　　　　　　　　room and a kitchen. The bedroom is
　　　　　　　　　　　　　　　　the same size as the one in the dorm
　　　　　　　　　　　　　　　　and the bathroom is a little smaller.

Vocabulary
生詞 Shēngcí

◎ **By Order of Appearance**

住		zhù	V	to live, to stay
習慣	习惯	xíguàn	SV	to get used to
路		lù	N	road (M: 條)
往前		wàng qián	V	[go toward-front] to go forward
往		wàng	Prep	to, toward
街		jiē	N	street (M: 條)
右轉	右转	yòu zhuǎn	V	[right-turn] to turn right
地址		dìzhǐ	N	[land-site] address
紅綠燈	红绿灯	hónglǜdēng	N	[red-green-lamp] traffic light
就是		jiù.shì	Adv	[then-is] exactly, that/it is
打		dǎ	M	dozen
夠	够	gòu	SV	(to be) enough
巧克力		qiǎokèlì	N	[clever-overcome-strength] chocolate
花兒	花儿	huār	N	flower (M: 朵 duǒ, 把 bǎ 'a bunch')
當然	当然	dāngrán	Adv	[ought to-so] of course
倆		liǎ	N	two (people)
球迷		qiúmí	N	[ball-enthrall] sports fan
舞迷		wǔmí	N	[dance-enthrall] dance fan
* 迷		mí	N	fan
受...影響	受...影响	shòu...yǐngxiǎng	V	[receive...shadow-loud] to be influenced by...
* 影響	影响	yǐngxiǎng	N/V	[shadow-sound] influence, to influence
聽見	听见	tīng.jiàn	RV	[hear-see] to hear, catch the sound of
恭喜		gōngxǐ	V	[respect-happy] to congratulate
熱鬧	热闹	rè.nào	SV	[hot-noisy] to have many things going on (hustle and bustle)
慶祝	庆祝	qìngzhù	V	[celebrate-wish] to celebrate
新年		xīnnián	N	[new-year] New Year
同學會	同学会	tóngxuéhuì	N	[same-learning-association] student association
舉辦	举办	jǔbàn	V	[raise hand-manage] to sponsor, to organize (an activity)
晚會	晚会	wǎnhuì	N	[evening-meeting] evening party
參加	参加	cānjiā	V	[participate-add] to participate; to attend (a conference, meeting)

幫忙	帮忙	bāngmáng	VO/N	[help-busy] to help, help, assistance
口		kǒu	M	[mouth] measure word for people (in a family)
家人		jiārén	N	[family-people] family member
又…又…		yòu...yòu…	Conj	[again-again] both... and...
養	养	yǎng	V	to raise
貓	猫	māo	N	cat (M:隻)
* 狗		gǒu	N	dog (M:隻)
怕		pà	V	(to be) afraid of, fear that
管…叫		guǎn...jiào	V	[manage-call] to call...X
王子		wángzǐ	N	[king-son] prince
孔子		Kǒngzǐ	N	Confucius, 551-479 BC, a philosopher and founder of Confucianism
老子		Lǎozǐ	N	Laotzu, 604-531 BC, a philosopher and founder of Taoism
哲學家	哲学家	zhéxuéjiā	N	[philosophy-study-expert] philosopher
孩子		hái.zi	N	[child-Suf] child (M:個)

◎ By Grammatical Categories

Nouns/Pronouns

路		lù	N	road (M: 條)
街		jiē	N	street (M: 條)
地址		dìzhǐ	N	[land-site] address
紅綠燈	红绿灯	hónglǜdēng	N	[red-green-lamp] traffic light
巧克力		qiǎokèlì	N	[clever-overcome-strength] chocolate
花兒	花儿	huār	N	flower (M: 朵 duǒ, 把 bǎ 'a bunch')
倆		liǎ	N	two (people)
球迷		qiúmí	N	[ball-enthrall] sports fan
舞迷		wǔmí	N	[dance-enthrall] dance fan
* 迷		mí	N	fan
* 影響	影响	yǐngxiǎng	N/V	[shadow-sound] influence, to influence
新年		xīnnián	N	[new-year] New Year
晚會	晚会	wǎnhuì	N	[evening-meeting] evening party
同學會	同学会	tóngxuéhuì	N	[same-learning-association] student association
家人		jiārén	N	[family-people] family member
貓	猫	māo	N	cat (M:隻)
* 狗		gǒu	N	dog (M:隻)

孔子		Kǒngzǐ	N	Confucius, 551-479 BC, a philosopher and founder of Confucianism
老子		Lǎozǐ	N	Laotzu, 604-531 BC, a philosopher and founder of Taoism
王子		wángzǐ	N	[king-son] prince
孩子		hái.zi	N	[child-Suf] child (M:個)
哲學家	哲学家	zhéxuéjiā	N	[philosophy-study-expert] philosopher

Measure Words

| 打 | | dǎ | M | dozen |
| 口 | | kǒu | M | [mouth] measure word for people (in a family) |

Verbs/Stative Verbs/Adjectives

住		zhù	V	to live, to stay
養	养	yǎng	V	to raise
怕		pà	V	(to be) afraid of, fear that
往前		wàng qián	V	[go toward-front] to go forward
右轉	右转	yòu zhuǎn	V	[right-turn] to turn right
恭喜		gōngxǐ	V	[respect-happy] to congratulate
慶祝	庆祝	qìngzhù	V	[celebrate-wish] to celebrate
舉辦	举办	jǔbàn	V	[raise hand-manage] to sponsor, to organize (an activity)
參加	参加	cānjiā	V	[participate-add] to participate; to attend (a conference, meeting)
幫忙	帮忙	bāngmáng	VO/N	[help-busy] to help, help, assistance
管...叫		guǎn...jiào	V	[manage-call] to call...X
受...影響	受...影响	shòu...yǐngxiǎng	V	[receive...shadow-loud] to be influenced by...
聽見	听见	tīng.jiàn	RV	[hear-see] to hear, catch the sound of
習慣	习惯	xíguàn	SV	to get used to
熱鬧	热闹	rè.nào	SV	[hot-noisy] to have many things going on (hustle and bustle)
夠	够	gòu	SV	(to be) enough
往		wàng	Prep	to, toward

Adverbs

| 就是 | | jiù.shì | Adv | [then-is] exactly, that/it is |
| 當然 | 当然 | dāngrán | Adv | [ought to-so] of course |

Conjunctions

又...又...	yòu...yòu...	Conj	[again-again] both... and...

✚ Supplementary Vocabulary

1. Odds and Ends

拐		guǎi	V	to turn
接		jiē	V	to receive (a gift); to pick up (a person)
摸		mō	V	to caress, to touch lightly with the fingers
敲門		qiāomén	VO	[knock-door] to knock (on a door)
上車	上车	shàngchē	VO	[ascend-car] to get in (a car)
下車	下车	xiàchē	VO	[descend-car] to get out of (a car)
四處	四处	sìchù	N	[four-place] everywhere
東南西北	东南西北	dōng nán xī běi	N	[east-south-west-north] all directions
西洋畫	西洋画	xīyánghuà	N	[west-ocean-drawing] western painting
舞會		wǔhuì	N	[dance-party] dancing party
跳舞		tiàowǔ	VO	[jump-dance] to dance

2. Chinese Festivals

除夕		Chúxì/Chúxī	N	[get rid of-eve] (Chinese) New Year's Eve
元宵節/ 燈節	元宵节/ 灯节	Yuánxiāojié/ Dēngjié	N	[beginning-night-festival] / [lantern-festival] Lantern Festival
清明節	清明节	Qīngmíngjié	N	[clear-bright-festival] Tomb-Sweeping Day
端午節	端午节	Duānwǔjié	N	[proper-noon-festival] Dragon Boat Festival
中秋節	中秋节	Zhōngqiūjié	N	[middle-autumn-festival] Autumn Festival

Characters
漢字 Hànzì

又 往 街 路

容 易 習 慣

怕 受 影 響

王 住 幫 管

花 謝 孩 夠

又…又   yòu…yòu   both…and

又

yòu
again   又
2   (again)

A: 你**又學日文又學中文**，不累嗎？
B: 累是累，可是我覺得這兩個語言都很有意思。

往

往   wàng   to, toward
往前   wàng qián   to go foward
*往後   wàng hòu   to go backward

wàng
to, toward   彳
8

A: 請問，圖書館在哪兒？
B: 你再**往前**走兩條街就到了。

街

*一條街   yì tiáo jiē   a street
*大街   dàjiē   main street
*街上   jiē .shàng   on the street

jiē
street   行
12   (to walk)

A: 大學門口的**那條街**真熱鬧。
B: 可不是嗎！早晚都有人在**街上**逛。

路

*走路   zǒulù   to walk, go on foot
*路上   lù .shàng   on the road

lù
road   足
13   (foot)

A: 晚上不要一個人在**路上**走。
B: 當然，要出門，我一定找你。

繁簡對照：	其他漢字： *條 SC51	✎ **My notes:**

容易　　　　róng.yì　　　　(to be) easy

容

róng
countenance, to
contain, tolerate
宀
10

A: 學中文眞難！
B: 學英文也**不容易**呀！

易

yì
(to be) easy, to
change　　日
8　　　(sun)

A: 學什麼比較**容易**找到工作？
B: 現在什麼工作都**不容易**找。

習

xí
to learn, to
familiarize
oneself with　羽
11　　(feather)

習慣　　　　xíguàn　　　　to get used to
*學習　　　xuéxí　　　　to learn, to study

A: 你在宿舍住，**習慣**嗎？
B: 剛開始的時候**不太習慣**，現在好一點兒了。

慣

guàn
to be used to,
spoil　　　忄
14　　(heart)

*吃得慣　　chī.deguàn　　to get used to eating
*住得慣　　zhù.deguàn　　to get used to living

A: 你**吃得慣吃不慣**美國飯？
B: **吃不慣**，但是還是得吃啊！

繁簡對照：	其他漢字：	✎ **My notes:**
習 慣	习 惯	

怕

pà
to be afraid 忄
8   (heart)

*害怕   hàipà   fear
*恐怕   kǒngpà   I'm afraid, perhaps

A: 你一個人住校外，**怕不怕**？
B: 有什麼好**怕**的 。

受 →

shòu
to receive, accept
又
8   (again)

受…影響   shòu…yǐngxiǎng   to be influenced by

A: 你一定是**受了小林的影響**，這麼喜歡吃糖。
B: 她對我一點兒影響也沒有。

影

yǐng
shadow, image,
reflection 彡
15

影響   yǐngxiǎng   influence
電影兒   diànyǐngr   movie
*影子   yǐng.zi   shadow

A: 你喜歡看什麼樣的**電影**？
B: 我什麼**電影**都喜歡看。

響

xiǎng
loudly   音
21   (sound)

*音響   yīnxiǎng   stereo

A: 什麼對孩子有很大的**影響**？
B: 電視對孩子有很大的**影響**。

繁簡對照：	其他漢字：	✎ **My notes:**
響 响	*隻 SC52 *貓 SC53 *狗 SC54	

王

| 王子 | wángzǐ | prince |
| *國王 | guówáng | king |

wáng
king, ruler,
common surname
玉
4 (jade)

A: 你管你的狗叫什麼？
B: 叫「王子」。

住

| *住址 | zhùzhǐ | address |

zhù
to live 亻
7 (person)

A: 我們明天晚上有個舞會，你來不來？
B: 好啊！可是我不知道你住哪兒。

幫

| *幫忙 | bāngmáng | to help |

bāng
to help 巾
17 (a towel)

A: 你今天中午有沒有空兒？幫我一個忙吧！
B: 幫你的忙可以，你得請我吃飯。

管

| 管…叫 | guǎn…jiào | to call…X |
| *管家 | guǎnjiā | housekeeper |

guǎn
to control, manage,
take care of 竹
14 (bamboo)

A: 美國人管整天坐著看電視吃東西的人叫什麼？
B: 我們管那種人叫 Couch Potato。

| 繁簡對照： | 其他漢字： | ✎ **My notes:** |
| 幫 帮 | | |

花兒	huār	flower
*花粉	huāfěn	pollen
*花粉熱	huāfěnrè	hay fever

huā
flower   艹
8   (grass)

A: 這兒的**花兒**眞漂亮！
B: 我一看見**花兒**就頭疼，我對**花粉**過敏。

| 謝謝 | xiè.xie | Thank you, |
| *不謝 | búxiè | You are welcome, |

xiè
to thank   言
17   (speech)

A: **謝謝**你來幫我的忙。
B: 哪裏，不客氣，這是我應該做的。

| 孩子 | hái.zi | child |
| *小孩兒 | xiǎoháir | child |

hái
child, infant,
baby   子
9   (son, child)

A: 你有沒有兄弟姐妹？
B: 沒有，我們家就我一個**孩子**。

| 不夠 | bú gòu | to not be enough |

gòu
enough   夕
11   (evening)

A: 一打啤酒**夠不夠**三個人喝？
B: **夠了，夠了**。

繁簡對照：	其他漢字：	✎ **My notes:**
謝 谢 夠=够	*草 SC55 *樹 SC56	

Grammar
語法 yǔfǎ

Ⓐ Major Sentence Patterns 主要句型 zhǔyào jùxíng

1. A 對 B 有影響 / B 受 A 的影響

1.1 A 對 B 有影響

Structure	Gloss
A 對 B 有影響	A has influence on B
A 對 B 有很大的影響	A has great influence on B
A 對 B 的影響很大	A has great influence on B
A 對 B 沒(有)影響	A has no influence on B
A 對 B 一點兒影響 都/也 沒有	A has no influence on B at all

1.　誰對你的影響最大？

Shéi duì nǐ .de yǐngxiǎng zuì dà?
Who has the greatest influence on you?

我的老師對我的影響最大。

Wǒ .de lǎoshī duì wǒ .de yǐngxiǎng zuì dà.
My teacher has the greatest influence on me.

2.　你爸爸對你有沒有影響？

Nǐ bà.bà duì nǐ yǒu .méi.yǒu yǐngxiǎng?
Does your father have any influence on you?

我爸爸對我有很大的影響。

Wǒ bà.bà duì wǒ yǒu hěn dà .de yǐngxiǎng.
My father has great influence on me.

我爸爸對我一點兒影響也沒有。

Wǒ bà.bà duì wǒ yì.diǎnr yǐngxiǎng yě méi.yǒu.
My father has no influence on me at all.

💡 影響 yǐngxiǎng may be a noun meaning "influence" or a verb meaning "to influence." In pattern 1.1, it functions as a noun. 對 duì is a preposition that means "to or toward"; it signals that the direction of 影響 is toward the object. Hence, A 對 B 的影響 means "the influence of A on B," and A 對 B 有影響 means "A has influence on B."

🔄 See L10–B2, L17–A4, L18–A2, L20–B4, L23–B4 for more on A 對 B...

1.2 B 受 A 的影響

Structure	Gloss
B 　　　受 A 的影響	B is/has been influenced by A
B 沒/不會 受 A 的影響	B was not/won't be influenced by A

1. 王華受誰的影響，每天都去鍛
    練？

    Wáng Huá shòu shéi .de yǐngxiǎng,
    měitiān dōu qù duàn.liàn?
    Who influenced Wang Hua to exercise
    every day?

    王華受美英的影響，每天都去鍛
    練。

    Wáng Huá shòu Měiyīng .de yǐngxiǎng,
    měitiān dōu qù duàn.liàn.
    Wang Hua has been influenced by
    Meiying; (she) goes to exercise every day.

2. 你受誰的影響最大？

    Nǐ shòu shéi .de yǐngxiǎng zuì dà?
    Who has greatly influenced you?

    我受我的朋友的影響最大。

    Wǒ shòu wǒ péng.yǒu .de yǐngxiǎng zuì dà.
    I has been greatly influenced by my friends.

3. 你有沒有受誰的影響？

    Nǐ yǒu .méi.yǒu shòu shéi .de yǐngxiǎng?
    Have you ever been influenced by anyone?

    我沒(有)受誰的影響。

    Wǒ méi(.yǒu) shòu shéi .de yǐngxiǎng.
    I have not been influenced by anybody.

 In pattern 1.2, 影響 yǐngxiǎng functions as a verb. In Chinese, there is no distinction of
voice in verbs and the direction of a verb may be outward from the subject as an actor or
inward toward the subject as a goal. 受 shòu is basically a verb that means "to receive,"
thus B 受 A 的影響 literally means "B receives A's influence." Since in English there is
a distinction between active and passive voice, you can translate this expression into
passive voice "B is/has been influenced by A."

2. 又...又... construction

Structure	Gloss
S 又 SV$_1$ 又 SV$_2$	S is both Adj$_1$ and Adj$_2$
S 又 (AuxV) VP$_1$ 又 (AuxV) VP$_2$	S (AuxV) does both VP$_1$ and VP$_2$

1. 誰又養魚又養貓？

    Shéi yòu yǎng yú yòu yǎng māo?
    Who raises both fish and cats?

    王華和美英又養魚又養貓。

    Wáng Huá hé Měiyīng yòu yǎng yú yòu
    yǎng māo.
    Wang Hua and Meiying raise both fish
    and cats.

2. 誰又會說英文又會說中文？

    Shéi yòu huì shuō Yīngwén yòu huì shuō
    Zhōngwén?

Who can speak both English and Chinese?

小高又會說英文又會說中文。

Xiǎo Gāo yòu huì shuō Yīngwén yòu huì shuō Zhōngwén.

Xiao Gao can speak both English and Chinese.

3. 什麼又有意思又熱鬧？

Shén.me yòu yǒuyì.si yòu rè.nào?
What is both interesting and exciting?

中國新年又有意思又熱鬧。

Zhōng.guó xīnnián yòu yǒuyì.si yòu rè.nào.
Chinese New Year is both interesting and exciting.

又...又... 'both...and...' is a set of correlative markers that connect two similar constructions. Because 又 is an adverb, it always precedes a verb (including stative verb/adjective and auxiliary verb).

See L13–B4 for more on 又.

B Usage of Common Phrases 詞組用法 cízǔ yòngfǎ

1. 往 X V expression

Structure	Gloss
往 X V	V toward X
往東走	walk toward the east
往西拐	turn to the west
往南轉	turn to the south
往北看	look to the north
往右滑	ski/slide to the right
往左跑	run toward the left
往上爬	climb upward/toward the top
往下走	walk downward/toward the bottom
往前開	drive forward
往後退	withdraw backward

1. 請問，到圖書館得怎麼走？

Qǐngwèn, dào túshūguǎn děi zěn.me zǒu?
Excuse me, how can I get to the library?

你先往東走，再往南拐，然後一直走就到了。

Nǐ xiān wàng dōng zǒu, zài wàng nán guǎi, ránhòu yìzhí zǒu jiù dào .le.
You go toward the east, then turn south, then go straight ahead, and then you'll be there.

2.   請問，到紐約得怎麼走？

Qǐngwèn, dào Niǔyuē děi zěn.me zǒu?
Excuse me, how can I get to New York?

你先往前開，開到80號公路，
再一直往東開就到了。

Nǐ xiān wàng qián kāi, kāi.dào bāshí hào
gōnglù, zài yìzhí wàng dōng kāi, jiù dào .le.
You drive straight ahead until you reach
highway 80, then (you) continue driving
to the east, and then you'll be there.

2. A 管 B 叫 X

Structure	Gloss
A 管 B 叫 X	A calls B (as) X

1.   中文管這個叫什麼？

Zhōngwén guǎn zhèi .ge jiào shén.me?
How do you say this in Chinese?

中文管這個叫貓。

Zhōngwén guǎn zhèi .ge jiào māo.
In Chinese this is "māo."

2.   美國人管房子叫什麼？

Měi.guórén guǎn "fáng.zi" jiào shén.me?
What do Americans call "fáng.zi"?

美國人管房子叫 "house."

Měi.guórén guǎn "fáng.zi" jiào "house."
Americans call "fáng.zi" "house."

3. The usage of 幫 (忙)

Structure	Gloss
A (AuxV)　幫　B　VO	A helps B to VO
A (AuxV)　來/去幫忙	A (AuxV) come/go to help
A (AuxV)　幫　B　的忙	A helps B out

1.   他下個星期要開舞會，需要很
     多人幫他做什麼？

Tā xià .ge xīngqī yào kāi wǔhuì, xūyào
hěn duō rén bāng tā zuò shén.me?
He is going to have a dance party next week.
What does he need all those people to do?

他下個星期要開舞會，需要很
多人幫他搬椅子。

Tā xià .ge xīngqī yào kāi wǔhuì, xūyào
hěn duō rén bāng tā bān yǐ.zi.
He is going to have a dance party next
week. He needs a lot of people to help
move the chairs.

2. 請問，你能不能幫我把花送到
林小姐家去？

Qǐngwèn, nǐ néng .bùnéng bāng wǒ bǎ
huā sòng.dào Lín xiǎo.jiě jiā qù?
Excuse me, could you deliver the flowers
to Miss Lin's house for me?

沒問題，我可以幫你把花送到
林小姐家去。

Méi wèntí, wǒ kě.yǐ bāng nǐ bǎ huā
sòng.dào Lín xiǎo.jiě jiā qù.
No problem, I can deliver the flowers to
Miss Lin's house for you.

3. 明天我要搬家，誰可以來幫忙？

Míng.tiān wǒ yào bānjiā, shéi kě.yǐ lái
bāngmáng?
I am moving tomorrow; who can come to
help?

你明天要搬家，我可以來幫忙。

Nǐ míng.tiān yào bānjiā, wǒ kě.yǐ lái
bāngmáng.
You are moving tomorrow. I can come
to help.

4. 小林要把書搬到樓上去，誰可
以去幫忙？

Xiǎo Lín yào bǎ shū bān.dào lóu.shàng
qù, shéi kě.yǐ qù bāngmáng?
Xiao Lin is going to move the books
upstairs, who can go to help?

我們可以去幫忙。

Wǒ.men kě.yǐ qù bāngmáng.
We can help.

5. 你後天得去幫誰的忙？

Nǐ hòu.tiān děi qù bāng shéi .de máng?
Whom will you help out the day after
tomorrow?

小林後天要搬家，我得去幫她
的忙。

Xiǎo Lín hòu.tiān yào bānjiā, wǒ děi qù
bāng tā .de máng.
Xiao Lin is moving the day after
tomorrow; I have to go to help her out.

6. 這個星期我得打三篇報告，你
可以幫我的忙嗎？

Zhèi .ge xīngqī wǒ děi dǎ sān piān
bàogào, nǐ kě.yǐ bāng wǒ .de máng .ma?
This week I have to type up three papers.
Can you help me out?

這個星期我不太忙，我可以幫你
的忙。

Zhèi .ge xīngqī wǒ bútài máng, wǒ kě.yǐ
bāng nǐ .de máng.
This week I am not very busy; I can help
you out.

幫 bāng 'to help' is a transitive verb that takes an object (see examples 1 and 2). 幫忙 bāngmáng [to help-busy] is a compound intransitive verb (VO) that doesn't take an object (see examples 3 and 4). If an object is inserted between 幫 and 忙, e.g., 幫 X 忙, then it means "to help X out" (see examples 5 and 6).

4. The usage of 夠

Function	Structure	Gloss
as a stative verb	S 夠了	S is enough
	S (不) 夠	S is not enough
as an adverb	X 夠 Adj 了	X is Adj enough
as an adverb	夠 No. M N V 了	to have enough amount/space for No. of N to V

1. 我請了十個朋友來吃飯，我們的菜夠不夠？

    Wǒ qǐng .le shí .ge péng.yǒu lái chīfàn, wǒ.men .de cài gòu .bugòu?
    I have invited ten friends to come to dinner. Do we have enough food?

    菜夠了，飯不夠。

    Cài gòu .le, fàn bú gòu.
    (We have) enough dishes, (but) not enough rice.

2. 這個房子夠不夠大，五個人住怎麼樣？

    Zhèi .ge fáng.zi gòu .bugòu dà, wǔ .ge rén zhù zěn.meyàng?
    Is this house big enough? How about five people living in it?

    這個房子夠大了，五個人住沒問題。

    Zhèi .ge fáng.zi gòu dà .le, wǔ .ge rén zhù méi wèntí.
    This house is big enough. There is plenty of room for five people.

3. 這些菜夠六個人吃嗎？

    Zhèixiē cài gòu liù .ge rén chī .ma?
    Is there enough food to feed six people?

    這些菜夠六個人吃的了。

    Zhèixiē cài gòu liù .ge rén chī .de .le.
    There is enough food to feed six people.

 夠 gòu 'enough' can be either a stative verb or an adverb. When you would like to say "We have enough X" or "We don't have enough X" in English, you should say 我們的 X夠了, or 我們的 X不夠.

✗   *Don't* say 我們有夠X or 我們不夠X.

5. The usage of SV 得很

Structure	Gloss
S SV 得很	S is very Adj

1. 你們宿舍熱鬧不熱鬧啊？

Nǐ.men sùshè rè.nào .burè.nào .a?
Are there lots of things going on in your dormitory?

熱鬧得很。

Rè.nào .de hěn.
There are lots of things going on.

2. 他們的公寓舒服不舒服啊？

Tā.men .de gōngyù shū.fú .bushū.fú .a?
Is their apartment comfortable?

舒服得很。

Shū.fú .de hěn.
(It's) very comfortable.

💡 很 'very' is an adverb that usually occurs in front of a verb or an adjective. When it follows SV得 it denotes the emphatic degree of "very."

ⓒ Reentry 複習 fùxí

1. 把…給… construction

Structure	Gloss
S (AuxV/Neg) 把 O 給 V complement 了	S (AuxV/Neg) do/did ... to O

1. 貓把魚給吃了嗎？

Māo bǎ yú gěi chī .le ma?
Did the cat eat the fish?

貓沒把魚給吃了。

Māo méi bǎ yú gěi chī .le.
No, the cat didn't eat the fish.

2. 你喝那麼多汽水兒，會把肚子給喝大了。

Nǐ hē nà.me duō qìshuǐr, huì bǎ dù.zi gěi hē dà .le.
You drank so much soda, (you) will have a big belly.

3. 別把我的巧克力糖都給吃了！

Bié bǎ wǒ .de qiǎokèlì táng dōu gěi chī .le!
Don't eat up all of my chocolate candies!

💡 In a bǎ construction, you may optionally add the verb 給 'to give' before the verb. The function of this 給 is to denote that the action has done harm or benefit to someone.

🔄 See L15–A1, L22–A1 for more on 把.

Cultural Notes
文化點滴 wénhuà diǎndī

1. 中國年 Zhōng.guónián 'Chinese New Year' is also known as 春節 Chūnjié 'Spring Festival' or 農歷(新)年 Nónglì(xīn)nián 'Farmer's Calendar New Year.' The celebration starts on the day of New Year's Eve (除夕 chúxì), when people who are away from home (one's paternal grandparents' home) must try to go home to the family reunion dinner (吃團圓飯 chī tuányuánfàn). After the reunion dinner, children and grandchildren kowtow to their grandparents and parents to wish them a prosperous year (辭歲 císuì 'to bid goodbye to the old year') and the grandparents and parents distribute lucky money (壓歲錢 yāsuìqian or 紅包 hóngbāo) to the children and grandchildren. On the first five days of Chinese New Year, when relatives and friends come to express their New Year's greetings, 恭喜發財 gōngxǐ fācái 'congratulatons and be rich,' they also distribute lucky money to younger children, and the host family offers tangarines or oranges (橘子 jú.zi), watermelon seeds (瓜子 guāzǐ), or New Year's cake (年糕 niángāo). 橘子 is homophonous with 吉 jí 'good luck' in most Chinese dialects; 瓜子 symbolizes "to have a lot of sons," and 年糕 is

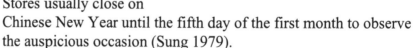

homophonous with 年年高 niánniángāo 'to have a promotion every year.' Stores usually close on Chinese New Year until the fifth day of the first month to observe the auspicious occasion (Sung 1979).

2. When invited to have dinner at a friend's house, Chinese usually bring fruit, candy, refreshments, or wine as a gift to the host family. Only Westernized young people bring flowers as a gift. When the host or hostess receives the gift, he or she is not supposed to open the gift in front of the guest(s). It is considered impolite if you do. While receiving the gift, the host or hostess must say, 謝謝，真不好意思，讓您破費了！ Xiè.xie, zhēn bù hǎo yì.si, ràng nín pòfèi .le. 'Thank you very much; it's really embarrassing to let you spend so much money (for a gift).'

3. 孔子 Kóngzǐ (Confucius, 551-479 BC), a philosopher and the founder of Confucianism, whose doctrine centered on 禮 lǐ 'propriety or rites,' has had a great influence on Chinese verbal and nonverbal behavior for 2,500 years.

4. 老子 Láozǐ (Laotzu, 604-531 BC), a philosopher and the founder of Taoism, whose doctrine centered on 自然主義 zìrán zhǔyì 'natualism,' advocated 無爲而治 wú wéi ér zhì 'to govern by doing nothing.' According to Laotzu, enlightened adminstration is possible only when the ruler can set a good example for the people to follow instead of proclaiming restrictive laws and regulations that tend to interfere with the orderly life of the masses.

5. In China people traditionally denote their birth times with four pairs of characters, the 生辰 八字 shēngchén bázì 'eight characters of one's age.' The first pair

Boar
1935, 1947, 1959, 1971, 1983
Galant and noble your friends will remain at your side.
Compatible with the Rabbit and Sheep; your opposite is the Boar.

Dog
1934, 1946, 1958, 1970, 1982
Generous and loyal you have the ability to work well with others. Compatible with the Horse and Tiger; your opposite is the Dragon.

Cock
1933, 1945, 1957, 1969, 1981
Seeking wisdom and truth you have a pioneering spirit. Compatible with the Snake and Ox; your opposite is the Rabbit.

Monkey
1932, 1944, 1956, 1968, 1980
Persuasive and intelligent you strive to excel. Compatible with the Dragon and Rat; your opposite is the Tiger.

Sheep
1931, 1943, 1955, 1967, 1979
Aesthetic and stylish you enjoy being a private person. Compatible with the Boar and Rabbit; your opposite is the Ox.

Rat
1936, 1948, 1960, 1972, 1984
Ambitious and sincere you can be generous with your financial resources. Compatible with the Dragon and Monkey; your opposite is the Horse.

Chinese Zodiac
Each of the 12 years of the Chinese Zodiac falls under a different animal sign. The sign under which you were born is believed to determine the circumstances of your life and the kind of person you are. What's your sign? Locate your birth year and find out. If you were born before 1925 add 12 to the year you were born to determine your sign.

Horse
1930, 1942, 1954, 1966, 1978
Physically attractive and popular you like the company of others. Compatible with the Tiger and Dog; your opposite is the Rat.

Ox
1925, 1937, 1949, 1961, 1973
A leader, you are bright and cheerful. Compatible with the Snake and Cock; your opposite is the Sheep.

Tiger
1926, 1938, 1950, 1962, 1974
Forthright and sensitive you possess great courage.
Compatible with the Horse and Dog; your opposite is the Monkey.

Rabbit
1927, 1939, 1951, 1963, 1975
Talented and affectionate you are a seeker of tranquility. Compatible with the Sheep and Boar; your opposite is the Cock.

Dragon
1928, 1940, 1952, 1964, 1976
Robust and passionate your life is filled with complexity. Compatible with the Monkey; your opposite is the Dog.

Snake
1929, 1941, 1953, 1965, 1977
Strong willed and intense you display great wisdom.
Compatible with the Cock and Ox; your opposite is the Boar.

denotes the year of one's birth, the second pair the month, the third the day, and the fourth the time (or hour). The character pairs are formed by combining 天干 tiāngān 'the Ten Celestial Stems' (hereafter abbreviated S) and 地支 dìzhī 'the Twelve Terrestrial

Branches' (abbreviated B) in a regular order, using S1 to S10 on the left side and B1 to B12 on the right side while cycling through both lists concurrently. The resulting combinations are: S1B1, S2B2,..., S10B10, S1B11, S2B12, S3B1, and so on. The list ends with a complete sixty-year cycle. Each of the twelve Terrestrial Branches is represented by a different animal sign, and together they form the 十二生肖 shí'èr shēngxiào 'Chinese Zodiac' (Sung 1981).

Names and Affinities of the Ten Celestial Stems
天干 tiāngān

Stems	Dual Combination	Corresponding Elements	Planets
S1 甲 jiǎ	甲乙 jiǎ yǐ	木 mù 'wood'	Jupiter
S2 乙 yǐ			
S3 丙 bǐng	丙丁 bǐng dīng	火 huǒ 'fire'	Mars
S4 丁 dīng			
S5 戊 wù	戊己 wù jǐ	土 tǔ 'earth'	Saturn
S6 己 jǐ			
S7 庚 gēng	庚辛 gēng xīn	金 jīn 'metal'	Venus
S8 辛 xīn			
S9 壬 rén	壬癸 rén guǐ	水 shuǐ 'water'	Mercury
S10 癸 guǐ			

The Twelve Terrestrial Branches
地支 dìzhī

Branches	Symbolic Animals		Zodiacal Signs	Corresponding Hours
B1 子 zǐ	鼠	shǔ 'Rat'	Aries	11pm-1am
B2 丑 chǒu	牛	niú 'Ox'	Taurus	1-3am
B3 寅 yín	虎	hǔ 'Tiger'	Gemini	3-5am
B4 卯 mǎo	兔	tù 'Rabbit'	Cancer	5-7am
B5 辰 chén	龍	lóng 'Dragon'	Leo	7-9am
B6 巳 sì	蛇	shé 'Snake'	Virgo	9-11am
B7 午 wǔ	馬	mǎ 'Horse'	Libra	11am-1pm
B8 未 wèi	羊	yáng 'Sheep'	Scorpio	1-3pm
B9 申 shēn	猴	hóu 'Monkey'	Sagittarius	3-5pm
B10 酉 yǒu	雞	jī 'Cock'	Capricorn	5-7pm
B11 戌 xū	狗	gǒu 'Dog'	Aquarius	7-9pm
B12 亥 hài	豬	zhū 'Boar'	Pisces	9-11pm

對話	92頁
小對話	98頁
生詞	99頁
漢字	104頁
語法	110頁
文化點滴	116頁

第十七課　你洗好澡了沒有？

對話

〔王華起床，發現林美英在浴室「高歌」。〕

小王：（敲門）小林！別唱了，快一點兒，好不好？我快遲到了。只剩十分鐘，要洗臉、刷牙、上廁所，真急死人了。你為什麼不能晚上洗澡呢？

小林：早上洗，才有精神上課呀！等（一）會兒，我快把頭髮吹乾了。（用吹風機，出來）你看，我的頭髮是不是太長了，應該去燙一下了。

小王：美英，晚上再研究你的頭髮吧。（自言自語）真倒霉，今天晚起，就蹚上她洗頭。這小姐，什麼都快，就是洗頭慢。

小林：看你，平常慢吞吞的，今天這麼急！

小王：我得趕去上課呀！

　　　　　　　（王華、林美英下午上完課後回來）

小林：你今天可不能再熬夜了，要不然，明天起晚了，又大喊大叫的。

小王：可不是嗎？我不像你是個夜貓子。（我要是）早睡早起，（就）什麼事兒也沒有，一晚睡就糟了。

小林：今天早上，你一直催我，害我頭髮沒吹好。

小王：你的頭髮太麻煩了，為什麼不剪短呢？剪短了，才好看，更容易找到男朋友。嗯！你看，高德中這個人怎麼樣？他好像對你挺有意思的。

小林：別胡說，我們不過是朋友。

小王：他好靜，你好動，正好是一對兒。而且他看起來很老實，没什麼脾氣，一定是個「好好先生」。

小林：這麼說，你應該配小李了，他外向，你內向嘛。

小王：我們倆說到哪兒去了。我得去洗澡、睡覺了。

对话

〔王华起床，发现林美英在浴室「高歌」。〕

小王：（敲门）小林！别唱了，快一点儿，好不好？我快迟到了。只剩十分钟，要洗脸、刷牙、上厕所，真急死人了。你为什么不能晚上洗澡呢？

小林：早上洗，才有精神上课呀！等（一）会儿，我快把头发吹干了。（用吹风机，出来）你看，我的头发是不是太长了，应该去烫一下了。

小王：美英，晚上再研究你的头发吧。（自言自语）真倒霉，今天晚起，就碰上她洗头。这小姐，什么都快，就是洗头慢。

小林：看你，平常慢吞吞的，今天这么急！

小王：我得赶去上课呀！

（王华、林美英下午上完课后回来）

小林：你今天可不能再熬夜了，要不然，明天起晚了，又大喊大叫的。

小王：可不是吗？我不象你是个夜猫子。（我要是）早睡早起，（就）什么事儿也没有，一晚睡就糟了。

小林：今天早上，你一直催我，害我头发没吹好。

小王：你的头发太麻烦了，为什么不剪短呢？剪短了，才好看，更容易找到男朋友。嗯！你看，高德中这个人怎么样？他好象对你挺有意思的。

小林：别胡说，我们不过是朋友。

小王：他好静，你好动，正好是一对儿。而且他看起来很老实，
　　　没什么脾气，一定是个「好好先生」。

小林：这么说，你应该配小李了，他外向，你内向嘛。

小王：我们俩说到哪儿去了。我得去洗澡、睡觉了。

My questions:

Duìhuà

(Wánghuá qǐchuáng, fāxiàn Lín Měiyīng zài yùshì "gāogē.")

Xiǎo Wáng: (Qiāomén) Xiǎo Lín! Bié chàng .le, kuài yì.diǎnr, hǎo
.bu.hǎo? Wǒ kuài chídào .le. Zhǐ shèng shí fēnzhōng,
yào xǐliǎn, shuāyá, shàng cèsuǒ, zhēn jí.sǐrén .le. Nǐ
wèishén.me bù néng wǎn.shàng xǐzǎo .ne?

Xiǎo Lín: Zǎo.shàng xǐ, cái yǒu jīng.shén .a! Děng (.yì)huǐr, wǒ
kuài bǎ tóu.fà chuīgān .le. (Yòng chuīfēngjī, chū.lái). Nǐ
kàn, wǒ .de tóu.fà shì.bú.shì tài cháng .le, yīnggāi qù tàng
.yíxià .le.

Xiǎo Wáng: Měiyīng, wǎn.shàng zài yánjiū nǐ .de tóu.fà .ba! (Zì yán
zì yǔ) Zhēn dǎoméi, jīn.tiān wǎn qǐ, jiù pèng.shàng tā
xǐtóu. Zhè xiǎo.jiě, shén.me dōu kuài, jiù.shì xǐtóu màn.

Xiǎo Lín: Kàn nǐ, píngcháng màntūntūn .de, jīn.tiān zhè.me jí!

Xiǎo Wáng: Wǒ děi gǎn qù shàngkè .a!

(Wáng Huá, Lín Měiyīng xià.wǔ shàngwán kè hòu huí.lái.)

Xiǎo Lín: Nǐ jīn.tiān kě bù néng zài áoyè .le, yào.burán, míng.tiān qǐ wǎn .le,
yòu dà hǎn dà jiào .de.

Xiǎo Wáng: Kě bú.shì ma! Wǒ bú xiàng nǐ, shì .ge yèmāo.zi. (Wǒ yào.shì) zǎo
shuì zǎo qǐ, (jiù) shén.me shìr yě méi.yǒu, yì wǎn shuì jiù zāo.le.

Xiǎo Lín: Jīn.tiān zǎo.shàng, nǐ yìzhí cuī wǒ, hài wǒ tóu.fà méi chuīhǎo.

Xiǎo Wáng: Nǐ .de tóu.fà tài má.fán .le. Wèishén.me bù jiǎnduǎn .ne? Jiǎnduǎn
.le, cái hǎokàn, gèng róng.yì zhǎo.dào nánpéng.yǒu. En! Nǐ kàn, Gāo
Dézhōng zhè .ge rén zěn.meyàng? Tā hǎo.xiàng duì nǐ tǐng yǒuyì.si
.de.

Xiǎo Lín: Bié húshuō. Wǒ.men búguò shì péng.yǒu.

Xiǎo Wáng: Tā hàojìng, nǐ hàodòng, zhènghǎo shì yíduìr. Érqiě tā kàn.qǐ.lái hěn
lǎoshí, méi shén.me pí.qì, yídìng shì .ge "hǎohǎo xiān.shēng."

Xiǎo Lín: Zhè.me shuō, nǐ yīnggāi pèi Xiǎo Lǐ .le. Tā wàixiàng, nǐ nèixiàng
.ma.

Xiǎo Wáng: Wǒ.men liǎ shuō.dào nǎr qù .le. Wǒ děi qù xǐzǎo, shuìjiào .le.

Dialogue

(After Wánghuá gets up, she finds that Lín Měiyīng is singing in the bathroom.)

Xiǎo Wáng: (Knocking at the door) Xiao Lin! Don't sing anymore. Could you hurry up? I'm going to be late. There are only ten minutes left. I need to wash my face, brush my teeth, and go to the bathroom. It really rushes me. Why can't you take a bath at night?

Xiǎo Lín: Taking a shower in the morning will keep me refreshed for classes. Just a minute. I'm going to blow-dry my hair. (She uses the hair dryer, then comes out of the bathroom.) Take a look of my hair; is it too long? Should I get a perm?

Xiǎo Wáng: Měiyīng, let's "study" your hair tonight. (Talking to herself:) How unlucky! Today I got up late and then she just had to wash her hair. This girl is quick at everything except washing her hair.

Xiǎo Lín: See, you are always slow. (Why are you) in such a hurry today?

Xiǎo Wáng: I have to hurry to go to my classes!

(Wánghuá and Lín Měiyīng come home after they finish their classes.)

Xiǎo Lín: You can't stay up late tonight. Otherwise, you'll get up late tomorrow and yell again.

Xiǎo Wáng: Isn't that true? I'm not a "night owl" like you. If I go to bed and get up early, everything will be all right. Once I stay up late, I will be in trouble.

Xiǎo Lín: This morning you kept rushing me, so I couldn't dry my hair well.

Xiǎo Wáng: Your hair is too much trouble. Why don't you cut it short? You'll look better with short hair and it'll be even easier to find a boyfriend. Hmm, what do you think of Gāo Dézhōng? He seems to be interested in you.

Xiǎo Lín: Don't talk nonsense. We are only friends.

Xiǎo Wáng: He is quiet and you are active. You are a perfect match. Besides, he seems to be honest and doesn't have a bad temper. He must be "Mr. Right."

Xiǎo Lín: With this logic, you should be matched with Xiǎo Lǐ. He is outgoing and you are introverted.

Xiǎo Wáng: What have we been saying? I have to take a bath and go to bed.

Mini-Dialogue
小對話 Xiǎoduìhuà

Complaining

1. A: 你今天早上一直趕我，害
      我頭髮没吹好。

   Nǐ jīn.tiān zǎo.shàng yìzhí gǎn wǒ,
   hài wǒ tóu.fà méi chuīhǎo.

   This morning you kept rushing me, so
   I couldn't dry my hair well.

   B: 誰叫你不早一點兒起床？

   Shéi jiào nǐ bù zǎo yì.diǎnr qǐchuáng?
   Who asked you to sleep so late?

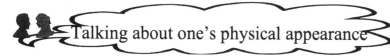

Talking about one's physical appearance

1. A: 你看，我的頭髮是不是太
      長了？

   Nǐ kàn, wǒ .de tóu.fà shì .bu.shì tài
   cháng .le?

   Look. My hair is too long, isn't it?

   B: 有一點兒。剪短了也好，
      現在流行短髮。

   Yǒu yì.diǎnr. Jiǎnduǎn .le yě hǎo,
   xiànzài liúxíng duǎnfà.

   It's a bit long. It's fine to cut it short.
   Now short hair is in.

Talking about a person's temperament

1. A: 你看他這個人怎麼樣？

   Nǐ kàn tā zhè .ge rén zěn.meyàng?
   What do you think of this guy?

   B: 還不錯，就是內向了一點
      兒。

   Hái búcuò, jiù.shì nèixiàng .le yì.diǎnr.
   Not bad. He is just a bit introverted.

Vocabulary
生詞 Shēngcí

◎ **By Order of Appearance**

	洗澡		xǐzǎo	VO	[wash-bath] to bathe
	快		kuài	SV/Adv	(to be) quick
*	慢		màn	SV/Adv	(to be) slow
	遲到	迟到	chídào	V	[late-arrive] to arrive late
	只		zhǐ	Adv	only
	剩		shèng	V	to remain, left over
	洗		xǐ	V	to wash
	臉	脸	liǎn	N	face (M: 張)
	刷牙		shuāyá	VO	to brush the teeth
*	牙(齒)	牙(齿)	yá(chǐ)	N	[tooth-tooth] tooth (M: 顆 kē)
	廁所	厕所	cèsuǒ	N	[toilet-building] toilet, lavatory (M: 間)
	急死人		jí.sǐrén	IE	[anxious-death-people] to rush anxiously
	精神		jīng.shén	N/Adj	vigor, vitality, spirited
	頭髮	头发	tóu.fà/tóu.fǎ	N	[hear-hair] hair on the head (M: 根 gēn, 頭)
	吹乾	吹干	chuīgān	RV	[blow-dry] to blow dry
*	吹風	吹风	chuīfēng	VO	[blow-wind] to blow
*	吹風機	吹风机	chuīfēngjī	N	[blow-wind-machine] hair dryer (M: 個)
	燙	烫	tàng	V	to perm, to iron (clothes)
	倒霉		dǎoméi	SV	[inverse-mold] (to be) out of luck (also written as 倒楣 dǎoméi—inverse-lintel)
	蹦上		pèng.shàng	V	[bump-up] to run into an unexpected situation; to bump into
	頭	头	tóu	N	head (M: 個)
	慢吞吞		màntūntūn	SV	(to be) very slow
	急		jí	SV	(to be) impatient, anxious
	趕	赶	gǎn	V	to hurry, to rush
	熬夜		áoyè	VO	[sustain-night] to burn the midnight oil
*	夜		yè	N	night, evening
	要不然		yào.burán	Conj	[want-not-although] otherwise
	起(來)	起(来)	qǐ(.lái)	V	[rise-come] to get up
	晚		wǎn	Adv/SV	(to be) late
*	早		zǎo	Adv/SV	(to be) early
	喊		hǎn	V	to shout, cry out, yell

糟了		zāo.le	SV	to become a mess
一直	一直	yìzhí	Adv	[one-straight] all the time
催		cuī	V	to urge, press
害		hài	V	to cause someone (trouble)
* 弄		nòng	V	to handle, to do (causative)
吹		chuī	V	to blow, puff, play (wind instrument)
剪		jiǎn	V	to cut (with scissors)
好像	好象	hǎo.xiàng	Adv	[good-like] (it) seems (often followed by 似的)
對...有意思	对...有意思	duì...yǒu yì.si	IE	to be interested in (a person)
胡說	胡说	húshuō	V	[foreign-say] nonsense!
不過	不过	búguò	Adv	only (=只)
好靜		hàojìng	SV	[love to-quiet] (to be) inactive (said of one's disposition)
好動	好动	hàodòng	SV	[love to-move] (to be) active or restless (said of one's disposition)
對兒	对儿	duìr	N/M	pair, couple
老實	老实	lǎoshí	SV	[old-solid] (to be) honest
脾氣	脾气	pí.qì	N	[spleen-air] temperament, disposition
配		pèi	V	to match
外向		wàixiàng	SV	[outside-face] (to be) outgoing, extroverted
內向		nèixiàng	SV	[inside-face] (to be) introverted

◎ By Grammatical Categories

Nouns/Pronouns

頭	头	tóu	N	head (M: 個)
頭髮	头发	tóu.fà/tóu.fǎ	N	[hear-hair] hair on the head (M: 根 gēn, 頭)
臉	脸	liǎn	N	face (M: 張)
* 牙(齒)	牙(齿)	yá(chǐ)	N	[tooth-tooth] tooth (M: 顆 kē)
精神		jīng.shén	N/Adj	vigor, vitality, spirited
脾氣	脾气	pí.qì	N	[spleen-air] temperament, disposition
對兒	对儿	duìr	N/M	pair, couple
廁所	厕所	cèsuǒ	N	[toilet-building] toilet, lavatory (M: 間)
* 夜		yè	N	night, evening
* 吹風機	吹风机	chuīfēngjī	N	[blow-wind-machine] hair dryer (M: 個)

Verbs/Stative Verbs/Adjectives

剩		shèng	V	to remain, left over
洗		xǐ	V	to wash
燙	烫	tàng	V	to perm, to iron (clothes)
吹		chuī	V	to blow, puff, play (wind instrument)
剪		jiǎn	V	to cut (with scissors)
趕	赶	gǎn	V	to hurry, to rush
催		cuī	V	to urge, press
害		hài	V	to cause someone (trouble)
* 弄		nòng	V	to handle, to do (causative)
配		pèi	V	to match
喊		hǎn	V	to shout, cry out, yell
胡說	胡说	húshuō	V	[foreign-say] nonsense!
踫上		pèng.shàng	V	[bump-up] to run into an unexpected situation; to bump into
起(來)	起(来)	qǐ(.lái)	V	[rise-come] to get up
遲到	迟到	chídào	V	[late-arrive] to arrive late
熬夜		áoyè	VO	[sustain-night] to burn the midnight oil
刷牙		shuāyá	VO	to brush the teeth
洗澡		xǐzǎo	VO	[wash-bath] to bathe
* 吹風	吹风	chuīfēng	VO	[blow-wind] to blow
吹乾	吹干	chuīgān	RV	[blow-dry] to blow dry
快		kuài	SV/Adv	(to be) quick
* 慢		màn	SV/Adv	(to be) slow
慢吞吞		màntūntūn	SV	(to be) very slow
急		jí	SV	(to be) impatient, anxious
好靜		hàojìng	SV	[love to-quiet] (to be) inactive (said of one's disposition)
好動	好动	hàodòng	SV	[love to-move] (to be) active or restless (said of one's disposition)
老實	老实	lǎoshí	SV	[old-solid] (to be) honest
外向		wàixiàng	SV	[outside-face] (to be) outgoing, extroverted
內向		nèixiàng	SV	[inside-face] (to be) introverted
倒霉		dǎoméi	SV	[inverse-mold] (to be) out of luck (also written as 倒楣 dǎoméi—inverse-lintel)
糟了		zāo.le	SV	to become a mess

Adverbs

只		zhǐ	Adv	only
* 早		zǎo	Adv/SV	(to be) early
晚		wǎn	Adv/SV	(to be) late
一直	一直	yìzhí	Adv	[one-straight] all the time

| 好像 | 好象 | hǎo.xiàng | Adv | [good-like] (it) seems (often followed by 似的) |
| 不過 | 不过 | búguò | Adv | only (=只) |

Conjunctions

| 要不然 | | yào.burán | Conj | [want-not-although] otherwise |

Idiomatic Expressions

| 急死人 | | jí.sǐrén | IE | [anxious-death-people] to rush anxiously |
| 對...有意思 | 对...有意思 | duì...yǒu yì.si | IE | to be interested in (a person) |

✚ Supplementary Vocabulary

1. Odds and Ends

興趣	兴趣	xìng.qù	N	interest
發現	发现	fāxiàn	V	[uncover-appear] to discover
浴室		yùshì	N	[bath-room] bathroom (M: 間)
洗手間	洗手间	xǐshǒujiān	N	[wash-hand-room] bathroom, restroom (M: 間)
洗澡間	洗澡间	xǐzǎojiān	N	[wash-bath-room] bathroom (M: 間)
化裝室	化裝室	huàzhuāngshì	N	[makeup-room] powder room
抽水馬桶	抽水马桶	chōushuǐ mǎtǒng	N	[pump-water-horse-bucket] toilet
洗臉盆	洗脸盆	xǐliǎnpén	N	[wash-face-tub] washbasin
洗澡盆		xǐzǎopén	N	[wash-bath-tub] bathtub
淋浴		línyù	V	[shower-bath] to take a shower

2. Daily Necessities

洗髮精	洗发精	xǐfǎjīng	N	[wash-hair-extract] shampoo
潤濕精	润湿精	rùnshījīng	N	[moist-wet-extract] conditioner
肥皂		féizào	N	[fat-soap] soap
牙刷		yáshuā	N	[tooth-brush] toothbrush
牙膏		yágāo	N	[tooth-paste] toothpaste
毛巾		máojīn	N	[wool-towel] towel
紙巾	纸巾	zhǐjīn	N	[paper-towel] paper towel
衛生紙	卫生纸	wèishēngzhǐ	N	[protect-life-paper] tissue, toilet paper
面紙	面纸	miànzhǐ	N	[face-paper] facial tissue

3. Appearance and Personalities

勤快		qínkuài	SV	[diligent-fast] (to be) diligent
懶	懒	lǎn	SV	(to be) lazy
聰明		cōngmíng	SV	(to be) smart
笨		bèn	SV	(to be) stupid
傻		shǎ	SV	(to be) foolish
大方		dàfāng	SV	[big-square] (to be) elegant and composed
活潑	活泼	huó.pō	SV	[live-splash] (to be) active, lively
可愛	可爱	kě'ài	SV	[may-love] (to be) lovable, cute
英俊		yīngjùn	SV	(to be) handsome (said of a man's manner)
瀟灑	潇洒	xiāosǎ	SV	(to be) casual yet refined (said of a man's manner)
帥		shuài	SV	(to be) handsome, skilled
慷慨		kāngkǎi	SV	(to be) generous
小氣	小气	xiǎoqì	SV	(to be) stingy

Characters
漢字 Hànzì

直　等　急　害

晚　慢　當　然

雖　更　內　向

洗　澡　睡　覺

臉　定　意　思

直

zhí
straight　目
8　　(eyes)

一直　　　yìzhí　　　all the time

A: 這幾天你們那兒冷不冷？
B: 冷死人了，這幾天一直在下雪。

等

děng
to wait　竹
12　　(bamboo)

等一下　　děng.yíxià　　to wait for a while
*等人　　　děngrén　　　to wait for people

A: 請問，美英在家嗎？
B: 在，請**等一下**，我去叫她。

急

jí
nervous　心
9　　(heart)

急死人　　jí.sǐrén　　to rush anxiously
*著急　　　zhāojí　　　worried

A: 快點兒，我們快遲到了。
B: **別急**，我馬上來。

害

hài
to injure, to
harm, harm　宀
10

*有害　　　yǒuhài　　　harmful
*利害　　　lìhài　　　serious

A: 你昨天叫我跟你一塊兒出去看電影，**害**我今天考不好。
B: 誰叫你不早一點兒開始學習？

繁簡對照：	其他漢字：	✎ **My notes:**

晚

晚上　　　wǎn.shàng　　　evening, night
*晚飯　　　wǎnfàn　　　　dinner, supper

wǎn
evening, late 日
11　　　(sun)

A: 今天**晚上**這頓飯眞好吃。
B: 別忘了，是我做的。

慢

慢吞吞　　màntūntūn　　　(to be) very slow

màn
slow　　　　　忄
14　　　(heart)

A: 他平常做事**慢吞吞**的，今天怎麼了？
B: 他明天得交兩個報告，還有一個考試。

當

當然　　　dāngrán　　　　of course

dāng
ought　　　田
13　　　(field)

A: 你明天去不去小林家吃飯？
B: **當然去**，明天是他的生日。

然

雖然　　　suīrán　　　　although
要不然　　yào.burán　　　otherwise

rán
thus, so　　灬
12　　　(fire)

A: **雖然**他脾氣不太好，但是他人不壞。
B: **要不然**我們也不會是朋友了。

繁簡對照：	其他漢字：	✎ **My notes:**
當 当	早 L5 快 L6	

雖然　　　　suīrán　　　　although

suí, suī
although　隹
17　　　(bird)

A: **雖然**我只學了兩百多個字，我會說的話很多。
B: 所以你們學的字都很有用。

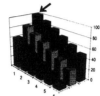

更容易　　gèng róng.yì　　even easier
更好　　　gèng hǎo　　　even better

gèng
even more　曰
7　　　(to say)

A: 那輛車好嗎？
B: 好，可是這輛**更好**。

內向　　　nèixiàng　　　introversion
*內人　　　nèi.rén　　　one's wife
*內衣　　　nèiyī　　　underwear

nèi
inner, within 入
4　　　(enter)

A: 他這個人太**內向**了，所以找不到朋友。
B: 才不呢！他的問題是脾氣不好。

外向　　　wàixiàng　　　(to be) outgoing
*向來　　　xiànglái　　　all along
*方向　　　fāngxiàng　　　direction

xiàng
to turn, fill, till
now　　　口
6　　　(mouth)

A: 這個孩子很**外向**，整天往外跑。
B: 那他的朋友一定很多了。

繁簡對照：	其他漢字：	**My notes:**
雖虽	外 L12	

洗

xǐ
to wash, rinse

氵
9   (water)

洗澡	xǐzǎo	to take a bath
*洗手	xǐshǒu	to wash hands
*洗臉	xǐliǎn	to wash the face
*洗碗	xǐwǎn	to wash dishes

A: 我做飯，你**洗碗**，怎麼樣？
B: 好啊！我們今天用紙碗吧！

澡

zǎo
to wash, bathe

氵
16   (water)

| 洗澡間 | xǐzǎojiān | bathroom |

A: 這個**洗澡間**比宿舍的大多了。
B: 這兒什麼都比宿舍的大。

睡

shuì
to sleep

目
13   (eyes)

睡覺	shuìjiào	to sleep
睡懶覺	shuìlǎnjiào	to get up late
*睡著	shuìzháo	to fall asleep

A: 你怎麼那麼累？不是**睡**了一整天嗎？
B: 我**睡**是**睡**了，可是**睡不著**。

覺

jué, jiào
perceive,
become
conscious of

見
20   (to see)

| 覺得 | jué.de | to feel, think |

A: 你現在**覺得**怎麼樣？
B: 很累，我一看書就想**睡覺**。

繁簡對照：	其他漢字：	✎ **My notes:**
覺觉	*醒 SC57	

臉

liǎn
face　　月
17　　(flesh)

洗臉　　　xǐliǎn　　　to wash the face
*臉色　　　liǎnsè　　　facial expression, complexion

A: 你的**臉色**很不好，是晚上沒睡好嗎？
B: 不是，是我牙痛。

定

dìng
to decide, surely
宀
8

一定　　　yídìng　　　certainly, definitely

A: 快走吧！我今天**一定**又要遲到了。
B: 別急，我開車送你去。

意

yì
thought,
meaning,
intention　心
13　　(heart)

沒意思　　　méiyì.si　　　not interesting, boring
對…有意思　　duì…yǒu yì.si　　(to be) interested in
*注意　　　zhùyì　　　attention to

A: 這部片子眞**沒意思**。
B: 可不是嗎！看來看去，只有那個女主
角演得還可以。

思

sī
to think, consider
contemplate　心
9　　(heart)

有意思　　　yǒuyì.si　　　interesting
*意思　　　yì.si　　　meaning

A: 老師，這句話什麼**意思**？
B: 你再想想看。

繁簡對照：	其他漢字：	✎ **My notes:**
臉脸	*牙 SC58	

Grammar
語法 yǔfǎ

A Major Sentence Patterns 主要句型 zhǔyào jùxíng

1. 什麼都..., 就是... **construction**

Structure	Gloss
S 什麼(N) 都...就是...	S can do everything (Adv) except...

    1.   她什麼都快，就是做什麼慢？   Tā shén.me dōu kuài, jiù.shì zuò shén.me màn?
She is quick at everything except what?

       她什麼都快，就是洗頭慢。   Tā shén.me dōu kuài, jiù.shì xǐtóu màn.
She is quick at everything except washing her hair.

    2.   老高什麼都好，就是不喜歡做什麼？   Lǎo Gāo shén.me dōu hǎo, jiù.shì bù xǐ.huān zuò shén.me?
Lao Gao is a fine person, except for the fact that (he) doesn't like to do what?

       老高什麼都好，就是不喜歡洗澡。   Lǎo Gāo shén.me dōu hǎo, jiù.shì bù xǐ.huān xǐzǎo.
Lao Gao is a fine person, except for the fact that (he) doesn't like to bathe.

    3.   我什麼(菜)都吃，就是不能吃生菜。   Wǒ shén.me (cài) dōu chī, jiù.shì bù néng chī shēngcài.
I eat everything except salads.

💡   Question word 什麼(N) followed by 都 denotes inclusiveness, whereas 就是 + VP (verb phrase) denotes the subject's determination to do an action or firm opposition against it.

🔄   See L11–A6, L14–A2 for more on 都.

2. 可..., 要不然... **construction**

Structure	Gloss
S 可(不/別) VO , 要不然 (S)...	S by all/no means do VO; otherwise (S) will...

1. 你可別起晚了，要不然你又要遲到了。

Nǐ kě bié qǐ wǎn .le, yào.burán nǐ yòu yào chídào .le.

By all means don't get up late; otherwise you'll be late to class again.

2. 我可不能把頭髮剪短了，要不然我的男朋友就會不喜歡。

Wǒ kě bù néng bǎ tóu.fǎ jiǎnduǎn .le, yào.burán wǒ .de nánpéng.yǒu jiù huì bù xǐ.huān.

I can by no means cut my hair short; otherwise my boyfreind won't like (it).

The adverb 可 serves as the emphatic marker for an action. The conjunction 要不然 must precede the second subject.

3. The conditional usage of 才

Structure	Gloss
S ... , (S) 才 VO	Only if S... then (S) will VO

1. 你把中文學好了，才容易做什麼？

Nǐ bǎ Zhōngwén xuéhǎo .le, cái róng.yì zuò shén.me?

Only if you learn Chinese well will it be easy to do what?

我把中文學好了，才容易找到工作。

Wǒ bǎ Zhōngwén xuéhǎo .le, cái róng.yì zhǎo.dào gōngzuò.

Only if I learn Chinese well will it be easy to find a job.

2. (我)累死了，可是沒有時間洗澡、休息，得立刻念書。

Wǒ lèi.sǐ .le, kě.shì méi.yǒu shíjiān xǐzǎo, xiū.xí, děi lìkè niànshū.

I am terribly tired, but I don't have time to take a bath and rest for a while. I have to study right away.

洗個澡，休息一下，(你)才有精神念書。

Xǐ .ge zǎo, xiū.xí.yíxià, (nǐ) cái yǒu jīng.shén niànshū.

Only if you take a bath and rest for a while will you have energy to study.

When a complex sentence consists of a conditional clause without an "if only" conjunction, the adverb 才 can be used as a conjunction in the consequence clause to denote the condition. Because 才 is an adverb, it must precede the verbal expression and follow the subject if it is present.

See L9–A5, L23–A2 for more on 才.

4. A 對 B 有意思 / 有興趣

4.1 A 對 B (person) 有意思

Structure	Gloss
A 對 B (person) (Adv) 有意思	A is (Adv) interested in B
A 對 B (person) 沒有意思	A is not interested in B
A 對 B (person) 一點兒意思 都/也沒有	A has no interest in B at all

1. 那個男孩子對小王有意思嗎？

    Nèi .ge nánhái.zi duì Xiǎo Wáng yǒu yì.si .ma?
    Is that boy interested in Xiao Wang?

    那個男孩子對小王很有意思。

    Nèi .ge nánhái.zi duì Xiǎo Wáng hěn yǒu yì.si.
    That boy is very interested in Xiao Wang.

    那個男孩子對小王沒有意思。

    Nèi .ge nánhái.zi duì Xiǎo Wáng méi.yǒu yì.si.
    That boy is not interested in Xiao Wang.

2. 你對小李有沒有意思？

    Nǐ duì Xiǎo Lǐ yǒu .méi.yǒu yì.si?
    Are you interested in Xiao Li?

    我對小李一點兒意思也沒有，
    我們只是朋友。

    Wǒ duì Xiǎo Lǐ yì.diǎnr yì.si yě méi.yǒu,
    wǒ.men zhǐ.shì péng.yǒu.
    I am not interested in Xiao Li at all; we are only friends.

 The idiomatic expression A 對 B 有意思 can only be used when "B" is a person.

4.2 A 對 B (thing) 有興趣

Structure	Gloss
A 對 B (thing) (Adv) 有興趣	A is (Adv) interested in B
A 對 B (thing) 沒有興趣	A is not interested in B
A 對 B (thing) 一點兒興趣 都/也沒有	A has no interest in B at all

1. 你對中國文學有興趣嗎？

   Nǐ duì Zhōng.guó wénxué yǒu xìng.qù .ma?
   Are you interested in Chinese literature?

   我對中國文學很有興趣。

   Wǒ duì Zhōng.guó wénxué hěn yǒu xìng.qù.
   I am very interested in Chinese literature.

2. 老王對電腦有興趣嗎？

   Lǎo Wáng duì diànnǎo yǒu xìng.qù .ma?
   Is Lao Wang interested in the computer?

   他對電腦一點兒興趣都没有。

   Tā duì diànnǎo yì.diǎnr xìng.qù dōu méi.yǒu.
   He is not interested in the computer at all.

If you would like to say that someone is interested in certain things/subject matters, you can use A 對 B 有興趣. 有興趣 yǒu xìng.qù means "to have an interest in."

See L10–B2, L16–A1, L18–A2, L20–B4, L23–B3 for more on A 對 B....

B Usage of Common Phrases 詞組用法 cízǔ yòngfǎ

1. The adverbial phrase 快/慢一點兒

Structure	Gloss
快/慢 一點兒！	Hurry up!/Slow down!
快/慢 一點兒 V！	V a little faster/slower!
(VO) V 快/慢 一點兒	does (O) a little faster/slower

1. 請你(開車)開慢一點兒。

   Qǐng nǐ (kāichē) kāi màn yì.diǎnr.
   Would you please drive a little slower?

2. 快一點兒走！我們要遲到了！

   Kuài yì.diǎnr zǒu! wǒ.men yào chídào .le.
   Walk a little faster! We'll be late!

The adverbial expression 快/慢 一點兒 as a whole can stand alone, precede a verb, or follow a verb. When it stands alone or precedes a verb, it denotes a command; when it follows a verb, it may either describe a state or denote a suggestion.

See L7–B2, L13–B1 for more on 一點兒.

2. The causative markers 害、弄

Structure	Gloss
S 害 (得) O V...	S causes/caused O to V...
S 弄 (得) O V...	S makes/made O to V...

1. 小王洗澡洗得很慢，害得你怎麼了？

Xiǎo Wáng xǐzǎo xǐ.de hěn màn, hài.de nǐ zěn.me .le?
Xiao Wang took a bath very slowly and therefore what happened to you?

小王洗澡洗得很慢，害得我不能上廁所。

Xiǎo Wáng xǐzǎo xǐ.de hěn màn, hài.de wǒ bù néng shàngcèsuǒ.
Xiao Wang took a bath very slowly and therefore I was unable to go to the bathroom.

2. 他一直催你，弄得你怎麼了？

Tā yìzhí cuī nǐ, nòng.de nǐ zěn.me .le?
He kept rushing you and therefore what happened to you?

他一直催我，弄得我頭髮沒吹好。

Tā yìzhí cuī wǒ, nòng.de wǒ tóu.fǎ méi chuīhǎo.
He kept rushing me and therefore I didn't dry my hair thoroughly.

 害 is a verb that means "to harm," and 弄 nòng is a verb that means "to handle, to do." But either one can be used as a causative marker to denote the person or the action of the preceding clause that caused the action in the second clause.

❸ Reentry 複習 fùxí

1. 為什麼 and 因為 ..., 所以...

Structure	Gloss
S 為什麼 (AuxV/Neg) V O (呢)? (MA)	Why is it that S (not) V O?
因為 S..., 所以 (S)... (MA)	Because S..., therefore S...

1. 你為什麼早上洗澡洗頭呢？/ 為什麼你早上洗澡洗頭呢？

Nǐ wèishén.me zǎo.shàng xǐzǎo xǐtóu .ne? / Wèishén.me nǐ zǎo.shàng xǐzǎo xǐtóu .ne?
Why is it that you take a bath and wash your hair in the morning?

因爲早上洗澡洗頭才有精神上課。

Yīn.wèi zǎo.shàng xǐzǎo xǐtóu cái yǒu jīng.shén shàngkè.
Because taking a shower and washing my hair in the morning will keep (me) refreshed for classes.

2. 他爲什麼不早睡早起呢？/
爲什麼他不早睡早起呢？

Tā wèishén.me bù zǎo shuì zǎo qǐ .ne?/
Wèishén.me tā bù zǎo shuì zǎo qǐ .ne?
Why is it that he doesn't want to go to bed early and get up early?

因爲他每天晚上都得熬夜做功課，所以他不能早睡早起。

Yīn.wèi tā měitiān wǎn.shàng dōu děi áo'yè zuò gōngkè, suǒ.yǐ tā bù néng zǎo shuì zǎo qǐ.
Because he has to burn the midnight oil to do homework every evening, he can't go to bed early and get up early.

3. 你爲什麼每天都遲到？/
爲什麼你每天都遲到？

Nǐ wèishén.me měitiān dōu chídào?/
Wèishén.me nǐ měitiān dōu chídào?
Why is it that you come to class late every day?

因爲我每天晚上都得打工打到半夜，所以(我)早上起不來。

Yīn.wèi wǒ měitiān wǎn.shàng dōu děi dǎgōng dǎ.dào bànyè, suǒ.yǐ (wǒ) zǎo.shàng qǐ.bu.lái.
Because I have to work every evening until midnight, (I) can't get up early in the morning.

💡 Questions with the movable adverb 爲什麼 can end with an optional particle 呢. When 呢 is attached to the end of an interrogative question with a question word, it softens the tone of the question.

Note: In a complex sentence that consists of two clauses beginning with the conjunctions 因爲 'because' and 所以 'therefore' respectively, the 因爲 is a movable adverb and thus can precede or follow the subject of the first clause, whereas 所以 is unmovable, and must precede the subject of the second clause if the subject is present.

🔄 See L8–A6 for more on 爲什麼 and 因爲.

Cultural Notes
文化點滴 wénhuà diǎndī

1. The Chinese usually take baths after work in the late afternoon or at night. The majority of Chinese are farmers or laborers who work during the day and consider it 不衛生 bú wèishēng 'unhygienic or unsanitary' not to take a bath before going to bed.

2. 上廁所 shàng cèsuǒ 'to go to the bathroom' and 洗手 xǐ shǒu '[wash-hands] go to bathroom' are modern Chinese words that are used in more formal settings. In more casual settings, Chinese say 大便 dàbiàn '[big-convenience] to defecate, feces,' 拉屎 lā shǐ '[to pull-feces] to go to stool,' 小便 xiǎobiàn '[small-convenience] to urinate, urine,' 拉尿 lā niào '[pull-urine] to urinate.' In Taiwan, students use the euphemism 上一號 shàng yī hào 'to go No. 1,' which has become a popular expression even among nonstudents.

3. (頭)髮 (tóu)fǎ refers only to the hair on the head of human beings. Human body hair is called 毛 máo, which is also a collective noun for all other animal hair.

4. People in China and Taiwan usually take naps at home or in the office after lunch. When you go to China or Taiwan, you will find it difficult to do business with anyone at lunchtime.

對　話	118頁
小對話	124頁
生　詞	127頁
漢　字	131頁
語　法	137頁
文化點滴	146頁

第十八課　你聽過中國音樂嗎？

對話

〔美英在校園內，邊走邊聽音樂，踫見高德中。〕

小高：（自言自語）看起來，怎麼不太像她？奇怪，她不是長頭
　　　髮嗎？（看著一個女孩的背影，叫美英！美英）

小林：（哼歌兒）噢，是你！

小高：這麼專心，叫了你幾次都沒聽見。怎麼一個多星期沒見，
　　　連樣子都變了，越
　　　來越漂亮了。

小林：你可真會說話，我
　　　不過把頭髮給剪短
　　　了罷。要不要聽聽
　　　這個CD, 最新的「中
　　　國搖滾」，我弟弟
　　　剛給我寄來的。

小高：中國也有搖滾樂嗎？我可沒聽過，跟美國的一樣嗎？

小林：當然有，還有中國式的爵士樂呢！中國現代音樂，尤其是
　　　流行歌曲，受了西方很大的影響。

小高：聽起來，你可真內行，難怪主修音樂。我就聽過一些中國
　　　傳統的民歌。上星期中文老師教我們唱了一首「茉莉花」
　　　，很好聽。

小林：那首歌兒，小時候媽媽也教我唱過，不過歌詞兒我都忘了
　　　，就記得調兒（哼……）。

小高：你唱得真好，不像我是個十足的音盲。

小林：別客氣。其實，真的中國音樂我也不懂，你聽過「二胡」
　　　嗎？我第一次聽的時候，還以為是貓叫呢！

小高：什麼時候，我們可以聚一聚，請王華和李明給我們好好兒
　　　地介紹一下中國音樂。我知道李明會拉胡琴兒。

小林：好啊！王華好
　　　像對京劇也有
　　　研究。這星期
　　　五她正好考完
　　　段考，可以好
　　　好兒地輕鬆一
　　　下。

小高：好極了！以後
　　　不必去聽演唱會了。咱們可以自己組一個「四人樂隊」，
　　　來個中美大合唱。

对话

〔美英在校园内，边走边听音乐，碰见高德中。〕

小高：（自言自语）看起来，怎么不太象她？奇怪，她不是长头
　　　发吗？（看着一个女孩的背影，叫美英！美英）

小林：（哼歌儿）噢，是你！

小高：这么专心，叫了你几次都没听见。怎么一个多星期没见
　　　，连样子都变了，越来越漂亮了。

小林：你可真会说话，我不过把头发给剪短了罢。要不要听听这
　　　个CD,最新的「中国摇滚」，我弟弟刚给我寄来的。

小高：中国也有摇滚乐吗？我可没听过，跟美国的一样吗？

小林：当然有，还有中国式的爵士乐呢！中国现代音乐，尤其是
　　　流行歌曲，受了西方很大的影响。

小高：听起来，你可真内行，难怪主修音乐。我就听过一些中国
　　　传统的民歌。上星期中文老师教我们唱了一首「茉莉花」
　　　，很好听。

小林：那首歌儿，小时候妈妈也教我唱过，不过歌词儿我都忘了
　　　，就记得调儿（哼……）。

小高：你唱得真好，不象我是个十足的音盲。

小林：别客气。其实，真的中国音乐我也不懂，你听过「二胡」
　　　吗？我第一次听的时候，还以为是猫叫呢！

小高：什么时候，我们可以聚一聚，请王华和李明给我们好好儿
　　　地介绍一下中国音乐。我知道李明会拉胡琴儿。

小林：好啊！王华好象对京剧也有研究。这星期五她正好考完段考，可以好好儿地轻鬆一下。

小高：好极了！以后不必去听演唱会了。咱们可以自己组一个「四人乐队」，来个中美大合唱。

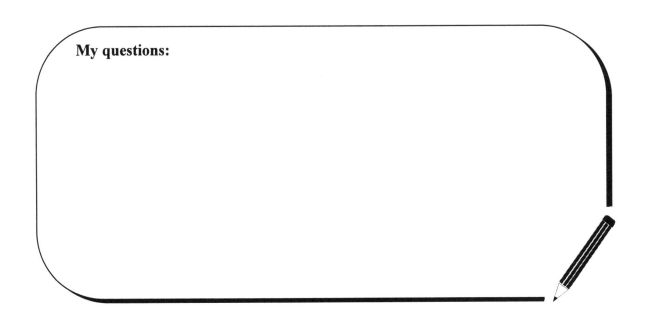

My questions:

Duìhuà

(Měiyīng zài xiàoyuán nèi, biān zǒu biān tīng yīnyuè, pèng.jiàn
Gāo Dézhōng.)

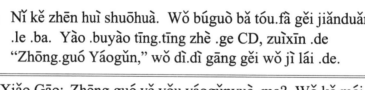

Xiǎo Gāo: (Zì yán zì yǔ) Kàn.qǐ.lái, zěn.me bútài xiàng tā? Qíguài, tā
bú.shì cháng tóu.fà .ma? (Kàn.zhe yí .ge nǚhái .de bèiyǐng,
jiào Měiyīng, Měiyīng.)

Xiǎo Lín: (Hēng gēr) Ou, shì nǐ!

Xiǎo Gāo: Zhè.me zhuānxīn, jiào .le nǐ jǐ cì dōu méi tīng.jiàn. Zěn.me
yí .ge duō xīngqī méi jiàn, lián yàng.zi dōu biàn .le, yuè lái
yuè piào.liàng .le.

Xiǎo Lín: Nǐ kě zhēn huì shuōhuà. Wǒ búguò bǎ tóu.fà gěi jiǎnduǎn
.le .ba. Yào .buyào tīng.tīng zhè .ge CD, zuìxīn .de
"Zhōng.guó Yáogǔn," wǒ dì.dì gāng gěi wǒ jì lái .de.

Xiǎo Gāo: Zhōng.guó yě yǒu yáogǔnyuè .ma? Wǒ kě méi tīng.guò,
gēn Měi.guó .de yíyàng .ma?

Xiǎo Lín: Dāngrán yǒu, hái yǒu Zhōng.guó shì .de juéshìyuè .ne!
Zhōng.guó xiàndài yīnyuè, yóuqí shì liúxíng gēqǔ, shòu
.le xīfāng hěn dà .de yǐngxiǎng.

Xiǎo Gāo: Tīng.qǐ.lái, nǐ kě zhēn nèiháng. Nánguài zhǔxiū yīnyuè.
Wǒ jiù tīng.guò yìxiē Zhōng.guó chuántǒng .de mín'gē.
Shàng xīngqī Zhōngwén lǎoshī jiāo wǒ.men chàng .le yì
shǒu "Mòlìhuā," hěn hǎotīng.

Xiǎo Lín: Nà shǒu gēr, xiǎoshí.hòu mā.mā yě jiāo wǒ chàng.guò,
búguò gēcír wǒ dōu wàng .le, jiù jì.de diàor (Hēng...).

Xiǎo Gāo: Nǐ chàng.de zhēn hǎo, bú xiàng wǒ shì .ge shízú .de
yīnmáng.

Xiǎo Lín: Bié kè.qi. Qíshí, zhēn .de Zhōng.guó yīnyuè wǒ yě
bù dǒng, nǐ tīng.guò "èrhú" .ma? Wǒ dì yí cì tīng .de
shí.hòu, hái yǐwéi shì māo jiào .ne!

Xiǎo Gāo: Shén.me shí.hòu, wǒ.men kě.yǐ jù.yíjù, qǐng Wáng Huá hé Lǐ Míng gěi wǒ.men
hǎo.hǎor.de jiè.shào.yíxià Zhōng.guó yīnyuè. Wǒ zhī.dào Lǐ Míng huì lā
húqínr.

Xiǎo Lín: Hǎo .a! Wáng Huá hǎo.xiàng duì jīngjù yě yǒu yánjiū. Zhè xīngqīwǔ tā zhèng
hǎo kǎowán duànkǎo, kě.yǐ hǎo.hǎor.de qīngsōng.yíxià.

Xiǎo Gāo: Hǎojí.le! Yǐhòu búbì qù tīng yǎnchànghuì .le. Zán.men kě.yǐ zìjǐ zǔ yí .ge "sì
rén yuèduì," lái .ge ZhōngMěi dà héchàng.

Dialogue

(Měiyīng is on campus. She's listening to music while walking. She runs into Gāo Dézhōng.)

Xiǎo Gāo: (Talking to himself:) How come it doesn't look like her? Strange, doesn't she have long hair? (Looking at the girl's back and yelling "Měiyīng, Měiyīng!")

Xiǎo Lín: (Humming.) Oh, it's you!

Xiǎo Gāo: You were concentrating so hard. I called you several times, but you didn't hear. How did you change so much in just over a week? You're getting prettier and prettier.

Xiǎo Lín: You are just being polite. I only got a haircut. Do you want to listen to this CD? It's the latest Chinese rock-and-roll. My younger brother just sent it to me.

Xiǎo Gāo: Does China also have rock-and-roll? I've never heard of it. Is it the same as in the US?

Xiǎo Lín: Of course, it does. There is also Chinese-style jazz! Contemporary Chinese music, especially popular songs, is greatly influenced by the West.

Xiǎo Gāo: You sound like an expert. No wonder you are majoring in music. I've only heard a few traditional Chinese folk songs. Last week our Chinese teacher taught us a song called "Jasmine Flowers." It sounded great.

Xiǎo Lín: My mother taught me that song when I was young, but I forgot the words. I only remember the melody. (Humming.)

Xiǎo Gāo: You sing really well, not like me, downright tone-deaf.

Xiǎo Lín: Don't be modest. Actually, I don't understand real Chinese music, either. Have you heard of the "two-stringed bowed instrument"? The first time I listened to it, I thought it sounded like cats howling.

Xiǎo Gāo: When can we get together and ask Wáng Huá and Lǐ Míng to give us a good introduction to Chinese music? I know that Lǐ Míng can play the húqínr.

Xiǎo Lín: That's good! Wáng Huá seems to know a lot about Beijing opera. This coming Friday she will finish her midterm. (Then) she can relax a little.

Xiǎo Gāo: That's great! Later on we don't need to go to concerts. We can organize a "four-person band" and have a huge Chinese-American chorus.

Mini-Dialogue
小對話 Xiǎoduìhuà

 Giving compliments

1. A: 怎麼幾個月沒見就變了這
      麼多？你越來越漂亮了。

   Zěn.me jǐ .ge yuè méi jiàn jiù biàn .le
   zhè.me duō? Nǐ yuè lái yuè piào.liàng
   .le.
   How did you change so much in just a
   few months? You're getting prettier
   and prettier.

   B: 你可真會說話，我不過
      把
      頭髮給剪短了罷。

   Nǐ kě zhēn huì shuōhuà, wǒ búguò bǎ
   tóu.fà gěi jiǎnduǎn .le .ba.

   You're just being polite. I only got a
   haircut.

 Expressing modesty

1. A: 你歌唱得真好，不像我是
      個十足的音盲。

   Nǐ gē chàng.de zhēn hǎo, bú xiàng wǒ
   shì .ge shízú .de yīnmáng.
   You sing really well, not like me,
   downright tone-deaf.

   B: 別客氣。你唱得不錯。

   Bié kè.qi. Nǐ chàng.de búcuò.
   Don't be modest. You sing quite well.

 Making plans for the weekend

1. A: 這星期六我們去聽音樂會
      ，怎麼樣？

   Zhè xīngqīliù wǒ.men qù tīng
   yīnyuèhuì, zěn.meyàng?
   How about going to a concert this
   Saturday?

   B: 好啊！聽說最近來的樂隊
      很不錯。

   Hǎo .a! Tīngshuō zuìjìn lái .de
   yuèduì hěn búcuò.

Great! I've heard that the band that just came is quite good.

2.　A:　咱們星期五輕鬆一下吧！

Zán.men xīngqīwǔ qīngsōng.yíxià .ba!
Let's relax a little this Friday.

　　B:　好啊！打球怎麼樣？

Hǎo .a! Dǎqiú zěn.meyàng?
O.K.! How about playing sports?

茉莉花
Mòlìhuā
Jasmine Flower

好　一　朵　美　麗的　茉　莉　花。
Hǎo　yì　duǒ měi　lì .de　mò　lì　huā.
Such　a　beau-ti-ful　Jas-mine flower.　(twice)

芬　芳　美　麗　滿　枝　椏，
Fēn fāng　měi　lì　mǎn　zhī　yá,
Branches　full　of　sweet　white　buds,

又　香　又　白　人　人　誇。
yòu xiāng　yòu　bái　rén　rén　kuā.
E- very　one　loves　their　beau - ty.

讓　我　來　將　你　摘　下，
Ràng wǒ　liá　jiāng　nǐ　zhāi　xià,
I will gather some　and　of - fer　them

送　給　別　人　家，　茉　莉
sòng gěi　bié　rén　jiā,　mò　lì
To the　one　I　love,　Jasmine

花　呀！茉　莉　花。
huā　yā! Mò　lì　huā.
flower,　Jasmine　flower.

Vocabulary
生詞 Shēngcí

◎ **By Order of Appearance**

奇怪		qíguài	SV	[strange-strange] (to be) strange
噢		.ou	Inter	oh! (realization of something)
專心	专心	zhuānxīn	SV	[specialize-mind] (to be) concentrated
連…都	连…都	lián…dōu	IE	even
樣子	样子	yàng.zi	N	appearance
變	变	biàn	V	to change
搖滾樂	摇滚乐	yáogǔnyuè	N	[rock-roll-music] rock-and-roll music
寄		jì	V	to send (by mail)
爵士樂	爵士乐	juéshìyuè	N	[Sir-scholar-music] jazz
現代	现代	xiàndài	Adj	[now-generation] current, modern
歌曲		gēqǔ	N	[song-music] song (M: 首 shǒu)
西方		xīfāng	N	[west-direction] Western
* 東方	东方	dōngfāng	N	[east-direction] Eastern, the East, Oriental
內行		nèiháng	SV	[inside-profession] (to be) professional, to specialize in
* 外行		wàiháng	SV	[outside-profession] (to be) amateurish, inexperienced, very much a layman
傳統	传统	chuántǒng	N	[pass on to-govern] tradition
民歌		mín'gē	N	[people-song] folk song
首		shǒu	M	measure word for songs
茉莉花		mòlǐhuā	N	[white jasmine-flower] white jasmine flower
歌兒	歌儿	gēr	N	[song-Suf] song (colloquial)
歌詞兒	歌词儿	gēcír	N	[song-word-Suf] lyrics of a song
忘了		wàng.le	V	forgot
* 忘記	忘记	wàngjì	V	[forget-record] to forget
記得	记得	jì.de	V	[record-able] to remember
調兒	调儿	diàor	N	[tone-Suf] tone (=聲調), tune (of music)
十足的		shízú .de	Adv	[ten-enough-part] completely
音盲		yīnmáng	N	[sound-blind] tone-deaf
* 聲音	声音	shēng.yīn	N	[sound-sound] sound
別客氣	别客气	bié kè.qì	IE	[don't-guest-atmosphere] don't be modest!
其實	其实	qíshí	Adv	[it-solid] actually, in fact
二胡		èrhú	N	[two-stringed violin] ＝胡琴

以爲	以为	yǐwéi	V	[by means of-for] to take (something) to be, to think incorrectly
聚		jù	V	to get together
好好兒		hǎohāor	Adv	[good-good-Suf] to do...well
胡琴兒	胡琴儿	húqínr	N	[northern tribe-organ-Suf] two-stringed violin—Chinese musical instrument (M: 把)
京劇	京剧	jīngjù	N	[Beijng-play] Beijing/Peking Opera
段考		duànkǎo	N	[section-test] midterm exam
* 考試	考试	kǎoshì	N/V	[test-try] test, to have a test
輕鬆	轻松	qīngsōng	SV	[light-loose] (to be) relaxed
* 緊張	紧张	jǐnzhāng	SV	[tight-stretch] (to be) nervous
演唱會	演唱会	yǎnchànghuì	N	[perform-sing-party] concert (V: 開)
組	组	zǔ	V	[organize-become] to organize
樂隊	乐队	yuèduì	N	[music-team] band
合唱		héchàng	N	[cooperate-sing] chorus

◎ By Grammatical Categories

Nouns/Pronouns

段考		duànkǎo	N	[section-test] midterm exam
* 考試	考试	kǎoshì	N/V	[test-try] test, to have a test
樣子	样子	yàng.zi	N	appearance
搖滾樂	摇滚乐	yáogǔnyuè	N	[rock-roll-music] rock-and-roll music
爵士樂	爵士乐	juéshìyuè	N	[Sir-scholar-music] jazz
京劇	京剧	jīngjù	N	[Beijng-play] Beijing/Peking Opera
民歌		mín'gē	N	[people-song] folk song
歌兒	歌儿	gēr	N	[song-Suf] song (colloquial)
歌曲		gēqǔ	N	[song-music] song (M: 首 shǒu)
歌詞兒	歌词儿	gēcír	N	[song-word-Suf] lyrics of a song
調兒	调儿	diàor	N	[tone-Suf] tone (=聲調), tune (of music)
* 聲音	声音	shēng.yīn	N	[sound-sound] sound
音盲		yīnmáng	N	[sound-blind] tone-deaf
合唱		héchàng	N	[cooperate-sing] chorus
樂隊	乐队	yuèduì	N	[music-team] band
演唱會	演唱会	yǎnchànghuì	N	[perform-sing-party] concert (V: 開)
二胡		èrhú	N	[two-stringed violin] = 胡琴
西方		xīfāng	N	[west-direction] Western
* 東方	东方	dōngfāng	N	[east-direction] Eastern, the East, Oriental

傳統	传统	chuántǒng	N	[pass on to-govern] tradition
胡琴兒	胡琴儿	húqínr	N	[northern tribe-organ-Suf] two-stringed violin—Chinese musical instrument (M: 把)
茉莉花		mòlìhuā	N	[white jasmine-flower] white jasmine flower

Measure Words

| 首 | | shǒu | M | measure word for songs |

Verbs/Stative Verbs/Adjectives

	變	变	biàn	V	to change
	寄		jì	V	to send (by mail)
	聚		jù	V	to get together
	組	组	zǔ	V	[organize-become] to organize
	忘了		wàng.le	V	forgot
*	忘記	忘记	wàngjì	V	[forget-record] to forget
	記得	记得	jì.de	V	[record-able] to remember
	以為	以为	yǐwéi	V	[by means of-for] to take (something) to be, to think incorrectly
	奇怪		qíguài	SV	[strange-strange] (to be) strange
	專心	专心	zhuānxīn	SV	[specialize-mind] (to be) concentrated
	內行		nèiháng	SV	[inside-profession] (to be) professional, to specialize in
*	外行		wàiháng	SV	[outside-profession] (to be) amateurish, inexperienced, very much a layman
	輕鬆	轻松	qīngsōng	SV	[light-loose] (to be) relaxed
*	緊張	紧张	jǐnzhāng	SV	[tight-stretch] (to be) nervous
	現代	现代	xiàndài	Adj	[now-generation] current, modern

Adverbs

其實	其实	qíshí	Adv	[it-solid] actually, in fact
十足的		shízú .de	Adv	[ten-enough-part] completely
好好兒		hǎohāor	Adv	[good-good-Suf] to do...well

Idiomatic Expressions

| 連...都 | 连...都 | lián...dōu | IE | even |
| 別客氣 | 别客气 | bié kè.qì | IE | [don't-guest-atmosphere] don't be modest! |

Others

噢		.ou	Inter	oh! (realization of something)

✚ Supplementary Vocabulary

1. Odds and Ends

校園	校园	xiàoyuán	N	[school-garden] campus
邊走邊聽	边走边听	biān zǒu biān tīng	IE	[side-walk-side-listen] listen to something while walking
哼		hēng	V	to hum
背影		bèiyǐng	N	[back-shadow] a view of someone's back

2. Music

古典音樂	古典音乐	gǔdiǎn yīnyuè	N	[classic-music] classical musical
輕音樂	轻音乐	qīng yīnyuè	N	[light-music] light music
交響樂	交响乐	jiāoxiǎngyuè	N	[cross-sound-music] orchestral music
歌劇	歌剧	gējù	N	[song-play] opera (M: 齣 chū)
歌舞劇	歌舞剧	gēwǔjù	N	[song-dance-play] musical (M: 齣 chū)
演奏		yǎnzòu	V	[perform-play music instrument] (of musicians) to perform
預演		yùyǎn	V/N	[in advance-perform] to rehearse, a preview, a rehearsal
獨唱	独唱	dúchàng	V	[alone-sing] solo
卡拉OK		kǎlā OK	N	[card-pull] karaoke
樂器	乐器	yuèqì	N	[music-utensil] musical instrument (M: 件)

Characters
漢字 Hànzì

考	唱	新	歌
研	究	音	樂
容	氣	漂	亮
忘	記	專	心
尤	其	實	連

考

段考	duànkǎo	midterm exam
*大考	dàkǎo	exam
*小考	xiǎokǎo	quiz
*考試	kǎoshì	test

kǎo
to test, examine
老
6   (old, aged)

A: 你今天中文**考得怎麼樣**？
B: 口試還可以，筆試不太好。

唱

唱歌	chànggē	to sing (a song)
合唱	héchàng	chorus
演唱會	yǎnchànghuì	concert
*唱片	chàngpiàn	gramophone record

chàng
to sing   口
11   (mouth)

A: 你可別說她**歌唱得不好**，要不然她一定
　　會生氣。
B: 她**唱得**我頭都疼了。

新

| 新年 | xīnnián | New Year |
| *新生 | xīnshēng | freshman |

xīn
new   斤
13   (a unit of
weight, ½
kilogram)

A: 今年中國**新年**是什麼時候？
B: 二月中。

歌

歌兒	gēr	song
歌曲	gēqǔ	song
歌詞兒	gēcír	lyrics of a song
民歌	mín'gē	folk song

gē
to sing, chant,
song   欠
14   (to owe)

A: 你喜歡唱什麼**歌兒**？
B: 我喜歡唱中國**民歌**，可是唱得不好。

| 繁簡對照： | 其他漢字： | ✎ **My notes:** |
| | *舊 SC59 | |

研究　　　　yánjiū　　　　　　　to study, research

研

yán
to study, grind
石
9　　(stone)

A: 你的專業是什麼？
B: 東亞**研究**，我學中國現代文學。

究

jiū
to study
carefully　穴
7　　(a cave)

*研究生　　yánjiūshēng　　　graduate student
*研究所　　yánjiūsuǒ　　　　graduate school
*研究院　　yánjiūyuàn　　　research institute

A: 你好像對中文**很有研究**。
B: 哪裏，我不過學了四年的中文。

音

yīn
sound, voice,
tone　　音
9　　(sound)

音樂　　　yīnyuè　　　　music
音盲　　　yīnmáng　　　tone-deaf
*聲音　　　shēng.yīn　　sound, voice

A: 你聽過中國**音樂**沒有？
B: 聽過，我剛買了一盤中國民歌的磁帶。

樂

yuè, lè
music, happy
木
15　　(wood)

音樂　　　yīnyuè　　　　music
快樂　　　kuàilè　　　　happy, joyful

A: 你不像我，對中國**音樂**很有研究。
B: 哪裏，我也是個外行。

繁簡對照：	其他漢字：	✎ **My notes:**
樂 乐	*聲 SC60	

別客氣　　bié kè.qi　　　Don't be modest!
好客　　　hàokè　　　　(to be) hospitable
*客人　　　kèrén　　　　guest

kè
guest　　宀
9

A: 聽說中國人很**好客**，對**客人**很好。
B: 沒錯，他們常說：「**別客氣**，多吃一點兒。」

脾氣　　　pí.qì　　　　temperament
*客氣　　　kè.qì　　　　(to be) polite
*生氣　　　shēngqì　　(to be) angry
*氣人　　　qìrén　　　　to make one mad

qì
air, gas, spirit,
character,
breath　　气
10　　　(air)

A: 小李這個人挺不錯的，沒什麼**脾氣**。
B: 他什麼都好，就是做事慢了一點兒。

漂亮　　　piào.liàng　　(to be) pretty, beautiful

piào
pretty, nice　氵
14　　　(water)

A: 這件衣服穿在你身上，特別**漂亮**。
B: 你真會說話。

liàng
(to be) bright
9　　　亠

A: 那個女演員真**漂亮**。
B: 她不只人長得**漂亮**，電影也演得好。

繁簡對照：	其他漢字：	**My notes:**

忘

| 忘了 | wàng .le | forgot |
| *忘記 | wàngjì | to forget |

wàng
to forget 心
7 (heart)

A: 今天我們不是要去聽演唱會嗎？
B: 對不起，我**把**這件事**給忘了**。

記

| 記得 | jì.de | to remember |
| *日記 | rìjì | diary |

jì
to record,
remember 言
10 (speech)

A: 你是哪一年到中國去的？
B: 我**不記得**了。

專

專心	zhuānxīn	(to be) concentrated
*專業	zhuānyè	major
*專長	zhuāncháng	specialty
*專家	zhuānjiā	expert

zhuān
to focus on one
thing, expert 寸
11 (a unit of
measure)

A: 這個學生上課不太**專心**。
B: 不知道他心裏在想什麼。

心

*小心	xiǎo.xīn	(to be) careful
*放心	fàngxīn	to relax, be assured
*擔心	dānxīn	(to be) worried

xīn
heart 心
4 (heart)

A: 你一個月没打電話回家，父母不**擔心**嗎？
B: 他們知道我最近很忙。

繁簡對照：	其他漢字：	✎ **My notes:**
記 记	*奇 SC61	
專 专	*怪 SC62	

尤

yóu
especially,
particularly 尢
4

尤其   yóuqí   especially

A: 你受誰的影響最大？
B: 我的父母，**尤其**是我爸爸。

其

qí
his, her, its,
their   八
8   (eight)

其實   qíshí   actually

A: 她會說中國話嗎？
B: 我**以為**她會，**其實**她一點兒也不會。

實

shí
solid, genuine,
reality   宀
14

A: 你好像很輕鬆，一點也不怕明天的考
試。
B: **其實**我心裏很緊張。

連

lián
including, to
connect   辶
11

連…都   lián…dōu   even
*一連   yìlián   in a row, in succession

A: 你對音樂有研究嗎？
B: 我**連**歌兒**都**不會唱，怎麼會對音樂有
研究？

繁簡對照：	其他漢字：	✎ **My notes:**
實实 連连		

Grammar
語法 yǔfǎ

Ⓐ Major Sentence Patterns 主要句型 zhǔyào jùxíng

1. 連...都... **construction**

Structure	Gloss
連 S　　　　　　都 V（了）	Even S...
S 連 O(generic N) 都 V（了）	S even V...
S 連一 M N 都/也不/沒 V	S doesn't even V...

1. 連中國人都喜歡搖滾樂嗎？

   Lián Zhōng.guórén dōu xǐ.huān yáogǔnyuè .ma?
   Even Chinese like rock-and-roll music?

   對了，連中國人都喜歡搖滾樂。

   Duì.le, lián Zhōng.guórén dōu xǐ.huān yáogǔnyuè.
   Yes, even Chinese like rock-and-roll music.

2. 她什麼都變了嗎？

   Tā shén.me dōu biàn .le .ma?
   Has she changed completely?

   對了，她什麼都變了，連樣子都變了。

   Duì.le, tā shén.me dōu biàn .le, lián yàng.zi dōu biàn .le.
   Yes, she has completely changed, even her appearance.

3. 你喜歡什麼音樂？

   Nǐ xǐ.huān shén.me yīnyuè?
   What kind of music do you like?

   我什麼音樂都喜歡，連流行歌曲都喜歡。

   Wǒ shén.me yīnyuè dōu xǐ.huān, lián liúxíng gēqǔ dōu xǐ.huān.
   I like all kinds of music, even popular songs.

4. 你會唱中國歌兒嗎？

   Nǐ huì chàng Zhōng.guó gēr .ma?
   Do you know how to sing Chinese songs?

   我連一句也不會唱。

   Wǒ lián yí jù yě bú huì chàng.
   I don't even know how to sing a line.

5. 你身上有錢嗎？

   Nǐ shēn.shàng yǒu qián .ma?
   Do you have any money (with you)?

   我身上連一毛錢也沒有。

   Wǒ shēn.shàng lián yì máo qián yě méi.you.
   I don't even have a dime (with me).

In this sentence pattern, 連 lián 'including, even' functions as a preposition that precedes the subject or the object of a sentence to stress the meaning of "even." It must occur with the adverb 都, which denotes "inclusiveness."

Note: In an affirmative sentence that includes 連 O 都/也 construction, the object (O) must be a generic noun that cannot be modified by "一 M." For example, 我們的公寓什麼都有，連鋼琴都有。 'Our apartment has everything, even a piano.' In the English translation for this sentence, you can say "a piano," but in Chinese you cannot say 一架鋼琴.

2. A 對 B 有研究

Structure	Gloss
A 對 B　　有研究	A has done research/study on B
A 對 B　沒有研究	A hasn't done research/study on B
A 對 B 一點兒研究 都/也 沒有	A hasn't done any research/study on B at all
A 對 B 沒什麼研究	A hasn't done much research/study on B

1. 你對中國音樂有沒有研究？

Nǐ duì Zhōng.guó yīnyuè yǒu .méi.yǒu yánjiū?
Have you done any research/study on Chinese music?

我對中國音樂很有研究。

Wǒ duì Zhōng.guó yīnyuè hěn yǒu yánjiū.
I have done much research/study on Chinese music.

我對中國音樂一點兒研究也沒有。

Wǒ duì Zhōng.guó yīnyuè yì.diǎnr yánjiū yě méi.yǒu.
I haven't done any research/study on Chinese music.

2. 他對京劇很有研究嗎？

Tā duì jīngjù hěn yǒu yánjiū .ma?
Has he done a lot of research/study on Beijing Opera?

他對京劇很有研究。

Tā duì jīngjù hěn yǒu yánjiū.
He has done a lot of research/study on Beijing Opera.

他對京劇沒什麼研究。

Tā duì jīngjù méi shén.me yánjiū.
He hasn't done much research/study on Beijing Opera.

3. 你對美國文學有研究沒有？

Nǐ duì Měi.guó wénxué yǒu yánjiū méi.yǒu?
Have you done any research on American literature?

我對美國文學有一點兒研究。

Wǒ duì Měi.guó wénxué yǒu yì.diǎnr yánjiū.
I have done some research on American literature.

4. 你對做飯有研究嗎？

Nǐ duì zuòfàn yǒu yánjiū .ma?
Have you done any research on (different) cooking (methods)?

我對做飯一點兒研究也沒有。

Wǒ duì zuòfàn yì.diǎnr yánjiū yě méi.yǒu.
I haven't done any research on (different) cooking (methods).

The word order of a sentence with the prepositional phrase 對...(沒)有研究 follows the Temporal Sequence Principle. The subject A has "to face" 對 the thing B first and then conduct the action of "research" 研究.

See L10–B2, L16–A1, L17–A4, L20–B4, L23–B3 for more on A 對 B...

3. A 給 B 寄 O 來/去

Structure	Gloss
A (Neg) 給 B 寄 O 來/去	A (Neg) sends O to B (here/there)
A (Neg) 給 B 寄 來/去 O	

1. 你媽媽給你寄什麼東西來？

Nǐ mā.mā gěi nǐ jì shén.me dōng.xī lái?
What did your mother send you?

我媽媽給我寄兩張光碟來。/
我媽媽給我寄來兩張光碟。

Wǒ mā.mā gěi wǒ jì liǎng zhāng guāngdié lái./ Wǒ mā.mā gěi wǒ jì lái liǎng zhāng guāngdié.
My mother sent me two CDs.

我媽媽沒給我寄東西來。

Wǒ mā.mā méi gěi wǒ jì dōng.xī lái.
My mother didn't send me anything.

2. 他給他弟弟寄了什麼東西去？

Tā gěi tā dì.dì jì .le shén.me dōng.xī qù?
What did he send his younger brother?

他給他弟弟寄了一本音樂書去。

Tā gěi tā dì.dì jì .le yì běn yīnyuèshū qù.
He sent his younger brother a music book.

他不給他弟弟寄音樂書去。 　　　Tā bù gěi tā dì.dì jì yīnyuèshū qù.
He doesn't want to send his younger
brother music books.

In this pattern, 給 functions as a co-verb that occurs before an indirect object (B). The negative marker 沒/不 must precede 給. The directional complements 來/去 denote the action of sending toward and sending away from the subject (A), respectively.

See L8–A1, L13–A3 for more on 給.

4. More resultative verb compounds

	Structure	Gloss
Actual form	V RE	do V
Positive potential form	V得RE	be able to V
Negative potential form	V不 RE	not be able to V

1. 這個字你們看得見嗎？ 　　　Zhèi .ge zì nǐ.men kàn.dejiàn .ma?
Can you see this character?

那個字很大，我們看得見。 　　　Nèi .ge zì hěn dà, wǒ.men kàn.dejiàn.
That character is big, (so) we can see it.

那個字太小，我們看不見。 　　　Nèi .ge zì tài xiǎo, wǒ.men kàn.bujiàn.
that character is too small, (so) we can't
see it.

2. 他說的話你聽得懂聽不懂？ 　　　Tā shuō .de huà nǐ tīng.dedǒng tīng.budǒng?
Can you understand what he is saying?

他說話說得很慢,我聽得懂。 　　　Tā shuōhuà shuō .de hěn màn, wǒ
tīng.dedǒng.
He speaks very slowly; I can understand
(what he is saying).

他說得太快,我聽不懂。 　　　Tā shuō.de tài kuài, wǒ tīng.budǒng.
He speaks too fast; I can't understand
(what he is saying).

Questions with resultative verb compounds can be formed either by adding just the question particle 嗎 to the end of a positive potential form or by combining the positive and negative form to form a choice-type question.

See L7–A6, L9–A6, L15–A2.3, L18–A4 for more on resultative verb compounds.
See L9–A6, L10–A1, L11–A3, L14–A6, L15–A2, L23–C1.5, for more on complement marker 得 .

The most common resultative verb endings

1. 懂 -dǒng: denotes the understanding of what is seen, heard, or read

	Structure		Gloss
Actual form	看懂	kàndǒng	understand by reading
	聽懂	tīngdǒng	understand by hearing
Positive potential form	看得懂	kàn.dedǒng	be able to understand by reading
	聽得懂	tīng.dedǒng	be able to understand by hearing
Negative potential form	看不懂	kàn.budǒng	be unable to understand by reading
	聽不懂	tīng.budǒng	be unable to understand by hearing

2. 見 -jiàn: denotes the perception of what is seen, heard, or smelled

	Structure		Gloss
Actual form	看見	kàn.jiàn	to see
	聽見	tīng.jiàn	to hear
	聞見	wén.jiàn	to smell
Positive potential form	看得見	kàn.dejiàn	can see (by seeing)
	聽得見	tīng.dejiàn	can hear (by listening)
	聞得見	wén.dejiàn	can smell (by smelling)
Negative potential form	看不見	kàn.bujiàn	cannot see (by seeing)
	聽不見	tīng.bujiàn	cannot hear (by listening)
	聞不見	wén.bujiàn	cannot smell (by smelling)

3. 到 -dào: denotes the arrival at the goal of an action

	Structure		Gloss
Actual form	看到	kàn.dào	to see
	聽到	tīng.dào	to hear
Positive potential form	看得到	kàn.dedào	can see (by seeing)
	聽得到	tīng.dedào	can hear (by listening)
Negative potential form	看不到	kàn.budào	cannot see (by seeing)
	聽不到	tīng.budào	cannot hear (by listening)

4. 好 -hǎo: denotes that an action is well done

	Structure		Gloss
Actual form	寫好	xiěhǎo	to write well
	做好	zuòhǎo	to do/make well
	辦好	bànhào	to manage/do well
Positive potential form	寫得好	xiě.dehǎo	can write well
	做得好	zuò.dehǎo	can do/make well
	辦得好	bàn.dehǎo	can manage/do well

Negative potential form	寫不好	xiě.buhǎo	cannot write well
	做不好	zuò.buhǎo	cannot do/make well
	辦不好	bàn.buhào	cannot manage/do well

5. 完 -wán: denotes the end or completion of an action

	Structure		Gloss
Actual form	吃完	chīwán	to finish eating
	念完	niànwán	to finish reading
	寫完	xiěwán	to finish writing
	做完	zuòwán	to finish doing/making
Positive potential form	吃得完	chī.dewán	can finish eating
	念得完	niàn.dewán	can finish reading
	寫得完	xiě.dewán	can finish writing
	做得完	zuò.dewán	can finish doing/making
Negative potential form	吃不完	chī.buwán	cannot finish eating
	念不完	niàn.buwán	cannot finish reading
	寫不完	xiě.buwán	cannot finish writing
	做不完	zuò.buwán	cannot finish doing/making

6. 起 -qǐ: denotes someone can afford to do something

	Structure		Gloss
Positive potential form	吃得起	chī.deqǐ	can afford to eat
	買得起	mǎi.deqǐ	can afford to buy
	住得起	zhù.deqǐ	can afford to live/stay
Negative potential form	吃不起	chī.buqǐ	cannot afford to eat
	買不起	mǎi.buqǐ	cannot afford to buy
	住不起	zhù.buqǐ	cannot afford to live/stay

7. 著 -zháo: denotes success in attaining the object of an action

	Structure		Gloss
Actual form	找著	zhǎozháo	to have found
	買著	mǎizháo	to have bought
	睡著	shuìzháo	to fall into sleep
Positive potential form	找得著	zhǎo.dezháo	to be able to find
	買得著	mǎi.dezháo	to be able to buy
	睡得著	shuì.dezháo	to be able to fall into sleep
Negative potential form	找不著	zhǎo.buzháo	to be unable to find
	買不著	mǎi.buzháo	to be unable to buy
	睡不著	shuì.buzháo	to be unable to fall into sleep

8. 了 -liǎo: denotes the capacity for doing something or for carrying it through to completion

	Structure		Gloss
Positive potential form	吃得了	chī.deliǎo	to be able to finish (all of the food)
	拿得了	ná.deliǎo	to be able to hold (all of the things)
	到得了	dào.deliǎo	to be able to arrive at a place (in a given time)
Negative potential form	吃不了	chī.buliǎo	to be unable to finish (all of the food)
	拿不了	ná.buliǎo	to be unable to hold (all of the things)
	到不了	dào.buliǎo	to be unable to arrive at a place (in a given time)

9. 上 -shàng: denotes satisfactory achievement of an upward action

	Structure		Gloss
Actual form	戴上	dài.shàng	to put on (hats, jewelry)
	關上	guān.shàng	to close up (doors, boxes)
Positive potential form	戴得上	dài.deshàng	can fit (jewelry)
	關得上	guān.deshàng	to be closable (doors, boxes)
Negative potential form	戴不上	dài.bushàng	doesn't fit (jewelry)
	關不上	guān.bushàng	doesn't close up (doors, boxes)

10. 下 -xià: denotes satisfactory achievement of a downward action

	Structure		Gloss
Actual form	放下	fàng.xià	to put down
	裝下	zhuāng.xià	to fill up (a container, box)
	吃下	chī.xià	to eat (down to the stomach)
Positive potential form	放得下	fàng.dexià	can put
	裝得下	zhuāng.dexià	can fit (to a container, box)
	吃得下	chī.dexià	can eat (up all the food)
Negative potential form	放不下	fàng.buxià	cannot put
	裝不下	zhuāng.buxià	cannot fit (to a container, box)
	吃不下	chī.buxià	cannot eat (up all the food)

11. 動 -dòng: denotes moving something or the start of an engine

	Structure		Gloss
Actual form	發動	fādòng	to start (an engine)
	搬動	bāndòng	to move (something)
Positive potential form	發得動	fā.dedòng	can start (an engine)
	搬得動	bān.dedòng	can move (something)
	走得動	zǒu.dedòng	can walk (to have strength to walk)

Negative potential form	發不動	fā.budòng	cannot start (an engine)
	搬不動	bān.budòng	cannot move (something)
	走不動	zǒu.budòng	cannot walk (too tired/weak to walk)

12. 開 -kāi: denotes the opening of container or walking away from work

		Structure	Gloss
Actual form	打開	dǎkāi	to open (a container, jar, box)
	開開	kāikāi	to open (a container, jar, box, door)
	走開	zǒukāi	to walk away (from work, a place)
Positive potential form	打得開	dǎ.dekāi	can open (a container, jar, box)
	開得開	kāi.dekāi	can open (a container, jar, box, door)
	走得開	zǒu.dekāi	can get away (from work, a place)
Negative potential form	打不開	dǎ.bukāi	can't open (a container, jar, box)
	開不開	kāi.bukāi	can't open (a container, jar, box, door)
	走不開	zǒu.bukāi	can't get away (from work, a place)

13. Idioms with resultative verb forms

		Structure	Gloss
Actual form	想到	xiǎngdào	to remember, to think of
	買到	mǎidào	to have bought
Positive potential form	想得到	xiǎng.dedào	to be able to remember
	買得到	mǎidedào	to be able to buy
	對得起	duì.deqǐ	to be able to look up to
	看得起	kàn.deqǐ	to have a high opinion of
Negative potential form	想不到	xiǎng.budào	to be unable to remember
	買不到	mǎi.budào	to be unable to buy
	對不起	duì.buqǐ	to let a person down
	看不起	kàn.buqǐ	to look down upon

B Usage of Common Phrases 詞組用法 cízǔ yòngfǎ

1. Vivid reduplicates

Structure
A Ā 兒地

1.   你要請他給我們做什麼？   Nǐ yào qǐng tā gěi wǒ.men zuò shén.me?
                                       What do you want to ask him to do for us?

我要請他給我們好好兒地介紹一下中國音樂。

Wǒ yào qǐng tā gěi wǒ.men hǎohāor.de jiè.shào.yíxià Zhōng.guó yīnyuè.
I want to ask him to give us a real good introduction to Chinese music.

2. 字要怎麼寫才會好看？

Zì yào zěn.me xiě cái huì hǎokàn?
How can one write the characters to make them look great?

字要慢慢兒地寫才會好看。

Zì yào mànmār.de xiě cái huì hǎokàn.
(Only when) you write the characters very slowly will they look great.

When a reduplicated adjective (A Ā) combines with the suffix 兒 followed by the subordinate particle 地 '.de' to modify an action, it has a vivid function. If the adjective is not in the first tone, then the second (reduplicated) syllable has to change to the first tone.

See L23–C1.4 for more on adverbial marker 地.

Cultural Notes
文化點滴 wénhuà diǎndī

1. Most traditional Chinese songs are classified as 藝術歌曲 yìshù gēqǔ 'art songs,' which basically are lyric songs and patriotic songs sung in Mandarin Chinese, and 民歌 mín'gē 'folk songs,' which are basically sung in local dialect or in the language of minority ethnic groups. Students of primary and secondary schools are required to take music courses, which teach only singing. Most of the songs that are taught at schools are 藝術歌曲. Other kinds of songs are learned by individuals outside of school. In the last few decades, 校園歌曲 xiàoyuán gēqǔ 'campus songs' have become very popular at colleges and universities in Taiwan. Most of the songs are composed and sung by college students.

2. There are different kinds of Chinese "operas," or 地方戲 dìfāngxì 'local operas,' which are sung in the local dialect. For example, 京劇/京戲/平劇 Jīngjù/Jīngxì/ Píngjù 'Beijing/Peking opera' is sung in Mandarin, 粵劇 Yuèjù 'Cantonese opera' is sung in Yuè/ Cantonese dialect, 越劇 Yuèjù 紹興 'Shàoxīng opera' is sung in Wú/Shanghainese dialect, and 歌仔戲 Gēzǎixì 'Taiwanese opera' is sung in Southern Min/Taiwanese dialect.

對話	148頁
小對話	155頁
生詞	157頁
漢字	161頁
語法	167頁
文化點滴	175頁

第十九課 哪一隊贏了？

對話

〔星期六上午，王華想叫美英跟她一塊兒看球。〕

小王：美英，別睡懶覺了，快起來。今天印大跟密西根比賽。

小林：我不想看了，昨晚唱到半夜，累死人了！讓我多睡一會兒
　　　，你自己看電視吧！

小王：（打開電視，看了一
　　　會兒，大叫）好球！

小林：（過了半小時，醒來
　　　，走進客廳）怎麼樣
　　　？哪一隊贏了？

小王：上半場印大領先，四
　　　十比三十二。下半場
　　　密西根的教練叫了兩
次暫停，換了兩個球員上來。那個高個兒的，九號，真厲
害，一下就進了三球，一個人就得了六分，快平手了。

小林：別緊張，再過五分鐘就知道輸贏了。

小王：（大叫）犯規！應該罰球，這裁判不公平，真氣人！

小林：別氣了，看人打球不如自己來，待會兒陪我去打網球吧！
　　　怎麼樣？

小王：先讓我看完了再說。

小林：真是個球迷。

　　　（王華看完電視球賽，和美英去網球場打網球。）

小林：來，你發球。

小王：這球拍太重了。

小林：別找藉口了，
　　　快發。

小王：（發了一球）
　　　太高了。

小林：還可以（把球
　　　打過去）。

小王：（沒打中）太
　　　低了，這不是打球，是撿球嘛！

小林：多練練就行了（繼續發球）。

小王：哎呀！我不行了，可把我累死了。打十分鐘的球比看一小
　　　時的球賽還累。

小林：小姐，現在你才知道什麼叫「看起來容易，做起來難」吧
　　　！

小王：打網球太累人了。咱們下次去打高爾夫球吧！

对话

〔星期六上午，王华想叫美英跟她一块儿看球。〕

小王：美英，别睡懒觉了，快起来。今天印大跟密西根比赛。

小林：我不想看了，昨晚唱到半夜，累死人了！让我多睡一会儿，你自己看电视吧！

小王：（打开电视，看了一会儿，大叫）好球！

小林：（过了半小时，醒来，走进客厅）怎么样？哪一队赢了？

小王：上半场印大领先，四十比三十二。下半场密西根的教练叫了两次暂停，换了两个球员上来。那个高个儿的，九号，真厉害，一下就进了三球，一个人就得了六分，快平手了。

小林：别紧张，再过五分钟就知道输赢了。

小王：（大叫）犯规！应该罚球，这裁判不公平，真气人！

小林：别气了，看人打球不如自己来，待会儿陪我去打网球吧！怎么样？

小王：先让我看完了再说。

小林：真是个球迷。

（王华看完电视球赛，和美英去网球场打网球。）

小林：来，你发球。

小王：这球拍太重了。

小林：别找藉口了，快发。

小王：（发了一球）太高了。

小林：还可以（把球打过去）。

小王：（没打中）太低了，这不是打球，是捡球嘛！

小林：多练练就行了（继续发球）。

小王：哎呀！我不行了，可把我累死了。打十分钟的球比看一小时的球赛还累。

小林：小姐，现在你才知道什么叫「看起来容易，做起来难」吧！

小王：打网球太累人了。咱们下次去打高尔夫球吧！

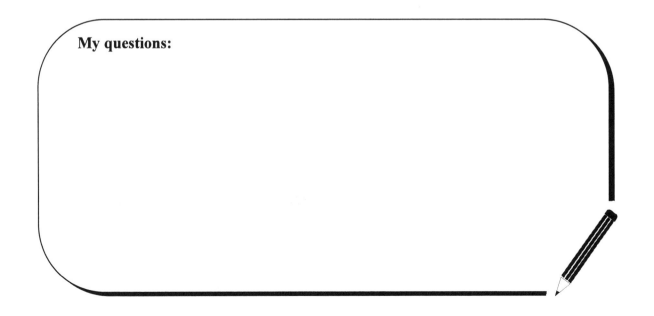

My questions:

Duìhuà

(Xīngqīliù shàng.wǔ, Wáng Huá xiǎng jiào Měiyīng gēn tā yíkuàir qù kànqiú.)

Xiǎo Wáng: Měiyīng, bié shuìlǎnjiào .le. Kuài.qǐ.lái. Jīn.tiān Yìndà
gēn Mìxīgēn bǐsài.

Xiǎo Lín: Wǒ bù xiǎng kàn .le, zuówǎn chàng.dào bànyè, lèi.sǐrén .le!
Ràng wǒ duō shuì yì.huǐr, nǐ zìjǐ kàn diànshì .ba!

Xiǎo Wáng: (Dǎkāi diànshì, kàn .le yì.huǐr, dà jiào) Hǎoqiú!

Xiǎo Lín: (Guò .le bàn xiǎoshí, xǐng.lái, zǒujìn kètīng) Zěn.meyàng?
Nǎ yí duì yíng .le?

Xiǎo Wáng: Shàng bànchǎng Yìndà lǐngxiān, sìshí bǐ sānshí'èr. Xià bàn
chǎng Mìxīgēn .de jiàoliàn jiào .le liǎng cì zhàntíng, huàn
.le liǎng .ge qiúyuán shàng.lái. Nà .ge gāogèr.de, jiǔ hào,
zhēn lì.hài, yí.xià jiù jìn .le sān qiú, yí .ge rén jiù dé .le liù
fēn, kuài píngshǒu .le.

Xiǎo Lín: Bié jǐnzhāng, zài guò wǔ fēn zhōng jiù zhī.dào shūyíng .le.

Xiǎo Wáng: (Dà jiào) Fànguī! Yīnggāi fáqiú, zhèi cáipàn bù gōngpíng,
zhēn qìrén!

Xiǎo Lín: Bié qì .le, kàn rén dǎqiú bùrú zìjǐ lái, dāi .huǐr péi wǒ qù dǎ
wǎngqiú .ba! Zěn.meyàng?

Xiǎo Wáng: Xiān ràng wǒ kànwán .le zài shuō.

Xiǎo Lín: Zhēn shì .ge qiúmí.

(Wáng Huá kànwán diànshì qiúsài, hé Měiyīng qù wǎngqiúchǎng dǎ wǎngqiú.)

Xiǎo Lín: Lái, nǐ fāqiú.

Xiǎo Wáng: Zhè qiúpāi tài zhòng .le.

Xiǎo Lín: Bié zhǎo jièkǒu .le, kuài fā.

Xiǎo Wáng: (Fā .le yì qiú) Tài gāo .le.

 Xiǎo Lín: Hái kě.yǐ (Bǎ qiú dǎ.guò.qù).

Xiǎo Wáng: (Méi dǎzhòng) Tài dī .le, zhè bú.shì dǎqiú, shì jiǎnqiú .ma!

Xiǎo Lín: Duō liàn.liàn jiù xíng .le (Jìxù fāqiú).

Xiǎo Wáng: .Ai.ya! Wǒ bùxíng.le, kě bǎ wǒ lèi.sǐ .le. Dǎ shí fēn zhōng .de qiú bǐ kàn yí .ge xiǎoshí .de qiúsài hái lèi.

Xiǎo Lín: Xiǎo.jiě, xiànzài nǐ cái zhī.dào shén.me jiào "kàn.qǐ.lái róng.yì, zuò .qǐ.lái nán" .ba!

Xiǎo Wáng: Dǎ wǎngqiú tài lèirén .le. Zán.men xià.cì qù dǎ gāo'ěrfūqiú .ba!

Dialogue

(Saturday morning Wáng Huá wants to ask Měiyīng to watch a basketball game with her.)

Xiǎo Wáng: Měiyīng, don't sleep too late. Get up quickly. Today IU is playing Michigan.

Xiǎo Lín: I don't want to watch the game. Last night we sang till midnight. I'm dead tired. Let me sleep a little longer. You watch TV yourself .

Xiǎo Wáng: (Turning on the TV, watching for a while, and yelling:) Good shot!

Xiǎo Lín: (After half an hour, waking up and entering the living room.) How is it? Which team won?

Xiǎo Wáng: The first half IU was ahead, 40 to 32. In the second half Michigan's coach called for two time-outs and changed two players. That tall guy, number nine, is really awesome. He made three baskets and scored six points. It's going to be a tie.

Xiǎo Lín: Don't be anxious, you will know the result in another five minutes.

Xiǎo Wáng: (Yelling:) Foul! We should get a penalty shot. This referee is not fair. It really makes me mad!

Xiǎo Lín: Don't be angry. To watch others play is not as good as playing the game yourself. After this go with me to play tennis; how's that?

Xiǎo Wáng: Let me finish watching the game first.

Xiǎo Lín: You are really a (basket)ball fan.

(After Wáng Huá finishes watching the game, she goes to the tennis court and plays tennis with Měiyīng.)

Xiǎo Lín: Here, you serve the ball.

Xiǎo Wáng: This racket is too heavy.

Xiǎo Lín: Don't find excuses; serve quickly.

Xiǎo Wáng: (Serving a ball.) It's too high.

Xiǎo Lín: It's O.K. (Hitting the ball back.)

Xiǎo Wáng: (Missing the ball.) It's too low. This is not playing tennis. It's picking up tennis balls!

Xiǎo Lín: You will get better after a little more practice. (Continuing to serve the ball.)

Xiǎo Wáng: Oh! I can't go on. This is tiring me. Playing tennis for ten minutes is more tiring than watching a ball game on TV for an hour.

Xiǎo Lín: (Hey) girl, now you know what it means, "it's easier to watch than do!"

Xiǎo Wáng: Playing tennis is too tiring. Let's play golf next time!

Mini-Dialogue
小對話 Xiǎoduìhuà

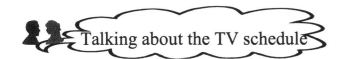

Talking about the TV schedule

1. A: 印大跟密西根的比賽幾點開始？

   Yìndà gēn Mìxīgēn .de bǐsài jǐ diǎn kāishǐ?

   When will the game between Indiana University and the University of Michigan start?

   B: 一點半，在第三台。

   Yī diǎn bàn, zài dì sān tái.
   One-thirty, on channel three.

2. A: 十二點有什麼節目？

   Shí'èr diǎn yǒu shén.me jiémù?
   What programs are showing at twelve o'clock?

   B: 第三台放電影，第五台播新聞。

   Dì sān tái fàng diànyǐng, dì wǔ tái bō xīnwén.

   Channel three will show a movie and channel five will have a news broadcast.

Talking about sports

1. A: 昨天的比賽怎麼樣？哪一
隊贏了？

Zuó.tiān .de bǐsài zěn.meyàng? Nǎ yí
duì yíng .le?

How was the game yesterday? Which
team won?

B: 印大贏了。三十比二十八
。眞緊張，幾乎平手。

Yìndà yíng .le. Sānshí bǐ èrshíbā.
Zhēn jǐn.zhāng, jīhū píngshǒu.

Indiana University won. Thirty to
twenty-eight. It was really tense.
There was almost a tie.

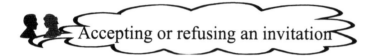

Accepting or refusing an invitation

1. A: 小王，待會兒陪我去打球
吧。

Xiǎo Wáng, dāi.huǐr péi wǒ qù dǎqiú
.ba.

Xiao Wang, go with me later to play
tennis.

B: 不行！我功課還沒做完，
明天再打吧。

Bù xíng! Wǒ gōngkè hái méi
zuòwán, míng.tiān zài dǎ .ba.

I can't. I haven't finished doing my
homework. Let's play tennis tomorrow.

2. A: 嘿！咱們去看籃球賽怎麼
樣？

Hèi! Zán.men qù kàn lánqiú sài
zěn.meyàng?

Hi! Let's go see a basketball game.
How's that?

B: 好啊！可是我没票。

Hǎo .a! Kě.shì wǒ méi piào.
Fine! But I don't have a ticket.

A: 我正好有兩張。

Wǒ zhènghǎo yǒu liǎng zhāng.
I happen to have two.

Vocabulary
生詞 Shēngcí

◎ **By Order of Appearance**

隊	队	duì	N	team
贏	赢	yíng	V	to win
* 輸	输	shū	V	to lose
密西根		Mìxīgēn	N	[tight-west-root] Michigan
比賽	比赛	bǐsài	N/V	[compare-compete] competition, to compete (M: 場)
半夜		bànyè	N	[half-night] midnight
好球		hǎoqiú	IE	[good-ball] good shot
半場	半场	bànchǎng	N	[half-field] half-time (of a game)
領先	领先	lǐngxiān	V	[lead-first] to lead (the score of a game)
* 落後	落后	luòhòu	V	[fall-behind] to fall behind (the score of a game)
# 比 #		bǐ	V	no. to no. (for the scores of a ball game)
教練	教练	jiàoliàn	N	[teach-train] coach (of sports)
暫停	暂停	zhàntíng	N	[temporary-stop] time-out
換	换	huàn	V	to change (player/money), exchange
球員	球员	qiúyuán	N	[ball-personnel] player
高個兒	高个儿	gāogèr	N	[tall-one-Suf] tall person
* 矮個兒	矮个儿	ǎigèr	N	[short-one-Suf] short person
厲害	厉害	lì.hài	SV	[severe-harm] (to be) awesome, be fierce
(投)進	(投)进	tóu(jìn)	V	[throw-enter] to shoot (a ball)
得		dé	V	[obtain] to score, obtain
分		fēn	N	point
平手		píngshǒu	V	[level-hand] to tie (in a ball game)
輸贏	输赢	shūyíng	N	[lose-win] result (of a game)
犯規	犯规	fànguī	V/VO	[offend-rule] to commit a foul
罰球	罚球	fáqiú	V/VO	[fine-ball] penalty shot
* 罰	罚	fá	V	to punish, to penalize, to fine
* 球		qiú	N	ball (M: 個)
裁判		cáipàn	N	[cut cloth-judge] referee, judge (M: 個)
公平		gōngpíng	SV	[public-level] (to be) fair
氣人	气人	qìrén	V	[anger-people] to make one mad
(生)氣	(生)气	(shēng)qì	SV	(to be) angry
打		dǎ	V	to hit, to play (ball)
* 打中		dǎzhòng	RV	[hit-hit target] to hit the ball/target
* 打到		dǎdào	RV	[hit-arrive] to hit the ball/target

不如		bùrú	V	[not-like] not as good as
待	待	dāi	V	to wait (= 等)
陪		péi	V	to accompany
網球	网球	wǎngqiú	N	[net-ball] tennis
發球	发球	fāqiú	VO	[issue-ball] to serve a ball
球拍		qiúpāi	N	[ball-pat] racket (M: 個)
* 球網	球网	qiúwǎng	N	[ball-net] net on a tennis/volleyball court
藉口	借口	jièkǒu	N	[rely on-mouth] excuse (M: 個)
低		dī	SV	(to be) low
撿	捡	jiǎn	V	to pick
嘛		.ma	Part	particle for dogmatic assertion
哎呀		ai.ya	Inter	my goodness! oh no!
不行了		bùxíng.le	IE	[not-work-Asp] (one) cannot go on (doing something), be too weak/sick to (do something)
球賽	球赛	qiúsài	N	[ball compete] ball game (M: 場)
累人		lèirén	V	[tired-people] to make one tired
高爾夫球	高尔夫球	gāo'ěrfūqiú	N	[tall-you-husband-ball] golf

◎ By Grammatical Categories

Nouns/Pronouns

密西根		Mìxīgēn	N	[tight-west-root] Michigan
比賽	比赛	bǐsài	N/V	[compare-compete] competition, to compete (M: 場)
球賽	球赛	qiúsài	N	[ball compete] ball game (M: 場)
隊	队	duì	N	team
分		fēn	N	point
* 球		qiú	N	ball (M: 個)
球拍		qiúpāi	N	[ball-pat] racket (M: 個)
* 球網	球网	qiúwǎng	N	[ball-net] net on a tennis/volleyball court
網球	网球	wǎngqiú	N	[net-ball] tennis
高爾夫球	高尔夫球	gāo'ěrfūqiú	N	[tall-you-husband-ball] golf
裁判		cáipàn	N	[cut cloth-judge] referee, judge (M: 個)
教練	教练	jiàoliàn	N	[teach-train] coach (of sports)
球員	球员	qiúyuán	N	[ball-personnel] player
高個兒	高个儿	gāogèr	N	[tall-one-Suf] tall person
* 矮個兒	矮个儿	ǎigèr	N	[short-one-Suf] short person
半場	半场	bànchǎng	N	[half-field] half-time (of a game)

暫停	暂停	zhàntíng	N	[temporary-stop] time-out
輸贏	输赢	shūyíng	N	[lose-win] result (of a game)
半夜		bànyè	N	[half-night] midnight
藉口	借口	jièkǒu	N	[rely on-mouth] excuse (M: 個)

Verbs/Stative Verbs/Adjectives

# 比 #		bǐ	V	no. to no. (for the scores of a ball game)
贏	赢	yíng	V	to win
* 輸	输	shū	V	to lose
得		dé	V	[obtain] to score, obtain
* 罰	罚	fá	V	to punish, to penalize, to fine
換	换	huàn	V	to change (player/money), exchange
待	待	dāi	V	to wait (= 等)
陪		péi	V	to accompany
(投)進	(投)进	tóu(jìn)	V	[throw-enter] to shoot (a ball)
撿	捡	jiǎn	V	to pick
打		dǎ	V	to hit, to play (ball)
* 打中		dǎzhòng	RV	[hit-hit target] to hit the ball/target
* 打到		dǎdào	RV	[hit-arrive] to hit the ball/target
平手		píngshǒu	V	[level-hand] to tie (in a ball game)
領先	领先	lǐngxiān	V	[lead-first] to lead (the score of a game)
* 落後	落后	luòhòu	V	[fall-behind] to fall behind (the score of a game)
不如		bùrú	V	[not-like] not as good as
犯規	犯规	fànguī	V/VO	[offend-rule] to commit a foul
罰球	罚球	fáqiú	V/VO	[fine-ball] penalty shot
發球	发球	fāqiú	VO	[issue-ball] to serve a ball
累人		lèirén	V	[tired-people] to make one tired
氣人	气人	qìrén	V	[anger-people] to make one mad
(生)氣	(生)气	(shēng)qì	SV	(to be) angry
屬害	厉害	lì.hài	SV	[severe-harm] (to be) awesome, be fierce
公平		gōngpíng	SV	[public-level] (to be) fair
低		dī	SV	(to be) low

Particles

| 嘛 | | .ma | Part | particle for dogmatic assertion |

Idiomatic Expressions

| 好球 | | hǎoqiú | IE | [good-ball] good shot |

不行了		bùxíng.le	IE	[not-work-Asp] (one) cannot go on (doing something), be too weak/sick to (do something)

Others

哎呀		ai.ya	Inter	my goodness! oh no!

✚ Supplementary Vocabulary

1. Odds and Ends

醒來	醒来	xǐnglái	V	[wake-come] to wake up
走進	走进	zǒujìn	V	[walk-enter] to walk into
繼續	继续	jìxù	V	[continue-continue] to continue

2. Sports and Related Terms

籃球	篮球	lánqiú	N	[basket-ball] basketball
橄欖球	橄榄球	gǎnlánqiú	N	[olive-ball] American football
美式足球		měishì zúqiú	N	[American-style-foot-ball] American football
英式足球		yīngshì zúqiú	N	[English-style-foot-ball] soccer
棒球		bàngqiú	N	[club-ball] baseball
排球		páiqiú	N	[row-ball] volleyball
乒乓球		pīngpāngqiú	N	[ping-pong-ball] ping pong
撞球		zhuàngqiú	N	[clash-ball] billiards
羽毛球		yǔmáoqiú	N	[feather-ball] badminton
游泳		yóuyǒng	V	[swim-swim] to swim
溜冰		liūbīng	V	[skate-ice] to ice skate
滑雪		huáxuě	V	[slip-snow] to ski
跑步		pǎobù	V	[run-step] to run
慢跑		mànpǎo	V	[slow-run] to jog
有氧舞蹈		yǒuyǎng wǔdào	N	[have-oxygen-dance] aerobics
體操	体操	tǐcāo	N	[body-exercise] gymnastics
武術	武术	wǔshù	N	[military-skill] martial arts
太極拳	太极拳	tàijíquán	N	[too-extreme-fist] Taichichuan, "shadow boxing"
踢毽子		tījiàn.zi	VO	[kick-shuttlecock] to kick shuttlecocks
跳繩	跳绳	tiàoshéng	VO	[jump-rope] to jump rope
球衣		qiúyī	N	[ball-clothes] sports uniform/shirts
球鞋		qiúxié	N	[ball-shoes] sport shoes
球隊	球队	qiúduì	N	[ball-team] team (of a ball game)
隊員	队员	duìyuán	N	[team-personel] team member
單打	单打	dāndǎ	N	[single-hit] singles game
雙打	双打	shuāngdǎ	N	[pair-hit] doubles game

Characters
漢字 Hànzì

隊　員　手　視

昨　夜　輸　贏

教　練　停　賽

難　拉　變　低

應　該　必　發

*球隊   qiúduì   ball team
*樂隊   yuèduì   band

隊

duì
team, group, line
阝
12   (a mound)

A: 今天是**哪一隊**跟**哪一隊**比賽？
B: 印大跟密西根比賽。

球員   qiúyuán   player
*隊員   duìyuán   team member
*服務員   fúwùyuán   attendant

員

yuán
a person engaged
in some field of
activity   口
10   (mouth)

A: 哪個**球員**打得好？
B: 那個高個兒的，八號。

平手   píngshǒu   to tie (in a ball game)
*歌手   gēshǒu   singer
*水手   shuǐshǒu   sailor

手

shǒu
hand   手
4   (hand)

A: 咱們倆去打網球吧！
B: 打網球沒意思，我們每次都**平手**。

電視   diànshì   television

視

shì
to look at   見
11   (to see)

A: 你看了昨天的**電視**沒有？
B: 沒有，我累得睡著了。

繁簡對照：	其他漢字：	✎ **My notes:**
隊 队 員 员 視 视	*腳 SC63	

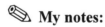

昨   zuó.tiān   yesterday

昨
zuó
yesterday 日
9   (sun)

A: **昨天**你上哪兒去了，我找你找不到？
B: 我上午去看球賽，下午去圖書館了。

半夜   bànyè   midnight
熬晚   áoyè   to burn the midnight oil
*夜晚   yèwǎn   night

夜
yè
night, dark,
darkness 夕
8   (evening)

A: 你昨天**一夜**沒睡覺。
B: 我在趕一個報告。

*輸贏   shūyíng   result (of a game)

輸
shū
to lose 車
16   (vehicle)

A: 昨天的比賽**誰贏誰輸**？
B: 我也不知道，我只看了上半場。

贏
yíng
to win 貝
20   (shells)

A: 那個教練很厲害，這幾年他的球隊每年
都**贏**。
B: 是嗎？

繁簡對照：	其他漢字：	✎ **My notes:**
輸 输 贏 赢	晚 L17	

教

jiào, jiāo
to educate, to
teach   攵
11   (tap)

教練	jiàoliàn	coach
*教育	jiàoyù	education
*教書	jiāoshū	to teach

A: 那個**教練**怎麼樣？
B: 十分厲害，每個球員都怕他。

練

liàn
practice, exercise,
to train   糸
15

| 練習 | liàn.xí | to practice, exercise |
| *練球 | liànqiú | to practice sports |

A: 你今天下午打算做什麼？
B: 我得去**練球**，我們明天比賽。

停

tíng
to stop, cease,
pause   亻
11   (person)

暫停	zhàntíng	time out
*停車	tíngchē	to park/stop cars
*停電	tíngdiàn	power cut
*停水	tíngshuǐ	to cut off the water supply
*停課	tíngkè	to suspend classes

A: 那個教練怎麼了？
B: 快打成平手了，所以他一直叫**暫停**。

賽

sài
to compete   貝
17   (shells)

| 比賽 | bǐsài | to compete, competition |
| 球賽 | qiúsài | ball game |

A: 昨天的**比賽**印大輸了。
B: 我覺得那個裁判不公平。

繁簡對照：	其他漢字：	✎ **My notes:**
練练	留 L23	
賽赛		

難

$E=MC^2$

nán
to be difficult 隹
19　(short-tailed
　　birds)

難過	nánguò	(to be) sad
*難說	nánshuō	hard to say
*難吃	nánchī	not tasty, tastes bad
*難看	nánkàn	(to be) ugly
*難寫	nánxiě	(to be) difficult to write

A: 那部電影怎麼樣？
B: 聽說很**難看**，我自己沒看過。

拉

lā
to pull, to drag 扌
8　　　(hand)

拉小提琴　lā xiǎotíqín　　to play the violin

A: 我想去學**拉小提琴**。
B: 學**拉小提琴**不如學**拉大提琴**。

變

biàn
to change, alter 言
23　　　(speech)

| *變化 | biànhuà | change |
| *改變 | gǎibiàn | to change |

A: 怎麼一個星期不見，你**變**了這麼多？
B: 我不過把頭髮燙了罷。

低

dī
low　　亻
7　　(person)

| *高低 | gāodī | height |

A: 你球發得**太低**了。
B: 看球容易，發球難呀！

繁簡對照：	其他漢字：	✎ **My notes:**
難难 變变	*推 SC64 高 L8	

應

應該　　　yīnggāi　　　should, ought to

yīng
should, ought to
心
17　　(heart)

A: 你**應該**把房間整理一下。
B: 你來幫我的忙吧。

該

gāi
should, deserve
言
13　　(speech)

A: 你**應該**把書放回書架上。
B: 我一會兒再放。

必

不必　　　búbì　　　not necessarily; need not

bì
must, necessarily
心
5　　(heart)

A: 我們今天得練球嗎？
B: **不必**，我們暫停一天。

發

發球　　　fāqiú　　　to serve a ball
*沙發　　　shāfā　　　sofa

fā
to rise, up,
develop
12

A: 你先**發球**。
B: 我**發得不好**，還是你先吧！

繁簡對照：	其他漢字：	✎ **My notes:**
應　应	*撿 SC65	
該　该		
發　发		

Grammar
語法 yǔfǎ

A Major Sentence Patterns 主要句型 zhǔyào jùxíng

1. 再過..., 就 ... construction

Structure	Gloss
(S) 再過多久 就 ... 呢 ？ 再過 多久 (S) 就 ... 呢 ？	In how long will (S) be...?
(S) 再過 Time Expression 就 ... 再過 Time Expression (S) 就 ...	In another Time Expression, (S) will be...

1. 再過多久就知道輸贏呢？

   Zài guò duójiǔ jiù zhī.dào shūyíng .ne?
   How long will it take to know the result (losing or winning)?

   再過五分鐘就知道輸贏了。

   Zài guò wǔ fēn zhōng jiù zhī.dào shūyíng .le.
   In another five minutes you'll know the result (losing or winning).

2. 我們再過多久就要考試呢？

   Wǒ.men zài guò duójiǔ jiù yào kǎoshì .ne?
   How long before we have a test?

   再過兩個星期就要考試了。

   Zài guò liǎng .ge xīngqī jiù yào kǎoshì .le.
   In another two weeks (we) will have a test.

3. 你們再過多久就要放假了？

   Nǐ.men zài guò duójiǔ jiù yào fàngjià .le?
   When will you have a vacation?

   再過三個星期我們就要放假了。

   Zài guò sān .ge xīngqī wǒ.men jiù yào fàngjià .le.
   In another three weeks we will have a vacation.

 In this sentence pattern, the adverbial expression 再過 Time Expression is movable. It may either precede or follow the subject if the subject is present.

2. Comparison of two events

Structure	Gloss
V_1O_1 比 V_2O_2 還/更 Adj	To do V_1O_1 is even Adj-er than V_2O_2
$V_1 O_1$ 沒(有)$V_2 O_2$ (那麼/這麼) Adj	To do V_1O_1 is not as Adj as V_2O_2

1. 打籃球比看籃球比賽更有意思
    嗎？

    Dǎ lánqiú bǐ kàn lánqiú bǐsài gèng
    yǒuyì.si .ma?
    Is playing basketball more interesting
    than watching a basketball game?

    打籃球比看籃球比賽更有意思。

    Dǎ lánqiú bǐ kàn lánqiú bǐsài gèng yǒuyì.si.
    Playing basketball is more interesting
    than watching a basketball game.

    打籃球沒(有)看籃球比賽那麼有
    意思。

    Dǎ lánqiú méi(.yǒu) kàn lánqiú bǐsài
    nà.me yǒuyì.si.
    Playing basketball is not as interesting as
    watching a basketball game.

2. 打十分鐘的球比看一小時的球
    賽還累嗎？

    Dǎ shí fēn zhōng .de qiú bǐ kàn yì xiǎoshí
    .de qiúsài hái lèi .ma?
    Is playing tennis for ten minutes more
    tiring than watching a ball game on TV
    for an hour?

    打十分鐘的球比看一小時的球
    賽還累。

    Dǎ shí fēn zhōng .de qiú bǐ kàn yì xiǎoshí
    .de qiúsài hái lèi.
    Playing tennis for ten minutes is even
    more tiring than watching a ball game on
    TV for an hour.

    打十分鐘的球沒有看一小時的
    球賽那麼累。

    Dǎ shí fēn zhōng .de qiú méi.yǒu kàn yì
    xiǎoshí .de qiúsài nà.me lèi.
    Playing tennis for ten minutes is not as
    tiring as watching a ball game on TV for
    an hour.

 You can always compare two events that belong to similar constructions. The word order
of a comparison sentence follows the Temporal Sequence Principle, since you must
compare the events first, then the result of the comparison follows.

更 and 還 are adverbs. 更 is used for emphatic superior degree and means "(even) more
–er," while 還 is used as an emphatic comparative form that means 'still...-er.'

See L10–A2, L12–A4, L19–A3, L21–A5 for more on comparisons.

3. Comparison of two performances

3.1 比 comparison

Structure	Gloss
A VO V得 比 B (更/還) Adj O, A V得 比 B (更/還) Adj	A VO Adj-er than B As for O, A V Adj-er than B
A VO V得 沒(有) B (那麼/這麼) Adj O, A V得 沒(有) B (那麼/這麼) Adj	A doesn't VO as Adj as B As for O, A doesn't V as Adj as B

1. 他打籃球打得比你(還)好嗎？/
   籃球，他打得比你(還)好嗎？

   Tā dǎ lánqiú dǎ.de bǐ nǐ (hái) hǎo .ma?/
   Lánqiú, tā dǎ.de bǐ nǐ (hái) hǎo .ma?
   Does he play basketball better than you do?

   對，他打籃球打得比我(還)好。/
   籃球，他打得比我(還)好。

   Duì, tā dǎ lánqiú dǎ.de bǐ wǒ (hái) hǎo./
   Lánqiú, tā dǎ.de bǐ wǒ (hái) hǎo.
   Yes, he plays basketball better than I do.

   不，他打籃球打得沒(有)我
   (這麼)好。/ 籃球，他打得沒(有)
   我(這麼)好。

   Bù, tā dǎ lánqiú dǎ.de méi(.yǒu) wǒ
   (zhè.me) hǎo./Lánqiú, tā dǎ.de méi(.yǒu)
   wǒ (zhè.me) hǎo.

   No, he doesn't play basketball as well as
   I do.

2. 他唱歌唱得比你(還)好嗎？/
   歌，他唱得比你(還)好嗎？

   Tā chànggē chàng.de bǐ nǐ (hái) hǎo .ma?/
   Gē, tā chàng.de bǐ nǐ (hái) hǎo .ma?
   Does he sing better than you do?

   對，他唱歌唱得比我(還)好 。/
   歌，他唱得比我(還)好 。

   Duì, tā chànggē chàng.de bǐ wǒ (hái) hǎo./
   Gē, tā chàng.de bǐ wǒ (hái) hǎo.
   Yes, he sings better than I do.

   不 ，他唱歌唱得沒(有)我(這麼)
   好 。/ 歌，他唱得沒(有)我(這麼)
   好。

   Bù, tā chànggē chàng.de méi(.yǒu) wǒ
   (zhè.me) hǎo./Gē, tā chàng.de méi(.yǒu)
   wǒ (zhè.me) hǎo.

   No, he doesn't sing as well as I do.

   不 ，他唱歌唱得跟我一樣好 。/
   歌，他唱得跟我一樣好。

   Bù, tā chànggē chàng.de gēn wǒ yíyàng
   hǎo./Gē, tā chàng.de gēn wǒ yíyàng hǎo.
   No, he sings as well as I do.

3.2 Equal comparison

Structure	Gloss
A VO V得跟　B 一樣　Adj	A VO as Adj as B does
A VO V得不跟 B 一樣　Adj	A doesn't VO equally Adj with B
A VO V得跟 B不一樣　Adj	A and B do not VO equally Adj
O, A V得跟　　B 一樣　Adj	As for O, A doesn't VO equally Adj with B
O, A V得不跟 B 一樣　Adj	As for O, A V as Adj as B does
O, A V得跟 B不一樣　Adj	As for O, A and B do not V equally Adj

1. 他打網球打得跟你 一樣好嗎？ /
    網球， 他打得跟你 一樣好嗎？

    Tā dǎ wǎngqiú dǎ.de gēn nǐ yíyàng hǎo
    .ma?/Wǎnqiú, tā dǎ.de gēn nǐ yíyàng hǎo
    .ma?
    Does he play tennis as well as you do?

    不，他打網球打得跟我不 一樣好
    。/網球，他打得跟我不一樣好
    。

    Bù, tā dǎ wǎnqiú dǎ.de gēn wǒ bù yíyàng
    hǎo./ Wǎnqiú, tā dǎ.de gēn wǒ bù yíyàng
    hǎo.
    No, he doesn't play tennis as well as I
    do.

2. 你看電視看得跟他一樣多嗎？ /
    電視，你看得跟他一樣多嗎？

    Nǐ kàn diànshì kàn.de gēn tā yíyàng duō
    .ma? /Diànshì, nǐ kàn.de gēn tā yíyàng
    duō .ma?
    Do you watch TV as much as he does?

    我 看電視看得跟他一樣多。/
    電視， 我 看得跟他一樣多。

    Wǒ kàn diànshì kàn.de gēn tā yíyàng
    duō./Diànshì, wǒ kàn.de gēn tā yíyàng
    duō.
    I watch TV as much as he does.

    我 看電視看得跟他不一樣多。 /
    電視， 我 看得跟他不一樣多。

    Wǒ kàn diànshì kàn.de gēn tā bù yíyàng
    duō./Diànshì, wǒ kàn.de gēn tā bù yíyàng
    duō.
    I don't watch TV as much as he does.

To compare the performance of two people performing a similar action, the second
verbal expression can be abbreviated as -V得 just as you would use the verb "do" in
English.

See L10–A2, L12–A4, L19–A2, L21–A5 for more on comparisons.

B Usage of Common Phrases 詞組用法 cízǔ yòngfǎ

1. A 不如 B... construction

Structure	Gloss
A 不如 B SV	A is not as Adj as B
V₁O₁ 不如 V₂O₂	To do V₁O₁ is not as good as to do V₂O₂
	It is better to do V₂O₂ than to do V₁O₁
一M 不如 一M	(It's) getting ...er M by M

1. 這個球員不如那個厲害嗎？

   Zhèi .ge qiúyuán bùrú nèi .ge lì.hài .ma?
   Is this player not as awesome as that one?

   對了，這個球員不如那個厲害。

   Duì.le, zhèi .ge qiúyuán bùrú nèi .ge lì.hài.
   (You are) right, this player is not as awesome as that one.

2. 打籃球不如打網球好嗎？

   Dǎ lánqiú bùrú dǎ wǎngqiú hǎo .ma?
   Is playing basketball not as good as playing tennis?

   對了，打籃球不如打網球好。

   Duì.le, dǎ lánqiú bùrú dǎ wǎngqiú hǎo.
   (You are) right, playing basketball is not as good as playing tennis/it's better to play tennis than to play basketball.

3. 你籃球打得怎麼樣？

   Nǐ lánqiú dǎ.de zěn.meyàng?
   How is your basketball game?

   我很久沒練籃球了，打得一天不如一天。

   Wǒ hěn jiǔ méi liàn lánqiú .le, dǎ .de yì tiān bùrú yì tiān.
   I haven't practiced basketball for a long while; (my) playing is getting worse day by day.

4. 你中文說得怎麼樣？

   Nǐ Zhōngwén shuō.de zěn.meyàng?
   How is your spoken Chinese?

   我很久沒說中文了，說得一天不如一天。

   Wǒ hěn jiǔ méi shuō Zhōngwén .le, shuō .de yì tiān bùrú yì tiān.
   I haven't spoken Chinese for a long time; (my) speaking is getting worse day by day.

2. The co-verb 跟

Structure	Gloss
A (AuxV)　　跟 B VO	A (AuxV)　VO　with B
A (不/沒/別)　跟 B VO	A (not)　　VO　with B

1. 今天是哪(一)隊跟哪(一)隊比賽
   啊？

   Jīn.tiān shì něi (yī) duì gēn něi (yī) duì
   bǐsài .a?
   Which teams are competing today?

   今天是印大跟普度比賽。

   Jīn.tiān shì Yìndà gēn Pǔdù bǐsài.
   Today IU will play against Purdue.

2. 現在誰跟誰在比賽啊？

   Xiànzài shéi gēn shéi zài bǐsài .a?
   Who is playing (competing) against
   whom now?

   現在小王跟小林在比賽打網球。

   Xiànzài Xiǎo Wáng gēn Xiǎo Lín zài
   bǐsài dǎ wǎngqiú.
   Now Xiao Wang is playing tennis against
   Xiao Lin.

3. 誰要跟你打乒乓球啊？

   Shéi yào gēn nǐ dǎ pīngpāngqiú .a?
   Who is going to play ping pong with you?

   小李要跟我打乒乓球。

   Xiǎo Lǐ yào gēn wǒ dǎ pīngpāngqiú.
   Xiao Li is going to play ping pong with me.

4. 去年你跟他學打籃球了嗎？

   Qù.nián nǐ gēn tā xué dǎ lánqiú .le .ma?
   Did you study basketball with him last year?

   對了，去年我跟他學打籃球了。

   Duì.le, qù.nián wǒ gēn tā xué dǎ lánqiú .le.
   Yes, I studied basketball with him last year.

   不，去年我沒跟他學打籃球。

   Bù, qù.nián wǒ méi gēn tā xué dǎ lánqiú.
   No, I didn't study basketball with him
   last year.

The co-verb 跟 cannot be suffixed by the aspect marker 了. In a past tense sentence, the
aspect marker 了 can be used as a suffix to the verb or verbal expression that follows the
object of 跟.

See L5–A2.3, L14–A7 for more on 跟.

3. Winning prizes and awards

Structure		Gloss
A 得了冠軍	A dé.le guànjūn	A won the championship
A 得了亞軍	A dé.le yàjūn	A was the runner-up
A 得了季軍	A dé.le jìjūn	A was the second runner-up
A 得了金牌	A dé.le jīnpái	A won the gold medal
A 得了銀牌	A dé.le yínpái	A won the silver medal
A 得了銅牌	A dé.le tóngpái	A won the bronze medal
A 得了第一名	A dé.le dìyīmíng	A won first place
A 得了第二名	A dé.le dì'èrmíng	A won second place
A 得了第三名	A dé.le dìsānmíng	A won third place

When someone has won a prize or an award, Chinese use the verb 得了 'obtained' or 贏得 yíngdé 'won.' For the first three awards or medals, the special terms are listed above. When expressing the standing of a game or competition, ordinal numbers are used, e.g., 第一名, 第二名 'first place, second place,' etc.

ⓒ Reentry 複習 fùxí

1. The difference between 跟、和、也

Structure	Gloss
NP₁ 跟 NP₂	NP₁ and NP₂
NP₁ 和 NP₂	NP₁ and NP₂
VP₁ 也 VP₂	VP₁ and VP₂

1. 什麼人喜歡看籃球比賽？

    Shén.me rén xǐ.huān kàn lánqiú bǐsài?
    Who likes to watch basketball?

    中國人跟/和美國人都喜歡看籃球比賽。

    Zhōng.guórén gēn/hé Měi.guórén dōu xǐ.huān kàn lánqiú bǐsài.
    Both Chinese and Americans like to watch basketball.

2. 做什麼很有意思？

    Zuò shén.me hěn yǒuyì.si?
    What is fun to do?

    打網球跟/和看網球比賽都很有意思。

    Dǎ wǎngqiú gēn/hé kàn wǎngqiú bǐsài dōu hěn yǒuyì.si.
    Playing tennis and watching tennis are both interesting.

3.　你喜歡打什麼球？

Nǐ xǐ.huān dǎ shén.me qiú?
What sports do you like to play?

我喜歡打網球，也喜歡打籃球。

Wǒ xǐ.huān dǎ wǎngqiú, yě xǐ.huān dǎ lánqiú.
I like to play tennis (and) also like to play basketball. (I like to play tennis and basketball.)

4.　他要學什麼？

Tā yào xué shén.me?
What does he want to study?

他要學中文，也要學日文。

Tā yào xué Zhōngwén, yě yào xué Rìwén.
He wants to study Chinese (and) also (wants to study) Japanese. (He wants to study Chinese and Japanese.)

The major difference between 跟/和 and 也 is that 跟 and 和 are conjunctions that connect two nominal expressions (nouns/noun phrases/gerunds) while 也 is an adverb that connects two verbs (including auxiliary verbs/stative verbs/adjectives). Because in English all three are translated "and," English-speaking students tend to use 也 mistakenly to connect two nominal expressions.

See L5–A2.3 for more on 跟.

Cultural Notes
文化點滴 wénhuà diǎndī

1. The average Chinese doesn't do as much exercise as Americans do because most of the working people must work really hard to make ends meet. Housewives are busy with their household chores and taking care of the children, whereas students are always overloaded with homework and after-school studies to prepare for the tough competition of entrance examinations. People just can't find much time for exercise. That is why, in mainland China and Taiwan, at parks and school campuses, early every morning there are volunteer teachers who teach people 打太極拳 dǎ tàijíquán 'to do shadow-boxing exercise' and 跳土風舞 tiào tǔfēngwǔ 'to

dance folk dances.' Traditionally, Taichiquan masters don't charge their disciples any fees.

2. In the old days when modern sports equipment was not available and people couldn't afford to play expensive sports, such as tennis, golf, swimming, skating, and skiing, the most popular sports for students at primary and secondary schools were 踢毽子 tī jiàn.zi 'kicking shuttlecocks' and 跳繩 tiàoshéng 'jumping rope' because these two kinds of sports didn't cost much and didn't take up much space, either. In the last few decades, there has been a revival of these two sports, which have been promoted to the level of national competition in Taiwan.

3. At a Chinese school game, you may find a 啦啦隊 lālāduì 'cheer-leader team' that encourages students 給球隊加油 gěi qiúduì jiāyóu 'to add oil to the team—to support their team.' For instance, they will yell, 印大，加油! 'Go IU!' 好球! 'Good ball!'

對話	178頁
小對話	184頁
生詞	185頁
漢字	191頁
語法	197頁
文化點滴	203頁

第二十課　你有沒有發燒？

對話

〔王華、林美英兩人互相抱怨。〕

小林：（打噴嚏）哈求！哈⋯⋯求！

小王：你看你，感冒了吧
　　　！叫你別一打完球
　　　就吹風、喝涼水。
　　　偏不聽。

小林：才不是感冒呢！我
　　　想是老毛病犯了——
　　　花粉熱。瞧你，（
　　　你）也好不到哪兒
　　　去，才打了半小時
　　　球，就全身酸疼。

小王：這得怪你，讓我滿場追球，摔了幾跤，腿傷得青一塊紫一
　　　塊的。

小林：好了，好了。咱們別再抱怨了，快給醫生打個電話，約個
　　　時間去看病吧！

小王：我自己抹點兒萬金油、跌打藥就行了。

　　　　　　　（美英去了印大學生保健中心的門診處。）

醫生：（看美英的病歷表）今天覺得怎麼樣？

小林：不太好。我一直流鼻涕，打噴嚏，眼睛癢得難受。

醫生：頭疼嗎？有沒有發燒？

小林：燒倒是沒有，頭有
　　　點兒疼。覺得很累
　　　，書也沒法子看。

醫生：這情況已經多久了
　　　？

小林：一個多星期吧！從
　　　我和同屋兒上星期
　　　打完球以後，我就

覺得不舒服，眼睛紅得像隻兔子。

醫生：（聽心跳、看喉嚨）說ㄚㄧ。

小林：ㄚㄧ。

醫生：沒什麼問題，你只是對空氣中的灰塵過敏。我給你打一針
　　　，再給你開個藥方就行了。

小林：要吃藥嗎？

醫生：不必，可是得按時點眼藥，過兩個星期還不好，再來看我
　　　。

小林：（拿藥方）謝謝。

对话

〔王华、林美英两人互相抱怨。〕

小林：（打喷嚏）哈求！哈……求！

小王：你看你，感冒了吧！叫你别一打完球就吹风、喝凉水。偏
　　　不听。

小林：才不是感冒呢！我想是老毛病犯了——花粉热。瞧你，
　　　（你）也好不到哪儿去，才打了半小时球，就全身酸疼。

小王：这得怪你，让我满场追球，摔了几跤，腿伤得青一块紫一
　　　块的。

小林：好了，好了。咱们别再抱怨了，快给医生打个电话，约个
　　　时间去看病吧！

小王：我自己抹点儿万金油、跌打药就行了。

（美英去了印大学生保健中心的门诊处。）

医生：（看美英的病历表）今天觉得怎么样？

小林：不太好。我一直流鼻涕，打喷嚏，眼睛痒得难受。

医生：头疼吗？有没有发烧？

小林：烧倒是没有，头有点儿疼。觉得很累，书也没法子看。

医生：这情况已经多久了？

小林：一个多星期吧！从我和同屋儿上星期打完球以后，我就觉
　　　得不舒服，眼睛红得像隻兔子。

医生：（听心跳、看喉咙）说丫一。

小林：ㄚ—。

医生：没什么问题，你只是对空气中的灰尘过敏。我给你打一针，再给你开个药方就行了。

小林：要吃药吗？

医生：不必，可是得按时点眼药，过两个星期还不好，再来看我。

小林：（拿药方）谢谢。

My questions:

Duìhuà

(Wáng Huá, Lín Měiyīng liǎng rén hùxiāng bàoyuàn.)

Xiǎo Lín: (Dǎ pēntì) Hāqiu! Hā.....qiu!

Xiǎo Wáng: Nǐ kàn nǐ, gǎnmào .le .ba! Jiào nǐ bié yī dǎwán qiú jiù
             chuīfēng, hē liángshuǐ, piān bù tīng.

Xiǎo Lín: Cái bú shì gǎnmào .ne! Wǒ xiǎng shì lǎomáobìng fàn .le —
             huāfěnrè. Qiáo nǐ, (nǐ) yě hǎo bú dào nǎr qù, cái dǎ .le bàn
             xiǎoshí qiú, jiù quánshēn suānténg.

Xiǎo Wáng: Zhè děi guài nǐ, ràng wǒ mǎnchǎng zhuīqiú, shuāi .le jǐ jiāo,
             tuǐ shāng .de qīng yí kuài zǐ yí kuài .de.

Xiǎo Lín: Hǎo.le, hǎo.le. Zán.men bié zài bàoyuàn .le, kuài gěi yī.shēng
             dǎ .ge diànhuà, yuē .ge shíjiān qù kànbìng .ba!

Xiǎo Wáng: Wǒ zìjǐ mǒ .diǎnr Wànjīnyóu, diédǎyào jiù xíng .le.

(Měiyīng qù .le Yìndà xué.shēng bǎojiàn zhōngxīn .de ménzhěnchù.)

Yīshēng: (Kàn Měiyīng .de bìnglìbiǎo) Jīn.tiān jué.de zěn.meyàng?

Xiǎo Lín: Bútài hǎo. Wǒ yìzhí liú bítì, dǎ pēntì, yǎn.jīng yǎng .de
             nánshòu.

Yīshēng: Tóuténg .ma? Yǒu .méi.yǒu fāshāo?

Xiǎo Lín: Shāo dào.shì méi.yǒu, tóu yǒu .diǎnr téng. Jué.de hěn lèi, shū
             yě méi fǎ.zi kàn.

Yīshēng: Zhè qíngkuàng yǐ.jīng duójiǔ .le?

Xiǎo Lín: Yí .ge duō xīngqī .ba! Cóng wǒ hé tóngwūr shàng xīngqī
             dǎwán qiú yǐhòu, wǒ jiù jué.de bù shū.fū, yǎn.jīng hóng .de
             xiàng zhī tù.zi.

Yīshēng: (Tīng xīntiào, kàn hóulóng) shuō Ah —.

Xiǎo Lín: Ah —.

Yīshēng: Méi shén.me wèntí. Nǐ zhǐ.shì duì kōngqì zhōng .de huīchén
             guòmǐn. Wǒ gěi nǐ dǎ yì zhēn, zài gěi nǐ kāi .ge yàofāng jiù
             xíng .le.

Xiǎo Lín: Yào chīyào .ma?

Yīshēng: Búbì, kě.shì děi ànshí diǎn yǎnyào, guò liǎng .ge xīngqī hái bù
             hǎo, zài lái kàn wǒ.

Xiǎo Lín: (Ná yàofāng) Xiè.xie.

Dialogue

(Wáng Huá and Lín Měiyīng are complaining to each other.)

Xiǎo Lín:　　(Sneezing:) Hachoo! Ha.....choo!

Xiǎo Wáng:　See, you caught a cold. I told you not to stand out in a draft and drink cold water right after playing ball. You just wouldn't listen.

Xiǎo Lín:　　It's not a cold! I think it's my old problem—hay fever. See, you are not very well, either. You just played ball for half an hour, and you are sore all over.

Xiǎo Wáng:　It's your fault. You made me chase the ball all over the court. I took a lot of falls. I've got bruises all over my legs.

Xiǎo Lín:　　All right, all right. Let's not complain to each other any more. Give the doctor a call and make an appointment to see him!

Xiǎo Wáng:　I will simply apply some Tiger Balm and "bruise ointment" myself.

(Měiyīng goes to the clinic of the Student Health Center at IU.)

Doctor:　　　(Looking at Měiyīng's record:) How do you feel today?

Xiǎo Lín:　　Not very good. I have a runny nose and I'm sneezing all the time. My eyes are also extremely itchy.

Doctor:　　　Do you have a headache or fever?

Xiǎo Lín:　　I don't have a fever, but I have a little headache. I am feeling very tired and I can't study (there is no way for me to study).

Doctor:　　　How long have you had this condition?

Xiǎo Lín:　　It's been about a week! Since I went to play tennis with my roommate last week, I've felt uncomfortable. My eyes are red like a rabbit.

Doctor:　　　(Listening to her heartbeat, and looking at her throat:) Say "Ah —."

Xiǎo Lín:　　Ah —.

Doctor:　　　No problem. You are only allergic to the dust in the air. I'll give you a shot and write you a prescription.

Xiǎo Lín:　　Do I have to take medicine?

Doctor:　　　No, but you have to use eyedrops and after two weeks come see me again if you are still not better.

Xiǎo Lín:　　(Taking the prescription:) Thank you.

Mini-Dialogue
小對話 Xiǎoduìhuà

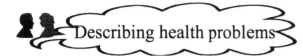 Describing health problems

1. A: 大夫，我頭疼，喉嚨也痛　Dài.fū, wǒ tóuténg, hóulóng yě tòng,
　　　　，一直咳嗽。　　　　　yìzhí késòu.
　　　　　　　　　　　　　　Doctor, I have a headache. My throat
　　　　　　　　　　　　　　aches, too. I'm coughing all the time.

    B: 什麼時候開始的？　　　Shén.me shí.hòu kāishǐ .de?
　　　　　　　　　　　　　　When did this condition start?

    A: 上星期二。　　　　　　Shàng xīngqī'èr.
　　　　　　　　　　　　　　Last Tuesday.

    B: 没什麼，小感冒，吃點兒藥　Méi shén.me, xiǎo gǎnmào, chī .diǎnr
　　　　，多喝水，多休息就好了。　yào, duō hēshuǐ, duō xiū.xí jiù hǎo.le.
　　　　　　　　　　　　　　It's nothing. Just a cold. It will be
　　　　　　　　　　　　　　fine if you take some medicine, drink
　　　　　　　　　　　　　　more water, and rest more.

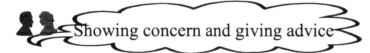 Showing concern and giving advice

1. A: 你怎麼了？　　　　　　Nǐ zěn.me .le?
　　　　　　　　　　　　　　What's wrong with you?

    B: 我想我是感冒了。　　　Wǒ xiǎng wǒ shì gǎnmào .le.
　　　　　　　　　　　　　　I think I have a cold.

    A: 快回家休息吧！　　　　Kuài huíjiā xiū.xí .ba!
　　　　　　　　　　　　　　Go home right away and rest.

Vocabulary
生詞 Shēngcí

◎ **By Order of Appearance**

(發)燒	(发)烧	(fā)shāo	N/VO	[issue-burn] a fever, to have a fever
燒	烧	shāo	N/V	fever, to have a fever
感冒		gǎnmào	V/VO	[feel-cold] to catch a cold
* 傷風	伤风	shāngfēng	V/VO	[injured-wind] to catch a cold (=感冒)
叫		jiào	CV	to cause, to tell (someone to do something)
吹風	吹风	chuīfēng	V	[blow-wind] to expose to cold wind
涼水	涼水	liángshuǐ	N	[cool-water] cool water
* 冷水		lěngshuǐ	N	[cold-water] cold water
偏(偏)		piān(piān)	Adv	deliberately (used before a verb to show contrariness or determination)
毛病		máo.bìng	N	[hair-sickness] illness; shortcoming
犯		fàn	V	to have a relapse, to fall back to an old illness or old bad habit
花粉熱	花粉热	huāfěnrè	N	[flower-powder-heat] hay fever
* 花粉		huāfěn	N	[flower-powder] pollen
過敏	过敏	guòmǐn	N	[over-sensitive] allergy
瞧		qiáo	V	to look at, to see (= 看)
酸疼		suānténg	SV	[sour-pain] (to be) sore (=酸痛)
* 疼		téng	SV	(to be) painful
怪		guài	V	to blame
滿場	满场	mǎnchǎng	N	[full-field] the whole field
追		zhuī	V	to chase
摔		shuāi	V	to fall
跤		jiāo	M	measure word for falling on the ground
腿		tuǐ	N	leg (M: 隻)
傷	伤	shāng	V	to injure
青	青	qīng	Adj/N	blue, green
紫		zǐ	Adj/N	purple
塊	块	kuài	M	lump, (hard) piece
抱怨		bàoyuàn	V	[embrace-complain] to complain
醫生	医生	yī.shēng	N	[medicine-teacher] doctor
* 大夫		dài.fu	N	[big-person] doctor (=醫生)
約	约	yuē	V	to make an appointment
看病		kànbìng	V/VO	[see-illness] to see a doctor
* 病		bìng	N/V	sickness, to be sick

生病		shēngbìng	V/VO	[birth-illness] to be sick (=病)
抹		mǒ	V	to smear
萬金油	万金油	Wànjīnyóu	N	[ten thousand-gold-oil] Tiger Balm
跌打藥	跌打药	diédǎyào	N	[fall-hit-medicine] "bruise ointment"
* 藥	药	yào	N	medicine, drug
流		liú	V	to flow, to run (water)
鼻涕		bítì	N	[nose-drip] nasal drip
噴嚏	喷嚏	pēn.tì	N	[blow out-sneeze] sneeze (M: 個)
眼睛		yǎn.jīng	N	[eye-eyeball] eye (M: 隻)
癢	痒	yǎng	SV	(to be) itchy
難受	难受	nánshòu	SV	[difficult-receive] (to be) unbearable, to feel bad
法子		fǎ.zi	N	[law-Suf] way, method (M: 個)
情況	情况	qíngkuàng	N	[matter-situation] situation
* 症狀	症状	zhèngzhuàng	N	[symptom-situation] symptom
從	从	cóng	Prep	since
同屋兒	同屋儿	tóngwūr	N	[same-room-Suf] roommate (China)
* 室友		shìyǒu	N	[room-friend] roommate
紅	红	hóng	SV/N	(to be) red, redness
兔子		tù.zi	N	[rabbit-Suf] rabbit (M: 隻)
問題	问题	wèntí	N	[ask-topic] question, problem
只是		zhǐ.shì	Adv	[only-be] merely, only, just
對...過敏	对...过敏	duì...guòmǐn	IE	[toward...over-sensitive] to be allergic to
空氣	空气	kōngqì	N	[empty-air] air
灰塵	灰尘	huīchén	N	[ash-dust] dust
打針	打针	dǎzhēn	VO	[strike-needle] to have a shot, injection
開藥方	开药方	kāi yàofāng	VO	[open-medicine-prescription] to give a prescription
* 藥方	药方	yàofāng	N	[medicine-prescription] prescription
按時	按时	ànshí	VO	[according to-time] according to schedule
點眼藥	点眼药	diǎn yǎnyào	VO	[point-eye-medicine] to use eyedrops
* 眼藥	眼药	yǎnyào	N	[eye-medicine] eyedrops

◎ By Grammatical Categories

Nouns/Pronouns

同屋兒	同屋儿	tóngwūr	N	[same-room-Suf] roommate (China)
* 室友		shìyǒu	N	[room-friend] roommate
醫生	医生	yī.shēng	N	[medicine-teacher] doctor
* 大夫		dài.fu	N	[big-person] doctor (=醫生)
* 病		bìng	N/V	sickness, to be sick
毛病		máo.bìng	N	[hair-sickness] illness; shortcoming
情況	情况	qíngkuàng	N	[matter-situation] situation
* 症狀	症状	zhèngzhuàng	N	[symptom-situation] symptom
燒	烧	shāo	N/V	fever, to have a fever
腿		tuǐ	N	leg (M: 隻)
眼睛		yǎn.jīng	N	[eye-eyeball] eye (M: 隻)
鼻涕		bítì	N	[nose-drip] nasal drip
噴嚏	喷嚏	pēn.tì	N	[blow out-sneeze] sneeze (M: 個)
過敏	过敏	guòmǐn	N	[over-sensitive] allergy
空氣	空气	kōngqì	N	[empty-air] air
灰塵	灰尘	huīchén	N	[ash-dust] dust
* 花粉		huāfěn	N	[flower-powder] pollen
花粉熱	花粉热	huāfěnrè	N	[flower-powder-heat] hay fever
涼水	凉水	liángshuǐ	N	[cool-water] cool water
* 冷水		lěngshuǐ	N	[cold-water] cold water
* 藥	药	yào	N	medicine, drug
* 藥方	药方	yàofāng	N	[medicine-prescription] prescription
* 眼藥	眼药	yǎnyào	N	[eye-medicine] eyedrops
跌打藥	跌打药	diédǎyào	N	[fall -hit-medicine] "bruise ointment"
萬金油	万金油	Wànjīnyóu	N	[ten thousand-gold-oil] Tiger Balm
問題	问题	wèntí	N	[ask-topic] question, problem
法子		fǎ.zi	N	[law-Suf] way, method (M: 個)
滿場	满场	mǎnchǎng	N	[full-field] the whole field
兔子		tù.zi	N	[rabbit-Suf] rabbit (M: 隻)

Measure Words

塊	块	kuài	M	lump, (hard) piece
跤		jiāo	M	measure word for falling on the ground

Verbs/Stative Verbs/Adjectives

叫		jiào	CV	to cause, to tell (someone to do something)
犯		fàn	V	to have a relapse, to fall back to an old illness or old bad habit
怪		guài	V	to blame
瞧		qiáo	V	to look at, to see (= 看)
追		zhuī	V	to chase
摔		shuāi	V	to fall
傷	伤	shāng	V	to injure
約	约	yuē	V	to make an appointment
抹		mǒ	V	to smear
流		liú	V	to flow, to run (water)
看病		kànbìng	V/VO	[see-illness] to see a doctor
生病		shēngbìng	V/VO	[birth-illness] to be sick (=病)
感冒		gǎnmào	V/VO	[feel-cold] to catch a cold
* 傷風	伤风	shāngfēng	V/VO	[injured-wind] to catch a cold (=感冒)
吹風	吹风	chuīfēng	V	[blow-wind] to expose to cold wind
(發)燒	(发)烧	(fā)shāo	VO	[issue-burn] to have a fever
抱怨		bàoyuàn	V	[embrace-complain] to complain
打針	打针	dǎzhēn	VO	[strike-needle] to have a shot, injection
開藥方	开药方	kāi yàofāng	VO	[open-medicine-prescription] to give a prescription
點眼藥	点眼药	diǎn yǎnyào	VO	[point-eye-medicine] to use eyedrops
按時	按时	ànshí	VO	[according to-time] according to schedule
紅	红	hóng	SV/N	(to be) red, redness
青	青	qīng	Adj/N	blue, green
紫		zǐ	Adj/N	purple
癢	痒	yǎng	SV	(to be) itchy
* 疼		téng	SV	(to be) painful
酸疼		suānténg	SV	[sour-pain] (to be) sore (=酸痛)
難受	难受	nánshòu	SV	[difficult-receive] (to be) unbearable, to feel bad
從	从	cóng	Prep	since

Adverbs

只是		zhǐ.shì	Adv	[only-be] merely, only, just
偏(偏)		piān(piān)	Adv	deliberately (used before a verb to show contrariness or determination)

Idiomatic Expressions

對...過敏	对...过敏	duì...guòmǐn	IE	[toward...over-sensitive] to be allergic to

✚ **Supplementary Vocabulary**

1. Odds and Ends

互相		hùxiāng	Adv	[mutual-mutual] mutually, each other
照顧	照顾	zhàogù	V	[relfect-see] to take care of

2. Medicine and Health

保健中心		bǎojiàn zhōngxīn	N	[protect-health-middle-heart] health center
門診部/處	门诊部/处	ménzhěnbù/chù	N	[door-diagnose-department/place] outpatient clinic
急診部/處	急诊部/处	jízhěnbù/chù	N	[urgent-diagnose-department/place] emergency room
救護車	救护车	jiùhùchē	N	[save-proctect-car] ambulance
護士	护士	hùshì	N	[protect-scholar] nurse
病歷表	病历表	bìnglìbiǎo	N	[illness-history-chart] health record
血壓	血压	xuěyā	N	[blood-pressure] blood pressure
心跳		xīntiào	N	[heart-jump] pulse
藥房/店	药房/店	yàofáng/diàn	N	[medicine-house/store] drugstore, pharmacy
中醫	中医	zhōngyī	N	[Chinese-medicine] Chinese medicine/doctor
西醫	西医	xīyī	N	[west-medicine] Western medicine/doctor
中藥	中药	zhōngyào	N	[Chinese-medicine] Chinese drug
西藥	西药	xīyào	N	[west-medicine] Western drug
草藥	草药	cǎoyào	N	[grass-medicine] herbal medicine
喉嚨痛	喉咙痛	hóulóng tòng	N/V	[throat-pain] sore throat, to have sore throat
咳嗽		ké.sòu	V	[cough-cough] to cough
頭暈	头晕	tóuyūn	N/V	[head-dizzy] to feel dizzy
惡心	恶心	ěxīn	N/V	[evil-heart] to feel nausea
肚子痛		dù.zi tòng	N/V	[belly-pain] bellyache
拉肚子		lā dù.zi	N/V	[pull-belly] diarrhea
胃痛		wèitòng	N/V	[stomach-pain] stomach pain

3. Body Parts

鼻子		bí.zi	N	[nose-Suf] nose
眉毛		méi.máo	N	[eyebrow-hair] eyebrow
嘴巴		zuǐ.bā	N	[mouth-Suf] mouth
下巴		xià.bā	N	[low-Suf] chin
耳朵		ěr.duō	N	[ear-bud] ear
脖子		bó.zi	N	[neck-Suf] neck
肩膀		jiānbǎng	N	[shoulder-upper arm] shoulder
背		bèi	N	back
腰		yāo	N	waist
屁股		pì.gǔ	N	[fart-butt] butt
大腿		dàtuǐ	N	[big-leg] upper leg
小腿		xiǎotuǐ	N	[small-leg] lower leg
脚	脚	jiǎo	N	foot

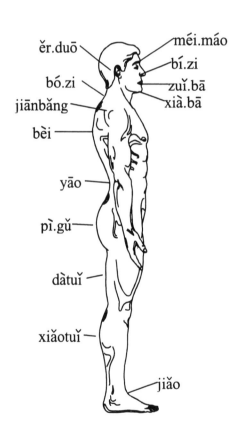

Characters
漢字 Hànzì

吹 風 病 瘆

熱 涼 舒 服

約 醫 藥 法

讓 眼 睛 紅

同 屋 倒 題

吹

吹風	chuīfēng	to expose to cold wind
吹乾	chuīgān	to blow dry
*吹風機	chuīfēngjī	hair dryer
*吹牛	chuīniú	to brag

chuī
to blow, brag,
boast   口
7   (mouth)

A: 屋子裏太熱了，咱們出去**吹吹風**吧！
B: 好啊！我的作業正好寫完了。

風

| *傷風 | shāngfēng | to catch a cold |
| *刮風 | guāfēng | to blow (wind) |

fēng
wind   風
9   (wind)

A: 今天外邊兒**風大**，你得加件外套。
B: 什麼時候了，還穿外套。

病

生病	shēngbìng	to fall ill, to get sick
看病	kànbìng	to see a doctor
毛病	máo.bìng	illness; shortcoming
*病人	bìngrén	patient
*病假	bìngjià	sick leave

bìng
ill, sick, disease
        疒
10

A: 你跟醫生約了去**看病**沒有？
B: 還沒有，我待會兒再給他打電話。

疼

酸疼	suānténg	(to be) sore
*頭疼	tóu.téng	headache
*牙疼	yáténg	toothache
*背疼	bèiténg	backache

téng
ache, pain   疒
10

A: 你看起來好像不太舒服。
B: 我**頭疼**得厲害。

繁簡對照：	其他漢字：	✎ **My notes:**
風风		

rè
hot
15   灬 (fire)

花粉熱	huāfěnrè	hay fever
熱鬧	rè.nào	hustle and bustle
*熱水	rèshuǐ	hot water

A: 今天天氣**真熱**。
B: 可不是嗎！我全身是汗。

liáng
cool, cold 冫
11   (water)

涼水	liángshuǐ	cool water
*涼鞋	liángxié	sandals
*涼快	liángkuài	nice and cool

A: 這麼冷的天，你怎麼還喝**涼水**？
B: 我喝不慣熱水。

shū
to relax,
leisurely 舌
12   (tongue)

| 舒服 | shū.fú | comfortable |

A: 你什麼時候開始頭疼的？
B: 自從上星期考完試後，我的頭就不**舒服**。

fú
clothing, dress,
to wear 月
8   (moon)

| 舒服 | shū.fú | comfortable |
| *衣服 | yī.fú | clothes |

A: 這兒真**舒服**。
B: 可不是嗎！又有花兒又有樹。

繁簡對照：	其他漢字：	✏ **My notes:**
熱热 涼涼	*燒 SC66 冷 L12	

約

A 約 B	A yuē B	A makes an appointment with B
約好	yuēhǎo	to have made an appointment
*大約	dàyuē	approximately, probably

yuē
to make an
appointment 糸
9

A: 你明天有没有空兒出去看電影？
B: 明天不行，我**跟醫**生**約好了**去看病。

醫

醫生	yī.shēng	doctor
*牙醫	yáyī	dentist
*醫院	yīyuàn	hospital

yī
to cure   酉
18 (tenth of the
twelve Terrestrial
Branches)

A: 你的**牙醫**好不好？
B: 很好，可是我一看見他，牙就疼。

藥

開藥方	kāi yàofāng	to give a prescription
點眼藥	diǎn yǎnyào	to use eyedrops
*吃藥	chīyào	to take medicine

yào
medicine   艹
19   (grass)

A: 你得記得每天要按時**吃藥**。
B: 是飯前吃還是飯後吃？

法

法子	fǎ.zi	way, method
*方法	fāngfǎ	way, method
*没法	méi fǎ	to have no way
*法律	fǎlǜ	law

fǎ, fǎ
method, law 氵
8   (water)

A: 我眼睛癢，頭疼，**沒法**念書。你幫我
   想個法子吧！
B: 我看你還是先去休息吧！

繁簡對照：	其他漢字：	✎ **My notes:**
約 约	*院 SC67	
醫 医	*針 SC68	
藥 药		

讓
ràng
to let　言
24　(speech)

| A 讓 B | A ràng B | A let B (do something) |

A: 快起來，別睡懶覺了。
B: 別吵！**讓我**多睡一會兒，行不行？

眼
yǎn
eyes　目
11　(eyes)

*眼鏡　　yǎnjìng　　glasses
*眼藥　　yǎnyào　　eyedrops

A: 我的**眼鏡**不見了。
B: 不是在你的鼻子上嗎？

睛
jīng
pupil (of the
eye)　目
13　(eyes)

眼睛　　yǎn.jīng　　eyes

A: 我的**眼睛**又紅又癢。
B: 是不是過敏了？

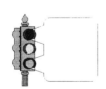

紅
hóng
red　糸
9

*紅色　　hóngsè　　red

A: 這件**紅色**的外套不夠大，你幫我找一件
　藍色的吧！
B: 他們沒有藍色的，有黑色的。

繁簡對照：	其他漢字：	✎ **My notes:**
讓让 紅红	*綠 SC69 *白 SC70 *黑 SC71 *色 SC72	

同

tóng
the same,
together with   口
6   (mouth)

同屋兒   tóngwūr   roommate
*同學   tóngxué   classmate
*同事   tóngshì   co-worker, colleague

A: 你的**同屋兒**怎麼樣？
B: 人不錯，只是不喜歡打掃。

屋

wū
room
9   (corpse)
尸

*屋子   wū.zi   room
*房屋   fángwū   house

A: 你喜歡**這間屋子**嗎？
B: 還可以，有沒有大一點兒的、便宜一
點兒的？

倒

dǎo, dào
to fall over; to
pour out   亻
10   (person)

倒是   dào.shì   on the contrary
倒盡   dǎojìn   to lose (one's appetite)
                      completely

A: 你現在覺得怎麼樣？
B: 眼睛癢**倒是**不癢，可是一直打噴嚏。

題

tí
topic, subject
頁
18   (head)

問題   wèntí   question, problem
*話題   huàtí   subject for a talk, topic of
                      conversation

A: 你**有問題沒有**？
B: **大問題**沒有，**小問題**很多。

繁簡對照：	其他漢字：	**My notes:**
題題	*室 SC73 房 L14	

Grammar
語法 yǔfǎ

 A Major Sentence Patterns 主要句型 zhǔyào jùxíng

1. The co-verbs 叫 and 讓

Structure	Gloss
S₁ 叫/讓 O₁/S₂ (別/不要) V₂ O₂	S₁ let/tell O₁/S₂ (don't) V₂ O₂

1. 我叫你別喝冷水，你爲什麼偏不聽呢？

Wǒ jiào nǐ bié hē lěngshuǐ, nǐ wèishén.me piān bù tīng .ne?
I told you not to drink ice water. Why didn't you listen to me?

因爲我剛打完球，口很渴。

Yīn.wèi wǒ gāng dǎwán qiú, kǒu hěn kě.
Because I just finished playing tennis, (I) was very thirsty.

2. 醫生讓你做什麼？

Yī.shēng ràng nǐ zuò shén.me?
What did the doctor tell you to do?

醫生讓我 按時吃藥跟多休息。

Yī.shēng ràng wǒ ànshí chīyào gēn duō xiū.xí.
The doctor told me to take the medicine on schedule and get a lot of rest.

叫 and 讓 are co-verbs that have a causative sense. They occur in a pivotal construction: the object (O₁) of 叫 and 讓 also serves as the subject (S₂) of the second verbal expression (V₂ O₂).

B Usage of Common Phrases 詞組用法 cízǔ yòngfǎ

1. The usage of 約

Structure	Gloss
A (想/要) 約 B Time Exp. (在 Place) VO	A (would/will make) made an appointment with B to VO at Time Exp. (at Place)
A 跟 B 約好 Time Exp. (在 Place) VO	A made an appointment with B to VO at Time Exp. (at Place)

1. 你約小林三點鐘在什麼地方見面？

Nǐ yuē Xiǎo Lín sān diǎnzhōng zài shén.me dì.fāng jiànmiàn?
Where will you meet Xiao Lin at three o'clock when you have the date?

我想約小林三點鐘在校門口見　　　　Wǒ xiǎng yuē Xiǎo Lín sān diǎnzhōng
面。　　　　　　　　　　　　　　　zài xiào ménkǒu jiànmiàn.
　　　　　　　　　　　　　　　　　I will make an appointment with Xiao
　　　　　　　　　　　　　　　　　Lin to meet at three o'clock in front of
　　　　　　　　　　　　　　　　　the school's main gate.

2.　老高跟誰約好了明天去打籃球？　　Lǎo Gāo gēn shéi yuēhǎo .le míng.tiān qù
　　　　　　　　　　　　　　　　　dǎ lánqiú?
　　　　　　　　　　　　　　　　　With whom did Lao Gao make an
　　　　　　　　　　　　　　　　　appointment to play basketball tomorrow?

　　老高跟小李約好了明天去打籃　　Lǎo Gāo gēn Xiǎo Lǐ yuēhǎo .le míng.tiān
　　球。　　　　　　　　　　　　　qù dǎ lánqiú.
　　　　　　　　　　　　　　　　　Lao Gao made an appointment with Xiao
　　　　　　　　　　　　　　　　　Li to play basketball tomorrow.

The word order of this pattern follows the Temporal Sequence Principle, since (A) must make an appointment with (B) first, then conduct the action later. In the expression A 跟 B 約好了, 跟 is a co-verb and 好 the resultative verb ending of resultative compound verb 約好 denotes that the appointment has already been made. The aspect marker 了 is optional.

2. The preposition 從

Structure	Gloss
從 S VO/Time Expression 以後, (S) 就 ...	S... ever since...
S 從 VO/Time Expression 以後, (S) 就 ...	

1.　他什麼時候開始發燒了？　　　　Tā shén.me shí.hòu kāishǐ fāshāo .le?
　　　　　　　　　　　　　　　　　When did the fever begin?

　　從上個星期他感冒了以後，他　　Cóng shàng .ge xīngqī tā gǎnmào .le
　　就一直發燒。　　　　　　　　　yǐhòu, tā jiù yìzhí fāshāo.

　　他從上個星期感冒了以後，他　　Tā cóng shàng .ge xīngqī gǎnmào .le
　　就一直發燒。　　　　　　　　　yǐhòu, tā jiù yìzhí fāshāo.
　　　　　　　　　　　　　　　　　He has had a fever ever since he caught a
　　　　　　　　　　　　　　　　　cold last week.

2.　你認識小高多久了？　　　　　　Nǐ rèn.shì Xiǎo Gāo duójiǔ .le?
　　　　　　　　　　　　　　　　　How long have you known Xiao Gao?

　　從我到美國以後，就認識他了。　Cóng wǒ dào Měi.guó yǐhòu, jiù rèn.shì
　　　　　　　　　　　　　　　　　tā .le.

我從到美國以後，就認識他了。

Wǒ cóng dào Měi.guó yǐhòu, jiù rèn.shì tā .le.

I have known Xiao Gao ever since the first day I arrived in the United States.

3. 他什麼時候開始沒(有)工作了？

Tā shén.me shí.hòu kāishǐ méi(.yǒu) gōngzuò .le?

How long has he been out of work?

從六月以後， 他就沒(有)工作了。

Cóng liùyuè yǐhòu, tā jiù méi(.yǒu) gōngzuò .le.

He has been out of work ever since June.

 The 從 VO/Time Expression is a movable adverb that may either precede or follow the subject of the clause. In the second clause, the subject must precede the adverb 就.

3. The interrogative adverb 多

Structure	Gloss
多 SV?	How Adj (is...)?
多久？	How long (is...)?
多好？	How good (is...)?
多重？	How heavy (is...)?

1. 他多久沒回來了？

Tā duójiǔ méi huí.lái .le?
How long has it been since he was back?

他兩年沒回來了。

Tā liǎng nián méi huí.lái .le.
He hasn't been back for two years.

2. 你多重？

Nǐ duó zhòng?
How much do you weigh?

我一百三十五磅。

Wǒ yì bǎi sānshíwǔ bàng.
I weigh 135 pounds.

3. 他中文說得多好？

Tā Zhōngwén shuō.de duó hǎo?
How good is his spoken Chinese?
(How well does he speak Chinese?)

他中文說得非常好。

Tā Zhōngwén shuō.de fēicháng hǎo.
He speaks Chinese very well.

 多 duó is an interrogative adverb that precedes a stative verb and denotes "how...?" The tone of this 多 is the second (rising).

4. A 對 B 過敏

Structure	Gloss
A 對 B 過敏	A is allergic to B

1. 春天的時候，你對什麼東西過敏？

    Chūntiān .de shí.hòu, nǐ duì shén.me dōng.xī guòmǐn?
    In the springtime, what are you allergic to?

    春天的時候，我對花粉過敏。

    Chūntiān .de shí.hòu, wǒ duì huāfěn guòmǐn.
    In the springtime, I am allergic to pollen.

2. 你為什麼不能喝牛奶？

    Nǐ wèishén.me bù néng hē niúnǎi?
    Why can't you drink milk?

    因為我對牛奶過敏。

    Yīn.wèi wǒ duì niúnǎi guòmǐn.
    Because I am allergic to milk.

See L10–B2, L16–A1, L17–A4, L18–A2, L23–B4 for more on A 對 B...

5. The adverb 只是

Structure	Gloss
S 只是...	It is only the case that...

1. 我怎麼了？有大問題嗎？

    Wǒ zěn.me .le? Yǒu dà wèntí .ma?
    What's wrong with me? Is my problem serious?

    沒有大問題。你只是對空氣中的灰塵過敏。

    Méi.yǒu dà wèntí. Nǐ zhǐ.shì duì kōngqì zhōng .de huīchén guòmǐn.
    No, your problem is not serious. You are only allergic to the dust in the air.

2. 他病得很重嗎？

    Tā bìng .de hěn zhòng .ma?
    Is he very sick?

    他病得不重。他只是有一點兒發燒。

    Tā bìng .de bú zhòng. Tā zhǐ.shì yǒu yì.diǎnr fāshāo.
    He is not very sick. He only has a little fever.

只是 is an adverb that precedes a verbal expression and denotes "it is only the case that..."

6. More on the co-verb 給

Structure		Gloss
A 給 B 打針	A gěi B dǎzhēn	A gives B a shot
A 給 B 點眼藥	A gěi B diǎn yǎnyào	A applies eyedrops for B
A 給 B 量血壓	A gěi B liáng xuěyā	A checks B's blood pressure
A 給 B 看病	A gěi B kànbìng	A examines B
A 給 B 開藥方	A gěi B kāi yàofāng	A writes a prescription for B

1. 誰給你打了針了？

    Shéi gěi nǐ dǎ .le zhēn .le?
    Who gave you the shot?

    醫生給我打了針了。

    Yī.shēng gěi wǒ dǎ .le zhēn .le.
    The doctor gave me the shot.

2. 誰給你點了眼藥了？

    Shéi gěi nǐ diǎn .le yǎnyào .le?
    Who put in the eyedrops (for you)?

    護士給我點了眼藥了。

    Hù.shì gěi wǒ diǎn .le yǎnyào .le.
    The nurse put in the eyedrops (for me).

3. 醫生給你做什麼了？

    Yī.shēng gěi nǐ zuò shén.me .le?
    What did the doctor do to you?

    醫生給我量了血壓了。

    Yī.shēng gěi wǒ liáng .le xuěyā .le.
    The doctor checked my blood pressure.

See L9–A1, L14–A3, L18–A3, L22–A1 for more on 給.

7. The usage of 打噴嚏

Structure		Gloss
S (一直) 打噴嚏	S (yìzhí) dǎ pēntì	S keeps sneezing
S 打了 (# 聲) 噴嚏	S dǎ.le (# shēng) pēntì	S has sneezed no. of times

1. 他對貓過敏，一直打噴嚏。

    Tā duì māo guòmǐn, yìzhí dǎ pēntì.
    He is allergic to the cat; (he) keeps sneezing.

2. 我感冒了，打了好幾聲噴嚏。

    Wǒ gǎnmào .le, dǎ .le hǎo jǐ shēng pēntì.
    I caught a cold; (I) have sneezed several times.

8. 難受 **vs.** 難過

Structure	Grammatical Function	Gloss
S 覺得 O 很/Adv 難受	descriptive complement	S feels that O is very/Adv unbearable/intolerable/bad
S Adj 得 很/Adv 難受	extent complement	S is so Adj that (S feels) uncomfortable
S 覺得 很/Adv 難過	descriptive complement	S feels very/Adv sorry/bad/ uncomfortable

1. 他吃了藥以後，覺得胃怎麼樣了？

   Tā chī .le yào yǐhòu, jué.de wèi zěn.meyàng .le?
   After taking the medicine, how does he feel?

   他吃了藥以後，覺得胃很難受。

   Tā chī .le yào yǐhòu, jué.de wèi hěn nánshòu.
   After taking the medicine, his stomach is upset.

2. 你喝了牛奶以後 覺 得肚子怎麼樣了？

   Nǐ hē .le niúnǎi yǐhòu, jué.de dù.zi zěn.meyàng .le?
   After drinking the milk, how does your stomach feel?

   我喝了牛奶以後，覺得肚子疼得很難受。

   Wǒ hē .le niúnǎi yǐhòu, jué.de dù.zi téng .de hěn nánshòu.
   After drinking the milk, my stomach is unbearably painful.

3. 看了那本小說以後，你覺得怎麼樣了？

   Kàn .le nèi běn xiǎoshuō yǐhòu, nǐ jué.de zěn.meyàng .le?
   After reading that novel, how do you feel?

   看了那本小說以後，我覺得很難過。

   Kàn .le nèi běn xiǎoshuō yǐhòu, wǒ jué.de hěn nánguò.
   After reading that novel, I feel sad.

Both 難受 and 難過 are stative verbs that can also be used as verb complements. But 難受 is always used to refer to the physical state of a certain body part that is suffering from pain or other uncomfortable situations, while 難過 is basically used to refer to the psychological state of feeling. The only case that can be used to refer to the body part is that of 胃/肚子 'stomach,' e.g., 我吃了藥以後，覺得胃很難過 Wǒ chī .le yào yǐhòu, jué.de wèi hěn nánguò 'After taking the medicine, my stomach is very uncomfortable.'

Cultural Notes
文化點滴 wénhuà diǎndī

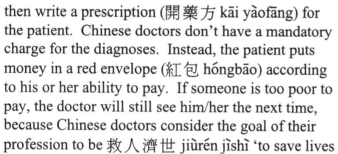

1. Traditionally, every Chinese drugstore maintains a medical station staffed by a Chinese doctor (中醫師 Zhōngyīshī). When doctors diagnose a patient's (病人) disease, instead of using a stethoscope (聽診器 tīngzhěnqì), they feel the patient's pulse (把脈 bǎmài or 診脈 zhěnmài) and examine the color of the patient's tongue (看舌頭 kàn shé.tóu). They then write a prescription (開藥方 kāi yàofāng) for the patient. Chinese doctors don't have a mandatory charge for the diagnoses. Instead, the patient puts money in a red envelope (紅包 hóngbāo) according to his or her ability to pay. If someone is too poor to pay, the doctor will still see him/her the next time, because Chinese doctors consider the goal of their profession to be 救人濟世 jiùrén jìshì 'to save lives and to benefit the world.' After receiving the prescription, the patient can purchase herbal medicine (草藥 cǎoyào) at the drugstore and bring the package of medicine home to "cook" it (煎藥 jiānyào) and drink it (服藥 fúyào).

2. For sports medicine, Chinese use several techniques to relieve the pain and cure the ailment, including 針灸 zhēnjiǔ 'acupuncture,' 艾灸 àijiǔ 'moxibustion,' 指壓推拿 zhǐyā tuīná 'to apply finger press and massage' and 拔罐子 bá guàn.zi 'to apply cup sucking.'

3. Chinese usually drink only hot boiled water (喝熱開水 hē rèkāishuǐ) or hot tea (熱茶 rèchá), thus their stomachs are not accustomed to ice water in the summer, not to mention the winter.

4. When you go to visit a sick person at the hospital or at home, don't take flowers as a get-well token (particularly for old people), because Chinese usually take flowers to bereaved families at funerals. Instead, you should take candy, cookies, fruit, or other foods that will help enhance the patient's nutrition.

對話	206 頁
小對話	214 頁
生詞	217 頁
漢字	222 頁
語法	228 頁
文化點滴	238 頁

第二十一課 你要寄平郵還是快信？

對話

〔王華在校園內踫見李明和高德中。〕

王華： 李明，好久不見，你上哪兒去？

李明： 我正準備上郵局
去寄封信，買些
郵票，順便領個
包裹。瞧！剛收
到的通知（搖搖
手上的領單）。

王華： 怎麼？家裏又寄
東西來了？

李明： 我想是吧！我父母老怕我在這兒餓著。其實，這兒什麼
都有，要買中國的食品，也可以去東方雜貨店。

王華： 天下父母心啊！我的爸媽也是整天擔心我飯吃不飽，書
讀不好。他們才剛給我寄來一張支票。

（李明在郵局）

李明： 我要領個包裹（拿出單子），還要寄這封信。

郵務員：（給李明包裹）這個包裹到的時候，盒子破了，我們用
膠帶把它貼好了。（看李明的信）這封信，你要寄平郵
還是快信？要不要掛號？

李明： 不要掛號。快信得多少錢？

郵務員：（看地址）寄到中國得十五塊。

李明：　　（大吃一驚）那麼貴！我不急，寄平信好了。我還要十二張郵票。現在寄到國外的平信郵資是多少？

郵務員：六毛，十二張就是七塊二。連信一共八塊二。

李明：　　（自言自語）以後還是發電子信好了。不但免費，而且國內的朋友也可以馬上收到。

（王華在銀行）

王華：　　高德中，眞巧！剛才踫見了小李，現在又踫見了你。我是來存錢的，你呢？

高德中：我是來提錢的。放春假的時候兒，我帶小李到芝加哥去玩兒了一趟，花了不少錢。小李來了美國這麼久，哪兒都沒去過。這兒離芝加哥不遠，開車五個小時就到了。

王華：　　你眞夠朋友，又當司機，又當導遊。我會在美英面前，替你說好話。（眨眨眼）

高德中：你這才夠朋友呢！（笑）

对话

〔王华在校园内碰见李明和高德中。〕

王华：　李明，好久不见，你上哪儿去？

李明：　我正准备上邮局去寄封信，买些邮票，顺便领个包裹。瞧！刚收到的通知（摇摇手上的领单）。

王华：　怎么？家裏又寄东西来了？

李明：　我想是吧！我父母老怕我在这儿饿着。其实，这儿什么都有，要买中国的食品，也可以去东方杂货店。

王华：　天下父母心啊！我的爸妈也是整天担心我饭吃不饱，书读不好。他们才刚给我寄来一张支票。

（李明在邮局）

李明：　我要领个包裹（拿出单子），还要寄这封信。

邮务员：（给李明包裹）这个包裹到的时候，盒子破了，我们用胶带把它贴好了。（看李明的信）这封信，你要寄平邮还是快信？要不要挂号？

李明：　不要挂号。快信得多少钱？

邮务员：（看地址）寄到中国得十五块。

李明：　（大吃一惊）那么贵！我不急，寄平信好了。我还要十二张邮票。现在寄到国外的平信邮资是多少？

邮务员：六毛，十二张就是七块二。连信一共八块二。

李明　：　（自言自语）以后还是发电子信好了。不但免费，而且国内的朋友也可以马上收到。

（王华在银行）

王华　：　高德中，真巧！刚才碰见了小李，现在又碰见了你。我是来存钱的，你呢？

高德中：我是来提钱的。放春假的时候儿，我带小李到芝加哥去玩儿了一趟，花了不少钱。小李来了美国这么久，哪儿都没去过。这儿离芝加哥不远，开车五个小时就到了。

王华　：　你真够朋友，又当司机，又当导游。我会在美英面前，替你说好话。（眨眨眼）

高德中：你这才够朋友呢！（笑）

My questions:

Duìhuà

(Wáng Huá zài xiàoyuán nèi pèng.jiàn Lǐ Míng hé Gāo Dézhōng.)

Wáng Huá: Lǐ Míng, hǎo jiǔ bú jiàn, nǐ shàng nǎr qù?

Lǐ Míng: Wǒ zhèng zhǔnbèi shàng yóujú qù jì fēng xìn, mǎi xiē yóupiào,
             shùnbiàn lǐng .ge bāoguǒ. Qiáo! Gāng shōu.dào .de tōngzhī (yáo.yáo
             shǒu .shàng .de lǐngdān).

Wáng Huá: Zěn.me? Jiā .lǐ yòu jì dōng.xī lái .le?

Lǐ Míng: Wǒ xiǎng shì .ba! Wǒ fùmǔ lǎo pà wǒ zài zhèr è.zhe. Qíshí, zhèr
             shén.me dōu yǒu, yào mǎi Zhōng.guó .de shípǐn, yě kě.yǐ qù dōngfāng
             záhuòdiàn.

Wáng Huá: Tiānxià fùmǔ xīn .a! Wǒ .de bàmā yě shì zhěngtiān dānxīn wǒ fàn chī
             .bubǎo, shū dú.buhǎo. Tā.men cái gāng gěi wǒ jì lái yì zhāng zhīpiào.

(Lǐ Míng zài yóujú)

Lǐ Míng: Wǒ yào lǐng .ge bāoguǒ (náchū dān.zi), hái yào jì zhè fēng xìn.

Yóuwùyuán: (Gěi Lǐ Míng bāoguǒ) Zhè .ge bāoguǒ dào .de shí.hòu, hé.zi pò .le,
             wǒ.men yòng jiāodài bǎ tā tiēhǎo .le. (Kàn Lǐ Míng .de xìn) Zhè
             fēng xìn, nǐ yào jì píngyóu hái.shì kuàixìn? Yào .buyào guàhào?

Lǐ Míng: Bú yào guàhào. Kuàixìn děi duō.shǎo qián?

Yóuwùyuán: (Kàn dìzhǐ) Jì.dào Zhōng.guó děi shíwǔ kuài.

Lǐ Míng: (Dà chī yì jīng) Nà.me guì! Wǒ bù jí, jì píngxìn hǎo.le. Wǒ hái yào
             shí'èr zhāng yóupiào. Xiànzài jì.dào guówài .de píngxìn yóuzī shì
             duō.shǎo?

Yóuwùyuán: Liù máo, shí'èr zhāng jiù.shì qī kuài èr. Lián xìn yígòng bā kuài èr.

Lǐ Míng: (Zì yán zì yǔ) Yǐhòu hái.shì fā diànzǐxìn hǎo.le. Búdàn miǎnfèi,
             érqiě guónèi .de péng.yǒu yě kě.yǐ mǎ.shàng shōu.dào.

(Wáng Huá zài yínháng)

Wáng Huá:　　Gāo Dézhōng.　Zhēn qiǎo! Gāngcái pèng.jiàn .le Xiǎo Lǐ, xiànzài
　　　　　　 yòu pèng.jiàn .le nǐ.　Wǒ shì lái cúnqián .de, nǐ .ne?

Gāo Dézhōng: Wǒ shì lái tíqián .de.　Fàng chūnjià .de shí.hòur, wǒ dài Xiǎo Lǐ
　　　　　　 dào Zhījiāgē qù wánr .le yí tàng, huā .le bù shǎo qián.　Xiǎo Lǐ lái
　　　　　　 .le Měi.guó zhè.me jiǔ, nǎr dōu méi qù.guò.　Zhèr lí Zhījiāgē bù
　　　　　　 yuǎn, kāichē wǔ .ge xiǎoshí jiù dào .le.

Wáng Huá:　　Nǐ zhēn gòu péng.yǒu, yòu dāng sījī, yòu dāng dǎoyóu.　Wǒ huì
　　　　　　 zài Měiyīng miànqián, tì nǐ shuō hǎohuà.　(Zhā.zhā yǎn)

Gāo Dézhōng: Nǐ zhè cái gòu péng.yǒu .ne! (Xiào)

Dialogue

(Wáng Huá runs into Lǐ Míng and Gāo Dézhōng on campus.)

Wáng Huá: Lǐ Míng, long time no see. Where are you going?

Lǐ Míng: I'm planning on going to the post office to send a letter, buy some stamps and also get a package. Look! (This is) the notice I just received. (Shaking the receipt in his hand.)

Wáng Huá: What happened? Your family sent you a package again?

Lǐ Míng: I think so. My parents always fear that I'm starving here. Actually, I have everything I need here. If I want to get Chinese food, I can go to the Oriental grocery store.

Wáng Huá: All parents are the same! My parents also always worry that I don't have enough to eat and I don't study enough. They just sent me a check.

(Lǐ Míng at the post office)

Lǐ Míng: I want to get a package (showing the notice), and I also want to send this letter.

Postmaster: (Handing the package over:) When this package arrived, the box was broken. We taped it again. (Looking at Lǐ Míng's letter:) Do you want to send it regular or express mail? Do you want it registered?

Lǐ Míng: No. I don't want it registered. How much is express mail?

Postmaster: (Looking at the address:) It costs fifteen dollars to send it to China.

Lǐ Míng: (Surprised:) So expensive! I am not in a hurry. Let me send it regular. I also need twelve stamps. What is the postage now to send air mail overseas?

Postmaster: Sixty cents (each). Twelve stamps will be seven dollars and twenty cents. The total is eight dollars and twenty cents, including the letter.

Lǐ Míng: (Talking to himself) It will be better to send e-mail in the future. Sending messages through e-mail is not only free but also my friends in China can receive it immediately.

(Wáng Huá at the bank)

Wáng Huá:　　Gāo Dézhōng.　What a coincidence!　I just ran into Xiǎo Lǐ, and now you.　I'm here to deposit a check.　How about you?

Gāo Dézhōng: I'm here to get some cash.　During spring break, I took Xiǎo Lǐ to Chicago on a trip.　We spent lots of money.　Xiǎo Lǐ has been in the States for a long time, but he hasn't been anywhere.　Chicago is not far from here.　It takes only five hours to drive there.

Wáng Huá:　　You are a real friend.　You work both as a driver and a tour guide.　I'll say something good for you in front of Měiyīng.　(Winking.)

Gāo Dézhōng: You are a real friend!　(Laughing.)

Mini-Dialogue
小對話 Xiǎoduìhuà

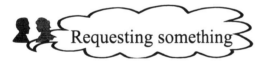
Expressing and correcting opinions

1. A: 他好像不懂中文似的。

Tā hǎo.xiàng bù dǒng Zhōngwén shì.de.
It seemed that he did not understand Chinese.

    B: 你別以爲他不懂中文，其實他中文好得很。

Nǐ bié yǐwéi tā bù dǒng Zhōngwén, qíshí tā Zhōngwén hǎo .de hěn.
You thought that he didn't understand Chinese. In fact, his Chinese is very good.

2. A: 這兒離芝加哥很遠吧？

Zhèr lí Zhījiāgē hěn yuǎn .ba?
Chicago is far away from here, I suppose?

    B: 其實不太遠，開車五個鐘頭就到了。

Qíshí bútài yuǎn, kāichē wǔ .ge zhōngtóu jiù dào .le.
Actually it's not too far. It takes only five hours to get there.

Requesting something

1. A: 我要寄這封信，還要買十張三毛二的郵票。

Wǒ yào jì zhè fēng xìn, hái yào mǎi shí zhāng sān máo èr .de yóupiào.
I want to mail this letter. I also need ten thirty-two cents stamps.

    B: 一共四塊八。

Yígòng sì kuài bā.
It's four dollars and eighty cents.

Giving alternative suggestions

1. A: 這兒沒有什麼好的中國飯館兒。

Zhèr méi.yǒu shén.me hǎo .de Zhōng.guó fànguǎnr.

There aren't any good Chinese restaurants here.

   B: 所以咱們以後還是自己做飯好了。

Suǒ.yǐ zán.men yǐhòu hái.shì zìjǐ zuòfàn hǎo.le.

So let's cook at home next time.

2. A: 出去玩兒一趟，真累！

Chū.qù wánr yí tàng, zhēn lèi!
It's really tiring to go on a trip!

   B: 可不是嗎！以後還是待在家裏好了。

Kě bú.shì .ma! Yǐhòu hái.shì dāi zài jiā .lǐ hǎo.le.

Isn't it true? We had better stay home next time.

3. A: 打電話到中國，十分鐘就要八塊錢。

Dǎ diànhuà dào Zhōng.guó, shí fēn zhōng jiù yào bā kuài qián.

It costs eight dollars to make a ten-minute phone call to China.

   B: 以後還是寫信好了。

Yǐhòu hái.shì xiěxìn hǎo.le.
(You) should write next time.

Inviting someone to come along

1. A: 你上哪兒去？

Nǐ shàng nǎr qù?
Where are you going?

   B: 我上銀行去提錢。

Wǒ shàng yínháng qù tíqián.
I'm going to the bank to withdraw some money.

   A: 真巧！我也要去那兒。咱們一起走吧！

Zhēn qiǎo! Wǒ yě yào qù nàr.
Zán.men yìqǐ zǒu .ba!
What a coincidence! I'm heading that way, too. Let's go together.

Talking about the past

1. A: 放春假的時候，我跟小王
        到紐約玩兒了一趟。

        Fàng chūnjià .de shí.hòu, wǒ gēn
        Xiǎo Wáng dào Niǔyuē wánr .le yí
        tàng.
        I went to New York with Xiao Wang
        during spring break.

    B: 誰當你們的導遊啊？

        Shéi dāng nǐ.men .de dǎoyóu .a?
        Who was your tour guide?

Showing appreciation to a friend

1. A: 這個星期六我可以帶你到
        芝加哥去買東西。

        Zhè .ge xīngqīliù wǒ kě.yǐ dài nǐ dào
        Zhījiāgē qù mǎi dōng.xī.
        I can take you to Chicago to shop this
        Saturday.

    B: 你這個人真夠朋友。

        Nǐ zhè .ge rén zhēn gòu péng.yǒu.
        You are a real friend.

2. A: 你從加州回來的時候，我
        可以去機場接你。

        Nǐ cóng Jiāzhōu huí.lái .de shí.hòu,
        wǒ kě.yǐ qù jīchǎng jiē nǐ.
        I can pick you up at the airport when
        you got back from California.

    B: 你真是個大好人。

        Nǐ zhēn shì .ge dàhǎorén.
        You are a real nice guy.

Vocabulary
生詞 Shēngcí

◎ **By Order of Appearance**

準備	准备	zhǔnbèi	V	[criterion-prepare] to prepare (=預備)
郵局	邮局	yóujú	N	[postal-bureau] post office
郵票	邮票	yóupiào	N	[postal-ticket] stamp (M: 張)
* 郵務員	邮务员	yóuwùyuán	N	[postal-business-personnel] postmaster, postal clerk
信		xìn	N	letter (M: 封)
順便	顺便	shùnbiàn	Adv	[follow-convenience] (to do something) while on one's way to perform a major task
領	领	lǐng	V	to pick up (things)
* 領單	领单	lǐngdān	N	[receive-slip] a slip of paper that entitles the bearer to get something; receipt (M: 張)
包裹	包裹	bāoguǒ	N	[wrap-wrap] package (M: 個)
通知		tōngzhī	V	[pass through-know] to notify, to inform
食品		shípǐn	N	[eat-thing] food
雜貨店	杂货店	záhuòdiàn	N	[mixed-goods-store] grocery store
心		xīn	N	heart, mind
讀	读	dú	V	to study, to read (=念)
盒子		hé.zi	N	[box-Suf] box
破		pò	SV	(to be) broken
用		yòng	V/CV	to use, with (instrument)
膠帶	胶带	jiāodài	N	[glue-belt] Scotch tape
平郵	平邮	píngyóu	N	[ordinary-postal] regular mail, surface mail
* 航空信		hángkōngxìn	N	[aviation-letter] airmail
* 普通航空		pǔtōng hángkōng	N	[common-letter] (regular) airmail
快信		kuàixìn	N	[fast-letter] express letter
貼	贴	tiē	V	to paste
掛號	挂号	guàhào	VO	[hang-number] to register (mail; or at the outpatient clinic of a hospital)
郵資	邮资	yóuzī	N	[postal-capital] postage
連	连	lián	Prep	including
發	发	fā	V	to issue, to send (a telegram or an e-mail)
電子信	电子信	diàn.zixìn	N	[electronic-letter] e-mail

不但...而且		búdàn...érqiě	Conj	[not-but...and yet-moreover] not only... but also...
免費	免费	miǎnfèi	SV	[avoid-fee] (to be) free of charge
國內	国内	guónèi	Adj	[country-inside] domestic
* 國際	国际	guójì	Adj	[country-border] international
馬上	马上	mǎ.shàng	Adv	[horse-up] immediately (=立刻)
* 銀行	银行	yínháng	N	[silver-company] bank
眞巧	真巧	zhēn qiǎo	IE	[real-skillful] what a coincidence!
踫見/到	碰见/到	pèng.jiàn/.dào	V	[bump-see] to meet someone unexpectedly; to bump into someone
存錢	存钱	cúnqián	VO	[save-money] to deposit (money)
提錢	提钱	tíqián	VO	[raise-money] to withdraw (money)
春假		chūnjià	N	[spring-holiday] spring vacation
芝加哥		Zhījiāgē	N	[a kind of fungus-add-older brother] Chicago
趟		tàng	M	measure word for trips
花錢	花钱	huāqián	VO	[spend-money] to spend money
離	离	lí	CV	to depart from, to separate
* 離開	离开	líkāi	V	[depart-open] to leave (a place)
遠	远	yuǎn	SV	(to be) far
* 近		jìn	SV	(to be) near, close
小時		xiǎoshí	N	[small-time] an hour (M: 個)
* 鐘頭	钟头	zhōngtóu	N	[clock-Suf] an hour (M: 個) (=小時)
夠朋友	够朋友	gòu péng.yǒu	IE	[enough-friend] to be a friend in need, be a true friend
當	当	dāng	V	to be (someone), to act as
司機	司机	sījī	N	[manage-machine] chauffeur, driver
* 師傅	师傅	shī.fù	N	[teacher-teacher] work master, chef
導遊	导游	dǎoyóu	N	[lead-play] tour guide
替		tì	CV	to substitute, to do... for...
說好話	说好话	shuō hǎohuà	VO	[say-good-language] to say something good
* 說壞話	说坏话	shuō huàihuà	VO	[say-bad-language] to say something bad, to slander

◎ **By Grammatical Categories**

Nouns/Pronouns

郵局	邮局	yóujú	N	[postal-bureau] post office
郵票	邮票	yóupiào	N	[postal-ticket] stamp (M: 張)
郵資	邮资	yóuzī	N	[postal-capital] postage
* 郵務員	邮务员	yóuwùyuán	N	[postal-business-personnel] postmaster, postal clerk
司機	司机	sījī	N	[manage-machine] chauffeur, driver
* 師傅	师傅	shī.fù	N	[teacher-teacher] work master, chef
導遊	导游	dǎoyóu	N	[lead-play] tour guide
信		xìn	N	letter (M: 封)
快信		kuàixìn	N	[fast-letter] express letter
電子信	电子信	diàn.zixìn	N	[electronic-letter] e-mail
平郵	平邮	píngyóu	N	[ordinary-postal] regular mail, surface mail
* 航空信		hángkōngxìn	N	[aviation-letter] airmail
* 普通航空		pǔtōng hángkōng	N	[common-letter] (regular) airmail
* 領單	领单	lǐngdān	N	[receive-slip] a slip of paper that entitles the bearer to get something; receipt (M: 張)
包裹	包裹	bāoguǒ	N	[wrap-wrap] package (M: 個)
盒子		hé.zi	N	[box-Suf] box
膠帶	胶带	jiāodài	N	[glue-belt] Scotch tape
食品		shípǐn	N	[eat-thing] food
雜貨店	杂货店	záhuòdiàn	N	[mixed-goods-store] grocery store
* 銀行	银行	yínháng	N	[silver-company] bank
春假		chūnjià	N	[spring-holiday] spring vacation
小時		xiǎoshí	N	[small-time] an hour (M: 個)
* 鐘頭	钟头	zhōngtóu	N	[clock-Suf] an hour (M: 個) (=小時)
心		xīn	N	heart, mind
芝加哥		Zhījiāgē	N	[a kind of fungus-add-older brother] Chicago

Measure Words

趟		tàng	M	measure word for trips

Verbs/Stative Verbs/Adjectives

讀	读	dú	V	to study, to read (=念)
領	领	lǐng	V	to pick up (things)

發	发	fā	V	to issue, to send (a telegram or an e-mail)
貼	贴	tiē	V	to paste
離	离	lí	CV	to depart from, to separate
替		tì	CV	to substitute, to do... for...
當	当	dāng	V	to be (someone), to act as
用		yòng	V/CV	to use, with (instrument)
準備	准备	zhǔnbèi	V	[criterion-prepare] to prepare (=預備)
通知		tōngzhī	V	[pass through-know] to notify, to inform
掛號	挂号	guàhào	VO	[hang-number] to register (mail; or at the outpatient clinic of a hospital)
存錢	存钱	cúnqián	VO	[save-money] to deposit (money)
提錢	提钱	tíqián	VO	[raise-money] to withdraw (money)
花錢	花钱	huāqián	VO	[spend-money] to spend money
踫見/到	碰见/到	pèng.jiàn/.dào	V	[bump-see] to meet someone unexpectedly; to bump into someone
* 離開	离开	líkāi	V	[depart-open] to leave (a place)
說好話	说好话	shuō hǎohuà	VO	[say-good-language] to say something good
* 說壞話	说坏话	shuō huàihuà	VO	[say-bad-language] to say something bad, to slander
破		pò	SV	(to be) broken
遠	远	yuǎn	SV	(to be) far
* 近		jìn	SV	(to be) near, close
免費	免费	miǎnfèi	SV	[avoid-fee] (to be) free of charge
國內	国内	guónèi	Adj	[country-inside] domestic
* 國際	国际	guójì	Adj	[country-border] international
連	连	lián	Prep	including

Adverbs

| 馬上 | 马上 | mǎ.shàng | Adv | [horse-up] immediately (=立刻) |
| 順便 | 顺便 | shùnbiàn | Adv | [follow-convenience] (to do something) while on one's way to perform a major task |

Conjunctions

| 不但...而且 | | búdàn...érqiě | Conj | [not-but...and yet-moreover] not only... but also... |

Idiomatic Expressions

眞巧	真巧	zhēn qiǎo	IE	[real-skillful] what a coincidence!
夠朋友	够朋友	gòu péng.yǒu	IE	[enough-friend] to be a friend in need, be a true friend

✚ Supplementary Vocabulary

1. Postal Service

郵遞員	邮递员	yóudìyuán	N	[postal-pass over-personnel] postman, mail carrier
郵差	邮差	yóuchāi	N	[postal-dispatch] postman, mail carrier
送信		sòngxìn	VO	[deliver-letter] to deliver letter
收信人		shōuxìnrén	N	[receive-letter-person] receiver (of a letter)
寄信人		jìxìnrén	N	[send-letter-person] sender (of a letter)
收據	收据	shōujù	N	[receive-proof] receipt
郵筒	邮筒	yóutǒng	N	[postal-cylinder] mail box
郵箱	邮箱	yóuxiāng	N	[postal-box] mail box
信箱		xìnxiāng	N	[letter-box] mail box (of a home/person)
郵區號碼	邮区号码	yóuqū hàomǎ	N	[postal-box] mail box
國際網路	国际网路	guójì wǎnglù	N	[country-border-net-road] Internet
電報	电报	diànbào	N	[electric-report] telegram
電傳	电传	diànchuán	N	[electric-transmit] telex
傳眞	传真	chuánzhēn	N	[transmit-real] fax
郵件	邮件	yóujiàn	N	[postal-piece] mail matter
郵購	邮购	yóugòu	V	[postal-purchase] to purchase something by mail

2. Banking

提款處	提款处	tíkuǎnchù	N	[carry-money-place] withdrawal counter (at a bank) (=cashier's counter)
存款處	存款处	cúnkuǎnchù	N	[save-money-place] deposit counter (at a bank) (=cashier's counter)
貸款處	贷款处	dàikuǎnchù	N	[to loan-money-place] loan department
匯款處	汇款处	huìkuǎnchù	N	[to remit-money-place] remittance department; cashier
外幣兌換	外币兑换	wàibì duìhuàn	N	[outside-currency-exchange-change] foreign currency exchange
取款機	取款机	qǔkuǎnjī	N	[fatch-money-machine] cash machine
匯票	汇票	huìpiào	N	[to remit-ticket] money order
匯率	汇率	huìlǜ	N	[to remit-rate] exchange rate
借錢	借钱	jièqián	VO	[borrow-money] to borrow money
貸款	贷款	dàikuǎn	VO/N	[to loan-money] to loan, a loan

Characters
漢字 Hànzì

存	提	擔	些
寄	封	郵	票
替	拿	帶	掛
遠	離	飛	機
場	馬	共	碰

存

cún
to deposit, to
exist　子
6　　(child)

存錢　　cúnqián　　to deposit (money)

A: 這幾年你**存了不少錢**吧？
B: 哪裏，都讓孩子花完了。

提

tí
to carry　扌
12　　(hand)

提錢　　tíqián　　to withdraw (money)

A: 我是來**提錢**的，我明天要出去玩兒。
B: 真巧，我也是。

擔

dān
to shoulder　扌
16　　(hand)

擔心　　dānxīn　　to worry

A: 你不念書，不**擔心**明天考不好嗎？
B: 我平常就準備好了。

些

xiē
some　二
8　　(two)

一些　　yìxiē　　some
這些　　zhèxiē　　these
*那些　　nàxiē　　those

A: **這些**東西一共多少錢？
B: 十塊三毛五。

繁簡對照：	其他漢字：	✎ **My notes:**
擔担	放 L13	

寄

| 寄來 | jì.lái | to send (to the speaker) |
| *寄信 | jìxìn | to send letters |

jì
to mail   宀
11

A: 你在聽什麼？
B: 聽中國民歌，我弟弟剛給我**寄來**的。

封

| 一封信 | yì fēng xìn | a letter |
| *信封 | xìnfēng | envelope |

fēng
M for letter   寸
9

A: 你上哪兒去？
B: 我正要去**寄封信**。

郵

郵局	yóujú	post office
郵票	yóupiào	stamp
郵資	yóuzī	postage

yóu
mail   阝
12   (a city)

A: 對不起，請問**郵局**怎麼走？
B: 我帶你去好了。

票

*電影票	diànyǐngpiào	movie ticket
*車票	chēpiào	bus/train ticket
*球票	qiúpiào	ticket for games

piào
ticket, ballet   示
11   (to show)

A: 我要買兩張**籃球票**。
B: **球票**早就賣完了。

繁簡對照：	其他漢字：	✎ **My notes:**
郵邮	收 L15 *貼 SC74	

替
tì
to replace, on
behalf of　曰
12　　(to say)

A替B　　　A tì B　　　　　A do...for B

A: 她病了，所以**我替她**把功課拿來。
B: 你没有**替**她做功課吧？

拿
ná
to take, to hold
　　　手
10　　(hand)

*拿來　　　ná.lái　　　　to bring over
*拿走　　　názǒu　　　　to take away

A: 你手上**拿的**是什麼？
B: 剛收到的一個包裹。

帶
dài
belt, band,
ribbon　巾
11　(a towel)

膠帶　　　jiāodài　　　　scotch tape
*錄音帶　　lùyīndài　　　audiotape
*錄影帶　　lùyǐngdài　　　videotape
*錄相帶　　lùxiàngdài　　videotape

A: 你寒假的時候，上哪兒去玩兒？
B: 哪兒也没去，我整天在家看**錄相帶**。

掛
guà
to hang　扌
11　　(hand)

掛號　　　guàhào　　　　to register (mail; or at the
　　　　　　　　　　　　　outpatient clinic of a
　　　　　　　　　　　　　hospital)

A: 這封信你要不要**掛號**？
B: 不要，平郵就好了。

繁簡對照：	其他漢字：	✎ **My notes:**
帶帶 掛挂		

遠

*多遠   duóyuǎn   how far
*遠近   yuǎnjìn   [far-near] distance

yuǎn
far, distant 辶
14

A: **你**家離學校有**多遠**？
B: 五哩路。

離

離…遠   lí…yuǎn   (to be) far from…
*離開   lí.kāi   to leave (a place)

lí
distance from
佳
19   (short-tail
         bird)

A: 這兒**離**芝加哥**遠不遠**？
B: 不太遠，開車五個小時就到了。

飛

飛機   fēijī   airplane
*起飛   qǐfēi   to take off

fēi
to fly   飛
9   (to fly)

A: 你是坐**飛機**來的嗎？
B: 不是，我是開車來的。

機

機場   jīchǎng   airport
*機會   jīhuì   opportunity
*洗衣機   xǐyījī   washer, washing machine

jī
machinery,
opportunity 木
16   (wood)

A: 你要我送你去**機場**嗎？
B: 不必了，我坐小巴很方便。

繁簡對照：	其他漢字：	✎ **My notes:**
遠 远 離 离 飛 飞 機 机	近 L11	

場

chǎng
area of level
ground, open
space 　 土
12 　 (soil)

| 飛機場 | fēijīchǎng | airport |
| *球場 | qiúchǎng | sports field, playing field, ball park |

A: 你得早一點兒去**飛機場**，晚了就不好。
B: 我馬上走。

馬

mǎ
horse 　 馬
10 　 (horse)

馬上　　mǎ.shàng　　immediately

A: 我好像發燒了，你幫我買藥 好嗎？
B: 好，我**馬上**去買 。

共

gòng
together 　 八
6 　 (eight)

一共　　yígòng　　altogether

A: 這兒**一共**多少錢？
B: **連**郵票**一共**十塊二毛八。

碰

pèng
to bump; to
collide 　 石
13 　 (stone)

| 碰見 | pèng.jiàn | to meet unexpectedly |
| 碰到 | pèng.dào | to meet unexpectedly |

A: 我昨天在街上**碰見**王文，她變了不少。
B: 聽說她最近剛生了一個孩子 。

繁簡對照：	其他漢字：	✎ **My notes:**
場场 馬马		

Grammar
語法 yǔfǎ

Ⓐ Major Sentence Patterns 主要句型 zhǔyào jùxíng

1. The adverb 正

Structure	Gloss
S 正 V₁/AuxV V₂ O 呢	S is in the midst of Ving to V₂ O

1. 我打電話給你的時候，爲什麼没
    人接？

    Wǒ dǎ diànhuà gěi nǐ .de shí.hòu,
    wèishén.me méi rén jiē?
    When I called you, how come nobody
    answered the phone?

    因爲我正準備去郵局買郵票呢！

    Yīn.wèi wǒ zhèng zhǔnbèi qù yóujú mǎi
    yóupiào .ne!
    Because I was just going to the post
    office to buy some stamps.

2. 喂，小林，你要上哪兒去？

    Wèi, Xiǎo Lín, nǐ yào shàng nǎr qù?
    Hey, Xiao Lin, where are you going?

    我正要去找你借幾個信封呢！

    Wǒ zhèng yào qù zhǎo nǐ jiè jǐ .ge
    xìnfēng .ne!
    I am in the midst of coming to your place
    to borrow some envelopes!

💡   In a sentence with a V₁-V₂ series, when 正 precedes the first verb, it denotes that the first action is in progress. The sentence may end with the sentence particle 呢.

🔄   See L8–A4 for more on the progressive aspect.

2. The co-verb 用

Structure	Gloss
S 用 X V O (instrument)	S V O with/by X

1. 這個盒子破了，怎麼辦？

    Zhèi .ge hé.zi pò .le, zěn.me bàn?
    This box is broken; what (should we) do
    about it?

    請你用膠帶把它貼好。

    Qǐng nǐ yòng jiāodài bǎ tā tiēhǎo.
    Please mend it with the Scotch tape.

2. 小高會用筷子吃飯嗎？

Xiǎo Gāo huì yòng kuài.zi chīfàn .ma?
Does Xiao Gao know how to eat with chopsticks?

小高很會用筷子吃飯。

Xiǎo Gāo hěn huì yòng kuài.zi chīfàn.
Xiao Gao knows very well how to eat with chopsticks.

3. 你會用中文寫報告嗎？

Nǐ huì yòng Zhōngwén xiě bàogào .ma?
Do you know how to write a paper in Chinese?

我不會用中文寫報告，我會
用英文寫報告。

Wǒ bú huì yòng Zhōngwén xiě bàogào, wǒ huì yòng Yīngwén xiě bàogào.
I don't know how to write a paper in Chinese; I know how to write a paper in English.

In a sentence where an instrument is used for doing something, the word order follows the Temporal Sequence Principle, since the actor must pick up the instrument, then perform the action. **Note**: Chinese regards language as an instrument for communication and writing. Thus when you would like to say "to speak/write in X language" in Chinese (see example 3), you should say 用X文說/寫.

3. 不但…, 而且/ 並且 …construction

Structure	Gloss
S 不但…, 而且/ 並且也 …	S not only…, but also…

1. 你覺得中國怎麼樣？

Nǐ jué.de Zhōng.guó zěn.meyàng?
What do you think about China?

中國不但很大，而且人也很多。

Zhōng.guó búdàn hěn dà, érqiě rén yě hěn duō.
China not only is huge but also has a lot of people.

2. 你覺得這本書怎麼樣？

Nǐ jué.de zhèi běn shū zěn.meyàng?
What do you think about this book?

我覺得這本書不但很便宜，而
且也很有意思。

Wǒ jué.de zhèi běn shū búdàn hěn pián.yí, érqiě yě hěn yǒuyì.si.
I think this book is not only inexpensive but also very interesting.

3. 你覺得小林怎麼樣？

Nǐ jué.de Xiǎo Lín zěn.meyàng?
What do you think about Xiao Lin?

我覺得小林不但很聰明, 並且也
很漂亮。

Wǒ jué.de Xiǎo Lín búdàn hěn
cōngmíng, bìngqiě yě hěn piàng.liàng.
I think that Xiao Lin is not only very
smart but also very pretty.

4. 你父母寄了什麼東西給你？

Nǐ fùmǔ jì .le shén.me dōng.xī gěi nǐ?
What did your parents send you?

我父母不但寄給我錢，並且也寄
給我很多食品。

Wǒ fùmǔ búdàn jì gěi wǒ qián, bìngqiě
yě jì gěi wǒ hěn duō shípǐn.
My parents not only sent me money but
also sent me a lot of food.

 The conjunctions 不但..., 而且/並且也 are the markers for two correlative
constructions.

4. Expressions of distance

4.1 A is far from/close to B

Structure	Gloss
A 離 B 遠不遠？	Is A far from B?
A 離 B 近不近？	Is A close to B?
A 離 B 很/Adv 遠/近	A is very/Adv far from/close to B
A 離 B 不 (太) 遠/近	A is not (very) far from/close to B

1. 北京離南京遠不遠？

Běijīng lí Nánjīng yuǎn .buyuǎn?
Is Beijing very far from Nanjing?

北京離南京非常遠。

Běijīng lí Nánjīng fēicháng yuǎn.
Beijing is very far from Nanjing.

2. 北京離天津近不近？

Běijīng lí Tiānjīn jìn .bujìn?
Is Beijing close to Tianjin?

北京離天津很近。

Běijīng lí Tiānjīn hěn jìn.
Beijing is very close to Tianjin.

4.2 A is very far from/close to B

Structure	Gloss
A 離 B 遠嗎？	Is A far from B?
A 離 B 遠/近 得很	A is very far from/close to B
A 離 B 遠/近 極了	A is extremely far from/close to B

1. 北京離上海遠嗎？

   Běijīng lí Shànghǎi yuǎn .ma?
   Is Beijing far from Shanghai?

   北京離上海遠極了。

   Běijīng lí Shànghǎi yuǎn jí .le.
   Beijing is extremely far from Shanghai.

2. 你家離學校近嗎？

   Nǐ jiā lí xuéxiào jìn .ma?
   Is your home close to the school?

   我家離學校不太近。

   Wǒ jiā lí xuéxiào bútài jìn.
   My home is not very close to the school.

4.3 A is no. of miles from B

Structure	Gloss
A 離 B 有 多遠？	How far is A from B?
A 離 B 有 no. 哩路	A is no. of miles from B

1. 東方食品店離這兒有多遠？

   Dōngfāng shípǐndiàn lí zhèr yǒu duó yuǎn?
   How far is the Oriental grocery store from here?

   東方食品店離這兒有十哩路。

   Dōngfāng shípǐndiàn lí zhèr yǒu shí lǐ lù.
   The Oriental grocery store is ten miles from here.

2. 你家 離電影院有多遠？

   Nǐ jiā lí diànyǐngyuàn yǒu duóyuǎn?
   How far is your home from the cinema?

   我 家離電影院只有三哩路。

   Wǒ jiā lí diànyǐngyuàn zhǐ yǒu sān lǐ lù.
   My home is only three miles from the cinema.

When expressing the distance between two places, you should bring up these two places first as a topic, then comment on the distance.

5. Comparison of distance

5.1 比 comparison

Structure	Gloss
A 離 C 比 B 離 C (還) 遠 嗎 ？	Is A (still) farther from C than B is?
A 離 C 比 B 離 C (還) 近 嗎 ？	Is A (still) closer to C than B is?
A 離 C 比 B 離 C (還) 遠	A is (still) farther from C than B is
A 離 C 比 B 離 C (還) 近	A is (still) closer to C than B is
A 離 C 比 B 離 C 遠 一點兒	A is a little bit farther from C than B is
A 離 C 比 B 離 C 近 一點兒	A is a little bit closer to C than B is

1. 你家離郵局比他家離郵局還遠嗎 ？

   Nǐ jiā lí yóujú bǐ tā jiā lí yóujú hái yuǎn .ma?

   Is your home farther from the post office than his?

   我家離郵局比他家離郵局遠一點兒。

   Wǒ jiā lí yóujú bǐ tā jiā lí yóujú yuǎn yì.diǎnr.

   My home is a little bit farther from the post office than his.

2. 你家離飯館兒比他家離飯館兒近嗎？

   Nǐ jiā lí fànguǎnr bǐ tā jiā lí fànguǎnr jìn .ma?

   Is your home closer to the restaurant than his?

   我家離飯館兒比他家離飯館兒還近。

   Wǒ jiā lí fànguǎnr bǐ tā jiā lí fànguǎnr hái jìn.

   My home is even closer to the restaurant than his.

Structure	Gloss
A 離 C 比 B 離 C 遠 得多 嗎 ？	Is A much farther from C than B is?
A 離 C 比 B 離 C 近 得多 嗎 ？	Is A much closer to C than B is?
A 離 C 比 B 離 C 遠 得多 了	A is much farther from C than B is
A 離 C 比 B 離 C 近 得多 了	A is much closer to C than B is

3. 紐約離舊金山比西雅圖離舊金山遠得多嗎 ？

   Niǔyuē lí Jiùjīnshān bǐ Xīyǎtú lí Jiùjīnshān yuǎn .de duō .ma?

   Is New York much farther from San Francisco than Seattle?

   對了，紐約離舊金山比西雅圖離舊金山遠得多了。

   Duì.le, Niǔyuē lí Jiùjīnshān bǐ Xīyǎtú lí Jiùjīnshān yuǎn .de duō .le.

Yes, New York is much farther from San Francisco than Seattle.

4. 芝加哥離舊金山比紐約離舊金山近得多嗎？

Zhījiāgē lí Jiùjīnshān bǐ Niǔyuē lí Jiùjīnshān jìn .de duō .ma?
Is Chicago much closer to San Francisco than New York?

對了，芝加哥離舊金山比紐約離舊金山近得多了。

Duì.le, Zhījiāgē lí Jiùjīnshān bǐ Niǔyuē lí Jiùjīnshān jìn .de duō .le.
Yes, Chicago is much closer to San Francisco than New York.

5.2 Equaling-degree comparison

A 離 C 有 沒有 B 離 C 那麼/這麼 遠？ A 離 C 有 沒有 B 離 C 那麼/這麼 近？	Is A as far from C as B is? Is A as near to C as B is?
A 離 C 沒有 B 離 C 　那麼/這麼 遠 A 離 C 沒有 B 離 C 　那麼/這麼 近	A is not as far from C as B is A is not as near to C as B is

1. 你家離郵局有沒有他家離郵局那麼遠？

Nǐ jiā lí yóujú yǒu měi.yǒu tā jiā lí yóujú nà.me yuǎn?
Is your home as far from the post office as his?

我家離郵局沒有他家離郵局那麼遠。

Wǒ jiā lí yóujú měi.yǒu tā jiā lí yóujú nà.me yuǎn.
My home is not as far from the post office as his.

2. 你家離飯館兒有沒有他家離飯館兒這麼近？

Nǐ jiā lí fànguǎnr yǒu méi.yǒu tā jiā lí fànguǎnr zhè.me jìn?
Is your home closer to the restaurant than his?

我家離飯館兒沒有他家離飯館兒這麼近。

Wǒ jiā lí fànguǎnr méi.yǒu tā jiā lí fànguǎnr zhè.me jìn.
My home is not as close to the restaurant as his.

3. 台北離台中有沒有台中離台南那麼遠？

Táiběi lí Táizhōng yǒu méi.yǒu Táizhōng lí Táinán nà.me yuǎn?
Is Taibei (Taipei) about as far from Taizhong as Taizhong is from Tainan?

台北離台中沒有台中離台南那
麼遠。

Táiběi lí Táizhōng méi.yǒu Táizhōng lí
Táinán nà.me yuǎn.
Taibei (Taipei) is not as far from
Taizhong as Taizhong is from Tainan.

4. 美國離日本有沒有美國離中國那
麼遠？

Měi.guó lí Rìběn yǒu méi.yǒu Měi.guó lí
Zhōng.guó nà.me yuǎn?
Is America about as far from Japan as
America is from China?

美國離日本沒有美國離中國那
麼遠。

Měi.guó lí Rìběn méi.yǒu Měi.guó lí
Zhōng.guó nà.me yuǎn.
America is not as far from Japan as
America is from China.

5.3 Equal-degree comparison

Structure	Gloss
A 離 C 跟 B 離 C　一樣 遠	A is about as far from/close to C as B is
A 離 C 跟 B 離 C　一樣 近	A is about as close to C as B is
A 離 C 跟 B 離 C 不 一樣 遠	A is not as far from/close to C as B is
A 離 C 跟 B 離 C 不 一樣 近	A is not as close to C as B is
A 離 C 不 跟 B 離 C 一樣 遠	A and B are not equally far from C
A 離 C 不 跟 B 離 C 一樣 近	A and B are not equally close to C

1. 你家離郵局跟他家離郵局一樣
遠嗎？

Nǐ jiā lí yóujú gēn tā jiā lí yóujú yíyàng
yuǎn .ma?
Is your home about as far from the post
office as his?

對了，我家離郵局跟他家離郵
局一樣遠。

Duì.le, wǒ jiā lí yóujú gēn tā jiā lí yóujú
yíyàng yuǎn.
Yes, my home is about as far from the
post office as his.

不，我家離郵局跟他家離郵局
不一樣遠。

Bù, wǒ jiā lí yóujú gēn tā jiā lí yóujú bù
yíyàng yuǎn.
No, my home and his home are not
equally distant from the post office.

2. 宿舍離圖書館跟宿舍離教室一樣
遠嗎？

Sùshè lí túshūguǎn gēn sùshè lí jiàoshì
yíyàng yuǎn .ma?
Is the dormitory about as far from the
library as it is from the classroom?

| 宿舍離圖書館跟宿舍離教室不一樣遠。 | Sùshè lí túshūguǎn gēn sùshè lí jiàoshì bù yíyàng yuǎn.
The dormitory is not as far from the library as it is from the classroom. |

See L10–A2, L12–C1, L19–A2, A3 for more on comparisons.

6. The co-verb/verb 帶

6.1 The co-verb 帶

Structure	Gloss
S (Neg) (AuxV) 帶 O	S (AuxV) (Neg) brings O
A(Neg) (AuxV) 帶 B 到 Place 去/來 VO	A (AuxV) (Neg) brings B along to Place to VO
S (Neg) (AuxV) 帶 O 到 Place 去/來 V(O)	S (AuxV) (Neg) brings O to Place to V

1. 下次你要帶誰到山上去滑雪？

Xià.cì nǐ yào dài shéi dào shān .shàng qù huáxuě?
Whom will you bring to ski in the mountains?

下次我要帶小李到山上去滑雪。

Xià.cì wǒ yào dài Xiǎo Lǐ dào shān .shàng qù huáxuě.
I will bring Xiao Li to ski in the mountains.

2. 你們明天得帶什麼來買書？

Nǐ.men míng.tiān děi dài shén.me lái mǎi shū?
What do you have to bring to buy books?

我們明天得帶錢來買書。

Wǒ.men míng.tiān děi dài qián lái mǎi shū.
We have to bring money to buy books.

帶 dài may serve as a verb or co-verb. When it serves as a co-verb, it may be followed by directional complement 來/去. Its object may be either [+ human] or [- human], where, for example, in the preceding sentences, it means "to lead, to bring along."

6.2 The verb 帶

Structure	Gloss
S (Neg) (AuxV) 帶孩子	S (AuxV) (Neg) takes care of a child
S (Neg) (AuxV) 帶路	S (AuxV) (Neg) leads the way

1. 你會帶孩子嗎？

Nǐ huì dài hái.zi .ma?
Do you know how to take care of children?

我不會帶孩子，我沒帶過孩子。   Wǒ bú huì dài hái.zi, wǒ cónglái méi
dài.guò hái.zi.
I don't know how to take care of children;
I have never taken care of children.

2. 你們要去芝加哥，誰帶路？   Nǐ.men yào qù Zhījiāgē, shéi dài lù?
You are going to Chicago. Who will lead
the way?

小高去過芝加哥很多次，他要   Xiǎo Gāo qù.guò Zhījiāgē hěn duō cì, tā
帶路。   yào dài lù.
Xiao Gao has been to Chicago many
times; he will lead the way.

 When 帶 dài serves as a main verb and if its object is [+ human], as in example 1, it means "to lead, to train, or to bring along"; if its object is [- human], as in example 2, it means "to lead, to bear, or to bring along."

7. The co-verb/verb 替

7.1 The verb 替

Structure	Gloss
A (Neg) (AuxV) 替 B VO	A (AuxV) (Neg) in place of B to VO

1. 我生病了，今天你可以替我教   Wǒ shēngbìng .le, jīn.tiān nǐ kě.yǐ tì wǒ
(書)嗎？   jiāo(shū) .ma?
I am sick; can you teach for me today?

没問題，我今天没課，我可以   Méi wèntí, wǒ jīn.tiān méi kè, wǒ kě.yǐ tì
替你教。   nǐ jiāo.
No problem, I don't have class today; I
can substitue teach for you.

2. 昨天你媽媽不在家，誰替她做   Zuó.tiān nǐ mā.mā bú zài jiā, shéi tì tā
飯？   zuòfàn?
Your mother was not at home yesterday.
Who cooked for her?

我爸爸替她做飯。   Wǒ bà.bà tì tā zuòfàn.
My dad cooked for her.

 When 替 tì serves as a main verb, it means "to substitute for," or "in place of."

7.2 The co-verb 替

Structure	Gloss
A (Neg) (AuxV) 替 B VO	A (AuxV) (Neg) VO for B

1. 誰在美英面前替小高說好話？

   Shéi zài Měiyīng miànqián tì Xiǎo Gāo shuō hǎohuà?
   Who said something good about Xiao Gao in front of Meiying?

   王華在美英面前替小高說好話。

   Wáng Huá zài Měiyīng miànqián tì Xiǎo Gāo shuō hǎohuà.
   Wang Hua said something good about Xiao Gao in front of Meiying.

2. 他不會說英文，你可以替他打電話嗎？

   Tā bú huì shuō Yīngwén, nǐ kě.yǐ tì tā dǎ diànhuà .ma?
   He doesn't know how to speak English. Can you make the phone call for him?

   没問題，我可以替他打電話。

   Méi wèntí, wǒ kě.yǐ tì tā dǎ diànhuà.
   No problem; I can make the phone call for him.

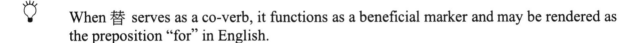

When 替 serves as a co-verb, it functions as a beneficial marker and may be rendered as the preposition "for" in English.

See L13–A3 for related beneficial marker 給.

Cultural Notes
文化點滴 wénhuà diǎndī

1. Chinese place great value on education. Chinese parents are always willing to sacrifice themselves in order to support their children's education, even if their children are already grown up and married. 天下父母心 'all parents' hearts are the same' is an idiom that refers to the way all Chinese parents care about their children's well-being.

2. In Chinese society, friends are supposed to help and to care for each other as they would for their own family members. Thus, when you receive a favor from a friend, you must return a favor to your friend when s/he is in need. Otherwise, you will be considered 不夠朋友 'not a friend in need, not a true friend.'

3. In the Chinese postal service, 平信 'ordinary/regular mail' may be via sea mail (海郵) or surface mail (陸郵). The postage is different. In Taiwan, you may send a package via 海空聯運 hǎikōngliányùn 'sea-air mail' to the United States (or other countries); the package is transported by air across the ocean, then by ground within the

United States. In this kind of service, the postage is cheaper than by airmail but more expensive than surface mail.

4. In modern China, officially people use the metric system for weights, measures and distance. (In the private sector, people may still use the traditional Chinese system instead.) Here is a comparison of the British and the metric system.

	British system 英制 Yīngzhì	Metric system 公制 Gōngzhì
1 foot	1 英尺/口尺 Yīngchǐ	0.3048 meter 公尺 Gōngchǐ
1 inch	1 英寸/口寸 Yīngcùn	2.54 centimeters 公分 Gōngfēn
1 pound	1 磅 Yīngbàng	0.45 kilogram 公斤 Gōngjīn
1 ounce	1 英兩/口兩 Yīngliǎng	0.28 hectogram 公兩 Gōngliǎng
1 mile	1 英里/哩 Yīnglǐ	1.6093 kilometers 公里 Gōnglǐ

5. Traditional letters are written vertically, from right to left. Here is the typical format of a Chinese letter.

親愛的爸爸媽媽：

您們好！謝謝您們寄來那麼多好吃的東西。最近特別想念親人和朋友們。

這個月我們很忙，因為大考快到了，還得寫兩篇報告。我的同學都對我很好。

我現在對吃美國食物也比較習慣了。功課也都沒問題。一切都很好。請不要掛念。

敬祝

大安

兒

小明　敬上

四月六日

When folding the letter, one must first fold it vertically two or three times into a long strip (about two inches in width), then fold the end up one third, so that the letter looks as if it were being handed to one's parent/reader by someone kneeling down on the floor.

6. Here is the typical format for addressing a Chinese envelope.

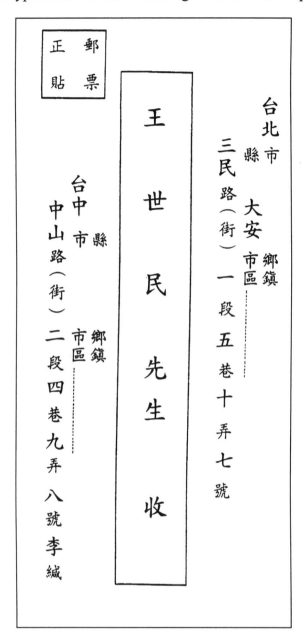

對話	242 頁
小對話	249 頁
生詞	252 頁
漢字	256 頁
語法	262 頁
文化點滴	268 頁

第二十二課　我的車怎麼不見了？

對話

〔美英在校園內看見高德中一臉是汗，走來走去。〕

小林 ： 高德中，怎麼了？ 在找什麼？

小高 ： 我的車怎麼不見了?剛才我
明明把車停在這兒。怎麼才
一會兒工夫就不見了？

小林 ： 會不會你把地方記錯了？

小高 ： 不可能。我平常都把車停
在這兒，從來都沒出過問題
。（ 左看右看）哎呀！什
麼時候這個停車位改了，就
許上午六點以前停車。我的
車八成兒叫人給拖走了。

小林 ： 真糟糕！我正想跟你借車來用一下呢！現在沒腿兒了，怎
麼辦？

小高 ： 你要開車去買東西嗎？

小林 ： 不是。是王華想練車，考駕駛執照，讓我當她的教練。從
前我總是叫她陪我練球，現在該我陪她練車了。

小高 ： 別著急，等我把車拿回來就借你們開。

（第二天一早王華、美英在街上練車）

小林 ： （大叫）小心！小心！過十字路口的時候，應該先往兩邊
兒看看再開。

小王： 別叫！你越叫我越緊張。

小林： （打開收音機）聽點兒音樂，輕鬆一下。

小王： 不行，我不能一邊兒開車，一邊兒聽音樂。我沒法子專心。

小林： 難道你還沒看見過有的人一邊兒開車，一邊兒化妝嗎？

小王： 那是美國人開車的法子。（慢慢兒地往前開）

小林： 你開得太慢了，這兒的時速是三十英哩。

小王： 開快車容易出事兒，如果萬一被警察發現了，還得吃罰單。

小林： 小王！你現在的時速才十五。

小王： 好吧！好吧！你的要求真多！（加油）你能不能說句好話，給我打打氣？（突然又慢下來）

小林： 怎麼了？

小王： 我看看（剎車）。
瞧！輪胎跟我一
樣，沒氣兒了。

对话

〔美英在校园内看见高德中一脸是汗，走来走去。〕

小林：高德中，怎么了？在找什么？

小高：我的车怎么不见了?刚才我明明把车停在这儿。怎么才一
　　　会儿工夫就不见了？

小林：会不会你把地方记错了？

小高：不可能。我平常都把车停在这儿，从来都没出过问题。（
　　　左看右看）哎呀！什么时候这个停车位改了，就许上午六
　　　点以前停车。我的车八成儿叫人给拖走了。

小林：真糟糕！我正想跟你借车来用一下呢！现在没腿儿了，怎
　　　么办？

小高：你要开车去买东西吗？

小林：不是。是王华想练车，考驾驶执照，让我当她的教练。从
　　　前我总是叫她陪我练球，现在该我陪她练车了。

小高：别着急，等我把车拿回来就借你们开。

（第二天一早王华、美英在街上练车）

小林：（大叫）小心！小心！过十字路口的时候，应该先往两边
　　　儿看看再开。

小王：别叫！你越叫我越紧张。

小林：（打开收音机）听点儿音乐，轻松一下。

小王： 不行，我不能一边儿开车，一边儿听音乐。我没法子专
　　　 心。

小林： 难道你还没看见过有的人一边儿开车，一边儿化妆吗？

小王： 那是美国人开车的法子。（慢慢儿地往前开）

小林： 你开得太慢了，这儿的时速是三十英哩。

小王： 开快车容易出事儿，如果万一被警察发现了，还得吃罚
　　　 单。

小林： 小王！你现在的时速才十五。

小王： 好吧！好吧！你的要求真多！（加油）你能不能说句好话
　　　 ，给我打打气？（突然又慢下来）

小林： 怎么了？

小王： 我看看（刹车）。瞧！轮胎跟我一样，没气儿了。

My questions:

Duìhuà

(Měiyīng zài xiàoyuán nèi kàn.jiàn Gāo Dézhōng yī liǎn shì hàn, zǒu lái zǒu qù.)

Xiǎo Lín: Gāo Dézhōng, zěn.me .le? Zài zhǎo shén.me?

Xiǎo Gāo: Wǒ .de chē zěn.me bújiàn.le? Gāngcái wǒ míngmíng bǎ chē tíng zài
              zhèr. Zěn.me cái yì.huǐr gōng.fu jiù bújiàn.le?

Xiǎo Lín: Huì .bu.huì nǐ bǎ dì.fāng jìcuò .le?

Xiǎo Gāo: Bù kěnéng. Wǒ píngcháng dōu bǎ chē tíng zài zhèr, cónglái dōu méi
              chū.guò wèntí. (Zuǒ kàn yòu kàn) .Ai.ya! Shén.me shí.hòur zhè .ge
              tíngchēwèi gǎi .le, jiù xǔ shàng.wǔ liù diǎn yǐqián tíngchē. Wǒ .de
              chē bāchéngr jiào rén gěi tuōzǒu .le.

Xiǎo Lín: Zhēn zāogāo! Wǒ zhèng xiǎng gēn nǐ jiè chē lái yòng.yíxià .ne!
              Xiànzài méi tuǐr .le, zěn.me bàn?

Xiǎo Gāo: Nǐ yào kāichē qù mǎi dōng.xī .ma?

Xiǎo Lín: Bú.shì. Shì Wáng Huá xiǎng liànchē, kǎo jiàshǐ zhízhào, ràng wǒ
              dāng tā .de jiàoliàn. Cóngqián wǒ zǒng.shì jiào tā péi wǒ liànqiú,
              xiànzài gāi wǒ péi tā liànchē .le.

Xiǎo Gāo: Bié zhāojí, děng wǒ bǎ chē nǎhuí.lái jiù jiè nǐ.men kāi.

(Dì èr tiān yīzǎo Wáng Huá, Měiyīng zài jiē .shàng liànchē.)

Xiǎo Lín: (Dà jiào) Xiǎo.xīn! Xiǎo.xīn! Guò shízì lùkǒu .de shí.hòu, yīnggāi
              xiān wàng liǎng biānr kàn.kàn zài kāi.

Xiǎo Wáng: Bié jiào! Nǐ yuè jiào wǒ yuè jǐn.zhāng.

Xiǎo Lín: (Dǎkāi shōuyīnjī) Tīng .diǎnr yīnyuè, qīngsōng.yíxià.

Xiǎo Wáng: Bù xíng, wǒ bù néng yìbiānr kāichē, yìbiānr tīng yīnyuè. Wǒ méi
              fá.zi zhuānxīn.

Xiǎo Lín: Nándào nǐ hái méi kàn.jiàn.guò yǒu .de rén yìbiānr kāichē, yìbiānr
              huàzhuāng .ma?

Xiǎo Wáng: Nà shì Měi.guórén kāichē .de fǎ.zi. (Mànmànr.de wàng qián kāi.)

Xiǎo Lín: Nǐ kāi .de tài màn .le, zhèr .de shísù shì sānshí yīnglǐ.

Xiǎo Wáng: Kāikuàichē róng.yì chūshìr, rúguǒ wànyī bèi jǐngchá fāxiàn .le, hái děi chī fádān.

Xiǎo Wáng: Hǎo .ba! Hǎo .ba! Nǐ .de yāo.qiú zhēn duō! (Jiā yóu) Nǐ néng .bu néng shuō jù hǎohuà, gěi wǒ dǎ.dǎ qì? (Tūrán yòu mànxià.lái.)

Xiǎo Lín: Zěn.me .le?

Xiǎo Wáng: Wǒ kàn.kàn (shāchē). Qiáo! Lúntāi gēn wǒ yíyàng, méi qìr .le.

30

Dialogue

(Měiyīng sees Gāo Dézhōng walking back and forth on campus, his face covered with sweat.)

Xiǎo Lín: Gāo Dézhōng, what has happened? What are you looking for?

Xiǎo Gāo: My car disappeared. I remember I just parked my car here a moment ago. How did it disappear in only a second?

Xiǎo Lín: Could it be that you parked at a different place?

Xiǎo Gāo: It's impossible. I usually park my car here and I have never had a problem. (Looking around:) Oh! When did this parking space change and allow people to park only before six a.m.? My car was probably towed away.

Xiǎo Lín: Oh! I wanted to borrow your car. Now there are no "wheels." What should I do?

Xiǎo Gāo: Do you want to go shopping by car?

Xiǎo Lín: No. It's Wáng Huá who wants to practice driving and get her driver's license. She asked me to be her coach. I used to ask her to accompany me for sports practice. Now it's my turn to go with her for driving practice.

Xiǎo Gāo: Don't worry. Wait till I get my car back and I'll lend it to you.

(On the morning of the next day, Wáng Huá and Měiyīng are practicing driving on the street.)

Xiǎo Lín: (Yelling:) Be careful! Be careful! When you cross the intersection, you should look around first before you go ahead.

Xiǎo Wáng: Don't yell! The more you yell, the more nervous I get.

Xiǎo Lín: (Turning on the radio:) Listen to some music and relax a little bit.

Xiǎo Wáng: No. I can't listen to music while I drive. I can't concentrate.

Xiǎo Lín: You don't mean to tell me you've never seen people drive and do makeup at the same time?

Xiǎo Wáng: That's the way Americans drive. (Driving forward slowly.)

Xiǎo Lín: You drive too slowly. The speed limit is thirty miles per hour here.

Xiǎo Wáng: Driving too fast will easily cause accidents. If I am caught speeding by a policeman, I will also get a ticket.

Xiǎo Lín: Xiao Wang! You're only driving fifteen miles per hour!

Xiǎo Wáng: All right, all right. You are really demanding. (Speeding up.) Could you say something nice and give me some encouragement? (Suddenly slowing down again.)

Xiǎo Lín: What happened?

Xiǎo Wáng: Let me see. (Stepping on the brake:) See! The tires are like me, losing their "spirit."

Mini-Dialogue
小對話 Xiǎoduìhuà

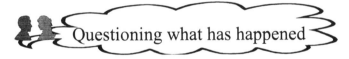
Questioning what has happened

1. A: 我今天明明把車子停在這兒，怎麼不見了？

   Wǒ jīn.tiān míngmíng bǎ chē.zi tíng zài zhèr, zěn.me bújiàn.le?

   I'm sure I parked my car here today. Why did it disappear?

   B: 會不會你把地方記錯了？

   Huì.buhuì nǐ bǎ dì.fāng jìcuò .le? Could it be that you remembered the place incorrectly?

2. A: 我昨天明明告訴過你，讓你今天三點鐘來，你怎麼沒來？

   Wǒ zuó.tiān míngíng gàosù.guò nǐ, ràng nǐ jīn.tiān sān diǎnzhōng lái, nǐ zěn.me méi lái?

   I'm sure I told you yesterday to come at three o'clock today. How come you didn't show up?

   B: 對不起，我把時間聽錯了。

   Duì.buqǐ, wǒ bǎ shíjiān tīngcuò .le. Sorry. I heard the time wrong.

Indicating and reacting to something wrong

1. A: 糟糕！我忘了把書帶來還   Zāogāo! Wǒ wàng .le bǎ shū dài.lái
        你。   huán nǐ.
                                    Oh! I forgot to bring your book back.

    B: 没關係，你可以下次再還。   Méi guān.xī, nǐ kě.yǐ xià.cì zài huán.
                                    It's O.K. You can return it next time.

2. A: 糟糕！我的車被拖走了，   Zāogāo! Wǒ .de chē bèi tuōzǒu .le,
        怎麼辦？   zěn.mebàn?
                                    Oh! My car was towed away. What
                                    should I do?

    B: 別著急，我待會兒就陪你   Bié zhāojí, wǒ dāi.huǐr jiù péi nǐ qù
        去把車拿回來。   bǎ chē náhuí.lái.
                                    Don't worry. I'll go with you to get
                                    your car back in a bit.

Expressing and responding to doubts

1. A: 你難道不知道這兒不許停   Nǐ nándào bù zhī.dào zhèr bù xǔ
        車嗎？   tíngchē .ma?
                                    Do you mean to say that you don't
                                    know that parking is forbidden here?

    B: 對不起，我真的不知道。   Duì.buqǐ, wǒ zhēn .de bù zhī.dào.
                                    Sorry, I was really unaware of this.

2. A: 你難道不知道我們今天有   Nǐ nándào bù zhī.dào wǒ.men jīn.tiān
        小考嗎？   yǒu xiǎokǎo .ma?
                                    Do you mean to say that you don't
                                    know we're having a quiz today?

    B: 對不起，我以爲我們後天   Duì.buqǐ, wǒ yǐwéi wǒ.men hòu.tiān
        才有小考。   cái yǒu xiǎokǎo.
                                    Sorry, I thought we didn't have a quiz
                                    till the day after tomorrow.

Giving and reacting to advice

1. A: 你開車的時候，可以聽點兒音樂，輕鬆一下。

Nǐ kāichē .de shí.hòu, kě.yǐ tīng .diǎnr yīnyuè, qīngsōng.yíxià.

You can listen to some music and relax while you're driving.

B: 不行，我不能一邊兒開車，一邊兒聽音樂。

Bù xíng. Wǒ bù néng yìbiānr kāichē, yìbiānr tīng yīnyuè.

No. I cannot listen to music while I drive.

2. A: 你過十字路口的時候，應該先往兩邊兒看看再開。

Nǐ guò shízì lùkǒu .de shí.hòu, yīngtāi xiān wàng liǎng biānr kàn.kàn zài kāi.

When you cross the intersection, you should look around first before you proceed.

B: 別說了，你越說我越緊張。

Bié shuō .le, nǐ yuè shuō wǒ yuè jǐn.zhāng.

Shut up. The more you talk about it, the more nervous I get.

Vocabulary
生詞 Shēngcí

◎ **By Order of Appearance**

不見了	不见了	bújiàn.le	IE	[not-see-Asp] to have disappeared
明明		míngmíng	Adv	[clear-clear] clearly
停(車)	停(车)	tíng(chē)	V/VO	[stop-car] to park (a car)
記錯	记错	jìcuò	RV	[record-error] to remember incorrectly
可能		kěnéng	Adv	[may-able] probably
從來都沒…	从来都没…	cónglái dōu méi...	Adv	[from-come-all-not] to have never...
停車位	停车位	tíngchēwèi	N	[stop-car-position] parking space
改		gǎi	V	to change (rule/situation), to correct
(允)許	(允)许	(yǔn)xǔ	V	[allow-permit] to allow, to permit
八成		bāchéng	N/Adv	[eight-one tenth] 80 percent, almost, very likely
拖		tuō	V	to tow, to drag
眞糟糕	真糟糕	zhēn zāogāo	IE	[real-sediment-cake] what a mess! too bad!
怎麼辦	怎么办	zěn.me bàn?	IE	[how-manage] what should (one) do?
練車	练车	liànchē	V/VO	[practice-car] to practice driving (=練習開車)
駕駛	驾驶	jiàshǐ	V	[drive a horse-run vehicle/sail] to drive (automobiles); to steer (boats)
執照	执照	zhízhào	N	[to hold-reflection] license
從前		cóngqián	MTA	[from-before] previously (=以前)
總是	总是	zǒng.shì	Adv	[total-is] always (= 老是)
該	该	gāi	AuxV	(it) should be X's turn
著急	着急	zhāojí	SV	[bear-urgent] (to be) anxious, worried (=急)
小心		xiǎo.xīn	SV	[small-heart] (to be) careful
十字路口		shízì lùkǒu	N	[ten-character-road-mouth] intersection
一邊兒…, 一邊兒	一边儿…, 一边儿	yìbiānr... yìbiānr	Conj	[one-side-Suf] on the one hand… on the other hand
難道	难道	nándào	MA	[hard-to say] do you mean to say (that)...?
化妝	化妆	huàzhuāng	V	[change-to doll up] to put on makeup
* 化妝品	化妆品	huàzhuāngpǐn	N	[make-up-thing] cosmetics

時速	时速	shísù	N	[time-speed] driving speed
出事兒	出事儿	chūshìr	V	[out-matter-Suf] to have an accident, to be in trouble
萬一	万一	wànyī	Adv	[ten thousands-one] a very tiny chance, just in case that...
被		bèi	CV	[passive marker] by
警察		jǐngchá	N	[alert-examine] police
發現	发现	fāxiàn	V/N	[issue-appear] to discover, discovery
罰單	罚单	fádān	N	[fine-slip] traffic ticket
要求		yāo.qiú	N/V	[want-beg] demand, request, to request (from senior to junior)
給...打氣	给...打气	gěi...dǎqì	IE	[give...hit-air] to give... encouragement, to fill with air (with an air pump)
* 突然		tūrán	Adv	[abrupt-like/-ly] suddenly
* 剎車	刹车	shāchē	V/N	[brake-car] to brake, brake(s)
輪胎	轮胎	lúntāi	N	[tire-fetus] tire (on a car)
沒氣了	没气了	méi qì.le	IE	[no-air-Suf] to have a flat tire, (to be) listless

◎ By Grammatical Categories

Nouns/Pronouns

警察		jǐngchá	N	[alert-examine] police
罰單	罚单	fádān	N	[fine-slip] traffic ticket
執照	执照	zhízhào	N	[to hold-reflection] license
要求		yāo.qiú	N/V	[want-beg] demand, request, to request (from senior to junior)
時速	时速	shísù	N	[time-speed] driving speed
輪胎	轮胎	lúntāi	N	[tire-fetus] tire (on a car)
停車位	停车位	tíngchēwèi	N	[stop-car-position] parking space
十字路口		shízì lùkǒu	N	[ten-character-road-mouth] intersection
* 化妝品	化妆品	huàzhuāngpǐn	N	[make-up-thing] cosmetics

Verbs/Stative Verbs/Adjectives

被		bèi	CV	[passive marker] by
該	该	gāi	AuxV	(it) should be X's turn
改		gǎi	V	to change (rule/situation), to correct
拖		tuō	V	to tow, to drag

(允)許	(允)许	(yǔn)xǔ	V	[allow-permit] to allow, to permit
駕駛	驾驶	jiàshǐ	V	[drive a horse-run vehicle/sail] to drive (automobiles); to steer (boats)
練車	练车	liànchē	V/VO	[practice-car] to practice driving (=練習開車)
停(車)	停(车)	tíng(chē)	V/VO	[stop-car] to park (a car)
* 刹車	刹车	shāchē	V/N	[brake-car] to brake, brake(s)
出事兒	出事儿	chūshìr	V	[out-matter-Suf] to have an accident, to be in trouble
化妝	化妆	huàzhuāng	V	[change-to doll up] to put on makeup
發現	发现	fāxiàn	V/N	[issue-appear] to discover, discovery
記錯	记错	jìcuò	RV	[record-error] to remember incorrectly
小心		xiǎo.xīn	SV	[small-heart] (to be) careful
著急	着急	zhāojí	SV	[bear-urgent] (to be) anxious, worried (=急)

Adverbs

總是	总是	zǒng.shì	Adv	[total-is] always (= 老是)
八成		bāchéng	Adv/N	[eight-one tenth] 80 percent, almost, very likely
萬一	万一	wànyī	Adv	[ten thousands-one] a very tiny chance, just in case that...
可能		kěnéng	Adv	[may-able] probably
* 突然		tūrán	Adv	[abrupt-like/-ly] suddenly
明明		míngmíng	Adv	[clear-clear] clearly
難道	难道	nándào	MA	[hard-to say] do you mean to say (that)...?
從前		cóngqián	MTA	[from-before] previously (=以前)
從來都沒...	从来都没...	cónglái dōu méi...	Adv	[from-come-all-not] to have never...

Conjuctions

| 一邊兒..., | 一边儿..., | yìbiānr... | Conj | [one-side-Suf] on the one hand...on the other hand |
| 一邊兒 | 一边儿 | yìbiānr | | |

Idiomatic Expressions

| 不見了 | 不见了 | bújiàn.le | IE | [not-see-Asp] to have disappeared |
| 眞糟糕 | 真糟糕 | zhēn zāogāo! | IE | [real-sediment-cake] what a mess! too bad! |

怎麼辦	怎么办	zěn.me bàn?	IE	[how-manage] what should (one) do?
給...打氣	给...打气	gěi...dǎqì	IE	[give...hit-air] to give... encourage-ment, to fill with air (with an air pump)
沒氣了	没气了	méi qì.le	IE	[no-air-Suf] to have a flat tire, (to be) listless

✚ Supplementary Vocabulary

1. Odds and Ends

一臉是汗	一脸是汗	yì liǎn shì hàn	IE	[one-face-is-sweat] to have sweat all over the face
滿頭大汗	满头大汗	mǎn tóu dà hàn	IE	[full-head-big-sweat] to have sweat all over the face
打開		dǎkāi	RV	[hit-open] to turn on (radio, range, etc.), to open (can, jar, book, etc.)
收音機	收音机	shōuyīnjī	N	[receive-sound-machine] radio
冷氣機	冷气机	lěngqìjī	N	[cold-air-machine] air-conditioning
空調	空调	kōngtiáo	N	[air-adjustment] air-conditioning

2. Driving and Parking

租車	租车	zūchē	V/VO	[rent-car] to rent a car
違規	违规	wéiguī	V	[disobey-rule] to violate the law
亂停車	乱停车	luàn tíngchē	VP	[chaotic-stop-car] to park illegally
發動車	发动车	fādòng chē	V/VO	[issue-move-car] to start a car's engine
踩剎車	踩刹车	cǎi shāchē	V/VO	[tread upon-brake] to apply the brakes
加油		jiāyóu	V/VO	[add-oil] to push down on the accelerator, to add gasoline/engine oil
汽油		qìyóu	N	[vapor-oil] gasoline
機油	机油	jīyóu	N	[machine-oil] engine oil
加速		jiāsù	V	[add-speed] to increase speed
減速		jiǎnsù	V	[substract-speed] to reduce speed
超速		chāosù	V	[exceed-speed] speeding
往前開	往前开	wàng qiánkāi	VP	[toward-front-drive] to drive forward
往後退	往后退	wàng hòutuì	VP	[toward-back-recede] to go backward
倒車	倒车	dàochē	V/VO	[backward-car] to move a vehicle backward
轉彎	转弯	zhuǎnwān	V/VO	[turn-wind] to make a turn
危險	危险	wéi/wēixiǎn	SV/N	[dangerous-dangerous] (to be) dangerous, danger
行人		xíngrén	N	[walk-people] pedestrian
過馬路	过马路	guò mǎlù	V/VO	[pass-horse-road] to go across the street
斑馬線	斑马线	bānmǎxiàn	N	[spots-horse-line] "zebra stripes" crossing
打訊號		dǎ xùnhào	V/VO	[hit-information-number] to signal (when driving)

Characters
漢字 Hànzì

求	借	單	位
剛	許	改	句
緊	張	腿	輕
千	萬	照	辦
總	非	被	陪

求

qiú
to seek, to beg 水
7　　　(water)

要求　　　yāo.qiú　　　demand, request, to request

A: 你在趕什麼？
B: 趕功課，老師**要求**我們明天交。

借

jiè
to borrow, to lend
亻
10　　　(person)

*借書　　　jièshū　　　to check out books
*借錢　　　jièqián　　　to borrow money

A: 你上哪兒去？
B: 我上圖書館**借書**去。

單

dān
single, individual
口
12　　　(mouth)

罰單　　　fádān　　　traffic ticket
*單子　　　dān.zi　　　form
*簡單　　　jiǎndān　　　simple
*單身　　　dānshēn　　　single

A: 你怎麼了？什麼事不高興？
B: 我剛**吃了一張罰單**。

位

wèi
AN for people 亻
7　　　(person)

*位子　　　wèi.zi　　　seat

A: 你認識坐在那兒喝茶的**那位**老師嗎？
B: 認識，她教我中文。

繁簡對照：	其他漢字：	✎ **My notes:**
單单	*罰 SC75	

剛

gāng
just, recently

10   (knife)

剛才   gāngcái   just now, a moment ago

A: 你**剛才**上哪兒去了，我找你，你不在。
B: 我出去寄信了。

許

xǔ
to promise, to
permit   言
11   (speech)

允許   yǔnxǔ   to allow, to permit
不許   bù xǔ   not to allow
*也許   yěxǔ   perhaps

A:這兒**許人**抽煙嗎？
B: 對不起，這兒**不許人**抽煙。

改

gǎi
to change, to
modify   攵
7

*改變   gǎibiàn   to change
*改成   gǎichéng   to change into

A: 這個地方三年沒來，**改了**很多。
B: 多了很多大樓。

句

jù
sentence   口
5   (mouth)

一句話   yí jù huà   one sentence
*句子   jù.zi   sentence

A: 你不是學過中文嗎？
B: 太久沒練習，我現在連**一句話**也說不
出來。

繁簡對照：	其他漢字：	✎ **My notes:**
剛剛 許许		

緊
jǐn
tight, close 糸
14

*緊張	jǐn.zhāng	(to be) nervous, tense
*要緊	yàojǐn	significant
*不要緊	bú yàojǐn	doesn't matter

A: 昨天的比賽怎麼樣？
B: 很**緊張**，八十比七十八，幾乎平手。

張
zhāng
AN for tables,
beds, etc;
surname 弓
11　　(a bow)

| *緊張 | jǐn.zhāng | (to be) nervous, tense |
| *一張紙 | yì zhāng zhǐ | piece of paper |

A: 我明天有口試。
B: 別**緊張**，**緊張**了就考不好。

腿
tuǐ
leg　　月
14　　(flesh)

腿兒	tuǐr	leg
*大腿	dàtuǐ	thigh
*小腿	xiǎotuǐ	shank

A: 我的**腿兒扭傷了**，都怪你。
B: 怎麼能怪我呢？只能怪你自己平常不運動。

輕
qīng
light　　車
14　　(vehicle)

| 輕鬆 | qīngsōng | (to be) relaxed |
| *輕重 | qīngzhòng | weight |

A: 剛考完試，你應該**輕鬆一下**。
B: 不行，我下星期又有一個考試。

繁簡對照：	其他漢字：	✎ **My notes:**
緊緊 張张 輕轻	重 L10	

一千　　　yì qiān　　　one thousand

qiān
one thousand 十
3　　　(ten)

A: 在美國上大學貴不貴？
B: 貴得很，一個學期就要**兩三千塊**。

萬一　　　wànyī　　　just in case that…
一萬　　　yí wàn　　　ten thousand
*千萬　　　qiānwàn　　　by all means

wàn
ten thousand 艹
13　　　(grass)

A: 你開車的時候，一定要小心。
B: 對，**不怕一萬，只怕萬一**。

照片　　　zhàopiàn　　　picture, photo
執照　　　zhízhào　　　license
*照相　　　zhàoxiàng　　　to take a photo

zhào
according to; to
shine　　　灬
13　　　(fire)

A: 你怎麼這麼高興？
B: 我剛考到**駕駛執照**。

怎麼辦　　　zěn.me bàn　　　what should one do?
舉辦　　　jǔbàn　　　to sponsor, to organize
*辦公室　　　bàngōngshì　　　office
*辦事　　　bànshì　　　to do things

bàn
to do　　　辛
16　　(eighth of
the ten
celestial stems)

A: 王老師的**辦公室**在哪兒？
B: 在新生大樓，三六五號。

繁簡對照：	其他漢字：	✎ **My notes:**
萬万 辦办	百 L15	

總

zǒng
always 糸
17

總是	zǒng.shì	always
*總想	zǒng xiǎng	always think about
*總要	zǒng yào	always want to

A: 你**總是**要我陪你去練球，你不能自己去嗎？

B: 兩個人打比較有意思。

非

fēi
is not 非
8 (not)

| 非常 | fēicháng | extremely, very |

A: 這個學生怎麼樣？

B: **非常**用功，可是學習的方法不對。

被

bèi
by (passive
marker) 衤
10 (clothing)

| A被B V | A bèi B V | A be V-ed by B |

A: 你那本中國文學的書在哪兒呢？

B: 我的書**被他**借走了。

陪

péi
to keep
company ß
11 (a mound)

| A陪B | A péi B | A accompany B |

A: **你陪我**去看球吧！一個人看沒意思。

B: 我才不要聽你大喊大叫的。

繁簡對照：	其他漢字：	✎ **My notes:**
總总		

Grammar
語法 yǔfǎ

Ⓐ Major Sentence Patterns 主要句型 zhǔyào jùxíng

1. The usage of 借

1.1 借 as "to borrow...from"

Structure	Gloss
A (Neg) (AuxV) 跟 B 借 X	A (AuxV) (Neg) borrows X from B

1. 你想跟誰借車呢？

    Nǐ xiǎng gēn shéi jièchē .ne?
    From whom are you going to borrow a car?

    我想跟小高借車。

    Wǒ xiǎng gēn Xiǎo Gāo jièchē.
    I would like to borrow a car from Xiao Gao.

2. 他打算跟誰借錢呢？

    Tā dǎsuàn gēn shéi jièqián .ne?
    From whom is he planning to borrow the money?

    他打算跟銀行借錢。

    Tā dǎsuàn gēn yínháng jièqián.
    He plans to borrow the money from the bank.

 借 means "to borrow" or "to lend." The direction of "borrowing" depends on whether it co-occurs with the co-verb 跟 or the indirect object marker 給. When 跟 occurs with 借, it means "to borrow (from)" in English.

1.2 借 as "to lend...to"

Structure	Gloss
A (Neg) (AuxV) 借 X 給 B	A (AuxV) (Neg) lends X to B
A (Neg) (AuxV) 借 給 B X	

1. 你能不能借五十塊錢給我？/
    你能不能借給我五十塊錢？

    Nǐ néng .bu.néng jiè wǔshí kuài qián gěi wǒ?/Nǐ néng .bu.néng jiè gěi wǒ wǔshí kuài qián?
    Can you lend me fifty dollars?

    對不起，我沒有錢，我不能借錢給你。/我不能借給你錢。

    Duì.buqǐ, wǒ méi.yǒu qián, wǒ bù néng jiè qián gěi nǐ./wǒ bù néng jiè gěi nǐ qián.
    I don't have the money, (so) I can't lend money to you.

2. 我可以借這本書給小李嗎？

Wǒ ké.yǐ jiè zhèi běn shū gěi Xiǎo Lǐ .ma?
May I lend this book to Xiao Li?

你可以借那本書給小李。

Nǐ ké.yǐ jiè nèi běn shū gěi Xiǎo Lǐ.
You may lend that book to Xiao Li.

When 借 precedes 給, it means "to lend (to)."

1.3 把 X 借給 as "to lend...to"

Structure	Gloss
A (Neg) (AuxV) 把 X 借 給 B	A (AuxV) (Neg) lends X to B

1. 我可以把車借給老王嗎？

Wǒ kě.yǐ bǎ chē jiè gěi Lǎo Wáng .ma?
May I lend the car to Lao Wang?

不可以把車借給老王，他開車不太小心。

Bù kě.yǐ bǎ chē jiè gěi Lǎo Wáng, tā kāichē bú tài xiǎo.xīn.
(You) may not lend the car to Lao Wang; he desn't drive very carefully.

2. 你可以把吹風機借給我用一下嗎？

Nǐ kě.yǐ bǎ chuīfēngjī jiè gěi wǒ yòng.yíxià .ma?
Can you lend me the hair dryer?

對不起，我自己要用，不能把它借給你。

Duì.buqǐ, wǒ zìjǐ yào yòng, bù néng bǎ tā jiè gěi nǐ.
Sorry, I need to use (it) myself, (so) can't lend it to you.

You may use 把 to prepose the direct object to the front of the verb.

See L9–A1, L14–A3, L18–A3 for more on 給.
See L15–A1, L16–C1 for more on 把.

2. 一邊兒... 一邊兒... construction

Structure	Gloss
S 一邊兒 V_1O_1, 一邊兒 V_2O_2	While one is VingO_1, he/she is VingO_2

1. 他一邊兒吃早飯，一邊兒做什麼？

Tā yìbiānr chī zǎofàn, yìbiānr zuò shén.me?
What is he doing while he is eating breakfast?

他一邊兒吃早飯，一邊兒看報
紙。

Tā yìbiānr chī zǎofàn, yìbiānr kàn bàozhǐ.

While he is eating breakfast, he is
reading a newspaper.

2. 你能一邊兒開車，一邊兒聽音
樂嗎？

Nǐ néng yìbiānr kāichē , yìbiānr tīng
yīnyuè .ma?
Can you listen to the music while you are
driving?

我不能一邊兒開車，一邊兒聽
音樂。我開車一定得專心。

Wǒ bù néng yìbiānr kāichē , yìbiānr tīng
yīnyuè. Wǒ kāichē yídìng děi zhuānxīn.
No, I can't listen to the music while I am
driving. I have to concentrate while I am
driving.

3. 你一邊兒聽老師講課，一邊
兒做什麼？

Nǐ yìbiānr tīng lǎoshī jiǎngkè , yìbiānr
zuò shén.me?
What were you doing while you were
listening to the teacher's lecture?

我一邊兒聽老師講課，一邊兒
記筆記。

Wǒ yìbiānr tīng lǎoshī jiǎngkè , yìbiānr jì
bǐjì.
While I was listening to the teacher's
lecture, I was taking down notes.

 一邊兒 is an adverbial expression; it always precedes the verb. When it is reduplicated,
it forms a correlative construction which denotes that two (or more) actions are
happening at the same time.

3. The passive marker 被

Structure	Gloss
A 被 B V 了	A was ... by B

1. 你的車怎麼不見了？

Nǐ .de chē zěn.me bújiàn.le?
How come your car has disappeared?

我違規停車，所以(我的)車被警
察拖走了。

Wǒ wéiguī tíngchē, suǒ.yǐ (wǒ .de) chē
bèi jǐngchá tuōzǒu .le.
I parked illegally; therefore (my) car was
towed away by the police.

2. 聽說他開車出事兒了，他人怎
麼樣了？有沒有受傷？

Tīngshuō tā kāichē chūshìr .le, tā rén
zěn.meyàng .le, yǒu méi.yǒu shòushāng?

(I) have heard that he had a car accident. How is he? Was (he) injured?

他的車被撞壞了，還好他人沒(有)受傷。

Tā .de chē bèi zhuànghuài .le, háihǎo tā rén méi(.yǒu) shòushāng.
His car was damaged by being bumped. Fortunately he was not injured.

3. 我們說的話被他聽見了嗎？

Wǒ.men shuō .de huà bèi tā tīng.jiàn .le .ma?
Did he hear what we have talked about ?

我們說的話被他聽見了。

Wǒ.men shuō .de huà bèi tā tīng.jiàn .le.
He has heard what we have talked about.

 In Chinese, there is no distinction of voice in verbs. But the direction of an action may be outward from the subject as actor or inward toward the subject as goal. The passive marker 被 is used if the inward action is to be expressed. Among the perception verbs, only 看見/看到 and 聽見/聽到 can occur with 被. Other perception verbs such as 聞到 wéndào 'to smell,' 感覺到 gǎnjuédào 'to feel' cannot occur with 被. Most of the sentences with 被 construction denote unfavorable meanings or adversity.

B Usage of Common Phrases 詞組用法 cízǔ yòngfǎ

1. The adverb 從來

Structure	Gloss
S 從來(都)不 VO	S never VO
S 從來(都)沒 V 過 O	S has never V-ed O

1. 你從來都沒看過中國電影兒嗎？

Nǐ cónglái dōu méi kàn.guò Zhōng.guó diànyǐngr .ma?
Have you ever seen a Chinese movie?

我從來都沒看過中國電影兒。

Wǒ cónglái dōu méi kàn.guò Zhōng.guó diànyǐngr.
I have never seen a Chinese movie.

2. 老高開車出過事兒嗎？

Lǎo Gāo kāichē chū.guò shìr .ma?
Has Lao Gao ever had a car accident?

老高開車開得很好，從來都沒出過事兒。

Lǎo Gāo kāichē kāi.de hěn hǎo, cónglái dōu méi chū.guò shìr.
Lao Gao drives very well; (he) has never had a car accident.

3. 你吸煙跟喝酒嗎？

Nǐ xīyān gēn hējiǔ .ma?
Do you smoke and drink (wine)?

我從來不吸煙也不喝酒。

Wǒ cónglái bù xīyān, yě bù hējiǔ.
I neither smoke nor drink (wine).

 從來 is an adverb that means "from the beginning." It is used only in a negative sentence that includes a negative adverb, such as 沒/不 (or 未 wèi in classical Chinese). In written Chinese, the compound 從來不 can be shortened to 從不. The adverb 都 may be inserted between 從來 and 沒/不 to function as an emphatic marker.

2. The movable adverb 難道

Structure	Gloss
難道　S　Neg VO 嗎？	Do you mean to say that...?/
S　難道　Neg VO 嗎？	Could it be possible that...?

1. 他難道不會開車嗎？／
    難道他不會開車嗎？

Tā nándào bú huì kāichē .ma?/
Nándào tā bú huì kāichē .ma?
Do you mean to say that he doesn't know how to drive?

他一直住在紐約，所以他不會開車。

Tā yìzhí zhù zài Niǔyuē, sǒu.yǐ tā bú huì kāichē.
He has been living in New York; therefore he doesn't know how to drive.

2. 你難道連一個中國字也不會寫嗎？／難道你連一個中國字也不會寫嗎？

Nǐ nándào lián yí .ge Zhōng.guózì yě bú huì xiě .ma?/Nándào nǐ lián yí .ge Zhōng.guózì yě bú huì xiě .ma?
Could it be possible that you don't even know how to write a single Chinese character?

我是在美國生的，我就會說中文，不會寫中國字。

Wǒ shì zài Měi.guó shēng .de, wǒ jiù huì shuō Zhōngwén, bú huì xiě Zhōng.guózì.
I was born in the United States. I only know how to speak Chinese, not how to write Chinese characters.

 難道 is a movable adverb that means 'Do you mean to say that...?/Could it be possible that...?' and is used only in a rhetorical question. It may either precede or follow the subject.

3. The reduplicated adverbs 偏偏 and 明明

Structure	Gloss
S 偏(偏) VO	S VO deliberately
S 明明 VO	Clearly S V

1. 我告訴你別吸煙跟喝酒，你為
什麼偏(偏)不聽？

Wǒ gào.sù nǐ bié xīyān gēn hējiǔ, nǐ wèishén.me piān(piān) bù tīng?
I told you not to smoke and drink. Why is it that you wouldn't listen?

2. 他爸爸叫他別開快車，他偏要
開快車。

Tā bà.bà jiào tā bié kāikuàichē, tā piān yào kāikuàichē.
His father told him don't speed; he did it deliberately.

3. 對不起，你還沒我錢呢！

Duì.buqǐ, nǐ hái méi gěi wǒ qián .ne!
Excuse me, you haven't given me the money yet!

我明明給了你錢，你怎麼說我
沒給呢？

Wǒ míngmíng gěi .le nǐ qián, nǐ zěn.me shuō wǒ méi gěi .ne?
I did give you the money; why is it that you said that I didn't?

4. 他說不要借車給我。

Tā shuō bú yào jiè chē gěi wǒ.
He said that he won't lend me the car.

可是昨天他明明說要借車給你
，怎麼今天他說不借給你呢？

Kě.shì zuó.tiān tā míngmíng shuō yào jiè chē gěi nǐ, zěn.me jīn.tiān tā shuō bú jiè gěi nǐ .ne?
But yesterday he did say that (he) would lend you the car. How come he said that he wouldn't lend it to you today?

偏 and 偏偏 both are adverbs and mean "(do something) deliberately or contrarily to (someone's expectation/rule)." 明明 is also an adverb that means "clearly, apparently, evidently." But it can only be used in reduplicated form and always occurs in a rhetorical question or denial statement.

Cultural Notes
文化點滴 wénhuà diǎndī

1. In Chinese, the concept "percentage" can be expressed in terms of 成 chéng 'one tenth.'

十成	100%	五成	50%
九成	90%	四成	40%
八成	80%	三成	30%
七成	70%	二成	20%
六成	60%	一成	10%

2. 氣 qì is a very ambiguous and interesting word in Chinese. Literally it means "air, gas, vapor, atmosphere, breath..." But it can be referred to as the inner qì 'immaterial substance' that forms the energy of one's life and spirit or the outer qì 'air or atmosphere of one's environment.' When used as a pun, 沒氣兒 méiqìr can mean either "losing one's breath/energy" or "losing the air (of tires)." Thus an expression such as 那個人沒氣兒了 nèi .ge rén méi qìr .le means "That person is dead." 打氣 dǎqì can be used as a pun to mean either "to pump air into a tire" or "to encourage (someone to do something)."

3. 加油 jiāyóu is also an ambiguous expression. It can mean "[to add oil/gasoline] to refuel, to step on the gas/to apply the accelerator, to step up effort." It is also very commonly used to cheer an athlete in competition or players in a game. For instance, 小王加油！Xiǎo Wáng jiāyóu means "Go! Xiao Wang!"

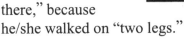

4. When someone goes someplace on foot, people may joke that 他是坐 11 號公車去的 "he/she took bus No. 11 to get there," because he/she walked on "two legs."

對話	270頁
小對話	276頁
生詞	279頁
漢字	286頁
語法	292頁
文化點滴	302頁

第二十三課 你們暑假打算做什麼？

對話

〔李明、高德中、王華、林美英在校園內討論暑假計劃。〕

小李 ： 小林、小王，最近怎麼樣？

小王 ： 忙死了，我下個星期有三個考試。

小林 ： 我也是，我還有一個重要的報告要交呢！

小高 ： 考完了就行了。你們放暑假打算做什麼？

小王 ： 我會留在這兒，繼續修課。

小林 ： 本來我也想修課，後來想想難得一個夏天，還是休息一下。五月底我會先去參加表妹的畢業典禮，然後回家給我父母慶祝銀婚。他們六月一號就結婚二十五週年了。七月也許會跟爸媽回台灣一趟，也許會在家附近找個工作，打工賺學費。你們呢？

小高 ： 我已經申請了兩家暑期語言學校，希望他們能收我。可是如果他們收了我，不給我獎學金，我看也上不起。

小林 ： 你難道不能一邊兒打工一邊兒學習嗎？

小高 ： 不行。那種強化班忙得不得了。學生一天到晚都得說中文。難是難，可是聽說對學生的中文水平很有幫助。

小王 ： 有道理。我來了美國以後，天天都說英文，所以進步了不少。尤其是我的聽力。李明，你呢？也上學嗎？

小李 ： 不，我可能會去實習。我們商學院的老師非常強調工作經驗。其實我自己想到東西兩岸走走，或者到加拿大去旅行，可是去旅行的話，我怕我的錢不夠。

小林：　你不要住旅館，露營可以省很多錢。

小王：　好了！好了！再聊下去就誤了我們的「大事」了。咱們
　　　　快回去準備期末考吧！

对话

〔李明、高德中、王华、林美英在校园内讨论暑假计划。〕

小李 ： 小林、小王，最近怎么样？

小王 ： 忙死了，我下个星期有三个考试。

小林 ： 我也是，我还有一个重要的报告要交呢！

小高 ： 考完了就行了。你们放暑假打算做什么？

小王 ： 我会留在这儿，继续修课。

小林 ： 本来我也想修课，后来想想难得一个夏天，还是休息一下。五月底我会先去参加表妹的毕业典礼，然后回家给我父母庆祝银婚。他们六月一号就结婚二十五週年了。七月也许会跟爸妈回台湾一趟，也许会在家附近找个工作，打工赚学费。你们呢？

小高 ： 我已经申请了两家暑期语言学校，希望他们能收我。可是如果他们收了我，不给我奖学金，我看也上不起。

小林 ： 你难道不能一边儿打工一边儿学习吗？

小高 ： 不行。那种强化班忙得不得了。学生一天到晚都得说中文。难是难，可是听说对学生的中文水平很有帮助。

小王 ： 有道理。我来了美国以后，天天都说英文，所以进步了不少。尤其是我的听力。李明，你呢？也上学吗？

小李 ： 不，我可能会去实习。我们商学院的老师非常强调工作经验。其实我自己想到东西两岸走走，或者到加拿大去旅行，可是去旅行的话，我怕我的钱不够。

小林： 你不要住旅馆，露营可以省很多钱。

小王： 好了！好了！再聊下去就误了我们的「大事」了。咱们快回去准备期末考吧！

My questions:

Duìhuà

(Lǐ Míng, Gāo Dézhōng, Wáng Huá, Lín Měiyīng zài xiàoyuán nèi tǎolùn shǔjià
  jìhuà.)

Xiǎo Lǐ:	Xiǎo Lín, Xiǎo Wáng, zuìjìn zěn.meyàng?
Xiǎo Wáng:	Máng.sǐ .le. Wǒ xià .ge xīngqī yǒu sān .ge kǎoshì.
Xiǎo Lín:	Wǒ yě shì, wǒ hái yǒu yí .ge zhòngyào .de bàogào yào jiāo .ne!
Xiǎo Gāo:	Kǎowán .le jiù xíng .le. Nǐ.men fàng shǔjià dǎsuàn zuò shén.me?

Xiǎo Wáng:	Wǒ huì liú zài zhèr, jì.xù xiūkè.
Xiǎo Lín:	Běnlái wǒ yě xiǎng xiūkè, hòulái xiǎng.xiǎng nándé yí .ge xiàtiān, hǎi.shì xiū.xī.yíxià. Wǔyuè dǐ wǒ huì xiān qù cānjiā biǎomèi .de bìyè diǎnlǐ, ránhòu huíjiā gěi wǒ fùmǔ qìngzhù yínhūn. Tā.men liùyuè yīhào jiù jiéhūn èrshíwǔ zhōunián .le. Qīyuè yěxǔ huì gēn bàmā huí Táiwān yí tàng, yěxǔ huì zài jiā fùjìn zhǎo .ge gōngzuò, dǎgōng zhuàn xuéfèi. Nǐ.men .ne?
Xiǎo Gāo:	Wǒ yǐ.jīng shēnqǐng .le liǎng jiā shǔqī yǔyán xuéxiào, xīwàng tā.men néng shōu wǒ. Kě.shì rúguǒ tā.men shōu .le wǒ, bù gěi wǒ jiǎngxuéjīn, wǒ kàn yě shàng.buqǐ.
Xiǎo Lín:	Nǐ nándào bù néng yìbiānr dǎgōng yìbiānr xuéxí .ma?
Xiǎo Gāo:	Bù xíng. Nà zhǒng qiánghuàbān máng .de bù.deliǎo. Xué.shēng yì tiān dào wǎn dōu děi shuō Zhōngwén. Nán shì nán, kě.shì tīngshuō duì xué.shēng .de Zhōngwén shuǐpíng hěn yǒu bāngzhù.

Xiǎo Wáng:	Yǒudào.lǐ. Wǒ lái .le Měi.guó yǐhòu, tiāntiān dōu shuō Yīngwén, suǒ.yǐ jìnbù .le bù shǎo, yóuqí shì wǒ .de tīnglì. Lǐ Míng, nǐ .ne? Yě shàngxué .ma?
Xiǎo Lǐ:	Bù, wǒ kěnéng huì qù shíxí. Wǒ.men shāngxuéyuàn .de lǎo.shī fēicháng qiángdiào gōngzuò jīngyàn. Qíshí wǒ zìjǐ xiǎng dào dōng xī liǎng'àn zǒu.zǒu, huò.zhě dào Jiā'nádà qù lǚxíng, kě.shì qù lǚxíng .de huà, wǒ pà wǒ .de qián bú gòu.
Xiǎo Lín:	Nǐ bú yào zhù lǚguǎn, lùyíng kě.yǐ shěng hěn duō qián.
Xiǎo Wáng:	Hǎo.le! Hǎo.le! Zài liáoxià.qù jiù wù .le wǒ.men .de "dàshì" .le. Zán.men kuài huí.qù zhǔnbèi qīmòkǎo .ba!

Dialogue

(Lǐ Míng, Gāo Dézhōng, Wáng Huá, and Lín Měiyīng are on campus discussing their summer plans.)

Xiǎo Lǐ: Xiǎo Lín, Xiǎo Wáng, how are you doing lately?

Xiǎo Wáng: (I'm) terribly busy. I have three tests next week.

Xiǎo Lín: So do I. I also have an important paper due.

Xiǎo Gāo: It will be all right after the exam is over. What do you plan to do during your summer vacation?

Xiǎo Wáng: I will stay here and continue to take courses.

Xiǎo Lín: Originally, I also planned to take courses, but then I thought we get only one summer a year. It's better for me to take a break. At the end of May, I will go to my cousin's graduation ceremony and then go home to celebrate the silver anniversary of my parents. They will have their twenty-fifth anniversary on June 1. In July, I will probably go to Taiwan with my parents or I will find a job near my home to earn some money for my tuition. How about you two?

Xiǎo Gāo: I have already applied to two summer language schools and hope that they will accept me. Even if they do accept me, I don't think I can go without a scholarship.

Xiǎo Lín: Can't you work part-time while you are studying?

Xiǎo Gāo: No. That kind of intensive class (keeps students) extremely busy. Students have to speak Chinese all day long. It's hard all right, but I have heard that it's very helpful in (bringing up) the students' level of Chinese.

Xiǎo Wáng: That makes sense. Since I came to the States, I speak English every day, so I have made considerable progress, especially in my listening comprehension skill. Lǐ Míng, how about you? Will you also go to summer school?

Xiǎo Lǐ: No. I may do an internship. The teachers in our business school emphasize work experience. Actually I personally would like to go to the East and the West Coasts, or take a trip to Canada. Still, if I travel, I'm afraid I won't have enough money.

Xiǎo Lín: You don't have to stay in motels. Camping will save you a lot of money.

Xiǎo Wáng: All right, all right. If we keep talking, we will hold up our "major duty." Let's go back and prepare for our finals.

Mini-Dialogue
小對話 Xiǎoduìhuà

 Talking about school

1. A: 你最近怎麼樣？

   Nǐ zuìjìn zěn.meyàng?
   How are you doing these days?

   B: 忙死了，我這星期有三個考試，下星期還要交兩個報告。

   Máng.sǐ .le, wǒ zhèi xīngqī yǒu sān .ge kǎoshì, xià xīngqī hái yào jiāo liǎng .ge bàogào.

   (I'm) terribly busy. I have three exams this week and I need to hand in two papers next week.

   A: 考完了就好了。

   Kǎowán .le jiù hǎo.le.
   Everything will be O.K. after the exams.

Talking about future plans

1. A: 你暑假的時候，打算做什麼？

   Nǐ shǔjià .de shí.hòu, dǎsuàn zuò shén.me?

   What are you planning to do during the summer break?

   B: 我想留在這兒，繼續修課。這樣可以早一點兒畢業。

   Wǒ xiǎng liú zài zhèr, jì.xù xiūkè. Zhèyàng kě.yǐ zǎo yì.diǎnr bìyè.

   I want to stay here taking more courses, so that I can graduate sooner.

2. A: 你放春假的時候，打算做什麼？

   Nǐ fàng chūnjià .de shí.hòu, dǎsuàn zuò shén.me?

   What are you planning to do during the spring break?

   B: 我本來想上芝加哥去玩玩，現在也許會回家。

   Wǒ běnlái xiǎng shàng Zhījiāgē qù wán.wán, xiànzài yěxǔ huì huíjiā.

   Originally I planned to go to Chicago for fun. Now I may be going home.

Showing agreement and disagreement

1. A: 你如果想進步，就應該一天到晚說中文。

   Nǐ rúguǒ xiǎng jìnbù, jiù yīnggāi yì tiān dào wǎn shuō Zhōngwén.

   If you want to make progress in Chinese, you should speak it all day long.

   B: 有道理，可是我跟誰說呢？

   Yǒudào.lǐ, kě.shì wǒ gēn shéi shuō .ne?

   That makes sense. But whom should I talk with?

2. A: 你如果想學好中文的話，就該上暑期語言學校。

   Nǐ rúguǒ xiǎng xuéhǎo Zhōngwén .de huà, jiù gāi shàng shǔqī yǔyán xuéxiào.

   If you want to study Chinese well, you should go to the summer language school.

   B: 有道理，可是哪裏來的錢呢？

   Yǒudào.lǐ, kě.shì nǎ.lǐ lái .de qián .ne?

   That makes sense. But where does the money come from?

Expressing and reacting to conjecture

1. A: 我看他們可能不會給我獎學金。

   Wǒ kàn tā.men kěnéng bú huì gěi wǒ jiǎngxuéjīn.

   I think they may not give me a scholarship.

   B: 不會吧！你不是研究做得很好，寫了好幾個報告嗎？

   Bú huì .ba! Nǐ bú.shì yánjiū zuò.de hěn hǎo, xiě .le hǎo jǐ .ge bàogào .ma?

   I don't think that will be the case. Isn't it true that you have done some research and written a couple of papers?

2. A: 我看他明年一定没法子畢業。

   Wǒ kàn tā míng.nián yídìng méi fǎ.zi bìyè.

   I think he won't be able to graduate next year.

B: 你怎麼知道呢？

Nǐ zěn.me zhī.dào .ne?
How do you know?

A: 他打工打得太厲害了，哪兒有時間學習？

Tā dǎgōng dǎ.de tài lì.hài .le, nǎr yǒu shíjiān xuéxí?
He has worked part-time a lot. When does he have time to study?

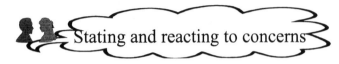

Stating and reacting to concerns

1. A: 我申請了這兒的研究所，可是不知道他們收不收我。

Wǒ shēnqǐng .le zhèr .de yánjiūsuǒ, kě.shì bù zhī.dào tā.men shōu .bushōu wǒ.
I've applied to the graduate school here, but I don't know if they will accept me or not.

   B: 別擔心，我想他們一定會收你的。

Bié dānxīn. Wǒ xiǎng tā.men yídìng huì shōu nǐ .de.
Don't worry. I think they will definitely accept you.

2. A: 我對中文有興趣，可是我怕以後找工作不容易。

Wǒ duì Zhōngwén yǒu xìng.qù, kě.shì wǒ pà yǐhòu zhǎo gōngzuò bù róng.yì.
I am interested in Chinese, but I'm afraid it won't be easy for me to find a job in the future.

   B: 你放心。我聽說學中文對找工作很有幫助。

Nǐ fàngxīn. Wǒ tīngshuō xué Zhōngwén duì zhǎo gōngzuò hěn yǒu bāngzhù.
Don't worry. I've heard that studying Chinese is very helpful in landing a job.

Vocabulary
生詞 Shēngcí

◎ **By Order of Appearance**

重要		zhòngyào	SV	[heavy-want] (to be) important
暑假		shǔjià	N	[summer-holiday] summer vacation
* 計劃	计划	jìhuà	V/N	[calculate-plan] to plan, plan, project
留		liú	V	to stay
繼續	继续	jì.xù	V	[continue-continue] to continue
本來	本来	běnlái	Adv	[origin-come] originally (=原來)
難得	难得	nándé	SV/Adv	[hard-obtain] (to be) hard to get, (to be) rare, once in a blue moon, rarely
夏天		xiàtiān	N	[summer-day] summertime
底		dǐ	N	bottom
表妹		biǎomèi	N	[outside-younger sister] daughter of father's sister or mother's sibling, who is younger than oneself
畢業	毕业	bìyè	V/N	[finish-profession] to graduate, graduation
典禮	典礼	diǎnlǐ	N	[display-ritual] ceremony
然後	然后	ránhòu	Adv	[still-back] then, afterwards, later (preceded by 先)
銀婚	银婚	yínhūn	N	[silver-marriage] silver anniversary
結婚	结婚	jiéhūn	V/N	[tie-marriage] to get married, marriage
* 離婚	离婚	líhūn	V/N	[depart-marriage] to divorce, divorce
* 訂婚	订婚	dìnghūn	V/N	[reserve-marriage] to engage/ betroth, engagement, betrothal
週年	周年	zhōunián	N	[period-year] anniversary
也許	也许	yěxǔ	Adv	[also-promise] perhaps
賺(錢)	赚(钱)	zhuàn(qián)	V/VO	[earn-money] to make money, to earn money
* 掙(錢)	挣(钱)	zhèng(qián)	V/VO	[earn-money] to make money, to earn money (=賺錢)
學費	学费	xuéfèi	N	[learn-fee] tuition
暑期		shǔqī	N	[summer-period] summer
希望		xīwàng	V/N	[hope-look] to hope, hope
收		shōu	V	to accept, to admit (to a study program), to collect (money, paper, tests, letters...)
獎學金	奖学金	jiǎngxuéjīn	N	[award-learn-gold] scholarship

上不起		shàng.buqǐ	RV	[up-not-raise] not to be able to afford to go to school
* V不起		V.buqǐ	RV	[V-not-raise] not to be able to afford to V
強化班		qiánghuàbān	N	[strong-ize-class] intensive course
一天到晚		yì tiān dào wǎn	IE	[one-day-to-evening] all day long (= 整天)
水平		shuǐpíng	N	[water-level] level, standard
對...有幫助	对...有帮助	duì...yǒu bāngzhù	IE	[to...have assistance] (to be) helpful to
有道理		yǒudào.lǐ	SV	[have-way-theory] (to be) logical
進步	进步	jìnbù	V/N	[progress-step] to progress, progression, progress
聽力	听力	tīnglì	N	[listen-strength] listening comprehension
實習	实习	shíxí	V/N	[practical-learn] to have an internship; internship
商學院	商学院	shāngxuéyuàn	N	[business-learn-yard] business school
強調	强调	qiángdiào	V	[strong-tone] to emphasize, to stress
東岸	东岸	dōng'àn	N	[east-coast] East Coast
西岸		xī'àn	N	[west-coast] West Coast
* 海岸		hǎi'àn	N	[sea-coast] coast
加拿大		Jiā'nādà	N	[add-take-big] Canada
旅行		lǚxíng	V/N	[travel-walk] to travel, traveling
旅館	旅馆	lǚguǎn	N	[travel-hall] hotel
露營	露营	lùyíng	V/N	[dew-camp] to camp, camping
省錢	省钱	shěngqián	SV/VO	[save-money] to save money
聊(天)		liáo(tiān)	V(O)	[chat-weather] to chat
(耽)誤	(耽)误	(dān)wù	V	[delay-error] to delay
期末考		qīmòkǎo	N	[period-end-test] final examination
* 大考		dàkǎo	N	[big-test] final examination (=期末考)

◎ By Grammatical Categories

Nouns/Pronouns

暑假		shǔjià	N	[summer-holiday] summer vacation
暑期		shǔqī	N	[summer-period] summer
夏天		xiàtiān	N	[summer-day] summertime
底		dǐ	N	bottom
表妹		biǎomèi	N	[outside-younger sister] daughter of father's sister or mother's sibling, who is younger than oneself
典禮	典礼	diǎnlǐ	N	[display-ritual] ceremony
銀婚	银婚	yínhūn	N	[silver-marriage] silver anniversary
週年	周年	zhōunián	N	[period-year] anniversary
學費	学费	xuéfèi	N	[learn-fee] tuition
獎學金	奖学金	jiǎngxuéjīn	N	[award-learn-gold] scholarship
強化班		qiánghuàbān	N	[strong-ize-class] intensive course
商學院	商学院	shāngxuéyuàn	N	[business-learn-yard] business school
期末考		qīmòkǎo	N	[period-end-test] final examination
* 大考		dàkǎo	N	[big-test] final examination (=期末考)
水平		shuǐpíng	N	[water-level] level, standard
聽力	听力	tīnglì	N	[listen-strength] listening comprehension
旅館	旅馆	lǚguǎn	N	[travel-hall] hotel
東岸	东岸	dōng'àn	N	[east-coast] East Coast
西岸		xī'àn	N	[west-coast] West Coast
* 海岸		hǎi'àn	N	[sea-coast] coast
加拿大		Jiā'nādà	N	[add-take-big] Canada

Verbs/Stative Verbs/Adjectives

留		liú	V	to stay
收		shōu	V	to accept, to admit (to a study program), to collect (money, paper, tests, letters...)
* 計劃	计划	jìhuà	V/N	[calculate-plan] to plan, plan, project
希望		xīwàng	V/N	[hope-look] to hope, hope
強調	强调	qiángdiào	V	[strong-tone] to emphasize, to stress
繼續	继续	jì.xù	V	[continue-continue] to continue
進步	进步	jìnbù	V/N	[progress-step] to progress, progression, progress
聊(天)		liáo(tiān)	V(O)	[chat-weather] to chat
(耽)誤	(耽)误	(dān)wù	V	[delay-error] to delay
旅行		lǚxíng	V/N	[travel-walk] to travel, traveling

露營	露营	lùyíng	V/N	[dew-camp] to camp, camping
實習	实习	shíxí	V/N	[practical-learn] to have an internship, internship
畢業	毕业	bìyè	V/N	[finish-profession] to graduate, graduation
結婚	结婚	jiéhūn	V/N	[tie-marriage] to get married, marriage
* 離婚	离婚	líhūn	V/N	[depart-marriage] to divorce, divorce
* 訂婚	订婚	dìnghūn	V/N	[reserve-marriage] to engage/betroth, engagement, betrothal
賺(錢)	赚(钱)	zhuàn(qián)	V/VO	[earn-money] to make money, to earn money
* 掙(錢)	挣(钱)	zhèng(qián)	V/VO	[earn-money] to make money, to earn money (=賺錢)
省錢	省钱	shěngqián	SV/VO	[save-money] to save money
重要		zhòngyào	SV	[heavy-want] (to be) important
難得	难得	nándé	SV/Adv	[hard-obtain] (to be) hard to get, (to be) rare, once in a blue moon, rarely
有道理		yǒudào.lǐ	SV	[have-way-theory] (to be) logical
上不起		shàng.buqǐ	RV	[up-not-raise] not to be able to afford to go to school
* V不起		V.buqǐ	RV	[V-not-raise] not to be able to afford to V

Adverbs

本來	本来	běnlái	Adv	[origin-come] originally (=原來)
然後	然后	ránhòu	Adv	[still-back] then, afterwards, later (preceded by 先)
也許	也许	yěxǔ	Adv	[also-promise] perhaps

Idiomatic Expressions

一天到晚		yì tiān dào wǎn	IE	[one-day-to-evening] all day long (=整天)
對...有幫助	对...有帮助	duì...yǒu bāngzhù	IE	[to...have assistance] (to be) helpful to

✚ Supplementary Vocabulary

1. Odds and Ends

旅遊		lǚyóu	V/N	[travel-play] to take a tour, a tour
旅遊團	旅游团	lǚyóutuán	N	[travel-play-group] tour group
旅行團	旅行团	lǚxíngtuán	N	[travel-walk-group] tour group
導遊	导游	dǎoyóu	N	[lead-play] tour guide
翻譯	翻译	fānyì	V/N	[turn over-translate] to translate, translation
陪同		péitóng	V/N	[accompany-same] to interpret, interpreter

2. Regions

部		bù	N	part, section
東部	东部	dōngbu	N	[east-part] eastern part of
西部		xībù	N	[west-part] western part of
南部		nánbù	N	[south-part] southern part of
北部		běibù	N	[north-part] northern part of
東南部	东南部	dōngnánbù	N	[east-south-part] southeastern part of
東北部	东北部	dōngběibù	N	[east-north-part] northeastern part of
西北部		xīběibù	N	[west-north-part] northwestern part of
西南部		xī'nánbù	N	[west-south-part] southwestern part of
中西部		zhōngxībù	N	[middle-west-part] midwest part of

3. American States[1]

			Abbre.	
Alabama	阿拉巴馬州	Ālābāma zhōu		
Alaska	阿拉斯加州	Ālāsijiā zhōu		
Arizona	亞利桑那州	Yǎlìsāngnà zhōu		
Arkansas	阿肯色州	Ākěnsè zhōu		
California	加利福尼亞州	Jiālìfúníyǎ zhōu	加州	Jiā zhōu
Colorado	科羅拉多州	Kēluóláduō zhōu		
Connecticut	康涅狄格州	Kāngnièdígé zhōu	康州	Kāng zhōu
Delaware	特拉華州	Tèlāhuá zhōu		
Florida	佛羅里達州	Fóluólǐdá zhōu	佛州	Fó zhōu
Georgia	佐治亞州	Zuǒzhìyà zhōu		
Hawaii	夏威夷州	Xiàwēiyí zhōu		
Idaho	愛達荷州	Aìdáhé zhōu		
Illinois	伊利諾伊州	Yīlìnuòyī zhōu	伊州	Yī zhōu
Indiana	印第安納州	Yìndì'ānnà zhōu	印州	Yìn zhōu
Iowa	艾奧瓦州	Aìàowǎ zhōu		
Kansas	堪薩斯州	Kānsàsī zhōu	堪州	Kān zhōu

---

[1] The transliterations of foreign places are from *Waiguo Diming Yiming Shouce* (外國地名譯名手冊), Beijing, Shangwu Yinshuguan, 1993.

Kentucky	肯塔基州	Kěntǎjī zhōu		
Louisiana	路易西安那州	Lùyìxī'ānnà zhōu		
Maine	緬因州	Miǎnyīn zhōu		
Maryland	馬里蘭州	Mǎlǐlán zhōu		
Massachusetts	馬薩諸塞州	Mǎsàzhūsè zhōu	麻州	Má zhōu
Michigan	密歇根州	Mìxiēgēn zhōu		
Minnesota	明尼蘇打州	Míngnísūdǎ zhōu		
Mississippi	密西西比州	Mìxīxībǐ zhōu		
Missouri	密蘇里州	Mìsūlǐ zhōu	密州	Mì zhōu
Montana	蒙大拿州	Méngdàná zhōu		
Nebraska	内布拉斯加州	Nèibùlāsījiā zhōu		
Nevada	内華達州	Nèihuádá zhōu		
New Hampshire	新罕布什爾州	Xīnhǎnbùshí'ér zhōu		
New Jersey	新澤西州	Xīnzéxī zhōu	新州	Xīn zhōu
New Mexico	新墨西哥州	Xīnmòxīgē zhōu		
New York	紐約州	Niǔyuē zhōu		
North Carolina	北卡羅來納州	Běikǎluóláinà zhōu	北卡	Běikǎ
North Dakota	北達科他州	Běidákētā zhōu		
Ohio	俄亥俄州	Éhài'é zhōu	俄州	É zhōu
Oklahoma	俄克拉何馬州	Ékèlāhémǎ zhōu		
Oregon	俄勒岡州	Élègāng zhōu		
Pennsylvania	賓夕法尼亞州	Bīnxìfǎ'níyǎ zhōu	賓州	Bīn zhōu
Rhode Island	羅得島州	Luódédǎo zhōu		
South Carolina	南卡羅來納州	Nánkǎluóláinà zhōu	南卡	Nánkǎ
South Dakota	南達科他州	Nándákētā zhōu		
Texas	得克薩斯州	Dékèsàsī zhōu	德州	Dé zhōu
Tennessee	田納西州	Tiánnàxī zhōu		
Utah	猶他州	Yóutā zhōu		
Vermont	佛蒙特州	Fóméngtè zhōu		
Virginia	弗吉尼亞州	Fújí'níyǎ zhōu		
Washington	華盛頓州	Huáshèngdùn zhōu	華州	Dé zhōu
West Virginia	西弗吉尼亞州	Xīfújí'níyǎ zhōu		
Wisconsin	威斯康星州	Wēisīkāngxīng zhōu	威州	Wēi zhōu
Wyoming	懷俄明州	Huái'émíng zhōu		

4. American Cities

Atlanta	亞特蘭大	Yàtèlándà		
Bloomington	布盧明頓	Bùlúmíngdùn	布城	Bùchéng
Boston	波士頓	Bōshìdùn		
Champaign	尚佩恩	Shàngpèi'ēn	香檳	Xiāngbīn
Chicago	芝加哥	Zhījiāgē		
Cleveland	克利夫蘭	Kèlìfūlán		

Columbus	哥倫布	Gēlúnbù		
Denver	丹佛	Dānfó		
Detroit	底特律	Dǐtèlǜ		
Houston	休斯敦	Xiūsīdūn		
Indianapolis	印第安那波利斯	Dìdì'ānnàbōlìsī	印地	Dìdì
Las Vegas	拉斯韋加斯	Lāsīwéijiāsī		
Los Angeles	洛杉磯	Luòshānjī	羅省	Luóshěng
Miami	邁阿密	Mài'āmì		
New York	紐約	Niǔyuē		
Philadelphia	費拉德爾菲亞	Fèilādé'ěrfēiyà	費城	Fèichéng
Pittsburgh	匹茲堡	Pǐzībǎo		
San Francisco	舊金山／三藩市	Jiùjīnshān/Sānfānshì		
Seattle	西雅圖	Xīyǎtú		
Washington	華盛頓	Huáshèngdùn		

5. Canadian Cities

| Toronto | 多倫多 | Duōlúnduō |
| Vancouver | 溫哥華 | Wēngēhuá |

6. Chinese Cities

Aòmén (Macau)	澳門	澳门
Běijīng	北京	
Chéngdū	成都	
Chóngqìng	重慶	重庆
Guǎngzhōu (Canton)	廣州	广州
Guìlín	桂林	
Hángzhōu	杭州	
Hā'ěrbīn	哈爾濱	哈尔滨
Jǐnán	濟南	济南
Kūnmíng	昆明	
Nánjīng	南京	
Shànghǎi	上海	
Shěnyáng	瀋陽	瀋阳
Shēnzhèn	深圳	
Táiběi (Taipei)	臺北	台北
Tiānjīn	天津	
Ulǔmùqí (Urumqi)	烏魯木齊	乌鲁木齐
Wǔhàn	武漢	武汉
Xiàmén (Amoy)	廈門	厦门
Xī'ān	西安	
Xiānggǎng (Hong Kong)	香港	

Characters
漢字 Hànzì

附	本	報	告
語	言	週	未
休	息	暑	底
妹	留	旅	費
已	經	驗	算

附　　　　　　fù
near to, close to
阝
8　　(a mound)

附近　　　　fùjìn　　　　　　nearby

A: **這附近**有沒有好的中國飯館兒？
B: 沒有，連一家也沒有。

本　　　　　　běn
root; origin　木
5　　　(tree)

本來　　　　běnlái　　　　originally
一本書　　　yì běn shū　　book
*本子　　　　běn.zi　　　　notebook

A: 你暑假的時候打算做什麼？
B: 本來打算回家，現在不回去了。

報　　　　　　bào
newspaper　土
12　　　(soil)

報告　　　　bàogào　　　　report, paper
*報紙　　　　bàozhǐ　　　　newspaper
*中文報　　　Zhōngwénbào　Chinese newspaper

A: 你看得懂**中文報**嗎？
B: 我只學了一年的中文，怎麼看得懂？

告　　　　　　gào
to tell, report　口
7　　　(mouth)

告訴　　　　gào.sù　　　　to tell

A: 他沒有**告訴**我他今天不來上課。
B: 我以爲他說了。

繁簡對照：	其他漢字：	✎ **My notes:**
報报	*訴 SC76	

語

yǔ
language,
speech   言
14   (speech)

 語言   yǔyán   language
 *外語   wàiyǔ   foreign language

A: 你會說幾種**外語**？
B: 五種 。

言

yán
speech, words
              言
7   (speech)

A: 你要留在這兒上**暑期語言強化班**嗎？
B: 我還不能決定 。

週

zhōu
week, a period
              辶
12

週年   zhōunián   anniversary
週末   zhōumò   weekend
*一週   yì zhōu   one week

A: 你給誰買禮物呀？
B: 給我爸媽，他們結婚已經**二十週年**了。

末

mò
end, last, final
              木
5   (tree)

期末考   qīmòkǎo   final examination

A: 你**期末考**準備好了沒有 ？
B: 還沒有呢！要念的書太多了。

繁簡對照：	其他漢字：	✎ **My notes:**
語语 週周	話 L9	

休

xiū
to rest, to stop
亻
6　(person)

休息　　　xiū.xí　　　to rest

A: 你別催我，我得**休息一會兒**。
B: 你已經**休息半天**了。

息

xí
news, tidings
心
10　(heart)

*消息　　　xiāo.xí　　　news

A: 你中午**休息不休息**？
B: 我一定**休息**。睡個午覺，晚上才有精
　神念書。

暑

shǔ
summer　日
13　(sun)

暑假　　shǔjià　　summer vacation
暑期　　shǔqī　　summer
*暑校　　shǔxiào　　summer school

A: 你**暑假的時候**，要去哪兒玩兒？
B: 我要先去西部，再去西北部玩兒。

底

dǐ
underside, base,
bottom　广
8

月底　　yuèdǐ　　at the end of a month
*底下　　dǐxià　　bottom, below
*到底　　dàodǐ　　after all

A: 你**五月底**會留在這兒嗎？
B: 可能不會，我那時候應該畢業了。

繁簡對照：	其他漢字：	✎ **My notes:**
	*寒 SC77	

妹

*妹妹	mèi.mèi	younger sister
*姐妹	jiěmèi	sisters
*兄妹	xiōngmèi	sisters and brothers
表妹	biǎomèi	a daughter of father's sister or mother's sibling (younger than oneself)

mèi
younger sister
　　女
8　　(female)

A: 你有幾個**妹妹**？
B: 我沒有**妹妹**，有兩個姐姐。

留

| *留學 | liúxué | to study abroad |
| *留學生 | liúxué.shēng | overseas student |

liú
to leave behind,
to keep　　田
10　　(field)

A: 你今年暑假打算做什麼？
B: 我打算去中國**留學**。

旅

旅行	lǚxíng	to travel
旅館	lǚguǎn	hotel
*旅客	lǚkè	traveler, passenger

lǚ
to travel　　方
10　　(square)

A: 你看我們**住旅館**怎麼樣？
B: 可以呀！我們的錢夠不夠？

費

學費	xuéfèi	tuition
*水費	shuǐfèi	water bill
*電費	diànfèi	electric bill
*電話費	diànhuàfèi	phone bill

fèi
expense, fee 貝
12　　(shell)

A: 那所學校好是好，可是**學費**太貴了。
B: 你可以利用暑假的時候**掙學費**。

繁簡對照：	其他漢字：	✎ **My notes:**
費 费	*父 SC78 *母 SC79 *親 SC80	

已

yǐ
to stop, to come
to an end　己
3　　　(self)

經

jīng
to pass through
or by　　糸
13

驗

yàn
to test, analyze
　　　　馬
23　　(horse)

算

suàn
to be considered
as, to count　竹
14　　(bamboo)

已經　　　　　yǐ.jīng　　　　　　already

A: 他能不能喝酒？
B: 可以，他**已經**十八歲了。

*經過　　　　　jīngguò　　　　　to pass by

A: 你想去西岸旅行嗎？
B: 我**已經**去過了。

經驗　　　　　jīngyàn　　　　　experience
*實驗　　　　　shíyàn　　　　　lab, experiment

A: 那位老師教得好不好？
B: 很好，她**很有經驗**。

打算　　　　　dǎsuàn　　　　　to plan, plan
*不算　　　　　búsuàn　　　　　not to consider

A: 你明年**打算**學中文嗎？
B: 當然，我的專業是中文，得一直學下
　　去。

繁簡對照：	其他漢字：	✎ **My notes:**
經 经 驗 验		

Grammar
語法 yǔfǎ

Ⓐ Major Sentence Patterns 主要句型 zhǔyào jùxíng

1. 先...然後... construction

Structure	Gloss
S 先 (AuxV) V₁O₁，然後(再/又/還)V₂ O₂ S (AuxV) 先 V₁O₁，然後(再/又/還)V₂ O₂	S (AuxV) V₁ O₁ first, (and) then V₂ O₂

1. 你要先回家，然後要到哪兒去？

    Nǐ yào xiān huíjiā, ránhòu yào dào nǎr qù?
    You will go home first, then where are you going?

    我要先回家，然後要到臺灣去。

    Wǒ yào xiān huíjiā, ránhòu yào dào Táiwān qù.
    I'll go home first, then I'll go to Taiwan.

2. 你畢業以後要做什麼？

    Nǐ bìyè yǐhòu yào zuò shén.me?
    What will you do after your graduation?

    畢業以後我先要工作一兩年，然後再申請商學院的研究所。

    Bìyè yǐhòu wǒ xiān yào gōngzuò yì liǎng nián, ránhòu zài shēnqǐng shāngxuéyuàn .de yánjiūsuǒ.
    After my graduation I would like to work for a couple years and then apply for the graduate school of business.

💡 然後 is a conjunction that occurs in the second clause of a complex sentence in which the first clause includes an adverb 先, as in example 1. 然後 may be followed by adverbs 再/又/還, as in example 2.

🔄 See L7–A5 and L9–A5 for more on actions in sequence.

2. More on 才 and 就

2.1 才 as "not until"

Structure	Gloss
S Time Expression 才 VO	S will not VO until Time Expression (the action won't be done/occur until later time)

1. 你今年要畢業嗎？

    Nǐ jīn.nián yào bìyè .ma?
    Will you graduate this year?

不，我明年才能畢業。

Bù, wǒ míng.nián cái néng bìyè.
No, I won't be able to graduate until next year.

2. 他父親這個月要到美國來嗎？

Tā fù.qīn zhèi .ge yuè yào dào Měi.guó lái .ma?
Is his father coming to America this month?

不，他下個月才來。

Bù, tā xià .ge yuè cái lái.
No, he won't come until next month.

才 is an adverb. In this pattern, when there is a time expression preceding 才, then 才 denotes that the action following it will occur later than expected. **Note:** In this pattern 才 *cannot* occur with the verb 有.

2.2 才 as "only"

Structure	Gloss
S Time Expression 才 No. M	S will be only No. M on Time Expression (the number is lesser/smaller than expected)

1. 你弟弟今年幾歲了？

Nǐ dì.dì jīn.nián jǐ suì .le?
How old is your younger brother now (this year)?

我弟弟今年四月才七歲。

Wǒ dì.dì jīn.nián sìyuè cái qī suì.
My younger brother is only seven years old this April.

2. 小李來美國幾年了？

Xiǎo Lǐ lái Měi.guó jǐ nián .le?
How long has Xiao Li been in America?

小李今年八月來美國才兩年。

Xiǎo Lǐ jīn.nián bāyuè lái Měi.guó cái liǎng nián.
Xiao Li will have been in America for only two years this August.

In this pattern, when there is a time expression preceding 才, 才 denotes that the number following it is lesser/smaller than expected. **Note:** The expression 才 No. M *cannot* be followed by 了.

See L9–A5, L17–A3 for more on 才.

2.3 就 as "on/in time"

Structure	Gloss
S Time Expression 就 VO 了	S has done VO on/in Time Expression (the action has already been done/occurred sooner than the expected time)

1. 你什麼時候考期末考？

   Nǐ shén.me shí.hòu kǎo qīmòkǎo?
   When will you have the final exam?

   我上個星期五就考完了。

   Wǒ shàng .ge xīngqīwǔ jiù kǎowán .le.
   I already had my final exam last Friday.

2. 小林的媽媽是不是六月要回臺灣去啊？

   Xiǎo Lín .de mā.mā shì .bu.shì liùyuè yào huí Táiwān qù .a?
   Is Xiao Lin's mother going back to Taiwan in June?

   小林的媽媽五月就回臺灣去了。

   Xiǎo Lín .de mā.mā wǔyuè jiù huí Táiwān qù .le.
   Xiao Lin's mother has already gone back to Taiwan (in May).

3. 你們是不是六月開始放暑假啊？

   Nǐ.men shì .bu.shì liùyuè kāishǐ fàng shǔjià .a?
   Do you start summer vacation in June?

   我們五月中就開始放暑假了。

   Wǒ.men wǔyuè zhōng jiù kāishǐ fàng shǔjià .le.
   We already started summer vacation in the middle of May.

4. 你們學了"把"字句没有？

   Nǐ.men xué .le "bǎ" zì jù méi.yǒu?
   Have you learned the "Ba-construction" yet?

   "把"字句我們上個月就學過了。

   "Bǎ" zì jù wǒ.men shàng .ge yuè jiù xué.guò .le.
   We have already learned the "ba-construction" (last month).

 就 is also an adverb. In this pattern, when there is a time expression preceding it, then 就 denotes that the action following it occurred sooner than expected.

2.4 就 as "on/in time"

Structure	Gloss
S Time Expression 就 No. M (N) 了	S was already No. M on/in Time Expression (the number is greater/larger than expected)

1. 你學中文已經學了幾年了？

    Nǐ xué Zhōngwén yǐng.jīng xué .le jǐ nián .le?
    How many years have you studied Chinese?

  今年六月就五年了。

    Jīn.nián liùyuè jiù wǔ nián .le.
    (It) will be five years this June.

2. 他的兒子今年幾歲了？

    Tā .de ér.zi jīn.nián jǐ suì .le?
    How old is his son (this year)?

  他的兒子今年就三十歲了。

    Tā .de ér.zi jīn.nián jiù sānshí suì .le.
    His son will be thirty years old this year.

In this pattern, when there is a time expression preceding 就, then 就 denotes that the number is greater/larger than expected. **Note:** The expression 就 No. M (N) is always followed by 了.

See L7–A4 for more on 就.

B Usage of Common Phrases 詞組用法 cízǔ yòngfǎ

1. The Chinese concept of location

Structure	Gloss
Whole 》 Part	
X 東部	the eastern part of X
X 西部	the western part of X
X 南部	the southern part of X
X 北部	the northern part of X
X 東南部	the southeastern part of X
X 東北部	the northeastern part of X
X 西北部	the northwestern part of X
X 西南部	the southwestern part of X
X 中西部	the midwestern part of X

1. 你去過美國的哪些地方？

    Nǐ qù.guò Měi.guó .de nǎ xiē dì.fāng?
    Where have you been in America?

我 去過美國的東南部跟西南部。   Wǒ qù.guò Měi.guó .de dōngnánbù gēn xī'nánbù.

I have been in the southeastern and southwestern parts of America.

2. 你們學校的學生是從什麼地方來 的？   Nǐ.men xuéxiào .de xué.shēng shì cóng shén.me dì.fāng lái .de?

Where did the students at your school come from?

有的是從西南部來的，有的是 從東北部來的，大部分是從中西 部來的。   Yǒu.de shì cóng xī'nánbù lái .de, yǒu.de shì cóng dōngběibù lái .de, dàbùfèn shì cóng zhōngxībù lái .de.

Some are from the southwestern part, some are from the northeastern part, (and) most of them are from the Midwest.

💡 For directions, Chinese uses "east" 東 and "west" 西 as initial points of reference, while English uses "north" and "south." For example, in Chinese you say 東北 dōngběi '[east-north],' whereas in English you say "northeast." The concept of location follows the From Whole to Part Principle. When one refers to a certain location of X, X as a whole is used as a reference point, whereas any part of X must follow X.

🔄 See L4–A1, L15–A3 for more on the From Whole to Part Principle.

2. VO 對 X 有幫助

Structure	Gloss
VO 對 X (很) 有幫助	Ving O is (very) helpful to X

1. 會說中文對找工作有幫助嗎？   Huì shuō Zhōngwén duì zhǎo gōngzuò yǒu bāngzhù .ma?

Will knowing how to speak Chinese be helpful in looking for a job?

對了，會說中文對找工作很有 幫助。   Duì.le, huì shuō Zhōngwén duì zhǎo gōngzuò hěn yǒu bāngzhù.

Yes, knowing how to speak Chinese will be very helpful in looking for a job.

2. 做運動對身體有幫助嗎？   Zuò yùndòng duì shēntǐ yǒu bāngzhù .ma?

Will exercise be helpful for (one's) health?

對了，做運動對身體有幫助。   Duì.le, zuò yùndòng duì shēntǐ yǒu bāngzhù.

Yes, doing exercise is very helpful for (one's) health.

3. 聽錄音帶對學中文有幫助嗎？

Tīng lùyīndài duì xué Zhōngwén yǒu bāngzhù .ma?
Will listening to the tapes be helpful in learning Chinese?

對了，聽錄音帶對學中文有幫助。

Duì.le, tīng lùyīndài duì xué Zhōngwén yǒu bāngzhù.
Yes, listening to the tapes is very helpful in learning Chinese.

See L10–B2, L16–A1, L17–A4, L18–A2, L20–B4 for more on A 對 B.

3. The complement 不得了

Structure	Gloss
不得了！S V O 了	Good Heavens! S did...!

1. 怎麼了？

Zěn.me .le?
What happened?

不得了！他的車出事兒了。

Bùdéliǎo! Tā .de chē chūshìr .le.
Good heavens! His car was in an accident!

2. 怎麼了？

Zěn.me .le?
What happened?

不得了！他發高燒了！

Bùdéliǎo! Tā fā gāoshāo .le!
Good heavens! He has a high fever!

不得了 bùdéliǎo is an idiom that means "Good heavens! It's serious!" It can occur alone at the beginning of a sentence and functions as an exclamation to indicate something serious has happened, as in examples1 and 2.

Structure	Gloss
S SV 得不得了	S is extremely/awfully Adj

3. 你最近怎麼樣？

Nǐ zuìjìn zěn.meyàng?
How have you been lately?

我最近忙得不得了。

Wǒ zuìjìn máng .de bùdéliǎo.
I have been extremely busy lately.

4. 你的胃怎麼樣了？

Nǐ .de wèi zěn.meyàng .le?
How is your stomach?

我的胃疼得不得了。

Wǒ .de wèi téng .de bùdéliǎo.
My stomach is extremely painful.

不得了 bùdéliǎo also means "extremely, awfully" and can be attached to the intransitive verb + 得 as a verb complement to indicate an extreme/awful situation, as in examples 3 and 4.

4. The successive aspect 下去

Structure	Gloss
O...V 下去	to continue Ving O
O...V 不下去	cannot continue Ving O

1. 這本小說你們還要念下去嗎？

Zhèi běn xiǎoshuō nǐ.men hái yào niàn.xià.qù .ma?
Do you still want to continue reading this novel?

那本小說很有意思，我們還要念下去。

Nèi běn xiǎoshuō hěn yǒuyì.si, wǒ.men hái yào niàn.xià.qù.
That novel is very interesting; we would like to continue reading (it).

那本小說太沒意思了，我們念不下去。

Nèi běn xiǎoshuō tài méi yì.si .le, wǒ.men niànbu.xià.qù.
That novel is very interesting; we would like to continue reading (it).

2. 這卷錄音帶你們還要聽下去嗎？

Zhèi juǎn lùyīndài nǐ.men hái yào tīng.xià.qù .ma?
Do you still want to continue listening to this tape?

那卷錄音帶太長了，我們不想聽下去了。

Nèi juǎn lùyīndài tài cháng .le, wǒ.men bù xiǎng tīng.xià.qù .le.
That tape is too long; we don't want to continue listening to (it) any more.

下去 denotes the successive aspect, which is suffixed to a verb to indicate that the action/situation will go on. It is different from the directional complement, as in 他從樓上走下去 Tā cóng lóushàng zǒu xiàqù 'He came down from upstairs.'

See L15–A2 for more on directional complements.

ⓒReentry 複習 fùxí

1. The differences between 的、地、得

1.1 的 as a possessive marker

Structure	Gloss
N₁/Pron 的 N	N₁'s N

1. 那位是商學院的教授嗎？

    Nèi wèi shì shāngxuéyuàn .de jiàoshòu .ma?
    Is that a professor in the business shcool?

    對，他是商學院的教授。

    Duì, tā shì shāngxuéyuàn .de jiàoshòu.
    Yes, he is a professor in the business shcool.

2. 這是你的車嗎？

    Zhèi shì nǐ .de chē .ma?
    Is this your car?

    不，那是小高的車。

    Bù, nà shì Xiao Gao .de chē.
    No, that is Xiao Gao's car.

的、地、得 are all pronounced as ".de" in modern Mandarin, but the function of each character is different. In this pattern, 的 serves as a possessive marker.

1.2 的 as a subordinate/modifier marker

Structure	Gloss
(S) V 的 N	The N that (S) V
(Adv) Adj 的 N	(Adv) Adj N

1. 你寫的報告交了沒有？

    Nǐ xiě .de bàogào jiāo .le méi.you?
    Have you turned in the paper that you wrote yet?

    我寫的報告昨天就交了。

    Wǒ xiě .de bàogào zuó.tiān jiù jiāo .le.
    I already turned in the paper that I wrote yesterday.

2. 他告訴你什麼？

    Tā gào.sù nǐ shén.me?
    What did he tell you?

    他告訴我一件非常重要的事情。

    Tā gào.sù wǒ yí jiàn fēicháng zhòngyào .de shì.qíng.
    He told me an unusally important mattter.

In this pattern, 的 serves as a subordinate marker (see example 1) or as a modifier (see example 2). **Note:** When 的 serves as possessive marker, subordinate marker, or modifier, the unit that follows it is always a noun.

1.3 的 as a nominalizer

Structure	Gloss
Adj 的 (N)	The Adj one
V 的 (N)	The one (that X) did V

1. 你喜歡大的還是小的？

    Nǐ xǐ.huān dà.de hái.shì xiǎo.de?
    Do you like the big one or the small one?

    我喜歡大的，不喜歡小的。

    Wǒ xǐ.huān dà.de, bù xǐ.huān xiǎo.de.
    I like the big one; (I) don't like the small one.

2. 這是你自己做的還是買的？

    Zhè shì nǐ zìjǐ zuò.de hái.shì mǎi.de?
    Is this made by you or (is this) the one you bought?

    這是我自己做的，不是買的。

    Zhè shì wǒ zìjǐ zuò.de, bú.shì mǎi.de.
    I made this myself; (it) is not the one that (I) bought.

 In this pattern, 的 serves as a nominalizer which indicates that the noun that follows the 的 is omitted. **Note:** The omitted noun must be a generic noun, such as 人 'person' or 東西 'thing.'

1.4 地 as an adverbial marker

Structure	Gloss
Adj Adj 地 V/Adj	Adj-ly

1. 考完試以後，你想做什麼？

    Kǎowánshì yǐhòu, nǐ xiǎng zuò shén.me?
    What do you want to do after the exam?

    考完試以後，我要好好兒地休息一下。

    Kǎowánshì yǐhòu, wǒ yào hǎohāor.de xiū.xí.yíxià.
    After the exam I am going to take a good rest.

2. 下了雪以後，你們開車得怎麼樣？

    Xià.le xuě yǐhòu, nǐ.men kāichē děi zěn.meyàng?

How should you drive on snow?

下了雪以後，路很滑，我們得 很小心地開。

Xià .le xuě yǐhòu, lù hěn huá, wǒ.men děi hěn xiǎo.xīn.de kāi.
When it has been snowing, the roads are very slippery. We should drive very carefully.

💡 In this pattern, 地 serves as an adverbial marker; it always precedes a verb or an adjective.

🔄 See L18–B1 for more on 地.

1.5 得 as a complement marker

Structure
V 得 Comp

1. 你中文學得怎麼樣？

Nǐ Zhōngwén xué.de zěn.meyàng?
How well are you learning Chinese?

說得還不錯，可是寫得不太好。

Shuō.de hái búcuò, kě.shì xiě.de bútài hǎo.
Speaking is pretty good, but writing is not very good.

2. 你快要畢業了，工作找得怎麼 樣？

Nǐ kuàiyào bìyè .le, gōngzuò zhǎo.de zěn.meyàng?
You are graduating soon; how is your job hunting (coming along)?

我學了中文，應該找得到工作。

Wǒ xué .le Zhōngwén, yīnggāi zhǎo.dedào gōngzuò.
I have learned Chinese. (I) should be able to find a job.

3. 他最近怎麼樣？

Tā zuìjìn zěn.meyàng?
How is he (lately)?

他最近忙得連吃飯的時間都沒 有！

Tā zuìjìn máng .de lián chīfàn .de shíjiān dōu méi.yǒu!
Lately he has been so busy that (he) doesn't even have time to eat!

4. 他三天沒睡覺，眼睛怎麼了？

Tā sān tiān méi shuìjiào, yǎn.jīng zěn.me .le?
He has not slept for three days. What happens to his eyes?

他的眼睛紅得像一隻兔子。   Tā .de yǎn.jīng hóng .de xiàng yì zhī
                                    tù.zi.
                                    His eyes are as red as a rabbit's.

得 is an infix that is placed between the verb and its complement. It serves as a complement marker for resultative verb compounds, verbs with descriptive complements, manner/degree complements, and extent complements.

See L7–A6, L9–A6, L10–A1, L11–A3, L14–A6, L15–A2, L18–A4 for more on 得 as a complement marker.

Cultural Notes
文化點滴 wénhuà diǎndī

1. Traditionally, Chinese people view a marriage as 終身大事 zhōngshēn dàshì "a great event affecting one's whole life" and a woman is supposed to follow the rule 從一而終 cóng yī ér zhōng "to be faithful to one's husband all her life (even after she is divorced or in widowhood)." Even with Westernization, it is still very difficult for a woman to get a divorce or to remarry in rural areas of Taiwan and China.

2. As we have mentioned before, Chinese pay great respect to their teachers. The accomplishments of students are generally accredited to their teachers. Therefore graduation is always the time for students to show their gratitude to their teachers. In Taiwan, many schools still hold the tradition that graduating students sponsor a 謝師宴 xièshīyàn 'dinner party given by graduating students in honor of their teachers.'

3. Owing to the keen competition on entrance examinations at high schools and colleges, middle school and high school students in Taiwan and China usually cannot enjoy any vacations at all. During winter or summer breaks, they have to go to school for 課外補習 kèwài bǔxí 'extra tutoring.' Teachers usually assign a lot of 寒假作業 hánjià zuòyè 'winter vacation homework' or 暑假作業 shǔjià zuòyè 'summer vacation homework' to students, or give them different 摹擬考試 mónǐ kǎoshì 'model examinations' to help them prepare for the competitions.

Appendixes

Appendix 1. Review of Lessons 14-18

Check ☑ the box in front of the sentence patterns and usages that you have forgotten or do not understand. Review them with your teachers and classmates.

A. Indicating Action

☐ 1. With 把 construction (L15, L16)

S (沒/不/別)　把 O V complement	S (doesn't/didn't) do... to O
S (AuxV/Neg) 把　O 給 V complement 了	S (AuxV/Neg) do/did... to O

☐ 2. With resultative verb compounds (L18)

Actual form	V　RE	do V
Positive potential form	V得RE	be able to V
Negative potential form	V不RE	not be able to V

☐ 3. With the verb 給 (L14)

main verb	S (沒/不) 給 O$_i$　O$_d$	S give O$_i$ O$_d$
preposition — indirect object marker	S (沒/不) V O$_d$　給 O$_i$	S VO to　O$_i$
co-verb/preposition — beneficial marker	S (沒/不)　給 O$_i$ V O$_d$.	S VO$_d$ for O$_i$

☐ 4. With A 給 B 寄 O 來/去 (L18)

A (Neg) 給 B 寄 O來/去	A (Neg) sends O to B (here/there)
A (Neg) 給 B 寄 來/去　O	

☐ 5. With the co-verb 跟 (L14)

A (Aux V)　　跟 B　VO	A (Aux V) VO with B
A (不/沒/別) 跟 B　VO	A (not)　　VO with B

☐ 6. With the causative markers 害、弄 (L17)

S 害 (得) O V...	S causes/caused O to V...
S 弄 (得) O V...	S makes/made O to V...

☐ 7. With A 對 B 有影響 / B 受 A 的影響 (L16)

A 對 B 有影響	A has influence on B
A 對 B 有很大的影響	A has great influence on B
A 對 B 的影響很大	A has great influence on B
A 對 B 沒 (有) 影響	A has no influence on B
A 對 B 一點兒影響 都/也 沒有	A has no influence on B at all
B 受 A 的影響	B is/has been influenced by A
B 沒/不會 受 A 的影響	B was not/won't be influenced by A

☐ 8. With A 對 B 有意思 / 有興趣 (L17)

A 對 B (person)(Adv) 有意思	A is (Adv) interested in B
A 對 B (person) 沒有意思	A is not interested in B
A 對 B (person) 一點兒意思 都/也沒有	A has no interest in B at all
A 對 B (thing) (Adv) 有興趣	A is (Adv) interested in B
A 對 B (thing) 沒有興趣	A is not interested in B
A 對 B (thing) 一點兒 興趣 都/也沒有	A has no interest in B at all

☐ 9. With A 對 B 有研究 (L18)

A 對 B 有研究	A has done research/study on B
A 對 B 沒有研究	A hasn't done research/study on B
A 對 B 一點兒研究 都/也 沒有	A hasn't done any research/study on B at all
A 對 B 沒什麼研究	A hasn't done much research/study on B

B. *Expressing Movement*

☐ 10. Through verbs with directional complements (L15)

搬 bān	來 /去	to move here/there
拿 ná	來 /去	to bring over here/there
走 zǒu	來 /去	to walk over here/there
跑 pǎo	來 /去	to run over here/there
上 shàng	來 /去	to go up here/there
下 xià	來 /去	to go down here/there
進 jìn	來 /去	to enter here/there
搬 bān	進來 /進去	to move over here/there
放 fàng	進來 /進去	to put over here/there
拿 ná	進來 /進去	to bring...in/out
拿 ná	上去/ 下來	to bring...up/down
走 zǒu	進來 /進去	to walk into/out
跑 pǎo	進來 /進去	to run into/out
穿 chuān	上去	to wear, to put on (clothes)
脫 tuō	下來	to take (clothes) off
戴 dài	上去	to put (jewelry, hat, glasses) on
拿 ná	下來	to take (jewelry, hat, glasses) off
寫 xiě	下來	to write/take (notes) down
記 jì	下來	to write/record...down

☐ 11. Through resultative verbs with directional complements (L15)

Actual form	回來/ 回去	huí.lái/ huí.qù	to come/go back
	進來/ 進去	jìn.lái/ jìn.qù	to come/go in
	上來/ 上去	shàng.lái/ shàng.qù	to come/go up
Positive potential form	回得來/ 回得去	huí.delái/ huí.dequ	can come/go back
	進得來/ 進得去	jìn.delái/ jìn.dequ	can come/go in
	上得來/ 上得去	shàng.delái/ shàng.dequ	can come/go up
Negative potential form	回不來/ 回不去	huí.bulái/ huí.buqù	cannot come/go back
	進不來/ 進不去	jìn.bulái/ jìn.buqù	cannot come/go in
	上不來/ 上不去	shàng.bulái/ shàng.buqù	cannot come/go up

❑ 12. With 往 X V expression (L16)

往 X V	V toward X
往 東 走	walk toward the east
往 西 拐	turn to the west
往 南 轉	turn to the south
往 北 看	look to the north
往 右 滑	ski/slide to the right
往 左 跑	run toward the left
往 上 爬	climb upward/toward the top
往 下 走	walk downward/toward the bottom
往 前 開	drive forward
往 後 退	withdraw backward

C. Expressing Time

❑ 13. With durative time expressions (L14)

S (VO) V 了 Time-Spent (了)	S did (has done) VO for Time-Spent
S V 了/過 Time-Spent (的) O	S did/has done VO for Time-Spent
S (AuxV) V Time-Spent (的) O	S (will/shall) VO for Time-Spent
S Time-Spent 沒/不 V O	S won't/didn't VO for Time-Spent

❑ 14. With 一 ...就... construction (L14)

S 一 V₁O₁ ,(S) 就 V₂ O₂...	As soon as S V₁O₁ ,(S) V₂ O₂...

D. Indicating Location

❑ 15. With the post-verbal preposition 在 (L14)

S (不)(要/想/喜歡) V₁ 在 Place (V₂O₂)	S (AuxV) V₁ at Place (V₂ O₂)

❑ 16. With place words (L15)

X 旁邊兒	side of X/next to X
X 左邊兒	left side of X/to the left of X
X 右邊兒	right side of X/to the right of X
X 前邊兒/前頭兒	front side of X/in front of X
X 後邊兒/後頭兒	back side of X/behind X
X 上 (邊兒)/上 (頭兒)	upper side of X/on top of X
X 下 (邊兒)/下 (頭兒)	lower side of X/underneath of X

E. Expressing Opinions/Comments/Commands

☐ 17. Using verbs with extent complements (L14)

S(VO) V 得 怎麼樣？ S(VO) V 得 Comp	After Ving O, what happened to S? After Ving O, S was so... that...

☐ 18. With the particle ... 的話 (L15)

(如果/要是) S V (O) 的話	If S V (O)

☐ 19. With the particle 吧 (L15)

S ... 吧？	S ... , I suppose/I guess

☐ 20. With the adverbial phrase 快/慢一點兒 (L17)

快/慢 一點兒！	Hurry up!/Slow down!
快/慢 一點兒 V!	V a little faster/slower!
(VO) V 快/慢 一點兒	does (O) a little faster/slower

☐ 21. With 又 ... 又 ... construction (L16)

S 又 SV$_1$　　又 SV$_2$	S is both Adj$_1$ and Adj$_2$
S 又 (AuxV) VP$_1$ 又 (AuxV) VP$_2$	S (AuxV) does both VP$_1$ and VP$_2$

☐ 22. With 為什麼 and 因為 ..., 所以 ...(L17)

S 為什麼 (AuxV/Neg) V O (呢)？ 　(MA)	Why is it that S (not) V O?
因為 S..., 所以 (S)... (MA)	Because S..., therefore S...

F. Expressing Emphasis

☐ 23. With 可..., 要不然... construction (L17)

S 可(不/別) VO , 要不然 (S)...	S by all/no means do VO; otherwise (S) will...

❏ 24. With the conditional usage of 才 (L17)

S ..., (S) 才 VO	Only if S... then (S) will VO

❏ 25. With question words (L14)

S 哪兒/什麼地方　　都　　　　　去過了	S has been everywhere
S 哪兒/什麼地方　　都/也 不/沒去	S doesn't/didn't go anywhere
S 什麼 N　　　　　都 Aux V　　V	S AuxV V everything
S 什麼 N　　　　　都　　　　　V過了	S has V-ed everything
S 什麼 (N)　　　　都/也 不/沒 V	S doesn't/didn't V O (at all)

❏ 26. With什麼都..., 就是... construction (L17)

S 什麼(N) 都... 就是...	S can do everything (Adv) except ...

❏ 27. With 連...都...construction (L18)

連 S　　　　　　都 V (了)	Even S...
S 連 O (generic N) 都 V (了)	S even V....
S 連一 M N 都/也 不/沒 V	S doesn't even V...

❏ 28. With vivid reduplicates (L18)

A Ā 兒地

❏ 29. With the usage of SV 得很 (L16)

S SV 得很	S is very Adj

G. Others

❏ 30. 知道 vs. 認識 (L15)

S₁ 知道　　[S₂　(Neg)　V　　　O]	S₁ knows (that)...
S₁ 不知道 [S₂　　V-not-V　　O]	S₁ doesn't know [(if)...]
S₁ 不知道 [QW Question] 　　　　　(information/fact/matter)	S₁ doesn't know [QW Question]
S (不) 認識　　　O 　　　　　(person/character/word)	S (doesn't) know (the person) S (doesn't) recognize/comprehend (the character/word)

❑ 31. The usage of 幫(忙) (L16)

A (AuxV)　幫　B　VO	A helps B to VO
A (AuxV)　來/去幫忙	A (AuxV) come/go to help
A (AuxV)　幫　B　的忙	A helps B out

❑ 32. The usage of 夠 (L16)

S 夠了	S is enough
S (不)夠	S is not enough
X 夠 Adj 了	X is Adj enough
夠 No. M N V 了	to have enough amount/space for No. of N to V

Review of Lessons 19-23

Check ☑ the box in front of the sentence patterns and usages that you have forgotten or do not understand. Review them with your teachers and classmates.

A. Indicating Actions

☐ 1. In passive voice (L22)

A 被 B V 了	A was ... by B

☐ 2. In progress (L21)

S 正 V₁/Aux V V₂ O 呢	S is in the midst of Ving to V₂ O

☐ 3. In sequence (L23)

S 先 (Aux V) V₁O₁，然後 V₂ O₂ S (Aux V) 先 V₁ O₁，然後 V₂ O₂	S (AuxV) V₁ O₁ first, (and) then V₂ O₂

☐ 4. Continued (L23)

O...V 下去	to continue Ving O
O...V 不下去	cannot continue Ving O

☐ 5. Occurring at the same time (L22)

S 一邊兒 V₁O₁，一邊兒 V₂O₂	While one is Ving O₁, he/she is Ving O₂

☐ 6. Has never occurred (L22)

S 從來(都)不 VO	S never V O
S 從來(都)沒 V 過 O	S has never V-ed O

☐ 7. Done with someone (L19)

A (Aux V) 跟 B VO	A (Aux V) VO with B
A (不/沒/別) 跟 B VO	A (not) VO with B

☐ 8. Done with something (L21)

S 用 X　V O (instrument)	S V O with/by X

☐ 9. With the co-verb/verb 帶 (L21)

S (Neg) (AuxV) 帶 O A(Neg) (AuxV) 帶 B 到 Place 去/來 VO S (Neg) (AuxV) 帶 O 到 Place 去/來 V(O)	S (AuxV) (Neg) brings O A (AuxV) (Neg) brings B along to Place to VO S (AuxV) (Neg) brings O to Place to V
S (Neg) (AuxV) 帶孩子 S (Neg) (AuxV) 帶路	S (AuxV) (Neg) takes care of a child S (AuxV) (Neg) leads the way

☐ 10. With the co-verb/verb 替 (L21)

A (Neg) (AuxV) 替 B VO	A (AuxV) (Neg) in place of B to VO
A (Neg) (AuxV) 替 B VO	A (AuxV) (Neg) VO for B

☐ 11. With the verb 借 (L22)

A (Neg) (AuxV) 跟 B 借 X	A (AuxV) (Neg) borrows X from B
A (Neg) (AuxV) 借 X 給 B A (Neg) (AuxV) 借 給 B X	A (AuxV) (Neg) lends X to B
A (Neg) (AuxV) 把 X 借 給 B	A (AuxV) (Neg) lends X to B

☐ 12. With the co-verb 給 (L20)

A 給 B 打針　　A gěi B dǎzhēn	A gives B a shot
A 給 B 點眼藥　A gěi B diǎn yǎnyào	A applies eyedrops for B
A 給 B 量血壓　A gěi B liáng xuěyā	A checks B's blood pressure
A 給 B 看病　　A gěi B kànbìng	A examines B
A 給 B 開藥方　A gei B kāi yàofāng	A writes a prescription for B

☐ 13. With 打噴嚏 (L20)

S (一直) 打噴嚏　　S (yìzhí) dǎ pēntì	S keeps sneezing
S 打了 (#聲) 噴嚏　S dǎ.le (# shēng) pēntì	S has sneezed no. of times

☐ 14. With 約 (L20)

A (想/要) 約 B Time Exp. (在 Place) VO	A (would/will make) made an appointment with B to VO at Time Exp. (at Place)
A 跟 B 約好 Time Exp. (在 Place) VO	A made an appointment with B to VO at Time Exp. (at Place)

☐ 15. With A 對 B 過敏 (L20)

A 對 B 過敏	A is allergic to B

B. Expressing Comparison

☐ 16. Of two events (L19)

V_1O_1 比　　V_2O_2　還/更　　　　Adj V_1O_1 沒(有)V_2O_2 (那麼/這麼) Adj	To do V_1O_1 is even Adj-er than V_2O_2 To do V_1O_1 is not as Adj as V_2O_2

☐ 17. Of two performances (L19)

A VO V得 比 B (更/還) Adj O, A　V得 比 B (更/還) Adj	A VO　Adj-er than B As for O, A　V Adj-er than B
A VO V得 沒(有) B (那麼/這麼) Adj O, A　V得 沒(有) B (那麼/這麼) Adj	A doesn't VO as Adj as B As for O, A doesn't V as Adj as B
A VO V得跟　 B 一樣　Adj A VO V得不跟 B 一樣　Adj A VO V得跟 B 不一樣　Adj	A VO as Adj as B does A doesn't VO equally Adj with B A and B do not VO equally Adj
O, A　V得跟　　B 一樣　Adj O, A　V得不跟 B 一樣　Adj O,　A　V得跟　B不一樣　Adj	As for O, A doesn't VO equally Adj with B As for O, A V as Adj as B does As for O, A and B do not V equally Adj

☐ 18. With A 不如 B... construction (L19)

A 不如 B SV	A is not as Adj as B
V_1O_1 不如　V_2O_2	To do V_1O_1 is not as good as to do V_2O_2. It is better to do V_1O_1 than to do V_2O_2.
一 M 不如 一 M	(It's) getting ...er M by M

C. Expressing Distance

□ 19. With 遠/近 (L21)

A 離 B 遠不遠？	Is A far from B?
A 離 B 近不近？	Is A close to B?
A 離 B 很 遠/近	A is very far from/close to B
A 離 B Adv 遠/近	A is Adv far from/close to B
A 離 B 不(太)遠/近	A is not (very) far from/close to B
A 離 B 遠 嗎？	Is A far from B?
A 離 B 遠/近 得很	A is very far from/close to B
A 離 B 遠/近 極了	A is extremely far from/close to B

□ 20. With no. 哩路 (L21)

A 離 B 有 多遠？	How far is A from B?
A 離 B 有 # 哩路	A is no. of miles from B

D. Comparing Distance

□ 21. With 比 construction (L21)

A 離 C 比 B 離 C (還) 遠 嗎？	Is A (still) farther from C than B is?
A 離 C 比 B 離 C (還) 近 嗎？	Is A (still) closer to C than B is?
A 離 C 比 B 離 C (還) 遠	A is (still) farther from C than B is
A 離 C 比 B 離 C (還) 近	A is (still) closer to C than B is
A 離 C 比 B 離 C 遠 一點兒	A is a little bit farther from C than B is
A 離 C 比 B 離 C 近 一點兒	A is a little bit closer to C than B is
A 離 C 比 B 離 C 遠 得多 嗎？	Is A much farther from C than B is?
A 離 C 比 B 離 C 近 得多 嗎？	Is A much closer to C than B is?
A 離 C 比 B 離 C 遠 得多 了	A is much farther from C than B is
A 離 C 比 B 離 C 近 得多 了	A is much closer to C than B is

□ 22. Of equaling-degree (L21)

A 離 C 有沒有 B 離 C 那麼/這麼 遠？	Is A as far from C as B is?
A 離 C 有沒有 B 離 C 那麼/這麼 近？	Is A as near to C as B is?
A 離 C 沒有 B 離 C 那麼/這麼 遠	A is not as far from C as B is
A 離 C 沒有 B 離 C 那麼/這麼 近	A is not as near to C as B is

❑ 23. Of Equal-degree (L21)

A 離 C 跟 B 離 C 　一樣 遠	A is about as far from/close to C as B is
A 離 C 跟 B 離 C 　一樣 近	A is about as close to C as B is
A 離 C 跟 B 離 C 不 一樣 遠	A is not as far from/close to C as B is
A 離 C 跟 B 離 C 不 一樣 近	A is not as close to C as B is
A 離 C 不 跟 B 離 C 一樣 遠	A and B are not equally far from C
A 離 C 不 跟 B 離 C 一樣 近	A and B are not equally close to C

E. Expressing Time

❑ 24. With 再過 ..., 就 ... construction (L19)

(S) 再過 多久 就 ...呢？ 再過 多久 (S) 就 ...呢？	In how long will (S) be...?
(S) 再過 Time Expression 就 ... 再過 Time Expression (S) 就 ...	In another Time Expression, (S) will be...

❑ 25. With the preposition 從 (L20)

從 S VO/Time Expression 以後, (S) 就 ... S 從 VO/Time Expression 以後, (S) 就 ...	S... ever since...

❑ 26. With 才 and 就 (L23)

S Time Expression 才 VO	S will not VO until Time Expression (the action won't be done/occur until later time)
S Time Expression 才 No. M	S will be only No. M on Time Expression (the number is lesser/smaller than expected)
S Time Expression 就 VO 了	S has done VO on/in Time Expression (the action has already been done/occurred sooner than the expected time)
S Time Expression 就 No. M (N) 了	S was already No. M on/in Time Expression (the number is greater/larger than expected)

F. Indicating Location

☐ 27. With X ... 部 (L23)

X 東部	the eastern part of X
X 西部	the western part of X
X 南部	the southern part of X
X 北部	the northern part of X
X 東南部	the southeastern part of X
X 東北部	the northeastern part of X
X 西北部	the northwestern part of X
X 西南部	the southwestern part of X
X 中西部	the midwestern part of X

G. Expressing Opinions/Comments

☐ 28. With 不但..., 而且/ 並且 ...construction (L21)

S 不但..., 而且/並且也...	S not only..., but also...

☐ 29. With the adverb 只是 (L20)

S 只是...	It is only the case that...

☐ 30. With the movable adverb 難道 (L22)

難道　S Neg VO 嗎 ?	Do you mean to say that...?/
S　難道 Neg VO 嗎 ?	Could it be possible that...?

☐ 31. With the co-verbs 叫 and 讓 (L20)

S_1 叫 / 讓 O_1/S_2 (別/不要) V_2 O_2	S_1 let/tell O_1/S_2 (don't) V_2 O_2

☐ 32. With the expression VO 對 X 有幫助 (L23)

VO 對 X(很)有幫助	Ving O is (very) helpful to X

☐ 33. With 難受 / 難過 (L20)

S 覺得 O 很/Adv 難受	S feels that O is very/Adv unbearable/intolerable/bad
S Adj 得 很/Adv 難受	S is so Adj that (S feels) uncomfortable
S 覺得　很/Adv 難過	S feels very/Adv sorry/bad/uncomfortable

H. Expressing Emphasis

☐ 34. With the reduplicated adverbs 偏偏 and 明明 (L22)

S 偏(偏) VO	S VO deliberately
S 明明　VO	Clearly S V

☐ 35. With the complement 不得了 (L23)

不得了！ S V O 了	Good Heavens!　S did...!
S SV 得不得了	S is extremely/awfully Adj

I. Others

☐ 36. The interrogative adverb 多 (L20)

多 SV？	How Adj (is...)?
多久？	How long (is...)?
多好？	How good (is...)?
多重？	How heavy (is...)?

☐ 37. The difference between 跟、和、也 (L19)

NP₁ 跟 NP₂	NP₁ and NP₂
NP₁ 和 NP₂	NP₁ and NP₂
VP₁ 也 VP₂	VP₁ and VP₂

☐ 38. The differences between 的、地、得 (L23)

N₁/Pron　的 N	N₁'s N	a possessive marker
(S)　　V 的 N (Adv) Adj 的 N	The N that (S) V (Adv) Adj N	a subordinate/ modifier marker
Adj 的 (N) V　　的 (N)	The Adj one The one (that X) did V	a nominalizer
Adj Adj 地 V/Adj V 得 Comp	Adj-ly	an adverbial marker a complement marker

Appendix 2. Supplementary Characters 41-80

SC 41-48

41

哥

gē
elder brother 口
10   (mouth)

45

雪

xuě
snow   雨
11   (rain)

42

運

yùn
to move;
transport 辶
13

46

雙

shuāng
pair   隹
18   (short-tail
              bird)

43

肚

dù
belly   月
7   (flesh)

47

認

rèn
to recognize 言
14   (speech)

44

雨

yǔ
rain   雨
8   (rain)

48

識

shì
to know,
recognize 言
19   (speech)

繁簡對照：

運 运   雙 双   識 识
             認 认

SC 49-56

49 牆
qiáng
wall; fence 爿
17

53 貓
māo
cat 豸
16　(reptiles
　　without feet)

50 活
huó
to live, survive,
be flexible 氵
9　(water)

54 狗
gǒu
dog 犭
8　(dog)

51 條
tiáo
strip; M for
animals, roads,
etc.　木
9　(tree)

55 草
cǎo
grass 艹
10　(grass)

52 隻
zhī
AN for animals
隹
10　(birds)

56 樹
shù
tree 木
16　(tree)

繁簡對照：

貓 猫
樹 树

SC 57-64

57
醒

xǐng
to wake up 酉
16   (the 10th
of the 12 Earthly
Branches)

58
牙

yá
teeth   牙
4   (teeth)

59
舊

jiù
old   臼
18   (mortar)

60
聲

shēng
sound   耳
17   (ear)

61
奇

qí
strange, rare,
wonderful 大
8   (big)

62
怪

guài
queer, to blame
          忄
8   (heart)

63
腳

jiǎo
foot   月
13   (flesh)

64
推

tuī
to push   扌
11   (hand)

繁簡對照：

舊旧
聲声

腳脚

SC 65-72

65
撿
jiǎn
to pick up, to
collect　扌
16　　(hand)

69
綠
lù
green　糸
14

66
燒
shāo
to burn, cook,
heat, roast;
fever　火
16　　(fire)

70
白
bái
white　白
5　　(white)

67
院
yuàn
yard　阝
10　(a mound)

71
黑
hēi
black　灬
12　　(fire)

68
針
zhēn
needle, stitch
金
10　　(metal)

72
色
sè
color, tint, hue
色
6　　(color)

繁簡對照：

撿捡
燒烧

綠绿

SC 73-80

73

室

shì
a room   宀
9

77

寒

hán
cold   宀
12

74

貼

tiē
to stick, to
paste   貝
12   (shell)

78

父

fù
father   父
4   (father)

75

罰

fá
to punish   网
14

79

母

mǔ
mother   母
5   (don't)

76

訴

sù
to tell, inform
言
12   (speech)

80

親

qīn
parent; closely
related   見
16   (to see)

繁簡對照：

貼 贴   訴 诉   親 亲
罰 罚

Appendix 3. Radicals (Arranged by Number of Strokes)

In the following table you will find the 213 standard radicals (R) which are included in *A New Practical Chinese-English Dictionary*, edited by Liang Shih-chiu (Taipei). They are listed according to the number of strokes (S No.) used to write them. The spoken form in Pinyin romanization and an English meaning are also given; note that some radicals have no meaning.[1] The last column shows you the order in which to write the strokes.

Of the 213 standard radicals, only 35 have been simplified in the PRC. For easier recognition, we list the simplifications along with their standard counterparts. We list the rest of the radicals, which are used in both traditional (or complicated) and simplified characters, only under the "Radical" column. The only simplified radical that has no standard counterpart is 业 yè, which is the simplified version of the traditional character 業 yè 'profession.' Traditionally, the character 業 yè belongs to the radical 木 mù 'tree or wood.' When you are familiar with the table, you will find that it is quite easy to convert from the traditional radicals to their simplified counterparts. Characters/graphs in parentheses under the radical column are variants of their corresponding radicals.

Since most of the Chinese characters (both the traditional and simplified) are made of one or more of these radicals, grasping them early on is the quickest way to learn Chinese characters well in a limited amount of time.

S No.	R No.	Radical/ Simplified	Pinyin/ English	Example	Stroke Order
1	1	一	yī one	丁不	
	2	丨	shù	中串	
	3	丶	diǎn dot	丸主	
	4	丿	piě	久乒	
	5	乙 乙 (乛乙乚)	yǐ a Celestial Stem	九也	
	6	亅	jué	了事	

---

[1] Radical 26 doesn't have sound or meaning.

2	7	二	èr two	云五	一	二	
	8	亠	tóu	京交	丶	亠	
	9	人（亻） 人（亻入）	rén man	位們	丿	人	
	10	儿	rén	元先	丿	儿	
	11	入	rù enter	内全	丿	入	
	12	八 八（丷）	bā eight	公六	丿	八	
	13	冂	jiōng	再册	丨	冂	
	14	冖	mì	冠冤	丶	冖	
	15	冫	bīng	冬冰	丶	冫	
	16	几 几（几）	jǐ a small table	凡凳	丿	几	
	17	凵	qū	出函	凵	凵	
	18	刀（刂） 刀（刂夕）	dāo knife	切刻	刁	刀	
	19	力	lì power	功勤	刁	力	
	20	勹	bāo	包勿	丿	勹	
	21	匕	bǐ a ladle	化匙	丿	匕	

	22	匚	fāng power	匡匠	一	匚		
	23	匸	xì	匹區	一	匸		
	24	十	shí ten	千午	一	十		
	25	卜 卜（卜）	bǔ to divine	卦卡	丨	卜		
	26	卩（㔾） 卩（㔾）		印即	㇖	卩		
	27	厂	hǎn	原厚	一	厂		
	28	厶	sǐ	去參	厶	厶		
	29	又	yòu again	友受	㇇	又		
3	30	口	kǒu mouth	叫可	丨	冂	口	
	31	囗	wéi	回國	丨	冂	囗	
	32	土	tǔ soil	坐地	一	十	土	
	33	士	shì a scholar	壬壯	一	十	士	
	34	夊	suī ten	夏夔	丿	夂	夊	
	35	夕	xì evening	多夢	丿	夕	夕	
	36	大	dà big	天太	一	大	大	

3	37	女	nǔ female	好姓	人	女	女	
	38	子	zǐ child, son	學孩	フ	了	子	
	39	宀	mián	安客	、	宀	宀	
	40	寸	cùn Chinese inch	對封	一	寸	寸	
	41	小 小 (⺌)	xiǎo small	少尖	亅	小	小	
	42	尢 (尤兀)	wāng	就尤	一	尢	尢	
	43	尸	shī a corpse	屋尺	ヿ	⼮	尸	
	44	屮	chè	屯	㇄	⼬	屮	
	45	山	shān mountain	島岸	丨	屮	山	
	46	巛	chuān a river	州巢	巜	巜	巛	
	47	工	gōng labor	左差	一	丁	工	
	48	己 己 (巳)	jǐ self	已巷	㇇	コ	己	
	49	巾	jīn towel	布師	丨	冂	巾	
	50	干	gān a Celestial Stem	年平	一	二	干	
	51	幺	yāo one	幼幾	幺	幺	幺	

52	广	yǎn	店座	、	亠	广		
53	廴	yǐn ten	建延	ㄱ	ㄋ	廴		
54	廾	gǒng	弄弊	一	十	廾		
55	弋	yì to catch	式	一	弋	弋		
56	弓	gōng a bow	弟張	ㄱ	コ	弓		
57	彐 (彑彐)	jì	彗彙	ㄱ	ㄱ	彐		
58	彡	shān	形影	ノ	ク	彡		
59	彳	chì	很得	ノ	ク	彳		
4	60	心 (忄小)	xīn heart	念忙	丶	心	心	心
	61	戈	gē a spear	我戰	一	弋	戈	戈
	62	戶	hù a door	房所	ノ	厂	戶	戶
	63	手 (扌)	shǒu hand	打抱	ノ	二	三	手
	64	支	zhī to pay, support	支	一	十	支	支
	65	攴 (攵)	pū a spear	放改	丨	卜	与	攴
	66	文	wén literature	斑斌	丶	亠	亣	文

4	67	斗	dǒu Chinese peck	料斜	丶	丬	三	斗
	68	斤	jīn catty	新斯	丿	厂	斤	斤
	69	方	fāng square	旁旅	丶	亠	方	方
	70	无	wú not, no	既	一	二	于	无
	71	日	rì sun	早明	丨	冂	日	日
	72	曰	yuē to say	書最	丨	冂	日	曰
	73	月	yuè moon	有朋	丿	刀	月	月
	74	木	mù tree, wood	李東	一	十	才	木
	75	欠	qiàn to owe	次歌	丿	𠂉	𠂊	欠
	76	止	zhǐ to stop	正步	丨	卜	止	止
	77	歹 (歺)	dǎi bad	死殖	一	丁	歹	歹
	78	殳	shū a weapon	段殺	丿	几	殳	殳
	79	毋 (母)	wù don't	每毒	乚	㇗	毋	毋
	80	比	bǐ to compare	毖毗	丿	上	比	比
	81	毛	máo hair	毯毽	丿	二	三	毛

	82	氏	shì family, clan	民氓	⺁	⺁	⺁	氏	
	83	气	qì air	氣氧	ノ	一	⺁	气	
	84	水 (氵氺)	shuǐ water	江洋	亅	刀	水	水	
	85	火 (灬)	huǒ fire	炒煮	丶	丷	少	火	
	86	爪 (爫)	zhuǎ claw	爬爭	⺁	⺁	⺆	爪	
	87	父	fù father	爸爹	ノ	八	少	父	
	88	爻	yáo line (of a divination diagram)	爽爾	ノ	メ	爻	爻	
	89	爿	qiáng	牆	㇄	丬	爿	爿	
	90	片	piàn a piece	牌版	丿	丿	广	片	
	91	牙	yá tooth	牙	一	匸	牙	牙	
	92	牛 (牜)	niú cow	物特	ノ	⺧	牛	牛	
	93	犬 (犭)	quǎn dog	狗狼	一	大	大	犬	
5	94	玄	xuán far and obscure	率	丶	亠	玄	玄	玄
	95	玉 (王)	yù jade	玩理	一	二	干	王	玉
	96	瓜	guā melon	瓢瓣	ノ	厂	瓜	瓜	瓜

5	97	瓦	wǎ a tile	瓶瓷	一	厂	厄	瓦	瓦
	98	甘	gān sweet	甜甚	一	十	廿	甘	甘
	99	生	shēng born, to live	產甥	ノ	⺧	牛	生
	100	用	yòng use	甫甬	ノ	门	月	月	用
	101	田	tián field	男當	丨	冂	冃	田	田
	102	疋(疋疋)	yǎ/pǐ	疑疏	乛	丆	疋	疋	疋
	103	疒	chuáng	病癌	丶	亠	疒	疒	疒
	104	癶	bō	發登	㇆	癶	癶	癶	癶
	105	白	bái white	的百	ノ	亻	竹	白	白
	106	皮	pí skin, leather	皺	乛	广	皮	皮	皮
	107	皿	mǐn saucer	盡益	丨	冂	皿	皿	皿
	108	目(罒)	mù eye	看睏	丨	门	月	目	目
	109	矛	máo a spear	矜	乛	乛	矛	予	矛
	110	矢	shǐ a dart	知短	ノ	广	乍	矢	矢
	111	石	shí stone	砂研	一	丆	不	石	石

	112	示（礻）	shì to show	祝神	一 二 亍 示 示
	113	内	róu	禹禽	丨 冂 内 内 内
	114	禾	hé rice plant	種科	一 二 千 禾 禾
	115	穴	xuè a cave	穿空	丶 八 宀 宀 穴
	116	立	lì to stand	站章	丶 亠 立 立 立
		业	yè profession	业邺	丨 丨丨 业 业 业
6	117	竹（⺮）	zhú bamboo	筆第	丿 ⺊ 个 竹 竹 竹
	118	米	mǐ rice	精粥	丶 丷 半 半 米 米
	119	糸（糹） 幺	mì	紅級	乙 幺 幺 糸 糸 糸
	120	缶	fǒu a crock	缺罐	丿 ⺊ 上 午 缶 缶
	121	网	wǎng	罷罰	丨 冂 冈 冈 网 网
	122	羊（⺶） 羊（⺷ 龸）	yáng a sheep, a goat	美義	丶 丷 立 兰 兰 羊
	123	羽	yǔ feather	習翁	ㄱ 刁 羽 羽 羽 羽
	124	老	lǎo old	考者	一 十 土 耂 老 老
	125	而	ér and yet	耐耍	一 丆 冇 而 而 而

6	126	耒	lěi handle of a plough	耕耙	ノ	二	三	丰	丰	耒
	127	耳	ěr ear	聲聞	一	T	TT	FT	耳	耳
	128	聿 聿(⺻聿)	yù pen, brush	肆肅	⁊	⁊	⁊	⁊	聿	聿
	129	肉 (月)	ròu flesh, meat	肌肚	丨	冂	内	内	肉	肉
	130	臣	chén a minister	臥臨	一	⻌	匚	臣	臣	臣
	131	自	zì self	臭臬	ノ	亻	门	自	自	自
	132	至	zhì to arrive at	致臺	一	丄	丂	죠	至	至
	133	臼(⺽)	jiù a mortar	舊興	ノ	亻	乍	臼	臼	臼
	134	舌	shé tongue	舍舒	ノ	二	千	千	舌	舌
	135	舛	chuǎn chaotic	舞舜	ノ	夕	夕	乑	舛	舛
	136	舟	zhōu boat	船航	ノ	亻	门	舟	舟	舟
	137	艮 艮 (⻗)	gēn name of a divination diagram	良艱	⁊	⁊	彐	艮	艮	艮
	138	色	sè color	艷	ノ	夕	纟	希	多	色
	139	屮屮(⺿) 艹	cǎo grass	花草	ㄴ	屮	屮	屮	艸	艸
	140	虍	hū rice	號虎	丨	卜	上	虍	虍	虎

141	虫	chóng worm	蛋蛇	丨 丨口 口 中 虫 虫
142	血	xuè/ xiě blood	衆	丿 丿 冂 血 血 血
143	行	xíng to walk	街衛	丿 彳 彳 行 行 行
144	衣 (衤)	yī clothing	裏褲	丶 亠 㐅 衣 衣 衣
145	襾 (覀) 西 (覀)	yà	要覆	一 冂 西 西 西 西
7	146	見 见	jiàn to see	視覺	丨 冂 冃 目 目 貝 見
	147	角 角	jiǎo angle	解觸	丿 ク 角 角 角 角 角
	148	言 言 (訁)	yán speech	說記	丶 亠 亠 言 言 言 言
	149	谷	gǔ a valley	谷	丿 八 父 谷 谷 谷
	150	豆	dòu bean	豇豌	一 冂 豆 豆 豆 豆 豆
	151	豕	shǐ hog	豬象	一 丆 豕 豕 豕 豕 豕
	152	豸	zhì reptiles without feet	貌豹	丿 豸 豸 豸 豸 豸 豸
	153	貝 贝	bèi shell	買貴	丨 冂 冃 目 目 貝 貝
	154	赤	chì red	赫赦	一 十 土 赤 赤 赤 赤
	155	走	zǒu to walk	起趕	一 十 土 走 走 走 走

156	足（足）	zú foot	跟跌	丨	口	口	𤴓	𤴔	𤴕	足		
157	身	shēn body	躺躬	丿	亻	勹	𠂤	自	身	身		
158	車 车	chē vehicle	輪輛	一	厂	戸	亘	百	亘	車		
159	辛	xīn a Celestial Stem	辣辦	丶	亠	㇒	立	立	立	辛		
160	辰	chén a Terrestrial Branch	農辱	一	厂	厂	辰	辰	辰	辰		
161	辵（辶/辶） 辶	chuò	進近	丿	㇉	彡	彳	辵	辵	辵		
162	邑（right ⻏）	yì a city	那都	丶	口	口	吕	吕	吕	邑		
163	酉	yǒu a Terrestrial Branch	酒酷	一	厂	门	丙	酉	酉	酉		
164	釆（采） 采	biàn/cǎi to gather	釋釉	丿	丷	爫	立	平	采	釆		
165	里	lǐ Chinese mile	重量	丨	冂	日	日	旦	里	里		
8	166	金 金（钅）	jīn gold, metal	錢銀	丿	人	스	仐	仝	余	金	金
	167	長（镸） 长	cháng long	長	一	厂	巨	巨	手	長	長	長
	168	門 门	mén door	開關	丨	冂	冎	門	門	門	門	門
	169	阜（left ⻖）	fù a mound	阿陳	丿	亻	𠂤	阜	阜	阜	阜	阜
	170	隶	tài long	隸	㇇	彐	彐	肀	肀	隶	隶	隶

	171	隹	zhuī short-tail birds	隻雖	ノ イ イ 亻 作 作 隹	隹
	172	雨 (⻗)	yǔ rain	雪雲	一 厂 厅 而 雨 雨 雨	雨
	173	青	qīng green	靜靖	一 二 圭 圭 青 青 青	青
	174	非	fēi not, un-	靠靡	) 刂 ヲ ヲ 非 非 非	非
9	175	面	miàn face	面	一 丆 丆 丏 而 面 面 面	面
	176	革	gé reform, leather	鞋靴	一 十 廿 廿 芐 苦 苦 革	革
	177	韋 韦	wěi tanned leather	韓韞	ヲ 立 乒 咅 吾 吾 章 章	韋
	178	韭	jiǔ leeks	韭	丨 刂 刲 丰 非 非 非	韭
	179	音	yīn sound	響韻	、 亠 亠 亣 立 音 音 音	音
	180	頁 页	yè a page	題預	一 丆 丆 丆 百 百 頁	頁
	181	風 风	fēng wind	颱颶	) 八 几 凡 凬 凮 風 風	風
	182	飛 飞	fēi to fly	飛	㇟ 飞 飞 ㇟ 飛 飛 飛	飛
	183	食 食 (飠)	shí to eat	飯餓	ノ 人 入 今 今 食 食 食	食
	184	首	shǒu head	首	、 丷 丷 艹 艹 首 首 首	首
	185	香	xiāng fragrant	馥馨	ノ 二 千 禾 禾 香 香	香
10	186	馬 马	mǎ horse	騎駛 馬	一 厂 厂 F 丐 馬 馬 馬 馬	

187	骨骨	gǔ bone	體	丶 骨	冂	冎	冎	冎	丹	丹	骨
188	高	gāo high, tall	高	丶 高	亠	宀	古	古	高	高	高
189	髟	biāo	髮髟	一 髟	丆	丆	镸	镸	镸	镸	髟
190	鬥斗	dòu to struggle	鬧	丨 鬥	冂	乊	乊	乊	乊	乊	乊
191	鬯	chàng sacrificial spirits	鬱	乚 鬯	凵	凶	凶	凶	凶	凶	鬯
192	鬲	gé name of an ancient state	鬻	一 鬲	丆	冎	冎	鬲	鬲	鬲	鬲
193	鬼	guǐ ghost	魅魔	丿 鬼	亻	冂	白	甶	甶	鬼	鬼
11	194	魚鱼	yú fish	鮭鮮	丿 魚	夕	夘	角	角	角	魚	魚
	195	鳥鸟	niǎo bird	鳳鴨	丿 鳥	亻	冂	白	鳥	鳥	鳥	鳥
	196	鹵卤	lǔ alkaline	鹹鹽	丨 鹵	卜	广	卤	鹵	鹵	鹵	鹵
	197	鹿	lù deer	麋麒	丶 鹿	亠	广	广	声	庶	鹿	鹿
	198	麥麦	mài wheat	麵麪	一 麥	丆	刄	双	夾	夾	夾	來
	199	麻	má hemp	麼	丶 麻	亠	广	广	庁	庐	麻	麻
12	200	黃黄	huáng yellow	黄	一 黃	十	艹	苎	芒	苦	苦	苗
	201	黍	shǔ millet	黍	丿 黍	二	千	禾	禾	禾	黍	黍
	202	黑	hēi black	點黛	丶 黑	冂	四	四	四	黑	黑	黑

	203	黹	zhǐ embroidery	黹								
	204	黽 黾	mǐn to strive	黽								
13	205	鼎	dǐng tripod	鼎								
	206	鼓	gǔ drum	鼓								
	207	鼠	shǔ mouse	鼬								
14	208	鼻	bí nose	鼾								
	209	齊 齐	qí equal, uniform	齋								
15	210	齒 齿	chǐ tooth	齡								
16	211	龍 龙	lóng dragon	龑								
	212	龜 龟	guī turtle	龜								
17	213	龠	yuè a kind of flute	龠								

Appendix 4. Characters with Two or More Readings

Character	Reading	Example			
長　长	cháng zhǎng	長短 長得很漂 亮	长短 长得很漂 亮	chángduǎn zhǎng .de hěn piào.liàng	length to look really pretty
待	dāi dài	待在家裏 招待	待在家里	dāi zài jiā .lǐ zhāodài	to stay at home to entertain
得	dé děi .de	得到 得上課 看得懂	得上课	dédào děi shàngkè kàn.dedǒng	to succeed in obtaining to have to attend the class can understand by reading
法	fǎ/fà fá	法國 法子	法国	Fǎ.guó/Fà.guó fá.zi	France method
好	hǎo hào	很好 好動 喜好	好动	hěn hǎo hàodòng xǐhào	very good to be active to like
教	jiāo jiào	教書 教室	教书	jiāoshū jiàoshì	to teach classroom
覺　觉	jué jiào	覺得 睡覺	觉得 睡觉	jué.de shuìjiào	to feel to sleep
空	kōng kòng	空氣 有空兒	空气 有空儿	kōngqì yǒukòngr	air to have free time
樂　乐	lè yuè	快樂 音樂	快乐 音乐	kuàilè yīnyuè	(to be) happy music
了	.le liǎo	來了 吃不了	来了	lái .le chī.bùliǎo	came cannot finish eating
爲　为	wèi wéi	因爲 以爲	因为 以为	yīnwèi yǐwéi	because to think incorrectly
行	xíng háng	不行 銀行	银行	bùxíng yínháng	won't do bank
要	yào yāo	要買 要求	要买	yào mǎi yāo.qiú	to want to buy to request
著　着	.zhe zháo	看著電視 睡著	看着电视	kàn.zhe diànshì shuìzháo	watching at TV to have fallen asleep
重	zhòng chóng	很重 重寫 重做	重写	hěn zhòng chóng xiě chóng zuò	very heavy to rewrite to redo

Appendix 5. Bibliography

Chang, Kuang-yuan (張光遠)

1995 "Shang Dynasty Bronze Inscriptions and Their Historical Significance: Bronze Inscriptions as Standard Script and Oracle Bone Inscriptions as Simplified Script." In National Palace Museum, *A Catalogue of Shang Dynasty Bronze Inscriptions : Ancient Chinese Script from the 1st Millenium BC* (商代金文圖錄—三千年前中國文字特展), 1-27.

Chao, Yuen Ren (趙元任)

1930 "A System of Tone Letters." *Le Maître phonétique,* troisième série, 30: 24-7. Reprinted in *Fangyan* (方言)1980, 2: 81-83.

1968 *A Grammar of Spoken Chinese.* Berkeley: University of California Press.

Gao, Shufan (高樹藩), ed.

1984 *Zhengzhong Xing Yin Yi Zonghe Da Zidian* (正中形音義綜合大字典). Rev. 5th ed. Taibei: Zhengzhong Shuju.

*Lianhebao*聯合報, January 6, 1992.

Liang, Shih-chiu (梁實秋)

1971 *A New Practical Chinese-English Dictionary* (最新實用漢英字典). Taipei: Far East Book Co. Ltd.

National Palace Museum (國立故宮博物院)

1995 *A Catalogue of Shang Dynasty Bronze Inscriptions : Ancient Chinese Script from the 1st Millenium BC* (商代金文圖錄—三千年前中國文字特展). Taipei: National Palace Museum.

Norman, Jerry

1988 *Chinese.* Cambridge: Cambridge University Press.

Ramsey, S. Robert

1987 *The Languages of China.* Princeton: Princeton University Press.

Sung, Margaret M. Yan (嚴棉)

1979 "Chinese Language and Culture: A Study of Homonyms, Lucky Words and Taboos." *Journal of Chinese Linguistics* 7.1: 15-28.

1981 "Chinese Personal Naming." *Journal of the Chinese Language Teachers Association* 16.2: 67-90.

Tai, James H-Y. (戴浩一)
    1985 "Temporal Sequence and Chinese Word Order." In *Iconicity in Syntax*, ed. John
             Haiman. Amsterdam: Benjamins.
    1987 "Temporal Sequence and Chinese Word Order." In *Wang Li Memorial Volumes,*
             English Volume, ed. the Chinese Language Society of Hong Kong, 377-404.
    1989 "Toward a Cognition-Based Functional Grammar of Chinese." In *Functionalism*
             and Chinese Grammar, ed. Tai and Hsueh, 187-226.

Tai, James H-Y. (戴浩一), and Frank F. S. Hsueh (薛鳳生), eds.
    1989 *Functionalism and Chinese Grammar* (功能學說與中文文法). Chinese
             Language Teachers Association Monograph Series No.1, Ohio State University,
             Columbus.

Wang, William S-Y. (王士元), ed.
    1991 *Languages and Dialects of China.* Monograph Series No. 3, Journal of Chinese
             Linguistics, University of California, Berkeley.

Wang, Yun-wu (王雲五)
    1967 *Zijiao Haoma Jianzifa* (四角號碼檢字法). Taipei: Taiwan Shangwu Yinshuguan
             (臺灣商務印書館).

Yan, Margaret Mian (嚴棉)
    1993 "Active Chinese—A Multimedia Beginning Chinese Text for College Students"
             (with computer technical assistance of I-feng Jeng). Paper presented at the Annual
             Meeting of the American Council on the Teaching of Foreign Languages, November
             20-22, San Antonio.

Yin, Binyong (尹斌庸), and Mary Felley (傅曼麗)
    1990 *Chinese Romanization: Pronunciation and Orthography* (漢語拼音和正詞法).
             Beijing: Sinolingua.

Zhongguo Da Baike Quanshu Chubanshe Bianjibu (中國大百科全書出版社編輯部編), eds.
    1988 *Zhongguo Da Baike Quanshu: Yuyan Wenzi* (中國大百科全書：語言文字).
             Beijing: Zhongguo Da Baike Quanshu Chubanshe.

Indexes
for All Lessons

Index 1. Vocabulary

◎ By Pinyin

Pinyin	Character		English	L
A				
.a	啊		particle for question	8
.ai.ya!	哎呀！		my goodness! oh no!	19
ǎi	矮		short	8
* ǎigèr	矮個兒	矮个儿	short person	19
ài	愛	爱	to love	8
ānjìng	安靜	安静	(to be) quiet	15
ànshí	按時	按时	according to schedule	20
áoyè	熬夜		to burn the midnight oil	17
B				
.ba	吧		particle for agreement	7
.ba	吧		particle for conjecture or supposition	15
bā	八		eight	4
bāchéng	八成		80 percent, almost, very likely	22
bǎ	把		executive/disposal construction marker	15
bà.bà	爸爸		father	8
bǎi	百		hundred	7
* bǎihuò	百貨	百货	goods, commodities	12
* bǎihuò dàlóu	百貨大樓	百货大楼	department store (M: 家) (China)	12
bǎihuò gōngsī	百貨公司	百货公司	department store (M: 家)	12
bǎi	擺	摆	to place, to spread out	15
* bān	搬		to move	14
bān.dào	搬到		to move to	14
bàn	半		half	9
bànchǎng	半場	半场	half-time (of a game)	19
bànyè	半夜		midnight	19
bāng	幫	帮	to help, to assist	12
bāngmáng	幫忙	帮忙	to help, help, assistance	16
bàng	磅		pound	13
bāo	包		to include, to wrap	15
bāoguǒ	包裹	包裹	package (M: 個)	21
* bǎo	飽		to eat to the full, (to be) satisfied (stomach)	11
bàogào	報告	报告	report, (term) paper (M: 篇/ 個)	13
bàoyuàn	抱怨		to complain	20

	bēi	杯		measure word for tea, wine, coffee; cup	7
	bēijù	悲劇	悲剧	tragedy	11
	běifāng	北方		the north	10
	bèi	被		by	22
	běn	本		measure word for books, notebooks	6
	běnlái	本來	本来	originally (=原來)	23
	běn.zi	本子		notebook (M: 本/個)	7
	bítì	鼻涕		nasal drip	20
	bǐ	筆	笔	pen (M: 枝 zhī)	7
*	bǐ	比		to compare	10
	bǐ	＃比＃		no. to no. (for the scores of a ball game)	19
	bǐjiào	比較	比较	comparatively, comparison	10
	bǐsài	比賽	比赛	competition, to compete (M: 場)	19
	bìyè	畢業	毕业	to graduate, graduation	23
*	biānr	邊兒	边儿	side (suffix), border	15
	biàn	變	变	to change	18
	biànchéng	變成	变成	to become	13
	biǎomèi	表妹		daughter of father's sister or mother's sibling, who is younger than oneself	23
	bié	別		don't	11
	bié.de	別的		other	7
	bié kè.qì	別客氣	别客气	don't be modest!	18
*	bìng	病		sickness, to be sick	20
	bù	不		no, not	4
*	búbì	不必		doesn't have to, need not (=不用)	5
	búbì	不必		not necessarily	10
	búcuò	不錯	不错	(to be) not bad, quite good	6
	búdàn...érqiě	不但...而且		not only... but also...	21
	búguò	不過	不过	and yet	8
	búguò	不過	不过	only (=只)	17
	bújiàn.le	不見了	不见了	to have disappeared	22
	bútài	不太		not quite, not very	6
*	búxiè	不謝	不谢	you're welcome	7
*	búyòng	不用		doesn't have to, need not (=不必)	5
*	bù hǎo yì.si	不好意思		(to be) ashamed, (to be) embarrassed, feel shy	13
*	V.buqǐ	V不起		not to be able to afford to V	23
	bùrú	不如		not as good as	19

	bùxíng .le	不行了		(one) cannot go on (doing something), be too weak/sick to (do something)	19
*	bù	部		a section, a part	8
	bù	部		measure word for films, cars, etc.	11

C

	cái	才		only	7
	cái	才		not until, only then	9
	cái bù .ne	才不呢		no!	14
	cáipàn	裁判		referee, judge (M: 個)	19
	cài	菜		dishes, vegetables (M: 盤 pán 'dish'; 道 dào 'course')	9
	cānjiā	參加	参加	to participate; to attend (a conference, meeting)	16
	cèsuǒ	廁所	厕所	toilet, lavatory (M: 間)	17
	chá	查		to check	7
	chá	茶		tea (M: 杯 bēi 'cup')	10
*	chà	差		to be short of, lack	6
	Chángchéng	長城	长城	the Great Wall	10
	chángdù	長度	长度	length	12
	chángduǎn	長短	长短	length	12
	chángtú	長途	长途	long distance	14
	chànggē	唱歌		to sing	8
	chāojí shìchǎng	超級市場	超级市场	supermarket (M: 個)	13
	chǎo	吵		(to be) noisy	15
	chǎo(jià)	吵(架)		to argue	14
	chē	車	车	car, vehicle (M: 輛 liàng, 部 bù)	10
	chènshān	襯衫	衬衫	shirt (M: 件, V: 穿)	12
	chéng	成		to constitute	8
	chī	吃		to eat	7
	chídào	遲到	迟到	to arrive late	17
	chū.qù	出去		to go out	9
	chūshìr	出事兒	出事儿	to have an accident, to be in trouble	22
	chú.le... yǐwài	除了...以外		besides, except for	12
	chúfáng	廚房		kitchen (M: 間)	15
	chūnjià	春假		spring vacation	21
	chūnjuǎnr	春捲兒	春卷儿	eggroll	10
	chōu	抽		to smoke (cigarettes, etc.) (=吸) , to inhale	10
*	chuān	穿		to wear (garments and shoes)	12
	chuān.chuān.kàn	穿穿看		to try (garments) on	12

	chuántǒng	傳統	传统	tradition	18
	chuī	吹		to blow, puff, play (wind instrument)	17
*	chuīfēng	吹風	吹风	to blow	17
	chuīfēng	吹風	吹风	to expose to cold wind	20
*	chuīfēngjī	吹風機	吹风机	hair dryer (M: 個)	17
	chuīgān	吹乾	吹干	to blow dry	17
	cídài	磁帶	磁带	audio tape (M: 盤 pán) (China)	7
	cì	次		measure word for frequency	11
	cóng	從	从	from	11
	cóng	從	从	since	20
	cóng...lái/qù	從...來/去	从...来/去	to come /go from (a place)	8
	cónglái dōu méi...	從來都沒...	从来都没...	to have never...	22
	cóngqián	從前		previously (=以前)	22
	cù	醋		vinegar	10
	cuī	催		to urge, hurry, press	17
	cúnqián	存錢	存钱	to deposit (money)	21

D

	dā	搭		to take (a vehicle, an airplane, a ship)	13
	dǎ	打		dozen	16
	dǎ	打		to hit, to play (ball)	19
	dǎcuò	打錯	打错	to dial a wrong number	9
*	dǎdào	打到		to hit the ball/target	19
	dǎ (diànhuà)	打(電話)	打(电话)	to make a telephone call	9
	dǎgōng	打工		to work (for a temporary job)	5
*	dǎsǎo	打掃	打扫	to clean up	15
	dǎsuàn	打算		to plan, a plan	14
	dǎzhé	打折		to give a discount	12
	dǎzhēn	打針	打针	to have a shot, injection	20
*	dǎzhòng	打中		to hit the ball/target	19
	dà	大		(to be) big, large, old (age)	4
	dà chī dà hē	大吃大喝		to eat and drink a lot	13
	dàjiā	大家		all, everybody	10
*	dàkǎo	大考		final examination (=期末考)	23
	dàxiǎo	大小		size	12
	dàxué	大學	大学	university, college (M: 個/間)	12
	dàyī	大衣		an overcoat (M: 件, V: 穿)	12
*	dài.fu	大夫		doctor (=醫生)	20
	dāi	待		to stay	14

	dāi	待	待	to wait (= 等)	19
*	dài	戴		to wear (glasses, gloves, jewelry)	12
	dài	帶	带	to bring along; to carry; to lead; to train	14
	(dān)wù	(耽)誤	(耽)误	to delay	23
	dānxīn	擔心	担心	to worry	14
	dàn	淡		(to be) light (taste, color), weak or thin (tea, coffee, etc.)	10
	dàn.shì	但是		but	8
	dāng	當	当	to be (someone), to act as	21
	dāngrán	當然	当然	of course	16
	dǎojìn	倒盡	倒尽	to lose completely (one's appetite)	11
	dǎoméi	倒霉		(to be) out of luck (also written as 倒楣 dǎoméi—inverse-lintel)	17
	dǎoyóu	導遊	导游	tour guide	21
	dào	道		measure word for dishes	10
*	dào.dì	道地		authentic, genuine (=地道)	9
	dào...qù/lái	到...去/來	到...去/来	to go there / come here	6
	dào.shì	倒是		on the contrary	8
	.de	的		possessive marker	4
	dé	得		to score, obtain	19
	Dé.guó	德國	德国	Germany	8
	děi	得		must, to have to	5
	děng	等		to wait	9
	dī	低		(to be) low	19
	dǐ	底		bottom	23
*	dì	第		an ordinalizing prefix	4
*	dì yī	第一		the first	4
	dì.dì	弟弟		younger brother	14
	dì.dào	地道		authentic, genuine	9
	dìwèi	地位		position (of a person), ranking, status	11
	dìzhǐ	地址		address	16
	diǎnlǐ	典禮	典礼	ceremony	23
	diǎn yǎnyào	點眼藥	点眼药	to use eyedrops	20
	diǎn(zhōng)	點(鐘)	点(钟)	o'clock	6
*	diànhuà	電話	电话	telephone (M: 個)	9
	diànnǎo	電腦	电脑	computer (M: 個 .ge)	7
	diànshì	電視	电视	TV	12
	diàn.zixìn	電子信	电子信	e-mail	21
	diànyǐngr	電影兒	电影儿	movie (M: 個/部 bù)	9

	diàor	調兒	调儿	tone (=聲調), tune (of music)	18
	diédǎyào	跌打藥	跌打药	"bruise ointment"	20
*	dìnghūn	訂婚	订婚	to engage/betroth, engagement, betrothal	23
	dìngjīn	定金		down payment, deposit	15
	dōng'àn	東岸	东岸	East Coast	23
	dōngbù	東部		eastern (America)	8
*	dōngfāng	東方	东方	Eastern, the East, Oriental	18
	dōng.xī	東西	东西	thing	7
	dōngjì	冬季		winter (season)	12
	dǒng	懂		to understand (=明白)	11
	dōu	都		all, both	5
	dú	讀	读	to study, to read (=念)	21
	dù.zi	肚子		stomach (belly)	13
	duànkǎo	段考		midterm exam	18
	duàn.liàn	鍛練	锻练	to do physical training	13
	duì	隊	队	team	19
*	duì	對	对	(to be) right, to face	4
	duì.buqǐ	對不起	对不起	(I am) sorry	6
	duìr	對兒	对儿	pair, couple	17
	duì...guòmǐn	對...過敏	对...过敏	(to be) allergic to	20
	duì...hǎo	對... 好	对... 好	be nice to...	10
	duì...yǒu bāngzhù	對...有幫助	对...有帮助	(to be) helpful to	23
	duì...yǒu yì.si	對...有意思	对...有意思	to be interested in (a person)	17
	duì.zhe	對著	对着	(to be) facing	14
	duìzhé	對折	对折	a 50% discount	12
	dùn	頓	顿	measure word for meals	13
	duō	多		(to be) much; many	6
	duōbànr	多半兒	多半儿	most of	11
	duō.shǎo	多少		how much, how many?	7
*	duójiǔ	多久		how long	14
E					
	érqiě	而且		furthermore, besides	9
	ér.shì	而是		but (preceded by 不是)	8
*	ér.zi	兒子	儿子	son (M: 個)	11
	è	餓	饿	(to be) hungry	11
	èr	二		two	4
	èrhú	二胡		=胡琴	18
F					
	fā	發	发	to issue, to send (a telegram or an e-mail)	21

	fāqiú	發球	发球	to serve a ball	19
	(fā)shāo	(發)燒	(发)烧	to have a fever	20
	fāxiàn	發現	发现	to discover, discovery	22
	fǎ.zi	法子		way, method	20
*	fá	罰	罚	to punish, to penalize, to fine	19
	fádān	罰單	罚单	traffic ticket	22
	fáqiú	罰球	罚球	penalty shot	19
	fàn	飯	饭	rice, meal (M: 頓 dùn)	7
	fànguǎnr	飯館兒	饭馆儿	restaurant (M: 家 jiā)	10
*	fàntīng	飯廳	饭厅	dining room (M: 間)	15
	fàn	犯		to have a relapse, to fall back to an old illness or old bad habit	20
	fànguī	犯規	犯规	to commit a foul	19
	fāng.biàn	方便		(to be) convenient	13
	fāngmiàn	方面		an aspect, (in this or that) respect	11
*	fángdōng	房東	房东	landlord, landlady	15
*	fángjiān	房間	房间	room (M: 間)	15
	fángkè	房客		tenant	15
	fáng.zi	房子		house (M: 所/個)	14
	fàng	放		to put	15
	fàngjià	放假		to have a holiday/vacation	13
*	fēicháng	非常		unusually, extraordinarily	6
	fēijī	飛機	飞机	airplane (M: 架 jià)	13
	(fēi)jīchǎng	(飛)機場	(飞)机场	airport (M: 個)	13
*	fēn	分		minute	6
	fēn	分		to divide	10
	fēn	分		point	19
*	fēn (qián)	分(錢)	分(钱)	cent	7
	fènr	份兒	份儿	measure word for gifts and newspapers	14
	fù	付		to pay (a bill)	15
	fùmǔ	父母		parents	8
*	fù.qīn	父親	父亲	father (formal)	8
	fùjìn	附近		nearby	15
	fùnǚ	婦女	妇女	woman, women (M: 個)	11
	fùxiū	副修		minor, to minor in	6
G					
	gāi	該	该	(it) should be X's turn	22
	gǎi	改		to change (rule/situation), to correct	22
	gǎn	趕	赶	to hurry, to rush	17

	gǎndòng	感動	感动	(to be) moved, (to be) touched	11
	Gǎn'ēnjié	感恩節	感恩节	Thanksgiving	13
	gǎnmào	感冒		to catch a cold	20
	gāng	剛	刚	just a moment ago (Adv)	14
	gāngcái	剛才	刚才	just now, a moment ago (MTA)	11
	Gāo	高		surname, high, tall	4
	gāo'ěrfūqiú	高爾夫球	高尔夫球	golf	19
	gāogèr	高個兒	高个儿	tall person	19
	gāojiàn	高見	高见	high opinion	11
	gāoxìng	高興	高兴	(to be) happy	11
	gào.sù	告訴	告诉	to tell	13
*	.ge	個	个	measure word for persons and things	5
	gēcír	歌詞兒	歌词儿	lyrics of a song	18
	gēqǔ	歌曲		song (M:首 shǒu)	18
	gēr	歌兒	歌儿	song (colloquial)	18
	gěi	給	给	to give	7
	gěi...dǎqì	給...打氣	给...打气	to give...encouragement, to fill with air (with an air pump)	22
	gēn	跟		and	5
	gēn	跟		to follow; with (person)	10
	gēn...qù/lái	跟...去/來	跟...去/来	to follow...to (there/here)	14
*	gèng	更		even	12
*	gōngchē	公車	公车	bus (M: 部/輛)	13
*	gōnggòng qìchē	公共汽車	公共汽车	bus (M: 部/輛)	13
	gōngpíng	公平		(to be) fair	19
*	gōngsī	公司		company (M: 家)	12
	gōngyù	公寓		apartment (M:間)	15
*	gōng.fū	功夫/工夫	工夫	time, leisure (=空兒), skill, work	9
	gōngkè	功課	功课	homework	5
*	gōngzuò	工作		to work	5
	gōngxǐ	恭喜		to congratulate	16
*	gǒu	狗		dog (M:隻)	16
	gòu	夠	够	(to be) enough	16
	gòu péng.yǒu	夠朋友	够朋友	to be a friend in need, be a true friend	21
	guà	掛	挂	to hang up	15
	guàhào	掛號	挂号	to register (mail; or at the outpatient clinic of a hospital)	21
	guài	怪		to blame	20
	guānmén	關門	关门	to close the door	6

	guān.xi	關係	关系	relationship	11
	guǎn...jiào	管...叫		to call...X	16
	guāng	光		just	14
	guāngdié	光碟		CD (compact disc)	7
	guàngjiē	逛街		to do window shopping	12
	guì	貴	贵	(to be) expensive	7
*	guójì	國際	国际	international	21
	guómào	國貿	国贸	international business	6
	guónèi	國內	国内	domestic	21
	.guò	過	过	experiential suffix to verbs	10
*	guò	過	过	to pass	6
	guòmǐn	過敏	过敏	allergy	20

H

	hái	還	还	still	6
	hái.shì	還是	还是	or	6
	hái.shì	還是	还是	had better	9
	hái.zi	孩子		child (M:個)	16
*	hǎi'àn	海岸		coast	23
	hǎixiān	海鮮	海鲜	seafood	10
	hài	害		to cause someone (trouble)	17
	hánjià	寒假		winter vacation	14
	hǎn	喊		to shout, cry out, yell	17
*	hàn	和		and	5
	hànbǎo(bāo)	漢堡	汉堡包	hamburger (M: 個)	7
	hànzì	漢字	汉字	Chinese character (M: 個)	8
*	hángkōngxìn	航空信		airmail	21
	hǎo	好		(to be) good	6
	hǎohāor	好好兒		to do...well	18
	hǎojǐ-	好幾-	好几-	several	13
	hǎojí .le	好極了	好极了	wonderful, bravo	8
	hǎo jiǔ bú jiàn	好久不見		(= 很久不見) I haven't seen ... for a long time	14
	hǎoqiú	好球		good shot	19
	hǎotīng	好聽	好听	(to be) delightful to listen to	8
	hǎowánr	好玩兒	好玩儿	(to be) fun	14
	hǎo.xiàng	好像	好象	(it) seems (often followed by 似的)	17
	hǎo.xiàng... shì.de/sì.de	好像...似的	好象...似的	it seems as if...	11
	hàodòng	好動	好动	(to be) active or restless	17

	hàojìng	好靜		(to be) inactive	17
	hàokè	好客		(to be) hospitable	13
	hào	號	号	number, day of the month (colloquial), size (clothing only)	4
	hē	喝		to drink	7
*	hé	和		and	5
	hé	合		to suit, fit	14
	héchàng	合唱		chorus	18
	héshì	合適	合适	(to be) suitable	12
	hé.zi	盒子		box	21
	hēisè	黑色		black	12
	hèi	嘿		an interjection	4
	hěn	很		very	6
	hú	壺	壶	pot	10
	Húnán	湖南		Hunan—name of a province	10
	húqínr	胡琴兒	胡琴儿	two-stringed violin—Chinese musical instrument (M: 把)	18
	húshuō	胡說	胡说	nonsense!	17
	hóng	紅	红	(to be) red, redness	20
	hónglǜdēng	紅綠燈	红绿灯	traffic light	16
*	hòu.biānr	後邊兒	后边儿	behind (= 後頭)	15
	hòu.tiān	後天	后天	the day after tomorrow	4
*	huāfěn	花粉		pollen	20
	huāfěnrè	花粉熱	花粉热	hay fever	20
	huā qián	花錢	花钱	to spend money	21
	huā shíjiān	花時間	花时间	(to be) time-consuming	8
	huār	花兒	花儿	flower (M: 朵 duǒ, 把 bǎ 'a bunch')	16
	huá	華	华	China (=中華), splendid, gorgeous (=華麗)	12
	huáxuě	滑雪		to ski	14
	huàr	畫兒	画儿	painting (M:張)	15
	huàzhuāng	化妝	化妆	to put on makeup	22
*	huàzhuāngpǐn	化妝品	化妆品	cosmetics	22
*	huán	還	还	to return (something)	6
	huàn	換	换	to change (player/money), exchange	19
	huīchén	灰塵	灰尘	dust	20
*	huí	回		to return (to a place; from a trip; to original state), go back	6
*	huì	會	会	will, can, to know how to	9

	huǒjī	火雞	火鸡	turkey (M: 隻)	13
	huò(.zhě)	或(者)		or	13

J

	jī	雞	鸡	chicken (M: 隻 zhī 'M for birds')	10
	jīhuì jiàoyù	機會教育	机会教育	on-the-spot lecture	14
	jí	急		(to be) impatient, anxious	17
	jí.sǐrén	急死人		to rush anxiously	17
	jǐ	幾	几	how many, how much	4
	jǐ	幾	几	few, some (+M+N) (indefinite)	6
*	jǐ diǎn zhōng	幾點鐘	几点钟	what time?	6
	jì	寄		to send (by mail)	18
	jìcuò	記錯	记错	to remember incorrectly	22
	jì.de	記得	记得	to remember	18
*	jìhuà	計劃	计划	to plan, plan, project	23
	jì.xù	繼續	继续	to continue	23
*	jiā	家		measure word for stores, restaurants, cinema; home	6
	jiārén	家人		family member	16
	jiā	加	加	to add	6
	Jiā'nādà	加拿大		Canada	23
	jiàqī	假期		holiday, vacation	14
	jià.qián	價錢	价钱	price	12
	jiàshǐ	駕駛	驾驶	to drive (a vehicle); to steer (boats)	22
*	jiān	間	间	measure word for rooms and buildings	15
	jiǎn	剪		to cut (with scissors)	17
	jiǎn	撿	捡	to pick	19
	jiǎnféi	減肥		to go on a diet	13
*	jiǎnjià	減價	减价	price reduction	12
	jiàn	件		measure word for upper garments and coats, affairs	12
	jiànshēnfáng	健身房		gym	13
	jiǎngxuéjīn	獎學金	奖学金	scholarship	23
	jiāo	交		to turn in (homework), to pay (a fee)	13
*	jiāo	教		to teach	5
	jiāo	跤		measure word for falling on the ground	20
	jiāodài	膠帶	胶带	Scotch tape	21
*	jiǎo	角	角	dime (as printed on real money)	7
	jiǎo.zi	餃子	饺子	dumpling (M: 個)	10
	jiào	叫		to call, be called	8

	jiào	叫		to order	10
	jiào	叫		to cause, to tell (someone to do something)	20
	jiàoliàn	教練	教练	coach (of sports)	19
*	jiē	接		to pick someone up	13
	jiē	街		street (M: 條)	16
	jiéhūn	結婚	结婚	to get married, marriage	23
*	jié	節	节	measure word for classes	5
*	jiéshí	節食	节食	to go on a diet (=減肥)	13
	jiě.jiě	姐姐		older sister	14
	jiè	借		to borrow	6
	jièkǒu	藉口	借口	excuse (M: 個)	19
	jiè.shào	介紹	介绍	to introduce	8
*	jīn.nián	今年		this year	5
	jīn.tiān	今天		today	4
	jǐn	緊	紧	(to be) tight	12
*	jǐn.zhāng	緊張	紧张	(to be) nervous	18
*	jìn	近		(to be) near, close	21
	jìn	進	进	to enter	15
	jìnbù	進步	进步	to progress, progression, progress	23
	jīngjù	京劇	京剧	Beijing/Peking Opera	18
	jīng.shén	精神		vigor, vitality, spirited	17
	jīngyàn	經驗	经验	experience	11
	jǐngchá	警察		police	22
	jiǔ	九		nine	4
	jiù	就		just, precisely, then	7
	jiù.shì	就是		exactly, that/it is	16
	jiù	舊	旧	old (for things), used	7
*	jú.zishuǐ	桔子水		orange juice	10
	jǔbàn	舉辦	举办	to sponsor, to organize (an activity)	16
	jù	聚		to get together	18
	jué.de	覺得	觉得	to feel, think	7
	juédìng	決定	决定	to decide	6
	juéshìyuè	爵士樂	爵士乐	jazz	18

K

	kāfēi	咖啡		coffee	7
	kāfēi	咖啡		brown (color)	12
	kāi	開	开	to drive (a vehicle), to open (a can, box, etc.)	10
*	kāimén	開門	开门	to open the door	6

	kāishǐ	開始	开始	to begin, to start	11
	kāiwánxiào	開玩笑	开玩笑	to crack a joke, to joke	13
	kāixué	開學	开学	to start school/classes	4
	kāi yàofāng	開藥方	开药方	to give a prescription	20
	kàn	看		to see, to think (when expressing one's opinion)	9
	kànbìng	看病		to see a doctor	20
	kàn.chū.lái	看出來	看出来	to figure out	11
	kàn.jiàn	看見	看见	to see, catch sight of	14
	…kàn.kàn	(VO) 看看		just VO and see what happens	7
	kàn.qǐ.lái	看起來	看起来	(it) looks, (it) seems	13
*	kǎoshì	考試	考试	test, to have a test	18
	kǎoyā	烤鴨	烤鸭	roast duck	10
	kě	可		emphatic marker	11
	kě bú.shì .ma	可不是嗎	可不是吗	isn't it true?	11
	kěnéng	可能		probably	22
	kě.shì	可是		but	6
	kě.yǐ	可以		may	7
*	kè	課	课	lesson, course	4
*	kè	刻		quarter; to engrave	6
*	kètīng	客廳	客厅	living room (M:間)	15
	kěndìng	肯定		certainly	12
	kōngfáng	空房		vacant room (M:間)	15
	kōngqì	空氣	空气	air	20
	Kǒngzǐ	孔子		Confucius	16
*	kòngr	空兒	空儿	unoccupied time or space, leisure	9
	kǒu	口		measure word for people (in a family)	16
	kǒufú	口福		enjoyment of the palate	13
	kǒuwèir	口味兒	口味儿	taste, flavor	10
	kū	哭		to cry	11
*	kù.zi	褲子	裤子	pants (M: 條, V: 穿)	12
	kuài	快		(to be) quick	17
	kuàilè	快樂	快乐	happiness; happy	4
	kuàixìn	快信		express letter	21
	kuài(yào)	快(要)		soon, before long	6
	kuài	塊	块	lump, (hard) piece	20
	kuài (qián)	塊(錢)	块钱	dollar (colloquial)	7
*	kuān	寬		(to be) loose	12

L

	lā	拉		to play (violin, viola), to pull	8
	là	辣		(to be) hot, spicy	10
*	lái	來	来	to come	6
	lánqiú	籃球	篮球	basketball (M: 個)	12
	lánsè	藍色	蓝色	blue	12
	lǎoshī	老師	老师	teacher (M: 位 wèi)	8
	lǎo.shí	老實	老实	(to be) honest	17
	Lǎozǐ	老子		Laotzu	16
	.le	了		aspect marker for completed action	6
	léishè chàngpán	雷射唱盤	雷射唱盘	laser disc (M: 個)	14
	lèi	累		(to be) tired	6
	lèirén	累人		to make one tired	19
	lèi.sǐ	累死		(to be) very tired	15
	lěng	冷		(to be) cold	12
*	lěngshuǐ	冷水		cold water	20
	lí	離	离	to depart from, to separate	21
*	líhūn	離婚	离婚	to divorce, divorce	23
*	lí.kāi	離開	离开	to leave (a place) (trans. V)	21
	Lǐ	李		surname	4
	lǐwù	禮物	礼物	gift, present (M: 個)	14
*	lǐbài	禮拜	礼拜	(colloquial) week	4
	lǐ.tóu	裏頭	里头	inside	12
	lìkè	立刻		immediately	14
	lì.hài	厲害	厉害	(to be) awesome, be fierce	19
	lìyòng	利用		to utilize, to use (time/tool/chance)	13
	liǎ	倆		two (people)	16
	lián	連	连	including	21
	lián…dōu	連…都	连…都	even	18
	Liánhéguó	聯合國	联合国	United Nations	8
	liǎn	臉	脸	face (M: 張)	17
	liàn chē	練車	练车	to practice driving (= 練習開車)	22
	liàn.xí	練習	练习	to practice	8
	liángshuǐ	涼水	凉水	cool water	20
	liǎng	兩	两	two (occurs only before a measure word)	5
	liáo(tiān)	聊(天)		to chat	23
	Lín	林		surname, forest (= 樹林)	8
*	líng	零		zero	4

	lǐng	領	领	to pick up (things)	21
*	lǐngdān	領單	领单	a slip of paper that entitles the bearer to get something; receipt (M: 張)	21
	lǐngxiān	領先	领先	to lead (said of the score of a game)	19
	lìngwài	另外		another, other (Adv), besides	15
	liú	流		to flow, to run (water)	20
	liúxíng	流行		(to be) in fashion, (to be) in vogue	11
	liú	留		to stay	23
	liù	六		six	4
	lúntāi	輪胎	轮胎	tire (on a car)	22
*	lóu.shàng	樓上	楼上	upstairs	15
	lóu.xià	樓下	楼下	downstairs	15
	lù	路		road (M: 條)	16
	lùyīn	錄音	录音	recording	8
	lùyīndài	錄音帶	录音带	audio tape (M: 卷 juǎn)	7
	lùyíng	露營	露营	to camp, camping	23
	lǚguǎn	旅館	旅馆	hotel	23
	lǚxíng	旅行		to travel, traveling	23
*	luòhòu	落後	落后	to fall behind (said of the score of a game)	19
M					
	.ma	嗎	吗	particle for yes-or-no question	4
	.ma	嘛		particle for dogmatic assertion	19
	mā.mā	媽媽	妈妈	mother	8
	má.fán	麻煩	麻烦	(to be) troublesome, trouble, hassle	9
	mǎ.shàng	馬上	马上	immediately (=立刻)	21
	mǎi	買	买	to buy	6
*	mài	賣	卖	to sell	6
	màiwán	賣完	卖完	sold out	7
	mǎnchǎng	滿場	满场	the whole field	20
*	màn	慢		(to be) slow	17
	màntūntūn	慢吞吞		(to be) very slow	17
*	máng	忙		(to be) busy	6
	māo	貓	猫	cat (M: 隻)	16
	máo.bìng	毛病		illness; shortcoming	20
	máo (qián)	毛(錢)	毛(钱)	dime (colloquial)	7
	máoyī	毛衣		sweater (M: 件, V: 穿)	12
	mào.zi	帽子		hat, cap (M: 頂 dǐng, V: 戴)	12
	méi cuò	沒錯	没错	(you are) right	7

	méi qì .le	沒氣了	没气了	to have a flat tire, (to be) listless	22
	méi(.yǒu)	沒(有)		to not have	5
	Měi.guó	美國	美国	America	8
	měitiān	每天		every day	5
	mén	門	门	measure word for courses	6
	ménkǒu	門口	门口	entrance	9
*	mí	迷		fan	16
	Mìxīgēn	密西根		Michigan	19
	miǎn.de	免得		to avoid, so as not to	14
	miǎnfèi	免費	免费	(to be) free of charge	21
	miànbāo	麵包	面包	bread (M: 個/片 piàn 'slice')	11
*	miǎo	秒		second	6
	mín'gē	民歌		folk song	18
	míng.bái	明白		to understand	11
	míngmíng	明明		clearly	22
*	míng.nián	明年		next year	5
	míng.tiān	明天		tomorrow	4
*	míng.zi	名字		name	8
	mǒ	抹		to smear	20
	mòlìhuā	茉莉花		white jasmine flower	18
*	mǔ.qīn	母親	母亲	mother (formal)	8
	mù	木		tree (=樹木)	8

N

	ná	拿		to take, to bring (something)	15
*	ná	拿		to take, to bring (something)	15
*	nǎ	哪		which	4
	nǎr	哪兒	哪儿	where?	6
	nǎ yì tiān	哪一天		which day?	4
	nà	那		that	6
	nà.me	那麼	那么	so (as that)	14
	nàr	那兒	那儿	there	7
*	nàyàng	那樣	那样	that way, so (as that)	15
*	nán	男		male (for human beings)	11
	nán	難	难	(to be) difficult, hard	8
	nándào	難道	难道	do you mean to say (that)...?	22
	nándé	難得	难得	(to be) hard to get, (to be) rare, once in a blue moon, rarely	23
	nánguài	難怪	难怪	no wonder	14
	nánguò	難過	难过	(to be) sad	11
	nánshòu	難受	难受	(to be) unbearable, to feel bad	20

nánfāng	南方		the south	10
nánguāpài	南瓜派		pumpkin pie	13
.ne	呢		particle for interest in additional information; how about...?	4
.ne	呢		particle for sarcastic retort	14
* něi	哪		which	4
něi yì tiān	哪一天		which day?	4
nèi	那		that	6
* nèixiē	那些		those	7
nèiháng	內行		(to be) professional, to specialize in	18
nèixiàng	內向		(to be) introverted	17
néng	能		can	9
nǐ	你		you (sing.)	4
nǐ .de	你的		your	4
* nǐ.men	你們	你们	you (pl.)	4
* nián	年		year	4
niàn	念		to study (a subject)	6
* niúnǎi	牛奶		milk	10
niúròu	牛肉		beef (M: 斤 jīn 'catty,' 磅 bàng 'pound')	10
niúyóu	牛油		butter	11
niúzǎikù	牛仔褲	牛仔裤	jeans (M: 條)	14
* nòng	弄		to handle, to do (causative)	17
nǚ	女		female (for human beings)	11
nǚ'ér	女兒	女儿	daughter (M: 個)	11
nǚláng	女郎		woman (derogatory)	12
nǔlì	努力		(to be) hard-working	13
O				
.ou	噢		oh! (realization of something)	18
P				
pà	怕		(to be) afraid of, fear that	16
pāimài	拍賣	拍卖	a sale, an auction	12
páng.biānr	旁邊兒	旁边儿	side	15
pàotāng	泡湯	泡汤	to be gone, finish	7
péi	陪		to accompany	19
pèi	配		to match	17
pèichéng	配成		to match and form	12
pēn.tì	噴嚏	喷嚏	sneeze (M: 個)	20
* péng.yǒu	朋友		friend	5

pèng.jiàn/.dào	踫見/到	碰见/到	to meet someone unexpectedly; to bump into someone	21
pèng.shàng	踫上		to run into an unexpected situation; to bump into	17
píjiǔ	啤酒		beer (M: 杯 bēi 'cup,' 罐 guàn 'can,' 瓶 píng 'bottle')	10
pí.qì	脾氣	脾气	temperament, disposition	17
piān(piān)	偏(偏)		deliberately	20
pián.yí	便宜		(to be) cheap	7
piàn.zi	片子		film (M: 部 bù)	11
piào.liàng	漂亮		(to be) pretty, (to be) beautiful	11
píngcháng	平常		ordinarily, usually, (to be) ordinary, (to be) usual	14
píngshǒu	平手		to tie (in a ball game)	19
píngyóu	平郵	平邮	regular mail, surface mail	21
pò	破		(to be) broken	21
* pǔtōng hángkōng	普通航空		(regular) airmail	21

Q

qī	七		seven	4
qīmò	期末		end of a semester	13
qīmòkǎo	期末考		final examination	23
qíshí	其實	其实	actually, in fact	18
qíguài	奇怪		(to be) strange	18
qǐ(.lái)	起(來)	起(来)	to get up	17
-qǐ.lái	起來	起来	to start (an action)	14
qìrén	氣人	气人	to make one mad	19
qìshuǐr	汽水兒	汽水儿	soft drink (M: 杯 bēi 'cup,' 罐 guàn 'can,' 瓶 píng 'bottle')	10
qián	錢	钱	money	7
* qián.biānr	前邊兒	前边儿	front (= 前頭)	15
qián.tiān	前天		the day before yesterday	4
qiáng	牆	墙	wall	15
qiángdiào	強調	强调	to emphasize, to stress	23
qiánghuàbān	強化班		intensive course	23
qiáo	瞧		to look at, to see (= 看)	20
qiǎokèlì	巧克力		chocolate	16
qīng	青	青	blue, green	20
* qīng	輕	轻	(to be) light (course load, weight)	6
qīngsōng	輕鬆	轻松	(to be) relaxed	18
qíngkuàng	情況	情况	situation	20

*	qǐng	請	请	please, to request	7
	qǐng	請	请	to invite, treat	9
	qǐngwèn	請問	请问	may I ask?	7
	qìngzhù	慶祝	庆祝	to celebrate	16
*	qiú	球		ball (M: 個)	19
	qiúmí	球迷		sports fan	16
	qiúpāi	球拍		racket (M: 個)	19
	qiúsài	球賽	球赛	ball game (M: 場)	19
*	qiúwǎng	球網	球网	net on a tennis/volleyball court	19
	qiúxié	球鞋		athletic shoes, sneakers (M: 雙/ 隻)	14
	qiúyuán	球員	球员	player	19
*	qù	去		to go	6
*	qù.nián	去年		last year	5
	quán	全		complete, whole	14
	qún	群		measure word for a group of people or animals	12
	qúnkù	裙褲	裙裤	skort (M: 條, V: 穿)	12
*	qún.zi	裙子		skirt (M: 條, V: 穿)	12

R

	ránhòu	然後	然后	then, afterwards, later (preceded by 先)	23
	ràng	讓	让	to make, let (causative)	11
*	rè	熱	热	(to be) hot (temperature)	12
	rè.nào	熱鬧	热闹	to have many things going on (hustle and bustle)	16
	rén	人		person, people	8
	rèn.shí/rèn.shì	認識	认识	to know (a person or a character/word)	8
*	rì	日		day of the month (written form)	4
	Rìwén	日文		Japanese language	5
	róng.yì	容易		(to be) easy	8
	rúguǒ	如果		if (= 要是)	14

S

	sān	三		three	4
	sānmíngzhì	三明治		sandwich (M: 個)	7
*	shāchē	刹車	刹车	to brake, brake(s)	22
	shālā	沙拉		salad	11
	shān	山		mountain (M: 座 zuò)	14
*	shānshuǐhuà	山水畫	山水画	landscape painting (M: 張)	15
	shāng	傷	伤	to injure	20
*	shāngfēng	傷風	伤风	to catch a cold (=感冒)	20

	shāngchǎng	商場	商场	mall (M: 個)	12
	shāngxuéyuàn	商學院	商学院	business school	23
*	shàng	上		to ascend; to go to (street/school/class/work)	4
	shàng...qù/lái	上...去/來	上...去/来	to go there /come here	6
*	shàng.biānr	上邊兒	上边儿	on top of, above (=上頭)	15
	shàng.bùqǐ	上不起		not to be able to afford to go to school	23
	shàngkè	上課	上课	to go to class; to attend class	4
	shàng.wǔ	上午		morning, forenoon	5
	shāo	燒	烧	fever, to have a fever	20
*	shǎo	少		(to be) little (quantity), few	6
	shèhuì	社會	社会	society	11
*	shéi	誰	谁	who, whoever, whom, whomever	4
*	shéi .de	誰的	谁的	whose	4
	shēn.shàng	身上		on one's body, with one's self	7
	shēntǐ	身體	身体	body, health	10
	shén.me	什麼/甚麼	什么	what?	5
	shén.me .de	什麼的	什么的	and so forth	10
*	shén.me dì.fāng	什麼地方	什么地方	what place? where?	6
*	shén.me shí.hòu	什麼時候	什么时候	what time? when?	6
	shēngbìng	生病		to be sick (=病)	20
	shēngcài	生菜		raw vegetables, lettuce	11
	shēng.huó	生活		life	15
	(shēng)qì	(生)氣	(生)气	(to be) angry	19
	shēng.rì	生日		birthday	4
	shēngdiào	聲調	声调	tone	8
*	shēng.yīn	聲音	声音	sound	18
	shěngqián	省錢	省钱	to save money	23
	shèng	剩		to remain, left over	17
*	Shèngdànjié	聖誕節	圣诞节	Christmas (M: 個)	14
*	shī.fù	師傅	师傅	work master, chef	21
	shí	十		ten	4
	shízì lùkǒu	十字路口		intersection	22
	shízú .de	十足的		completely	18
*	shí.hòu	時候	时候	time	6
	shíjiān	時間	时间	time	9
	shísù	時速	时速	driving speed	22
	shípǐn	食品		food	21

	shíxí	實習	实习	to have an internship; internship	23
	shíyànshì	實驗室	实验室	laboratory (M: 間 jiān)	8
	shì	是		to be (is, was, are, were)	4
	shì	事		matters, affairs, undertaking (M: 件 jiàn)	9
	shì	式		style (Suf)	13
	shì(.yí)shì	試(一)試	试(一)试	to try, to give it a try	10
*	shìyǒu	室友		roommate	20
	shū.fú	舒服		(to be) comfortable	11
	shū	書	书	book	6
	shūdiàn	書店	书店	bookstore (M: 家 jiā)	6
	shūjià	書架	书架	bookcase (M: 個)	15
*	shū	輸	输	to lose	19
	shūyíng	輸贏	输赢	result (of a game)	19
	shǔjià	暑假		summer vacation	23
	shǔqī	暑期		summer	23
	shōu	收		to accept, to admit (to a study program), to collect (money, paper, tests, letters...)	23
	shōu.dào	收到		to receive	14
	shǒu	首		measure word for songs	18
	shǒutào	手套		gloves (M: 雙 /付 fù, V: 戴)	12
	shòu.bùliǎo	受不了		cannot stand it	11
	shòu...yǐngxiǎng	受...影響	受...影响	to be influenced by...	16
	shuāyá	刷牙		to brush the teeth	17
	shuāi	摔		to fall	20
	shuāng	雙	双	double, measure word for a pair (of things)	8
	shuǐdiàn	水電	水电	utilities charge	15
	shuǐpíng	水平		level, standard	23
*	shuìjiào	睡覺	睡觉	to sleep	14
	shuìlǎnjiào	睡懶覺	睡懒觉	to get up late	14
	shùnbiàn	順便	顺便	(to do something) while on one's way to perform a major task	21
	shuō	說	说	to say	7
	shuō.bùliǎo	說不了	说不了	(to be) unable to say	14
	shuō hǎohuà	說好話	说好话	to say something good	21
*	shuō huàihuà	說壞話	说坏话	to say something bad, to slander	21
	shuō zhēn .de	說真的	说真的	be serious!; quit kidding/joking!	13
	sījī	司機	司机	chauffeur, driver	21
	sì	四		four	4

	sòng	送		to take (someone to some place); to see (a person) off	13
*	sòng(gěi)	送(給)	送(给)	to present as a gift	14
	sùshè	宿舍		dormitory (M: 棟 dòng, 間 jiān)	7
	suān	酸		(to be) sour	10
	suānténg	酸疼		(to be) sore (=酸痛)	20
	suāntòng	酸痛		(to be) sore, (muscle) ache	14
	suàn.le	算了		forget it	10
	suīrán/suírán	雖然	虽然	although	8
	suíshēntīng	隨身聽	随身听	portable stereo, Walkman (M: 個 .ge)	7
	suǒ.yǐ	所以		therefore	11
T					
*	tā	他		he, she, him, her	4
*	tā	它		it	4
*	tā	她		she, her	4
*	tā .de	他的		his/her	4
	tā.men	他們	他们	they, them	4
	tándào	談到	谈到	to talk about	11
	tāng	湯	汤	soup (M: 碗 wǎn 'bowl')	10
	táng	糖		sugar, candy (M: 塊/盒 hé 'box')	10
	táng	堂		measure word for classes	5
	tàng	燙	烫	to perm, to iron (clothes)	17
	tàng	趟		measure word for trips	21
	tào	套		a set	12
	tèbié	特別		especially, particularly	11
*	téng	疼		(to be) painful	20
	tíqián	提錢	提钱	to withdraw (money)	21
	tǐyùguǎn	體育館	体育馆	gym (M: 個) (=健身房)	14
	tì	替		to substitute, to do... for...	21
*	tiān	天		day, sky	4
	tiān.qì	天氣	天气	weather	12
	tiāntiān	天天		every day	5
	tián	甜		(to be) sweet	10
	tiē	貼	贴	to paste	21
*	tīng	聽	听	to hear	8
	tīng.jiàn	聽見	听见	to hear, catch the sound of	16
	tīnglì	聽力	听力	listening comprehension	23
	tīngshuō	聽說	听说	to hear someone say	8
	tíng(chē)	停(車)	停(车)	to park (a car)	22

	tíngchēwèi	停車位	停车位	parking space	22
	tǐng	挺		very, quite (=很)	9
	tōngzhī	通知		to notify, to inform	21
	tóngwūr	同屋兒	同屋儿	roommate (China)	20
	tóngxuéhuì	同學會	同学会	student association	16
	tóu	頭	头	head (M: 個)	17
	tóu.fà/tóu.fǎ	頭髮	头发	hair on the head (M: 根 gēn, 頭)	17
	tóu(jìn)	(投)進	(投)进	to shoot (a ball)	19
*	tūrán	突然		suddenly	22
	túshūguǎn	圖書館	图书馆	library (M: 個 .ge)	6
	tù.zi	兔子		rabbit	20
	tuǐ	腿		leg	20
	tuì	退		to drop (a course), to withdraw (from school), to return (something to the store)	6
	tuō	拖		to tow, to drag	22

W

*	wàiháng	外行		(to be) inexperienced, amateurish, very much a layman	18
	wàitào	外套		an overcoat (M: 件, V: 穿) (=大衣)	12
*	wài.tóu	外頭	外头	outside	12
	wàixiàng	外向		(to be) outgoing, extroverted	17
*	wán	完		to finish	7
	wán	玩		to play	14
	wǎn	晚		(to be) late	17
	wǎnhuì	晚會	晚会	evening party	16
*	wǎn.shàng	晚上		evening, night	5
	Wànjīnyóu	萬金油	万金油	Tiger Balm	20
	wànyī	萬一	万一	a very tiny chance, just in case that...	22
	Wáng	王		surname	9
	wángzǐ	王子		prince	16
	wǎngqiú	網球	网球	tennis	19
	wǎngqiúchǎng	網球場	网球场	tennis court (M: 個)	15
	wàng .le	忘了		forgot	18
*	wàngjì	忘記	忘记	to forget	18
	wàng qián	往前		to go forward	16
	wàng	往		to, toward	16
	wéi	喂		hello	9
*	wéi	圍	围	to wear (scarf), to surround	12
	wéibór	圍脖兒	围脖儿	scarf (M: 條, V: 圍)	12

	wéijīnr	圍巾兒	围巾儿	scarf (M: 條, V: 圍) (=圍巾兒)	12
	wèi	位		measure word for people (polite)	10
*	wèi	胃		stomach	11
	wèikǒu	胃口		appetite	11
	wèidào	味道		taste, flavor (=口味兒), odor	10
*	wèishén.me	爲什麼	为什么	why	8
*	wèn	問	问	to ask	7
	wèntí	問題	问题	question, problem	20
	wǒ	我		I, me	4
	wǒ .de	我的		my	4
*	wǒ.men	我們	我们	we, us	4
*	wū.zi	屋子		room (M:間) (=房間)	15
	wǔ	五		five	4
	wǔmí	舞迷		dance fan	16

X

*	xī	吸		to smoke (cigarettes, etc.) (= 抽), to inhale	10
	xī'àn	西岸		West Coast	23
	xībù	西部		western (America)	8
	xīfāng	西方		Western	18
	xīwàng	希望		to hope, hope	23
	xíguàn	習慣	习惯	to get used to	16
	xǐ	洗		to wash	17
	xǐyīfáng	洗衣房		laundry room (M:間)	15
	xǐzǎo	洗澡		to bathe	17
	xǐzǎojiān	洗澡間	洗澡间	bathroom (M:間)	15
	Xǐfúhuì	喜福會	喜福会	*Joy Luck Club*—title of a movie	11
	xǐ.huān	喜歡	喜欢	to like	6
	xǐjù	喜劇	喜剧	comedy	11
*	xià	下		to descend, to go down; to get off (class/work)	4
*	xià.biānr	下邊兒	下边儿	underneath, below (=下頭)	15
	xià.cì	下次		next time	11
*	xiàkè	下課	下课	class dismissed	4
	xià.wǔ	下午		afternoon	5
	xiàtiān	夏天		summertime	23
	xiān	先		first	7
	xiàndài	現代	现代	current, modern	18
	xiànjīn	現金	现金	cash	15
*	xiànzài	現在	现在	now	6

	xiāng.zi	箱子		suitcase, box (M:個/隻)	15
	xiāngdāng	相當	相当	quite, rather (=挺)	11
	xiǎng	想		would like to; to think (=覺得)	8
*	xiàng	像	象	to resemble	8
	xiàng...yíyàng	像...一樣	象...一样	(it) seems the same as...	8
*	xiàngpiàn	相片		picture, photo (M:張) (=照片)	15
*	xiǎo	小		(to be) small, little (size), young (age)	4
	xiǎobā	小巴		van, mini-bus (M:部/輛)	13
	xiǎo.jiě	小姐		miss, young lady	14
	xiǎoshí	小時		an hour (M:個)	21
	xiǎoshuō	小說	小说	novel, fiction (M:本běn)	7
	xiǎotíqín	小提琴		violin	8
	xiǎo.xīn	小心		(to be) careful	22
*	xiào	笑		to laugh	11
	xiàowài	校外		off campus	14
	xiē	些		measure word for plural nouns; some (of plural N)	7
	xiē	歇		to rest (=休息)	15
	xiě	寫	写	to write	8
	xiě.bùliǎo	寫不了	写不了	(to be) unable to write	14
	xiěxìn	寫信	写信	to write a letter	14
	xiè.xie	謝謝	谢谢	thank (you)	7
	xīn	心		heart, mind	21
	xīn.lǐ	心裏	心里	in the heart, in mind	11
*	xīn	新		new	7
	xīnnián	新年		New Year	16
	xìn	信		letter (M:封)	21
	xìnyòngkǎ	信用卡		credit card (M:張)	15
	xīngqī	星期		(literary) week	4
	xíng	行		(to be) all right, can do, O.K.	13
	xìng	姓		to be surnamed	8
	xiū.xí	休息		to take a rest, to rest from work	5
	xuǎn	選	选	to take (a course) , to elect	6
	xuē.zi	靴子		boots (M:雙, V:穿)	12
*	xué	學	学	to learn, to study (=學習)	5
	xuéfèi	學費	学费	tuition	23
	xuéfēn	學分	学分	credits (M:個 .ge)	6
	xuéqī	學期	学期	semester (M:個 .ge)	6

*	xué.shēng	學生	学生	student	4
*	xuéxí	學習	学习	to learn, to study (=學)	5
*	xuéxiào	學校	学校	school	4
	xuě	雪		snow	14

Y

	.ya	呀		sentence particle–a variant of 啊	12
*	yājīn	押金		deposit	15
*	yá(chǐ)	牙(齒)	牙(齿)	tooth (M: 顆 kē)	17
	yān	煙	烟	cigarette, smoke	10
	yán	嚴	严	(to be) strict, stern	8
	yánjiū/yánjiù	研究	研究	to research	11
	yánsè	顏色	颜色	color	12
	yǎn	演		to act	11
	yǎnchànghuì	演唱會	演唱会	concert (V: 開)	18
	yǎnyuán	演員	演员	actor (M: 個)	11
	yǎn.jīng	眼睛		eye (M: 隻)	20
*	yǎnyào	眼藥	眼药	eyedrops	20
	yǎng	養	养	to raise	16
	yǎng	癢	痒	(to be) itchy	20
	yàng.zi	樣子	样子	style	12
	yàng.zi	樣子	样子	appearance	18
	yāo.qiú	要求		demand, request, to request (from senior to junior)	22
	yáogǔnyuè	搖滾樂	摇滚乐	rock-and-roll music	18
	yào	要		to want, will (=會), shall	6
	yào.bùrán	要不然		otherwise	17
	yào.shì	要是		if, suppose, in case	11
*	yào	藥	药	medicine, drug	20
*	yàofāng	藥方	药方	prescription	20
	Yēdànjié	耶誕節	耶诞节	Christmas (M: 個)	14
	yě	也		also, too	4
	yěxǔ	也許	也许	perhaps	23
	yè	頁	页	page	7
*	yè	夜		night, evening	17
*	yī.fú	衣服		clothes (M: 件, V: 穿)	12
	yī.shēng	醫生	医生	doctor	20
	yī	一		one	4
	yī...jiù...	一...就...		as soon as	14
	yídìng	一定		certainly, definitely	15

	yígòng	一共		altogether	7
	yíkuàir	一塊兒	一块儿	together	8
	…yíxià	V 一下		just V...	7
*	yíyàng	一樣	一样	(to be) the same	8
	yìbiānr... yìbiānr	一邊兒…, 一邊兒	一边儿…, 一边儿	on the one hand… on the other hand	22
	yì.diǎnr	一點兒	一点儿	a little bit	7
	yì.huǐr	一會兒	一会儿	a little while, a moment	15
	yì jiā rén	一家人		the whole family	14
	yì tiān dào wǎn	一天到晚		all day long	23
	yìzǎo	一早		early morning	13
	yìzhí	一直	一直	all the time	17
	yǐhòu	以後	以后	after (a given time), later	9
*	yǐqián	以前		before (a given time), previously	9
	yǐwéi	以爲	以为	to take (something) to be, to think incorrectly	18
	yǐ.jīng	已經	已经	already	6
	yīn.wèi	因爲	因为	because	8
	yīnmáng	音盲		tone-deaf	18
	yīnyuè	音樂	音乐	music	8
*	yínháng	銀行	银行	bank	21
	yínhūn	銀婚	银婚	silver anniversary	23
	Yìndà	印大		IU (Indiana University)	15
	Yīng.guó	英國	英国	England	8
	Yīngwén	英文		English	5
	yīnggāi	應該	应该	should, ought to, must （=得）	8
	yíng	贏	赢	to win	19
*	yǐngxiǎng	影響	影响	influence, to influence	16
	yòng	用		to use, with (instrument)	21
*	yònggōng	用功		(to be) diligent	6
	yóuqí	尤其		especially	10
	yóuyǒngchí	游泳池		swimming pool (M: 個)	15
	yóujú	郵局	邮局	post office	21
	yóupiào	郵票	邮票	stamp (M: 張)	21
*	yóuwùyuán	郵務員	邮务员	postmaster, postal clerk	21
	yóuzī	郵資	邮资	postage	21
	yǒu	有		to have	5
	yǒudào.lǐ	有道理		(to be) logical	23

*	yǒu .de	有的		some (+N)	7
*	yǒu gōng.fū	有功夫		to have free time	9
	yǒu kòngr	有空兒	有空儿	to have free time	9
	yǒu shén.me hǎo guàng .de?	有什麼好逛的	有什么好逛的	what is there to see window shopping?	12
	yǒushí.hòu	有時候	有时候	sometimes	14
	yǒuyì.si	有意思		interesting	8
	yòu	又		again, moreover	12
	yòu...yòu...	又...又...		both... and...	16
	yòu.biānr	右邊兒	右边儿	right side	15
	yòuzhuǎn	右轉	右转	to turn right	16
	yú	魚	鱼	fish (M: 條 tiáo 'stripe,' M for long and soft things)	10
	yǔyán	語言	语言	language (M: 種 zhǒng 'kind')	8
	yù.bèi	預備	预备	to prepare	5
*	yuán	元		dollar (written form)	7
*	yuán	圓	圆	dollar (as printed on real money)	7
	yuánlái	原來	原来	originally	12
	yuǎn	遠	远	(to be) far	21
	yuē	約	约	to make an appointment	20
	yuè	月		month	4
	yuèduì	樂隊	乐队	band	18
	yuè lái yuè...	越來越...	越来越...	(it's becoming) more/much Adj-er	12
	(yǔn)xǔ	(尤)許	(尤)许	to allow, to permit	22
	yùndòngchǎng	運動場	运动场	athletic field	13
Z					
	záhuòdiàn	雜貨店	杂货店	grocery store	21
	zài	在		(be) located at, in, on	7
	zài	再		then	7
	zàijiàn	再見	再见	goodbye	6
	zán.men	咱們	咱们	we, us (including the person addressed)	9
	zāo.le	糟了		to become a mess	17
*	zǎo	早		(to be) early	17
	zǎojiù	早就		to have already...	7
*	zǎo.shàng	早上		morning, forenoon (= 上午)	5
	zěn.me?	怎麼	怎么	how come?	11
	zěn.me bàn?	怎麼辦	怎么办	What should (one) do?	22
	zěn.me hǎo yì.si	怎麼好意思	怎么好意思	how can (one) let someone do...	13
	zěn.meyàng?	怎麼樣	怎么样	how is it?	6

*	zhàn	站		to stand	7
	zhàn	站		station	15
	zhàntíng	暫停	暂停	time-out	19
	zhǎng	長	长	to grow	11
	zhāojí	著急	着急	(to be) anxious, be worried	22
	zhǎo	找		to look for, to seek	9
	zhàopiàn	照片		picture, photo (M:張)	15
	.zhe	著	着	durative aspect marker	10
*	zhè/zhèi	這	这	this	6
	zhè.me	這麼	这么	this way (as…), so (as this)	8
	zhèr	這兒	这儿	here	7
	zhèixiē	這些	这些	these	7
	zhèyàng	這樣	这样	this way, so (as this), such	15
	zhéxuéjiā	哲學家	哲学家	philosopher	16
	zhēn	眞	真	really, real	11
	zhēn qiǎo	眞巧	真巧	what a coincidence!	21
	zhēn.shì .de	眞是的	真是的	give me a break!; (someone is) impossible; (something is) a little too much	12
	zhēn zāogāo	眞糟糕！	真糟糕！	what a mess! too bad!	22
	zhěng.lǐ	整理		to put in order, to tidy up	15
	zhěngtiān	整天		all day long	14
	zhènghǎo	正好		exactly right (at the moment/amount)	13
	(zhèng)zài	(正)在		V-ing	8
*	zhèng(qián)	挣(錢)	挣 (钱)	to make money, to earn money (=賺錢)	23
*	zhèngzhuàng	症狀	症状	symptom	20
	zhī.dào	知道		to know	15
	Zhījiāgē	芝加哥		Chicago	21
	zhīpiào	支票		check (M:張 zhāng)	15
	zhízhào	執照	执照	license	22
	zhǐ	只		only	17
	zhǐhǎo	只好		the only alternative is …	7
	zhǐ.shì	只是		merely, only, just (to be)	20
	zhǐ yào	只要		only (if/takes)	13
	Zhōng.guó	中國	中国	China	8
	Zhōngwén	中文		Chinese	5
*	zhōng.wǔ	中午		noon	5
*	zhōngtóu	鐘頭	钟头	an hour (M: 個) (= 小時)	21
	zhòng	重		(to be) heavy (course load, taste, weight)	6

	zhòng	重		to gain weight	13
	zhòngyào	重要		(to be) important	23
	zhōumò	週末	周末	weekend	5
	zhōunián	週年	周年	anniversary	23
	zhǔjué/jiǎo	主角	主角	leading actor	11
	zhǔxiū	主修		major, to major in	6
*	zhù	祝		to wish	4
	zhù	住		to live, to stay	16
	zhùcè	註冊	注册	to register (at school)	4
	zhuānxīn	專心	专心	(to be) concentrated	18
*	zhuānyè	專業	专业	specialty, major	6
	zhuàn(qián)	賺(錢)	赚(钱)	to make money, to earn money	23
	zhuī	追		to chase	20
	zhǔnbèi	準備	准备	to prepare (=預備)	21
	zǐ	紫		purple	20
	zìdiǎn	字典		dictionary (M: 本)	7
	zìjǐ	自己		oneself	9
	zìrán	自然		(to be) natural	11
	zǒng.shì	總是	总是	always (= 老是)	22
	zǒu	走		to walk, to leave (a place) (intrans. V)	8
	zǒu.búdòng	走不動	走不动	(to be) too tired to walk	14
*	zū	租		to rent	15
	zǔ	組	组	to organize	18
	zuìjìn	最近		recently, lately	11
*	zuó.tiān	昨天		yesterday	4
	zuǒ.biānr	左邊兒	左边儿	left side	15
	zuò	坐		to sit	7
	zuò	坐		to go by (bus, airplane, ship)	13
	zuò	做		to do, to make	5
	zuòwén	作文		composition (M: 篇 piān)	9
*	zuòyè	作業	作业	homework (= 功課)	13

◎ By English

English	Pinyin	Character		L
A				
* above (=上頭)	shàng.biānr	上邊兒	上边儿	15
accept, to	shōu	收		23
accompany, to	péi	陪		19
according to schedule	ànshí	按時	按时	20
ache (muscle)	suāntòng	酸痛		14
act as, to	dāng	當	当	21
act, to	yǎn	演		11
active or restless, (to be)	hàodòng	好動	好动	17
actor	yǎnyuán	演員	演员	11
actually	qíshí	其實	其实	18
add, to	jiā	加	加	6
address	dìzhǐ	地址		16
admit (to a study program), to	shōu	收		23
affairs	shì	事		9
afraid of, (to be)	pà	怕		16
after (a given time)	yǐhòu	以後	以后	9
afternoon	xià.wǔ	下午		5
afterwards	ránhòu	然後	然后	23
again	yòu	又		12
air	kōngqì	空氣	空气	20
* airmail	hángkōngxìn	航空信		21
* airmail (regular)	pǔtōng hángkōng	普通航空		21
airplane	fēijī	飛機	飞机	13
airport	(fēi)jīchǎng	(飛)機場	(飞)机场	13
all (Adv)	dōu	都		5
all (N)	dàjiā	大家		10
all day long	zhěngtiān	整天		14
all day long (=整天)	yì tiān dào wǎn	一天到晚		23
all right, (to be)	xíng	行		13
all the time	yìzhí	一直	一直	17
allergic to, to be	duì...guòmǐn	對...過敏	对...过敏	20
allergy	guòmǐn	過敏	过敏	20
allow, to	(yún)xǔ	(允)許	(允)许	22
almost	bāchéng	八成		22
already	yǐ.jīng	已經	已经	6

also	yě	也		4
although	suīrán/suírán	雖然	虽然	8
altogether	yígòng	一共		7
always (=老是)	zǒng.shì	總是	总是	22
* amateurish, (to be)	wàiháng	外行		18
America	Měi.guó	美國	美国	8
and	gēn	跟		5
* and (= 和)	hé/hàn	和		5
and so forth	shén.me .de	什麼的	什么的	10
and yet	búguò	不過	不过	8
angry, (to be)	(shēng)qì	(生)氣	(生)气	19
anniversary	zhōunián	週年	周年	23
another	lìngwài	另外		15
anxious, (to be)	jí	急		17
anxious, (to be) (= 急)	zhāojí	著急	着急	22
apartment	gōngyù	公寓		15
appearance	yàng.zi	樣子	样子	18
appetite	wèikǒu	胃口		11
argue, to	chǎo(jià)	吵(架)		14
arrive late, to	chídào	遲到	迟到	17
as soon as	yī...jiù...	一...就...		14
* ascend, to	shàng	上		4
* ashamed, (to be)	bù hǎo yì.si	不好意思		13
* ask, to	wèn	問	问	7
aspect marker for completed action	.le	了		6
aspect marker, durative	.zhè	著	着	10
aspect, an	fāngmiàn	方面		11
assist, to	bāng	幫	帮	12
assistance	bāngmáng	幫忙	帮忙	16
athletic field	yùndòngchǎng	運動場	运动场	13
athletic shoes	qiúxié	球鞋		14
attend (a conference, meeting), to	cānjiā	參加	参加	16
attend class, to	shàngkè	上課	上课	4
auction, an	pāimài	拍賣	拍卖	12
audio tape	lùyīndài	錄音帶	录音带	7
audio tape (China)	cídài	磁帶	磁带	7
authentic	dì.dào	地道		9

* authentic (= 地道)	dào.dì	道地		9
avoid, to	miǎn.de	免得		14
awesome, (to be)	lì.hài	屬害	厉害	19

B

* ball	qiú	球		19
ball game	qiúsài	球賽	球赛	19
band	yuèduì	樂隊	乐队	18
* bank	yínháng	銀行	银行	21
basketball	lánqiú	籃球	篮球	12
bathe, to	xǐzǎo	洗澡		17
bathroom	xǐzǎojiān	洗澡間	洗澡间	15
be (someone), to	dāng	當	当	21
be in trouble, to	chūshìr	出事兒	出事儿	22
be nice to...	duì...hǎo	對... 好	对... 好	10
be serious!	shuō zhēn .de	說眞的	说真的	13
be too weak/sick to (do something)	bùxíng.le	不行了		19
be, to	shì	是		4
beautiful, (to be)	piào.liàng	漂亮		11
because	yīn.wèi	因爲	因为	8
become a mess, to	zāo.le	糟了		17
become, to	biànchéng	變成	变成	13
beef	niúròu	牛肉		10
beer	píjiǔ	啤酒		10
* before (a given time)	yǐqián	以前		9
before long	kuài(yào)	快(要)		6
begin, to	kāishǐ	開始	开始	11
* behind (= 後頭)	hòu.biānr	後邊兒	后边儿	15
Beijing/Peking Opera	jīngjù	京劇	京剧	18
* below (=下頭)	xià.biānr	下邊兒	下边儿	15
besides (Adv)	lìngwài	另外		15
besides (Conj)	chú.le... yǐwài	除了...以外		12
besides (Conj)	érqiě	而且		9
* betroth, to/-al	dìnghūn	訂婚	订婚	23
big, (to be)	dà	大		4
birthday	shēng.rì	生日		4
black	hēisè	黑色		12
blame, to	guài	怪		20
blow dry, to	chuīgān	吹乾	吹干	17

	English	Pinyin	Traditional	Simplified	Lesson
	blow, to	chuī	吹		17
*	blow, to	chuīfēng	吹風	吹风	17
	blue	qīng	青	青	20
	blue (colloquial)	lánsè	藍色	蓝色	12
	body	shēntǐ	身體	身体	10
	book	shū	書	书	6
	bookcase	shūjià	書架	书架	15
	bookstore	shūdiàn	書店	书店	6
	boots	xuē.zi	靴子		12
*	border	.biānr	邊兒	边儿	15
	borrow, to	jiè	借		6
	both	dōu	都		5
	both... and...	yòu...yòu...	又...又...		16
	bottom	dǐ	底		23
	box	hé.zi	盒子		21
	box	xiāng.zi	箱子		15
*	brake, a/to	shāchē	刹車	刹车	22
	bravo	hǎojí.le	好極了	好极了	8
	bread	miànbāo	麵包	面包	11
	bring along, to	dài	帶	带	14
*	bring, to	ná	拿		15
	broken, (to be)	pò	破		21
	brown (color)	kāfēi	咖啡		12
	bruise ointment	diédǎyào	跌打藥	跌打药	20
	brush the teeth, to	shuāyá	刷牙		17
	bump into someone, to	pèng.jiàn/.dào	踫見/到	碰见/到	21
	bump into, to	pèng.shàng	踫上		17
	burn the midnight oil, to	áoyè	熬夜		17
*	bus	gōnggòng qìchē	公共汽車	公共汽车	13
*	bus (= 公共汽車)	gōngchē	公車	公车	13
	business school	shāngxuéyuàn	商學院	商学院	23
*	busy, (to be)	máng	忙		6
	but	kě.shì	可是		6
	but (= 可是)	dàn.shì	但是		8
	but (preceded by 不是)	ér.shì	而是		8
	butter	niúyóu	牛油		11
	buy, to	mǎi	買	买	6
	by	bèi	被		22

C

call, to	jiào	叫		8
call...X, to	guǎn...jiào	管...叫		16
called, to be	jiào	叫		8
camp, to/-ing	lùyíng	露營	露营	23
can	néng	能		9
* can (to know how to)	huì	會	会	9
can do	xíng	行		13
Canada	Jiā'nādà	加拿大		23
candy	táng	糖		10
cannot go on (doing something)	bùxíng.le	不行了		19
cannot stand it	shòu.bùliǎo	受不了		11
cap	mào.zi	帽子		12
car	chē	車	车	10
careful, (to be)	xiǎo.xīn	小心		22
carry, to	dài	帶	带	14
cash	xiànjīn	現金	现金	15
cat	māo	貓	猫	16
catch a cold, to	gǎnmào	感冒		20
* catch a cold, to (=感冒)	shāngfēng	傷風	伤风	20
catch sight of, to	kàn.jiàn	看見	看见	14
catch the sound of, to	tīng.jiàn	聽見	听见	16
cause (someone to do something), to	jiào	叫		20
cause someone (trouble), to	hài	害		17
CD (compact disc)	guāngdié	光碟		7
celebrate, to	qìngzhù	慶祝	庆祝	16
* cent	fēn (qián)	分(錢)	分(钱)	7
ceremony	diǎnlǐ	典禮	典礼	23
certainly	kěndìng	肯定		12
certainly (=肯定)	yídìng	一定		15
change (player/money), to	huàn	換	换	19
change (rule/situation), to	gǎi	改		22
change, to	biàn	變	变	18
chase, to	zhuī	追		20
chat, to	liáo(tiān)	聊(天)		23
chauffeur	sījī	司機	司机	21
cheap, (to be)	pián.yí	便宜		7
check	zhīpiào	支票		15

	check, to	chá	查		7
*	chef	shī.fù	師傅	师傅	21
	Chicago	Zhījiāgē	芝加哥		21
	chicken	jī	雞	鸡	10
	child	hái.zi	孩子		16
	China	Zhōng.guó	中國	中国	8
	China (=中華)	huá	華	华	12
	Chinese	Zhōngwén	中文		5
	Chinese character	hànzì	漢字	汉字	8
	chocolate	qiǎokèlì	巧克力		16
	chorus	héchàng	合唱		18
	Christmas	Yēdànjié	耶誕節	耶诞节	14
*	Christmas (=耶誕節)	Shèngdànjié	聖誕節	圣诞节	14
	cigarette	yān	煙	烟	10
*	class dismissed	xiàkè	下課	下课	4
*	clean up, to	dǎsǎo	打掃	打扫	15
	clearly	míngmíng	明明		22
	close the door, to	guānmén	關門	关门	6
*	close, (to be)	jìn	近		21
*	clothes	yī.fú	衣服		12
	coach (of sports)	jiàoliàn	教練	教练	19
*	coast	hǎi'àn	海岸		23
	coffee	kāfēi	咖啡		7
*	cold water	lěngshuǐ	冷水		20
	cold, (to be)	lěng	冷		12
	collect (money, paper, tests, letters...), to	shōu	收		23
	college	dàxué	大學	大学	12
	color	yánsè	顏色	颜色	12
	come /go from (a place), to	cóng...lái/qù	從...來/去	从...来/去	8
*	come, to	lái	來	来	6
	comedy	xǐjù	喜劇	喜剧	11
	comfortable, (to be)	shū.fú	舒服		11
	commit a foul, to	fànguī	犯規	犯规	19
*	commodities	bǎihuò	百貨	百货	12
*	company	gōngsī	公司		12
	comparatively	bǐjiào	比較	比较	10
*	compare, to	bǐ	比		10

comparison	bǐjiào	比較	比较	10
compete, to	bǐsài	比賽	比赛	19
competition	bǐsài	比賽	比赛	19
complain, to	bàoyuàn	抱怨		20
complete	quán	全		14
completely	shízú .de	十足的		18
composition	zuòwén	作文		9
computer	diànnǎo	電腦	电脑	7
concentrated, (to be)	zhuānxīn	專心	专心	18
concert	yǎnchànghuì	演唱會	演唱会	18
Confucius	Kǒngzǐ	孔子		16
congratulate, to	gōngxǐ	恭喜		16
constitute, to	chéng	成		8
continue, to	jì.xù	繼續	继续	23
convenient, (to be)	fāng.biàn	方便		13
cool water	liángshuǐ	涼水	凉水	20
correct, to	gǎi	改		22
* cosmetics	huàzhuāngpǐn	化妝品	化妆品	22
couple	duìr	對兒	对儿	17
* course	kè	課	课	4
crack a joke, to	kāiwánxiào	開玩笑	开玩笑	13
credit card	xìnyòngkǎ	信用卡		15
credits	xuéfēn	學分	学分	6
cry out, to	hǎn	喊		17
cry, to	kū	哭		11
cup	bēi	杯		7
current	xiàndài	現代	现代	18
cut (with scissors), to	jiǎn	剪		17

D

dance fan	wǔmí	舞迷		16
daughter	nǚ'ér	女兒	女儿	11
daughter of father's sister or mother's sibling, who is younger than oneself	biǎomèi	表妹		23
* day	tiān	天		4
day after tomorrow, the	hòu.tiān	後天	后天	4
day before yesterday, the	qián.tiān	前天		4
day of the month (colloquial)	hào	號	号	4
* day of the month (written)	rì	日		4

	decide, to	juédìng	決定	决定	6
	definitely	yídìng	一定		15
	delay, to	(dān)wù	(耽)誤	(耽)误	23
	deliberately	piān(piān)	偏(偏)		20
	delightful to listen to, (to be)	hǎotīng	好聽	好听	8
	demand	yāo.qiú	要求		22
	depart from, to	lí	離	离	21
	department store	bǎihuò gōngsī	百貨公司	百货公司	12
*	department store (China)	bǎihuò dàlóu	百貨大樓	百货大楼	12
	deposit	dìngjīn	定金		15
*	deposit (=定金)	yājīn	押金		15
	deposit (money), to	cúnqián	存錢	存钱	21
*	descend, to	xià	下		4
	dial a wrong number, to	dǎcuò	打錯	打错	9
	dictionary	zìdiǎn	字典		7
	difficult, (to be)	nán	難	难	8
*	diligent, (to be)	yònggōng	用功		6
	dime (colloquial)	máo (qián)	毛(錢)	毛(钱)	7
*	dime (as printed on real money)	jiǎo	角	角	7
*	dining room	fàntīng	飯廳	饭厅	15
	discover, to, discovery	fāxiàn	發現	发现	22
	dishes	cài	菜		9
	disposition	pí.qì	脾氣	脾气	17
	divide, to	fēn	分		10
*	divorce, a/to	líhūn	離婚	离婚	23
	do physical training, to	duàn.liàn	鍛練	锻练	13
	do something while on one's way to perform a major task, to	shùnbiàn	順便	顺便	21
	do window shopping, to	guàngjiē	逛街		12
	do you mean to say that...?	nándào	難道	难道	22
	do, to	zuò	做		5
*	do, to (causative)	nòng	弄		17
	do... for... , to	tì	替		21
	do...well, to	hǎohāor	好好兒		18
	doctor	yī.shēng	醫生	医生	20
*	doctor (=醫生)	dài.fu	大夫		20
*	doesn't have to	búyòng	不用		5
*	doesn't have to (=不必)	búbì	不必		5

* dog	gǒu	狗		16
dollar (colloquial)	kuài (qián)	塊 (錢)	块钱	7
* dollar (written form)	yuán	元		7
* dollar (as printed on real money)	yuán	圓	圆	7
domestic	guónèi	國內	国内	21
don't	bié	別		11
don't be modest!	bié kè.qì	別客氣	别客气	18
dormitory	sùshè	宿舍		7
double	shuāng	雙	双	8
down payment	dìngjīn	定金		15
downstairs	lóu.xià	樓下	楼下	15
dozen	dǎ	打		16
drag, to	tuō	拖		22
drink, to	hē	喝		7
drive (a vehicle), to	kāi	開	开	10
drive (a vehicle), to (literary)	jiàshǐ	駕駛	驾驶	22
driver	sījī	司機	司机	21
driving speed	shísù	時速	时速	22
drop (a course), to	tuì	退		6
* drug	yào	藥	药	20
dumpling	jiǎo.zi	餃子	饺子	10
dust	huīchén	灰塵	灰尘	20
E				
early morning	yìzǎo	一早		13
* early, (to be)	zǎo	早		17
* earn money, to	zhèngqián	掙(錢)	挣(钱)	23
earn money, to	zhuànqián	賺(錢)	赚(钱)	23
East Coast	dōng'àn	東岸	东岸	23
* East, the	dōngfāng	東方	东方	18
* Eastern	dōngfāng	東方	东方	18
eastern (America)	dōngbù	東部		8
easy, (to be)	róng.yì	容易		8
eat and drink a lot, to	dà chī dà hē	大吃大喝		13
* eat to the full, to	bǎo	飽	饱	11
eat, to	chī	吃		7
eggroll	chūnjuǎnr	春捲兒	春卷儿	10
eight	bā	八		4
eighty percent	bāchéng	八成		22

elect, to	xuǎn	選	选	6
e-mail	diàn.zixìn	電子信	电子信	21
* embarrassed, (to be)	bù hǎo yì.si	不好意思		13
emphasize, to	qiángdiào	強調	强调	23
emphatic marker	kě	可		11
end of a semester	qīmò	期末		13
* engage, to/-ment	dìnghūn	訂婚	订婚	23
England	Yīng.guó	英國	英国	8
English	Yīngwén	英文		5
enjoyment of the palate	kǒufú	口福		13
enough, (to be)	gòu	夠	够	16
enter, to	jìn	進	进	15
entrance	ménkǒu	門口	门口	9
especially	tèbié	特別		11
especially	yóuqí	尤其		10
* even (Adv)	gèng	更		12
even (Conj)	lián...dōu	連...都	连...都	18
* evening (MTA)	wǎn.shàng	晚上		5
* evening (N)	yè	夜		17
evening party	wǎnhuì	晚會	晚会	16
everybody	dàjiā	大家		10
every day	měitiān	每天		5
every day (=每天)	tiāntiān	天天		5
exactly right (at the moment/amount)	zhènghǎo	正好		13
exactly, that/it is	jiù.shì	就是		16
except for	chú.le...yǐwài	除了...以外		12
exchange, to	huàn	換	换	19
excuse	jièkǒu	藉口	借口	19
executive/disposal construction marker	bǎ	把		15
expensive, (to be)	guì	貴	贵	7
experience	jīngyàn	經驗	经验	11
expose to cold wind, to	chuīfēng	吹風	吹风	20
express letter	kuàixìn	快信		21
* extraordinarily	fēicháng	非常		6
extroverted, (to be)	wàixiàng	外向		17
eye	yǎn.jīng	眼睛		20
* eyedrops	yǎnyào	眼藥	眼药	20

F

	face	liǎn	臉	脸	17
*	face, to	duì	對	对	4
	facing, (to be)	duì.zhe	對著	对着	14
	fair, (to be)	gōngpíng	公平		19
	fall back to an old illness or old bad habit, to	fàn	犯		20
*	fall behind (said of the score of a game), to	luòhòu	落後	落后	19
	fall, to	shuāi	摔		20
	family member	jiārén	家人		16
*	fan	mí	迷		16
	far, (to be)	yuǎn	遠	远	21
	father	bà.bà	爸爸		8
*	father (formal)	fù.qīn	父親	父亲	8
	fear that, to	pà	怕		16
	feel bad, to	nánshòu	難受	难受	20
*	feel shy, to	bù hǎo yì.si	不好意思		13
	feel, to	jué.de	覺得	觉得	7
	female (for human beings)	nǚ	女		11
	fever	shāo	燒	烧	20
	few (indefinite)	jǐ	幾	几	6
*	few, (to be)	shǎo	少		6
	fiction	xiǎoshuō	小說	小说	7
	fierce, (to be)	lì.hài	厲害	厉害	19
	fifty percent discount, a	duìzhé	對折	对折	12
	figure out, to	kàn.chū.lái	看出來	看出来	11
	fill with air (with an air pump), to	gěi…dǎqì	給…打氣	给…打气	22
	film	piàn.zi	片子		11
	final examination	qīmòkǎo	期末考		23
*	final examination (=期末考)	dàkǎo	大考		23
*	fine, to	fá	罰	罚	19
	finish	pàotāng	泡湯	泡汤	7
*	finish, to	wán	完		7
	first	xiān	先		7
*	first, the	dìyī	第一		4
	fish	yú	魚	鱼	10
	fit, to	hé	合		14
	five	wǔ	五		4

flavor	kǒuwèir	口味兒	口味儿	10
flavor (=口味兒)	wèidào	味道		10
flow, to	liú	流		20
flower	huār	花兒	花儿	16
folk song	mín'gē	民歌		18
follow... to (there/here), to	gēn...qù/lái	跟...去/來	跟...去/来	14
follow, to	gēn	跟		10
food	shípǐn	食品		21
forenoon	shàng.wǔ	上午		5
* forenoon (=上午)	zǎo.shàng	早上		5
forest (= 樹林)	lín	林		8
forget it	suàn.le	算了		10
* forget, to	wàngjì	忘記	忘记	18
forgot	wàng.le	忘了		18
four	sì	四		4
free of charge, (to be)	miǎnfèi	免費	免费	21
* friend	péng.yǒu	朋友		5
friend in need, be a true friend, to be a	gòu péng.yǒu	夠朋友	够朋友	21
from	cóng	從	从	11
* front (= 前頭)	qián.biānr	前邊兒	前边儿	15
fun, (to be)	hǎowánr	好玩兒	好玩儿	14
furthermore	érqiě	而且		9

G

gain weight, to	zhòng	重		13
genuine	dì.dào	地道		9
* genuine (=地道)	dào.dì	道地		9
Germany	Dé.guó	德國	德国	8
get married, to	jiéhūn	結婚	结婚	23
* get off (class, work), to	xià	下		4
get together, to	jù	聚		18
get up late, to	shuìlǎnjiào	睡懶覺	睡懒觉	14
get up, to	qǐ(.lái)	起(來)	起(来)	17
get used to, to	xíguàn	習慣	习惯	16
gift	lǐwù	禮物	礼物	14
give a discount, to	dǎzhé	打折		12
give a prescription, to	kāi yàofāng	開藥方	开药方	20
give it a try, to	shì(.yí)shì	試(一)試	试(一)试	10
give me a break!	zhēn.shì.de	眞是的	真是的	12

	give, to	gěi	給	给	7
	give... encouragement, to	gěi...dǎqì	給...打氣	给...打气	22
	gloves	shǒutào	手套		12
*	go back, to	huí	回		6
	go by (bus, airplane, ship), to	zuò	坐		13
*	go down, to	xià	下		4
	go forward, to	wàng qián	往前		16
	go on a diet, to	jiǎnféi	減肥		13
*	go on a diet, to (=減肥)	jiéshí	節食	节食	13
	go out, to	chū.qù	出去		9
	go there /come here, to	dào...qù/lái	到...去/來	到... 去/来	6
	go there /come here, to	shàng...qù/lái	上... 去/來	上... 去/来	6
*	go to (street/school/class/work), to	shàng	上		4
	go to class, to	shàngkè	上課	上课	4
*	go, to	qù	去		6
	golf	gāo'ěrfū qiú	高爾夫球	高尔夫球	19
	gone, to be	pàotāng	泡湯	泡汤	7
	good shot	hǎoqiú	好球		19
	good, (to be)	hǎo	好		6
	goodbye	zàijiàn	再見	再见	6
*	goods	bǎihuò	百貨	百货	12
	gorgeous (=華麗)	huá	華	华	12
	graduate, to	bìyè	畢業	毕业	23
	graduation	bìyè	畢業	毕业	23
	Great Wall, the	Chángchéng	長城	长城	10
	green	qīng	青	青	20
	grocery store	záhuòdiàn	雜貨店	杂货店	21
	grow, to	zhǎng	長	长	11
	gym	jiànshēnfáng	健身房		13
	gym (=健身房)	tǐyùguǎn	體育館	体育馆	14
H					
	had better	hái.shì	還是	还是	9
*	hair dryer	chuīfēngjī	吹風機	吹风机	17
	hair on the head	tóu.fà/tóu.fǎ	頭髮	头发	17
	half	bàn	半		9
	half-time (of a game)	bànchǎng	半場	半场	19
	hamburger	hànbǎo(bāo)	漢堡	汉堡包	7
*	handle, to	nòng	弄		17

	hang up, to	guà	掛	挂	15
	happiness	kuàilè	快樂	快乐	4
	happy	kuàilè	快樂	快乐	4
	happy	gāoxìng	高興	高兴	11
	hard to get, (to be)	nándé	難得	难得	23
	hard, (to be)	nán	難	难	8
	hard-working, (to be)	nǔlì	努力		13
	hassle	má.fán	麻煩	麻烦	9
	hat	mào.zi	帽子		12
	have a fever, to	(fā)shāo	(發)燒	(发)烧	20
	have a flat tire, to	méi qì .le	沒氣了	没气了	22
	have a holiday/vacation, to	fàngjià	放假		13
	have a relapse, to	fàn	犯		20
	have a shot, to	dǎzhēn	打針	打针	20
*	have a test, to	kǎoshì	考試	考试	18
	have already... , to	zǎojiù	早就		7
	have an accident, to	chūshìr	出事兒	出事儿	22
	have an internship, to	shíxí	實習	实习	23
	have disappeared, to	bújiàn.le	不見了	不见了	22
*	have free time, to	yǒu gōng.fū	有功夫		9
	have free time, to	yǒu kòngr	有空兒	有空儿	9
	have many things going on (hustle and bustle), to	rè.nào	熱鬧	热闹	16
	have never... , to	cónglái dōu méi...	從來都沒...	从来都没...	22
	have to, to	děi	得		5
	have, to	yǒu	有		5
	haven't seen... for a long time (＝很久不見)	hǎo jiǔ bú jiàn	好久不見		14
	hay fever	huāfěnrè	花粉熱	花粉热	20
*	he	tā	他		4
	head	tóu	頭	头	17
	health	shēntǐ	身體	身体	10
	hear someone say, to	tīngshuō	聽說	听说	8
*	hear, to	tīng	聽	听	8
	hear, to (RV)	tīng.jiàn	聽見	听见	16
	heart	xīn	心		21
	heavy (course load, taste, weight), (to be)	zhòng	重		6
	hello	wéi	喂		9

	help, to	bāng	幫	帮	12
	help, to (VO)	bāngmáng	幫忙	帮忙	16
	helpful to, (to be)	duì...yǒu bāngzhù	對... 有幫助	对... 有帮助	23
*	her	tā	她		4
	here	zhèr	這兒	这儿	7
	high	gāo	高		4
	high opinion	gāojiàn	高見	高见	11
*	him	tā	他		4
*	his/her	tā .de	他的		4
*	hit the ball/target, to	dǎdào	打到		19
*	hit the ball/target, to	dǎzhòng	打中		19
	hit, to	dǎ	打		19
	holiday	jiàqī	假期		14
	home	jiā	家		6
	homework	gōngkè	功課	功课	5
*	homework (= 功課)	zuòyè	作業	作业	13
	honest, (to be)	lǎo.shí	老實	老实	17
	hope, a/to	xīwàng	希望		23
	hospitable, (to be)	hàokè	好客		13
*	hot (temperature), (to be)	rè	熱	热	12
	hot, (to be)	là	辣		10
	hotel	lǚguǎn	旅館	旅馆	23
	hour, an	xiǎoshí	小時		21
*	hour, an (=小時)	zhōngtóu	鐘頭	钟头	21
	house	fáng.zi	房子		14
	how about...?	.ne	呢		4
	how can (one) let someone do…	zěn.me hǎo yì.si	怎麼好意思	怎么好意思	13
	how come?	zěn.me?	怎麼	怎么	11
	how is it?	zěn.meyàng?	怎麼樣	怎么样	6
*	how long	duójiǔ	多久		14
	how many, how much	jǐ	幾	几	4
	how many	duō.shǎo	多少		7
	how much	duō.shǎo	多少		7
	Hunan—name of a province	Húnán	湖南		10
	hundred	bǎi	百		7
	hungry, (to be)	è	餓	饿	11
	hurry, to	gǎn	趕	赶	17

I

I	wǒ	我		4
if	yào.shì	要是		11
if (= 要是)	rúguǒ	如果		14
illness	máo.bìng	毛病		20
immediately	lìkè	立刻		14
immediately (=立刻)	mǎ.shàng	馬上	马上	21
impatient, (to be)	jí	急		17
important, (to be)	zhòngyào	重要		23
impossible, (someone is)	zhēnshì.de	眞是的	真是的	12
in case	yào.shì	要是		11
in fact	qíshí	其實	其实	18
in fashion, (to be)	liúxíng	流行		11
in mind	xīn.lǐ	心裏	心里	11
in the heart	xīn.lǐ	心裏	心里	11
in vogue, (to be)	liúxíng	流行		11
inactive, (to be)	hàojìng	好靜		17
include, to	bāo	包		15
including	lián	連	连	21
* inexperienced, (to be)	wàiháng	外行		18
* influence, a/to	yǐngxiǎng	影響	影响	16
influenced by, to be	shòu...yǐngxiǎng	受...影響	受...影响	16
inform, to	tōngzhī	通知		21
inhale, to	chōu	抽		10
* inhale, to (= 抽)	xī	吸		10
injection	dǎzhēn	打針	打针	20
injure, to	shāng	傷	伤	20
inside	lǐ.tóu	裏頭	里头	12
intensive course	qiánghuàbān	強化班		23
interested in (a person), to be	duì...yǒuyì.si	對...有意思	对...有意思	17
interesting	yǒuyì.si	有意思		8
interjection, an	hèi	嘿		4
* international	guójì	國際	国际	21
international business	guómào	國貿	国贸	6
internship	shíxí	實習	实习	23
intersection	shízì lùkǒu	十字路口		22
introduce, to	jiè.shào	介紹	介绍	8
introverted, (to be)	nèixiàng	内向		17

	invite, to	qǐng	請	请	9
	iron (clothes), to	tàng	燙	烫	17
	isn't it true?	kě bú.shì .ma?	可不是嗎	可不是吗	11
	issue (a telegram or an e-mail), to	fā	發	发	21
*	it	tā	它		4
	it seems as if...	hǎo.xiàng... shì.de/ sì.de	好像...似的		11
	it seems…	kàn.qǐ.lái…	看起來	看起来	13
	itchy, (to be)	yǎng	癢	痒	20
	IU (Indiana University)	Yìndà	印大		15
J					
	Japanese language	Rìwén	日文		5
	jazz	juéshìyuè	爵士樂	爵士乐	18
	jeans	niúzǎikù	牛仔褲	牛仔裤	14
	joke, to	kāiwánxiào	開玩笑	开玩笑	13
	Joy Luck Club—title of a movie	Xǐfúhuì	喜福會	喜福会	11
	judge	cáipàn	裁判		19
	just	guāng	光		14
	just	jiù	就		7
	just	zhǐ.shì	只是		20
	just (V...)	….yíxià	V一下		7
	just a moment ago (Adv)	gāng	剛	刚	14
	just in case that...	wànyī	萬一	万一	22
	just now (MTA)	gāngcái	剛才	刚才	11
K					
	kitchen	chúfáng	廚房		15
	know (a person or a character/ word), to	rèn.shí/rèn.shì	認識	认识	8
*	know how to, to	huì	會	会	9
	know, to	zhī.dào	知道		15
L					
	laboratory	shíyànshì	實驗室	实验室	8
*	lack, to	chà	差		6
*	landlady	fángdōng	房東	房东	15
*	landlord	fángdōng	房東	房东	15
*	landscape painting	shānshuǐhuà	山水畫	山水画	15
	language	yǔyán	語言	语言	8
	Laotzu	Lǎozǐ	老子		16
	large, (to be)	dà	大		4
	laser disc	léishè chàngpán	雷射唱盤	雷射唱盘	14

*	last year	qù.nián	去年		5
	late, (to be)	wǎn	晚		17
	lately	zuìjìn	最近		11
	later	yǐhòu	以後	以后	9
	later (preceded by 先)	ránhòu	然後	然后	23
*	laugh, to	xiào	笑		11
	laundry room	xǐyīfáng	洗衣房		15
	lavatory	cèsuǒ	廁所	厕所	17
	lead (said of the score of a game), to	lǐngxiān	領先	领先	19
	lead, to	dài	帶	带	14
	leading actor	zhǔjué/jiǎo	主角	主角	11
*	learn, to	xuéxí	學習	学习	5
*	learn, to (=學習)	xué	學	学	5
	leave (a place), to (intrans. V)	zǒu	走		8
*	leave (a place), to (trans. V)	lí.kāi	離開	离开	21
	left over	shèng	剩		17
	left side	zuǒ.biānr	左邊兒	左边儿	15
	leg	tuǐ	腿		20
*	leisure	kòngr	空兒	空儿	9
	leisure (=空兒)	gōng.fū	功夫/工夫	工夫	9
	length	chángduǎn	長短	长短	12
	length	chángdù	長度	长度	12
*	lesson	kè	課	课	4
	let, to	ràng	讓	让	11
	letter	xìn	信		21
	lettuce	shēngcài	生菜		11
	level	shuǐpíng	水平		23
	library	túshūguǎn	圖書館	图书馆	6
	license	zhízhào	執照	执照	22
	life	shēng.huó	生活		15
*	light (course load, weight), (to be)	qīng	輕	轻	6
	light (taste, color), (to be)	dàn	淡		10
	like, to	xǐ.huān	喜歡	喜欢	6
	listening comprehension	tīnglì	聽力	听力	23
	listless, (to be)	méi qì.le	沒氣了	没气了	22
*	little (quantity), (to be)	shǎo	少		6
*	little (size, age), (to be)	xiǎo	小		4

	little bit, a	yì.diǎnr	一點兒	一点儿	7
	little while, a	yì.huǐr	一會兒	一会儿	15
	live, to	zhù	住		16
*	living room	kètīng	客廳	客厅	15
	located at/in/on, (be)	zài	在		7
	logical, (to be)	yǒudào.lǐ	有道理		23
	long distance	chángtú	長途	长途	14
	look at (= 看), to	qiáo	瞧		20
	look for, to	zhǎo	找		9
	looks…, (it)	kàn.qǐ.lái	看起來	看起来	13
*	loose, (to be)	kuān	寬		12
	lose completely (one's appetite), to	dǎojìn	倒盡	倒尽	11
*	lose, to	shū	輸	输	19
	love, to	ài	愛	爱	8
	low, (to be)	dī	低		19
	lump	kuài	塊	块	20
	lyrics of a song	gēcír	歌詞兒	歌词儿	18

M

	major	zhuānyè	專業	专业	6
*	major, to/a	zhǔxiū	主修		6
	make a telephone call, to	dǎ (diànhuà)	打(電話)	打(电话)	9
	make an appointment, to	yuē	約	约	20
	make money, to	zhuànqián	賺(錢)	赚(钱)	23
*	make money, to (=賺錢)	zhèngqián	掙(錢)	挣(钱)	23
	make one mad, to	qìrén	氣人	气人	19
	make one tired, to	lèirén	累人		19
	make, to	zuò	做		5
	make, to (causative)	ràng	讓	让	11
*	male (for human beings)	nán	男		11
	mall	shāngchǎng	商場	商场	12
	many, (to be)	duō	多		6
	marriage	jiéhūn	結婚	结婚	23
	match and form, to	pèichéng	配成		12
	match, to	pèi	配		17
	matters	shì	事		9
	may	kě.yǐ	可以		7
	may I ask?	qǐngwèn	請問	请问	7
	me	wǒ	我		4

	meal	fàn	飯	饭	7
	measure word for a group of people or animals	qún	群		12
	measure word for a pair (of things)	shuāng	雙	双	8
	measure word for books, notebooks	běn	本		6
*	measure word for classes	jié	節	节	5
	measure word for classes	táng	堂		5
	measure word for courses	mén	門	门	6
	measure word for dishes	dào	道		10
	measure word for falling on the ground	jiāo	跤		20
	measure word for films, cars, etc.	bù	部		11
	measure word for frequency	cì	次		11
	measure word for gifts and newspapers	fènr	份兒	份儿	14
	measure word for meals	dùn	頓	顿	13
	measure word for people (in a family)	kǒu	口		16
	measure word for people (polite)	wèi	位		10
*	measure word for persons and things	.ge	個	个	5
	measure word for plural nouns	xiē	些		7
*	measure word for rooms and buildings	jiān	間	间	15
	measure word for songs	shǒu	首		18
*	measure word for stores, restaurants, cinema; home	jiā	家		6
	measure word for tea, wine, coffee	bēi	杯		7
	measure word for trips	tàng	趟		21
	measure word for upper garments and coats, affairs	jiàn	件		12
*	medicine	yào	藥	药	20
	meet someone unexpectedly, to	pèng.jiàn/.dào	踫見/到	碰见/到	21
	merely	zhǐ.shì	只是		20
	method	fǎ.zi	法子		20
	Michigan	Mìxīgēn	密西根		19
	midnight	bànyè	半夜		19
	midterm exam	duànkǎo	段考		18
*	milk	niúnǎi	牛奶		10
	mind	xīn	心		21

	mini-bus	xiǎobā	小巴		13
	minor, a/to	fùxiū	副修		6
*	minute	fēn	分		6
	miss	xiǎo.jiě	小姐		14
	modern	xiàndài	現代	现代	18
	moment ago, a	gāngcái	剛才	刚才	11
	moment, a	yì.huǐr	一會兒	一会儿	15
	money	qián	錢	钱	7
	month	yuè	月		4
	more/much Adj-er, (it's becoming)	yuè lái yuè…	越來越…	越来越…	12
	moreover	yòu	又		12
	morning	shàng.wǔ	上午		5
*	morning (=上午)	zǎo.shàng	早上		5
	most of	duōbànr	多半兒	多半儿	11
	mother	mā.mā	媽媽	妈妈	8
*	mother (formal)	mǔ.qīn	母親	母亲	8
	mountain	shān	山		14
	mouth	kǒu	口		16
	move to, to	bān.dào	搬到		14
*	move, to	bān	搬		14
	moved, (to be)	gǎndòng	感動	感动	11
	movie	diànyǐngr	電影兒	电影儿	9
	much, (to be)	duō	多		6
	music	yīnyuè	音樂	音乐	8
	musical instrument (=胡琴)	èrhú	二胡		18
	must	děi	得		5
	must (=得)	yīnggāi	應該	应该	8
	my	wǒ .de	我的		4
	my goodness!	.ai.ya!	哎呀！		19
N					
*	name	míng.zi	名字		8
	nasal drip	bítì	鼻涕		20
	natural, (to be)	zìrán	自然		11
*	near, (to be)	jìn	近		21
	nearby	fùjìn	附近		15
*	need not	búyòng	不用		5
*	need not (=不用)	búbì	不必		5
*	nervous, (to be)	jǐn.zhāng	緊張	紧张	18

*	net on a tennis/volleyball court	qiúwǎng	球網	球网	19
*	new	xīn	新		7
	New Year	xīnnián	新年		16
	next time	xià.cì	下次		11
*	next year	míng.nián	明年		5
*	night (MTA)	wǎn.shàng	晚上		5
*	night (N)	yè	夜		17
	nine	jiǔ	九		4
	no	bù	不		4
	no wonder	nánguài	難怪	难怪	14
	no!	cái bù .ne	才不呢		14
	noisy, (to be)	chǎo	吵		15
	nonsense!	húshuō	胡說	胡说	17
*	noon	zhōng.wǔ	中午		5
	north, the	běifāng	北方		10
	not	bù	不		4
	not as good as	bùrú	不如		19
	not bad, (to be)	búcuò	不錯	不错	6
	not have, to	méi(.yǒu)	没(有)		5
	not necessarily	búbì	不必		10
	not only... but also...	búdàn...érqiě...	不但... 而且		21
	not quite	bútài	不太		6
	not to be able to afford to go to school	shàng.bùqǐ	上不起		23
*	not to be able to afford to V	V .bùqǐ	V不起		23
	not until	cái	才		9
	not very	bútài	不太		6
	notebook	běn.zi	本子		7
	notify, to	tōngzhī	通知		21
	novel	xiǎoshuō	小說	小说	7
*	now	xiànzài	現在	现在	6
	number	hào	號	号	4

O

	o'clock	diǎn(zhōng)	點(鐘)	点(钟)	6
	obtain, to	dé	得		19
	odor	wèidào	味道		10
	of course	dāngrán	當然	当然	16
	off campus	xiàowài	校外		14
	oh no!	.ai.ya!	哎呀！		19

oh! (realization of something)	.ou	噢		18
O.K.	xíng	行		13
old (age), (to be)	dà	大		4
old (things), (to be)	jiù	舊	旧	7
older sister	jiě.jiě	姐姐		14
on one's body	shēn.shàng	身上		7
on the contrary	dào.shì	倒是		8
on the one hand ... on the other hand	yìbiānr... yìbiānr	一邊兒..., 一邊兒	一边儿..., 一边儿	22
* on top of (=上頭)	shàng.biānr	上邊兒	上边儿	15
once in a blue moon	nándé	難得	难得	23
one	yī	一		4
oneself	zìjǐ	自己		9
only	cái	才		7
only	zhǐ	只		17
only (=只)	búguò	不過	不过	17
only (if/takes)	zhǐ yào	只要		13
only (to be)	zhǐ.shì	只是		20
only alternative is ... , the	zhǐhǎo	只好		7
only then	cái	才		9
on-the-spot lecture	jīhuì jiàoyù	機會教育	机会教育	14
open (a can, box, etc.), to	kāi	開	开	10
* open the door, to	kāimén	開門	开门	6
or	hái.shì	還是	还是	6
or	huò(.zhě)	或 (者)		13
* orange juice	jú.zishuǐ	桔子水		10
order, to	jiào	叫		10
ordinarily, (to be) ordinary	píngcháng	平常		14
organize (an activity), to	jǔbàn	舉辦	举办	16
organize, to	zǔ	組	组	18
* Oriental	dōngfāng	東方	东方	18
originally	yuánlái	原來	原来	12
originally (=原來)	běnlái	本來	本来	23
other	bié .de	別的		7
other (Adv)	lìngwài	另外		15
otherwise	yào.bùrán	要不然		17
ought to	yīnggāi	應該	应该	8
out of luck, (to be)	dǎoméi	倒霉		17

	outgoing, (to be)	wàixiàng	外向		17
*	outside	wài.tóu	外頭	外头	12
	overcoat, an	dàyī	大衣		12
	overcoat, an (=大衣)	wàitào	外套		12

P

	package	bāoguǒ	包裹	包裹	21
	page	yè	頁	页	7
*	painful, (to be)	téng	疼		20
	painting	huàr	畫兒	画儿	15
	pair	duìr	對兒	对儿	17
*	pants	kù.zi	褲子	裤子	12
	paper (term)	bàogào	報告	报告	13
	parents	fùmǔ	父母		8
	park (a car), to	tíng(chē)	停(車)	停(车)	22
	parking space	tíngchēwèi	停車位	停车位	22
*	part, a	bù	部		8
	participate, to	cānjiā	參加	参加	16
	particle for agreement	.ba	吧		7
	particle for conjecture or supposition	.ba	吧		15
	particle for dogmatic assertion	.ma	嘛		19
	particle for interest in additional information	.ne	呢		4
	particle for question	.a	啊		8
	particle for sarcastic retort	.ne	呢		14
	particle for yes-or-no question	.ma	嗎	吗	4
	particle–a variant of 啊	.ya	呀		12
	particularly	tèbié	特別		11
*	pass, to	guò	過	过	6
	paste, to	tiē	貼	贴	21
	pay (a bill) , to	fù	付		15
	pay (a fee) , to	jiāo	交		13
	pen	bǐ	筆	笔	7
*	penalize, to	fá	罰	罚	19
	penalty shot	fáqiú	罰球	罚球	19
	people	rén	人		8
	perhaps	yěxǔ	也許	也许	23
	perm, to	tàng	燙	烫	17
	permit, to	(yǔn)xǔ	(尤)許	(尤)许	22

	person	rén	人		8
	philosopher	zhéxuéjiā	哲學家	哲学家	16
	photo	zhàopiàn	照片		15
*	photo (=照片)	xiàngpiàn	相片		15
*	pick someone up, to	jiē	接		13
	pick up (things), to	lǐng	領	领	21
	pick, to	jiǎn	撿	捡	19
	picture	zhàopiàn	照片		15
	picture (=照片)	xiàngpiàn	相片		15
	piece (hard)	kuài	塊	块	20
	place, to	bǎi	擺	摆	15
	plan, a/to	dǎsuàn	打算		14
*	plan, a/to	jìhuà	計劃	计划	23
	play (ball), to	dǎ	打		19
	play (violin, viola), to	lā	拉		8
	play (wind instrument), to	chuī	吹		17
	play, to	wán	玩		14
	player	qiúyuán	球員	球员	19
*	please	qǐng	請	请	7
	point	fēn	分		19
	police	jǐngchá	警察		22
*	pollen	huāfěn	花粉		20
	portable stereo	suíshēntīng	隨身聽	随身听	7
	position (of a person)	dìwèi	地位		11
	possessive marker	.de	的		4
	post office	yóujú	郵局	邮局	21
	postage	yóuzī	郵資	邮资	21
*	postal clerk	yóuwùyuán	郵務員	邮务员	21
*	postmaster	yóuwùyuán	郵務員	邮务员	21
	pot	hú	壺	壶	10
	pound	bàng	磅		13
	practice driving (=練習開車), to	liàn chē	練車	练车	22
	practice, to	liàn.xí	練習	练习	8
	precisely	jiù	就		7
*	prefix, an ordinalizing	dì	第		4
	prepare, to	yù.bèi	預備	预备	5
	prepare, to (=預備)	zhǔnbèi	準備	准备	21
*	prescription	yàofāng	藥方	药方	20

present	lǐwù	禮物	礼物	14
* present as a gift, to	sòng(gěi)	送(給)	送(给)	14
press, to	cuī	催		17
pretty, (to be)	piào.liàng	漂亮		11
* previously	yǐqián	以前		9
previously (=以前)	cóngqián	從前		22
price	jià.qián	價錢	价钱	12
* price reduction	jiǎnjià	減價	减价	12
prince	wángzǐ	王子		16
probably	kěnéng	可能		22
problem	wèntí	問題	问题	20
professional, (to be)	nèiháng	內行		18
progress, a/to, progression	jìnbù	進步	进步	23
* project	jìhuà	計劃	计划	23
puff, to	chuī	吹		17
pull, to	lā	拉		8
pumpkin pie	nánguāpài	南瓜派		13
* punish, to	fá	罰	罚	19
purple	zǐ	紫		20
put in order, to	zhěng.lǐ	整理		15
put on makeup, to	huàzhuāng	化妝	化妆	22
put, to	fàng	放		15

Q

* quarter	kè	刻		6
question	wèntí	問題	问题	20
quick, (to be)	kuài	快		17
quiet, (to be)	ānjìng	安靜	安静	15
quit kidding/joking!	shuō zhēn .de	說真的	说真的	13
quite	tǐng	挺		9
quite (=挺)	xiāngdāng	相當	相当	11
quite good, (to be)	búcuò	不錯	不错	6

R

rabbit	tù.zi	兔子		20
racket	qiúpāi	球拍		19
raise, to	yǎng	養	养	16
ranking	dìwèi	地位		11
rare, (to be), rarely	nándé	難得	难得	23
rather	xiāngdāng	相當	相当	11
raw vegetables	shēngcài	生菜		11

	read, to	dú	讀	读	21
	real,-ly	zhēn	眞	真	11
*	receipt	lǐngdān	領單	领单	21
	receive, to	shōu.dào	收到		14
	recently	zuìjìn	最近		11
	recording	lùyīn	錄音	录音	8
	red, (to be)/-ness	hóng	紅	红	20
	referee	cáipàn	裁判		19
	register (at school), to	zhùcè	註冊	注册	4
	register (mail; or at the outpatient clinic of a hospital), to	guàhào	掛號	挂号	21
	regular mail	píngyóu	平郵	平邮	21
	relationship	guān.xi	關係	关系	11
	relaxed, (to be)	qīngsōng	輕鬆	轻松	18
	remain, to	shèng	剩		17
	remember incorrectly, to	jìcuò	記錯	记错	22
	remember, to	jì.de	記得	记得	18
*	rent, to	zū	租		15
	report	bàogào	報告	报告	13
	request, a/to (from senior to junior)	yāo.qiú	要求		22
*	request, to	qǐng	請	请	7
	research, to	yánjiū/yánjiù	研究	研究	11
*	resemble, to	xiàng	像	象	8
	respect, (in this or that)	fāngmiàn	方面		11
	rest from work, to	xiū.xí	休息		5
	rest, to (=休息)	xiē	歇		15
	restaurant	fànguǎnr	飯館兒	饭馆儿	10
	result (of a game)	shūyíng	輸贏	输赢	19
	return (something to the store), to	tuì	退		6
*	return (something), to	huán	還	还	6
*	return (to a place; from a trip; to original state), to	huí	回		6
	rice	fàn	飯	饭	7
	right side	yòu.biānr	右邊兒	右边儿	15
*	right, (to be)	duì	對	对	4
	right, (you are)	méicuò	沒錯	没错	7
	road	lù	路		16
	roast duck	kǎoyā	烤鴨	烤鸭	10
	rock-and-roll music	yáogǔnyuè	搖滾樂	摇滚乐	18

*	room	fángjiān	房間	房间	15
*	room (=房間)	wū.zi	屋子		15
*	roommate	shìyǒu	室友		20
	roommate (China)	tóngwūr	同屋兒	同屋儿	20
	run (water), to	liú	流		20
	run into an unexpected situation, to	pèng.shàng	碰上		17
	rush anxiously, to	jí.sǐrén	急死人		17
	rush, to	gǎn	趕	赶	17
S					
	sad, (to be)	nánguò	難過	难过	11
	salad	shālā	沙拉		11
	sale, a	pāimài	拍賣	拍卖	12
*	same, (to be) the	yíyàng	一樣	一样	8
	sandwich	sānmíngzhì	三明治		7
*	satisfied (stomach), (to be)	bǎo	飽	饱	11
	save money, to	shěngqián	省錢	省钱	23
*	say something bad, to	shuō huàihuà	說壞話	说坏话	21
	say something good, to	shuō hǎohuà	說好話	说好话	21
	say, to	shuō	說	说	7
	scarf	wéijīnr	圍巾兒	围巾儿	12
	scarf (=圍巾兒)	wéibór	圍脖兒	围脖儿	12
	scholarship	jiǎngxuéjīn	獎學金	奖学金	23
*	school	xuéxiào	學校	学校	4
	score, to	dé	得		19
	Scotch tape	jiāodài	膠帶	胶带	21
	seafood	hǎixiān	海鮮	海鲜	10
*	second	miǎo	秒		6
*	section, a	bù	部		8
	see (= 看), to	qiáo	瞧		20
	see (a person) off, to	sòng	送		13
	see a doctor, to	kànbìng	看病		20
	see what happens, just (VO) and	...kàn.kàn	(VO) 看看		7
	see, to	kàn	看		9
	see, to (RV)	kàn.jiàn	看見	看见	14
	seek, to	zhǎo	找		9
	seems the same as... (it)	xiàng...yíyàng	像 ... 一樣	象 ... 一样	8
	seems, (it)	kàn.qǐ.lái	看起來	看起来	13
	seems, (it) (followed by 似的)	hǎo.xiàng	好像	好象	17

*	sell, to	mài	賣	卖	6
	semester	xuéqī	學期	学期	6
	send (a telegram or an e-mail), to	fā	發	发	21
	send (by mail), to	jì	寄		18
	separate, to	lí	離	离	21
	serve a ball, to	fāqiú	發球	发球	19
	set, a	tào	套		12
	seven	qī	七		4
	several	hǎojǐ-	好幾-	好几-	13
	shall	yào	要		6
*	she	tā	她		4
	shirt	chènshān	襯衫	衬衫	12
	shoot (a ball) , to	tóu(jìn)	(投)進	(投)进	19
	short	ǎi	矮		8
*	short of, to be	chà	差		6
*	short person	ǎigèr	矮個兒	矮个儿	19
	shortcoming	máo.bìng	毛病		20
	should	yīnggāi	應該	应该	8
	should be X's turn, (it)	gāi	該	该	22
	shout, to	hǎn	喊		17
	sick, to be (=病)	shēngbìng	生病		20
*	sick, to be/-ness	bìng	病		20
	side	páng.biānr	旁邊兒	旁边儿	15
*	side (Suf)	.biānr	邊兒	边儿	15
	silver anniversary	yínhūn	銀婚	银婚	23
	since	cóng	從	从	20
	sing, to	chànggē	唱歌		8
	sit, to	zuò	坐		7
	situation	qíngkuàng	情況	情况	20
	six	liù	六		4
	size	dàxiǎo	大小		12
	size (clothing only)	hào	號	号	4
	ski, to	huáxuě	滑雪		14
*	skill	gōng.fū	功夫	工夫	9
*	skirt	qún.zi	裙子		12
	skort	qúnkù	裙褲	裙裤	12
*	sky	tiān	天		4
*	slander, to	shuō huàihuà	說壞話	说坏话	21

*	slander, to	shuō huàihuà	說壞話	说坏话	21
*	sleep, to	shuìjiào	睡覺	睡觉	14
*	slip of paper that entitles the bearer to get something, a	lǐngdān	領單	领单	21
*	slow, (to be)	màn	慢		17
*	small (size/age), (to be)	xiǎo	小		4
	smear, to	mǒ	抹		20
	smoke	yān	煙	烟	10
*	smoke (cigarettes), to	xī	吸		10
	smoke (cigarettes), to (=吸)	chōu	抽		10
	sneakers	qiúxié	球鞋		14
	sneeze	pēn.tì	噴嚏	喷嚏	20
	snow	xuě	雪		14
	so (as that)	nà.me	那麼	那么	14
*	so (as that)	nàyàng	那樣	那样	15
	so (as this)	zhèyàng	這樣	这样	15
	so as not to	miǎn.de	免得		14
	society	shèhuì	社會	社会	11
	soft drink	qìshuǐr	汽水兒	汽水儿	10
	sold out	màiwán	賣完	卖完	7
*	some (+ N)	yǒu .de	有的		7
	some (+M+N)	jǐ	幾	几	6
	some (of plural N)	xiē	些		7
	sometimes	yǒushí.hòu	有時候	有时候	14
*	son	ér.zi	兒子	儿子	11
	song	gēqǔ	歌曲		18
	song (colloquial)	gēr	歌兒	歌儿	18
	soon	kuài(yào)	快(要)		6
	sore, (to be)	suāntòng	酸痛		14
	sore, (to be) (=酸痛)	suānténg	酸疼		20
	sorry, (I am)	duì.buqǐ	對不起	对不起	6
*	sound	shēng.yīn	聲音	声音	18
	soup	tāng	湯	汤	10
	sour, (to be)	suān	酸		10
	south, the	nánfāng	南方		10
	specialize in, to	nèiháng	內行		18
*	specialty	zhuānyè	專業	专业	6
	spend money, to	huāqián	花錢	花钱	21

	spicy, (to be)	là	辣		10
	spirited	jīng.shén	精神		17
	splendid (=華麗)	huá	華	华	12
	sponsor (an activity), to	jǔbàn	舉辦	举办	16
	sports fan	qiúmí	球迷		16
	spread out, to	bǎi	擺	摆	15
	spring vacation	chūnjià	春假		21
	stamp	yóupiào	郵票	邮票	21
*	stand, to	zhàn	站		7
	standard	shuǐpíng	水平		23
	start (an action), to	qǐ.lái	起來	起来	14
	start school/classes, to	kāixué	開學	开学	4
	start, to	kāishǐ	開始	开始	11
	station	zhàn	站		15
	status	dìwèi	地位		11
	stay, to	dāi	待		14
	stay, to	liú	留		23
	stay, to	zhù	住		16
	steer (boats), to	jiàshǐ	駕駛	驾驶	22
	stern, (to be)	yán	嚴	严	8
	still	hái	還	还	6
*	stomach	wèi	胃		11
	stomach (belly)	dù.zi	肚子		13
	strange, (to be)	qíguài	奇怪		18
	street	jiē	街		16
	stress, to	qiángdiào	強調	强调	23
	strict, (to be)	yán	嚴	严	8
*	student	xué.shēng	學生	学生	4
	student association	tóngxuéhuì	同學會	同学会	16
	study (a subject), to	niàn	念		6
*	study, to	xué	學	学	5
	study, to (=念)	dú	讀	读	21
*	study, to (=學)	xuéxí	學習	学习	5
	style	yàng.zi	樣子	样子	12
	style (Suf)	shì	式		13
	substitute, to	tì	替		21
	such	zhèyàng	這樣	这样	15
*	suddenly	tūrán	突然		22

	suffix, experiential	.guò	過	过	10
	sugar	táng	糖		10
	suit, to	hé	合		14
	suitable, (to be)	héshì	合適	合适	12
	suitcase	xiāng.zi	箱子		15
	summer	shǔqī	暑期		23
	summertime	xiàtiān	夏天		23
	summer vacation	shǔjià	暑假		23
	supermarket	chāojí shìchǎng	超級市場	超级市场	13
	suppose	yào.shì	要是		11
	surface mail	píngyóu	平郵	平邮	21
	surname, a	Gāo	高		4
	surname, a	Lǐ	李		4
	surname, a	Lín	林		8
	surname, a	Wáng	王		9
	surnamed, to be	xìng	姓		8
*	surround, to	wéi	圍	围	12
	sweater	máoyī	毛衣		12
	sweet, (to be)	tián	甜		10
	swimming pool	yóuyǒngchí	游泳池		15
*	symptom	zhèngzhuàng	症狀	症状	20
T					
	take (a course), to	xuǎn	選	选	6
	take (a vehicle, an airplane, a ship), to	dā	搭		13
	take (someone to some place), to	sòng	送		13
	take (something) to be, to	yǐwéi	以爲	以为	18
*	take (something), to	ná	拿		15
	take a rest, to	xiū.xí	休息		5
	talk about, to	tándào	談到	谈到	11
	tall	Gāo	高		4
	tall person	gāogèr	高個兒	高个儿	19
	taste	kǒuwèir	口味兒	口味儿	10
	taste (=口味兒)	wèidào	味道		10
	tea	chá	茶		10
*	teach	jiāo	教		5
	teacher	lǎoshī	老師	老师	8
	team	duì	隊	队	19
*	telephone	diànhuà	電話	电话	9

	tell (someone to do something), to	jiào	叫		20
	tell, to	gào.sù	告訴	告诉	13
	temperament	pí.qì	脾氣	脾气	17
	ten	shí	十		4
	tenant	fángkè	房客		15
	tennis	wǎngqiú	網球	网球	19
	tennis court	wǎngqiúchǎng	網球場	网球场	15
*	test	kǎoshì	考試	考试	18
	thank (you)	xiè.xie	謝謝	谢谢	7
	Thanksgiving	Gǎn'ēnjié	感恩節	感恩节	13
	that	nà/nèi	那		6
*	that way	nàyàng	那樣	那样	15
	them	tā.men	他們	他们	4
	then	jiù	就		7
	then	ránhòu	然後	然后	23
	then	zài	再		7
	there	nàr	那兒	那儿	7
	therefore	suǒ.yǐ	所以		11
	these	zhèixiē	這些	这些	7
	they	tā.men	他們	他们	4
	thing	dōng.xī	東西	东西	7
	think (when expressing one's opinion), to	kàn	看		9
	think incorrectly, to	yǐwéi	以爲	以为	18
	think, to	jué.de	覺得	觉得	7
	think, to (=覺得)	xiǎng	想		8
*	this	zhè/zhèi	這	这	6
	this way	zhèyàng	這樣	这样	15
	this way (as…)	zhè.me	這麼	这么	8
*	this year	jīn.nián	今年		5
*	those	nèixiē	那些		7
	three	sān	三		4
	tidy up, to	zhěng.lǐ	整理		15
	tie (in a ball game), to	píngshǒu	平手		19
	Tiger Balm	Wànjīnyóu	萬金油	万金油	20
	tight, (to be)	jǐn	緊	紧	12
*	time	gōng.fū	功夫/ 工夫	工夫	9
*	time	shí.hòu	時候	时候	6

time (=功夫)	shíjiān	時間	时间	9
time-out	zhàntíng	暫停	暂停	19
time-consuming, (to be)	huā shíjiān	花時間	花时间	8
tire (on a car)	lúntāi	輪胎	轮胎	22
tired, (to be)	lèi	累		6
… to... (for the scores of a ball game)	bǐ	#比#		19
to	wàng	往		16
today	jīn.tiān	今天		4
together	yíkuàir	一塊兒	一块儿	8
toilet	cèsuǒ	廁所	厕所	17
tomorrow	míng.tiān	明天		4
tone	shēngdiào	聲調	声调	8
tone (=聲調)	diàor	調兒	调儿	18
tone-deaf	yīnmáng	音盲		18
too	yě	也		4
too bad!	zhēn zāogāo	眞糟糕	真糟糕	22
too much, (something is) a little	zhēnshì.de	眞是的	真是的	12
too tired to walk, (to be)	zǒu.búdòng	走不動	走不动	14
* tooth	yá(chǐ)	牙(齒)	牙(齿)	17
touched, (to be)	gǎndòng	感動	感动	11
tour guide	dǎoyóu	導遊	导游	21
tow, to	tuō	拖		22
toward	wàng	往		16
tradition	chuántǒng	傳統	传统	18
traffic light	hónglǜdēng	紅綠燈	红绿灯	16
traffic ticket	fádān	罰單	罚单	22
tragedy	bēijù	悲劇	悲剧	11
train, to	dài	帶	带	14
travel, to/-ing	lǚxíng	旅行		23
treat, to	qǐng	請	请	9
tree (=樹木)	mù	木		8
trouble, (to be) troublesome	má.fán	麻煩	麻烦	9
try (garments) on, to	chuān.chuān.kàn	穿穿看		12
try, to	shì(.yí)shì	試(一)試	试(一)试	10
tuition	xuéfèi	學費	学费	23
tune (of music)	diàor	調兒	调儿	18
turkey	huǒjī	火雞	火鸡	13

turn in (homework), to	jiāo	交		13
turn right, to	yòuzhuǎn	右轉	右转	16
TV	diànshì	電視	电视	12
two	èr	二		4
two (only occurs before a measure word)	liǎng	兩	两	5
two (people)	liǎ	倆		16
two-stringed violin	húqínr	胡琴兒	胡琴儿	18
U				
unable to say, (to be)	shuō.bùliǎo	說不了	说不了	14
unable to write, (to be)	xiě.bùliǎo	寫不了	写不了	14
unbearable, (to be)	nánshòu	難受	难受	20
* underneath (=下頭)	xià.biānr	下邊兒	下边儿	15
understand, to	míng.bái	明白		11
understand, to (=明白)	dǒng	懂		11
undertaking	shì	事		9
university	dàxué	大學	大学	12
* unoccupied time or space	kòngr	空兒	空儿	9
United Nations	Liánhéguó	聯合國	联合国	8
* unusually	fēicháng	非常		6
* upstairs	lóu.shàng	樓上	楼上	15
urge, to	cuī	催		17
* us	wǒ.men	我們	我们	4
us (including the person addressed)	zán.men	咱們	咱们	9
use (time/tool/chance), to	lìyòng	利用		13
use eyedrops, to	diǎn yǎnyào	點眼藥	点眼药	20
use, to	yòng	用		21
used	jiù	舊	旧	7
usually, (to be) usual	píngcháng	平常		14
utilities charge	shuǐdiàn	水電	水电	15
utilize, to	lìyòng	利用		13
V				
vacant room	kōngfáng	空房		15
vacation	jiàqī	假期		14
van	xiǎobā	小巴		13
vegetables	cài	菜		9
vehicle	chē	車	车	10
very	hěn	很		6

very likely	bāchéng	八成		22
very slow, (to be)	màntūntūn	慢吞吞		17
very tiny chance, a	wànyī	萬一	万一	22
very tired, (to be)	lèi.sǐ	累死		15
vigor	jīng.shén	精神		17
vinegar	cù	醋		10
V-ing	(zhèng)zài	(正)在		8
violin	xiǎotíqín	小提琴		8
vitality	jīng.shén	精神		17

W

wait (= 等), to	dāi	待	待	19
wait, to	děng	等		9
walk, to	zǒu	走		8
Walkman	suíshēntīng	隨身聽	随身听	7
wall	qiáng	牆	墙	15
want, to	yào	要		6
wash, to	xǐ	洗		17
way	fǎ.zi	法子		20
* we	wǒ.men	我們	我们	4
we (including the person addressed)	zán.men	咱們	咱们	9
weak or thin (tea, coffee, etc.), (to be)	dàn	淡		10
* wear (garments and shoes), to	chuān	穿		12
* wear (glasses, gloves, jewelry), to	dài	戴		12
* wear (scarf), to	wéi	圍	围	12
weather	tiān.qì	天氣	天气	12
* week (colloquial)	lǐbài	禮拜	礼拜	4
week (literary)	xīngqī	星期		4
weekend	zhōumò	週末	周末	5
West Coast	xī'àn	西岸		23
Western	xīfāng	西方		18
western (America)	xībù	西部		8
what a coincidence!	zhēn qiǎo	真巧	真巧	21
what a mess!	zhēn zāogāo!	真糟糕！	真糟糕！	22
what is there to see window shopping?	yǒu shén.me hǎo guàng .de?	有什麼好逛的	有什么好逛的	12
what should (one) do?	zěn.me bàn	怎麼辦	怎么办	22

* what time?	jǐ diǎn zhōng	幾點鐘	几点钟	6
what?	shén.me	什麼/甚麼	什么	5
* when? /what time?	shén.me shí.hòu	什麼時候	什么时候	6
where?	nǎr	哪兒	哪儿	6
* where? /what place?	shén.me dì.fāng	什麼地方	什么地方	6
* which	nǎ/něi	哪		4
which day	nǎ yì tiān/něi yì tiān	哪一天		4
white jasmine flower	mòlìhuā	茉莉花		18
* who	shéi	誰	谁	4
* whoever	shéi	誰	谁	4
whole	quán	全		14
whole family, the	yì jiā rén	一家人		14
whole field, the	mǎnchǎng	滿場	满场	20
* whom	shéi	誰	谁	4
* whomever	shéi	誰	谁	4
* whose	shéi .de	誰的	谁的	4
* why	wèishén.me	爲什麼	为什么	8
* will	huì	會	会	9
will (=會)	yào	要		6
win, to	yíng	贏	赢	19
winter (season)	dōngjì	冬季		12
winter vacation	hánjià	寒假		14
* wish, to	zhù	祝		4
with (instrument)	yòng	用		21
with (person)	gēn	跟		10
with one's self	shēn.shàng	身上		7
withdraw (from school), to	tuì	退		6
withdraw (money), to	tíqián	提錢	提钱	21
woman (derogatory)	nǚláng	女郎		12
woman, women	fùnǚ	婦女	妇女	11
wonderful	hǎojí.le	好極了	好极了	8
* work	gōng.fū	功夫/工夫	工夫	9
work (for a temporary job), to	dǎgōng	打工		5
* work master	shī.fù	師傅	师傅	21
* work, to	gōngzuò	工作		5
worried, (to be)	zhāojí	著急	着急	22
worry, to	dānxīn	擔心	担心	14
would like to	xiǎng	想		8

wrap, to	bāo	包		15
write a letter, to	xiěxìn	寫信	写信	14
write, to	xiě	寫	写	8

Y

* year	nián	年		4
yell, to	hǎn	喊		17
* yesterday	zuó.tiān	昨天		4
* you (pl.)	nǐ.men	你們	你们	4
you (sing.)	nǐ	你		4
* you're welcome	búxiè	不謝	不谢	7
* young (for age), (to be)	xiǎo	小		4
young lady	xiǎo.jiě	小姐		14
younger brother	dì.dì	弟弟		14
your	nǐ.de	你的		4

Z

* zero	líng	零		4

Index 2. Characters

◎ By Pinyin

Pinyin	Character		S No.	L
A				
* ǎi	矮		13	SC13
* ài	愛	爱	13	SC21
B				
.ba	吧		7	L7
bǎ	把		7	L15
bà	爸		8	L14
* bái	白		5	SC70
bǎi	百		6	L15
bān	搬		13	L15
bàn	半		5	L9
bàn	辦	办	16	L22
bāng	幫	帮	17	L16
bāo	包		5	L11
* bǎo	飽	饱	13	SC27
bào	報	报	12	L23
* bēi	杯		8	SC20
běi	北		5	L10
bèi	被		10	L22
běn	本		5	L23
bǐ	比		4	L10
* bǐ	筆	笔	12	SC6
bì	必		5	L19
biān	邊	边	19	L15
biàn	變	变	23	L19
bié	別		7	L11
* bīng	冰		6	SC19
bìng	病		10	L20
bù	不		4	L4
* bù	部		11	SC25
C				
cái	才		3	L7
cài	菜		12	L10
* cǎo	草	草	10	SC55
chá	茶		10	L10
cháng	長	长	8	L12
cháng	常		8	L14
chǎng	場	场	12	L21

Pinyin	Character		S No.	L
chàng	唱		11	L18
chǎo	吵		7	L15
chē	車	车	7	L10
chī	吃		6	L7
chóng	重		9	L10
* chōu	抽		8	SC22
chū	出		5	L9
chú	除		10	L12
chuān	穿		9	L12
chuī	吹		7	L20
cì	次		6	L11
cóng	從	从	11	L8
cún	存		6	L21
cuò	錯	错	16	L10
D				
dǎ	打		5	L9
dà	大		3	L4
dài	帶	带	11	L21
* dài	戴		18	SC30
dān	單	单	12	L22
dān	擔	担	16	L21
dàn	但		7	L8
dāng	當	当	13	L17
dǎo	倒		10	L20
dào	到		8	L6
dào	道		13	L15
.de	的		8	L4
.de	得		11	L6
děng	等		12	L17
dī	低		7	L19
dǐ	底		8	L23
dì	弟		7	L14
dì	第		11	L14
diǎn	點	点	17	L6
diàn	店		8	L6
diàn	電	电	13	L9
dìng	定		8	L17
dōng	東	东	8	L7

dǒng	懂		16	L11
dòng	動	动	11	L14
dōu	都		11	L5
* dù	肚		7	SC43
duǎn	短		12	L12
duì	隊	队	12	L19
duì	對	对	14	L9
* dùn	頓	顿	13	SC10
duō	多		6	L6

E

è	餓	饿	15	L11
ér	而		6	L8
ér	兒	儿	8	L6

F

fā	發	发	12	L19
* fá	罰	罚	14	SC75
fǎ	法		8	L20
fàn	飯	饭	12	L7
fāng	方		4	L10
fáng	房		8	L14
fàng	放		8	L13
fēi	非		8	L22
fēi	飛	飞	9	L21
fèi	費	费	10	L23
fēn	分		4	L6
fēng	風	风	9	L20
fēng	封		9	L21
fú	服		8	L20
* fù	父		4	SC78
fù	付		5	L15
fù	附		8	L23

G

gāi	該	该	13	L19
gǎi	改		7	L22
gāng	剛	刚	10	L22
gāo	高		10	L8
gào	告		7	L23
.ge	個	个	10	L5
* gē	哥		10	SC41
gē	歌		14	L18
gěi	給	给	12	L7
gēn	跟		13	L5
gèng	更		7	L17

gōng	工		3	L9
* gōng	公		4	SC33
* gōng	功		5	SC18
gòng	共		6	L21
* gǒu	狗		8	SC54
gòu	夠		11	L16
guà	掛	挂	11	L21
* guài	怪		8	SC62
* guān	關	关	19	SC24
guǎn	管		14	L16
guǎn	館	馆	16	L10
guàn	慣	惯	14	L16
guì	貴	贵	12	L12
guó	國	国	11	L5
guǒ	果		8	L14
guò	過	过	13	L8

H

hái	孩		9	L16
hái	還	还	17	L12
hài	害		10	L17
* hán	寒		12	SC77
* hàn	漢	汉	14	SC15
hǎo	好		6	L6
hào	號	号	13	L12
hē	喝		12	L10
hé	和		8	L9
* hēi	黑		12	SC71
hěn	很		9	L6
hóng	紅	红	9	L20
hòu	後	后	9	L9
hòu	候		10	L14
huā	花		8	L16
* huà	畫	画	12	SC5
huà	話	话	13	L9
* huài	壞	坏	19	SC8
huān	歡	欢	22	L10
huí	回		6	L13
huì	會	会	13	L11
* huó	活		9	SC50
huǒ	火		4	L13

J

jī	機	机	16	L21

	繁	简		
jī	雞	鸡	18	L13
jí	急		9	L17
jǐ	己		3	L11
jǐ	幾	几	12	L4
jì	記	记	10	L18
jì	寄		11	L21
jiā	家		10	L13
jià	假		11	L13
jiān	間	间	12	L9
* jiǎn	撿	捡	16	SC65
* jiàn	件		6	SC31
jiàn	見	见	7	L9
* jiǎo	腳	脚	13	SC63
jiào	叫		5	L8
jiào	教		11	L19
jiào	覺	觉	20	L17
* jiē	接		11	SC35
jiē	街		12	L16
jié	節	节	15	L13
jiě	姐		8	L14
* jiè	介		4	SC11
jiè	借		10	L22
jīn	今		4	L5
jǐn	緊	紧	14	L22
jìn	近		8	L11
jìn	進	进	13	L15
jīng	經	经	13	L20
jīng	睛		13	L23
jiū	究		7	L18
jiǔ	久		3	L14
jiǔ	酒		10	L10
jiù	就		12	L7
* jiù	舊	旧	18	SC59
jù	句		5	L22

K

kāi	開	开	12	L10
kàn	看		9	L7
kǎo	考		7	L18
kě	可		5	L7
kè	客		9	L18
kè	課	课	15	L4
* kū	哭		10	SC37

kòng	空		8	L15
kǒu	口		3	L13
kuài	快		7	L6
kuài	塊	块	13	L12

L

lā	拉		8	L19
lái	來	来	8	L8
lǎo	老		6	L8
.le	了		2	L6
lèi	累		11	L15
lěng	冷		7	L12
lí	離	离	19	L21
lǐ	裏	里	13	L12
lián	連	连	11	L18
liǎn	臉	脸	17	L17
liàn	練	练	15	L19
liáng	涼	凉	11	L20
liǎng	兩	两	8	L5
liàng	亮		9	L18
liú	留		10	L23
lóu	樓	楼	15	L15
lù	路		13	L16
lǚ	旅		10	L23
* lù	綠	绿	14	SC69

M

.ma	嗎	吗	13	L4
mā	媽	妈	13	L14
mǎ	馬	马	10	L21
mǎi	買	买	12	L6
* mài	賣	卖	15	SC9
màn	慢		14	L17
máng	忙		6	L6
* māo	貓	猫	16	SC53
máo	毛		4	L12
.me	麼	么	14	L5
méi	沒		7	L5
měi	每		7	L11
měi	美		9	L8
mèi	妹		8	L23
.men	們	们	10	L9
mén	門	门	13	L13
miàn	麵	面	20	L12
míng	名		6	L8

	míng	明	8	L4
	mò	末	5	L23
*	mǔ	母	5	SC79

N				
	ná	拿	10	L21
	nǎ	哪	10	L4
	nà	那	7	L7
	nán	男	7	L11
	nán	南	9	L10
	nán	難　难	19	L19
	nǎo	腦　脑	9	L14
	.ne	呢	8	L5
	něi	哪	10	L4
	nèi	内	4	L17
	néng	能	10	L9
	nǐ	你	7	L4
	nián	年	6	L5
	niàn	念	8	L15
*	nín	您	11	SC1
	niú	牛	4	L11
	nǚ	女	3	L11

P				
	pà	怕	8	L16
	páng	旁	10	L15
*	pǎo	跑	12	SC16
	péi	陪	11	L22
	péng	朋	8	L5
	pèng	踫	13	L21
*	pián	便	9	SC28
	piào	票	11	L21
	piào	漂	14	L18
	píng	平	5	L14

Q				
	qī	期	12	L13
	qí	其	8	L18
*	qí	奇	8	SC61
	qǐ	起	10	L9
*	qì	汽	7	SC26
	qì	氣　气	10	L18
	qiān	千	3	L22
	qián	前	9	L9
	qián	錢　钱	16	L12
*	qiáng	牆　墙	17	SC49

	qiě	且	5	L12
*	qīn	親　亲	16	SC80
	qīng	輕　轻	14	L22
	qǐng	請　请	15	L7
	qiú	求	7	L22
	qiú	球	11	L12
	qù	去	5	L6
	quán	全	6	L14

R				
	rán	然	12	L17
	ràng	讓　让	24	L20
	rè	熱　热	15	L20
*	rén	人	2	SC2
*	rèn	認　认	14	SC47
	rì	日	3	L4
	róng	容	10	L16
	ròu	肉	6	L10
	rú	如	6	L14

S				
	sài	賽　赛	17	L19
*	sè	色	6	SC72
	shàng	上	3	L4
*	shāo	燒　烧	16	SC66
	shǎo	少	4	L6
*	shào	紹　绍	11	SC12
	shè	舍	8	L13
	shéi	誰　谁	15	L6
	shēn	身	7	L14
	shén	什	4	L5
	shēng	生	5	L4
*	shēng	聲　声	17	SC60
	shī	師　师	10	L8
	shí	時　时	10	L9
	shí	實　实	14	L18
	shì	市	5	L13
*	shì	式	6	SC39
	shì	事	8	L9
	shì	是	9	L4
*	shì	室	9	SC73
	shì	視　视	11	L19
*	shì	識　识	19	SC48
	shōu	收	6	L15

	Pinyin	Character	Simplified	Strokes	Lesson
	shǒu	手		4	L19
	shòu	受		8	L16
	shū	書	书	10	L6
	shū	舒		12	L20
	shū	輸	输	16	L19
	shǔ	暑		13	L23
*	shù	樹	树	16	SC56
*	shuāng	雙	双	18	SC46
	shuǐ	水		4	L10
	shuì	睡		13	L17
	shuō	說	说	14	L7
*	sī	司		5	SC34
	sī	思		9	L17
	sǐ	死		6	L15
	sòng	送		10	L13
	sù	宿		11	L13
*	sù	訴	诉	12	SC76
	suàn	算		14	L23
	suī	雖	虽	17	L17
	suǒ	所		8	L11

T

	Pinyin	Character	Simplified	Strokes	Lesson
	tā	他		5	L4
*	tā	它		5	SC4
*	tā	她		6	SC3
	tài	太		4	L6
	tán	談	谈	15	L11
	tāng	湯	汤	12	L10
	téng	疼		10	L20
	tí	提		12	L21
	tí	題	题	18	L20
	tì	替		12	L21
	tiān	天		4	L4
*	tiáo	條	条	9	SC51
*	tiào	跳		13	SC17
*	tiē	貼	贴	12	SC74
	tīng	聽	听	22	L12
	tíng	停		11	L19
	tóng	同		6	L20
	tóu	頭	头	16	L12
*	tuī	推		11	SC64
	tuǐ	腿		14	L22

W

	Pinyin	Character	Simplified	Strokes	Lesson
	wài	外		5	L12
	wán	完		7	L7
	wán	玩		8	L13
	wǎn	晚		11	L17
*	wǎn	碗		13	SC32
	wàn	萬	万	13	L22
	wáng	王		4	L16
	wàng	忘		7	L18
	wàng	往		8	L16
	wèi	位		7	L22
	wèi	爲	为	9	L8
	wén	文		4	L5
	wèn	問	问	11	L7
	wǒ	我		7	L4
	wū	屋		9	L20
	wǔ	午		4	L5

X

	Pinyin	Character	Simplified	Strokes	Lesson
	xī	西		6	L7
	xí	息		10	L23
	xí	習	习	11	L16
	xǐ	洗		9	L17
	xǐ	喜		12	L10
	xià	下		3	L4
	xiàn	現	现	11	L15
	xiǎng	想		13	L8
	xiǎng	響	响	21	L16
	xiàng	向		6	L17
	xiàng	像	象	14	L11
	xiǎo	小		3	L4
	xiào	笑		10	L13
*	xiào	校		10	SC36
	xiē	些		8	L21
	xié	鞋		15	L14
	xiě	寫	写	15	L12
	xiè	謝	谢	17	L16
	xīn	心		4	L18
	xīn	新		13	L18
	xìn	信		9	L14
	xīng	星		9	L13
	xíng	行		6	L13
*	xǐng	醒		16	SC57
	xìng	姓		8	L8

	pinyin	字		筆	课
	xiū	休		6	L23
	xǔ	許	许	11	L22
	xué	學	学	16	L4
*	xuě	雪	雪	11	SC45

Y

	pinyin	字		筆	课
*	yā	鴨	鸭	16	SC38
*	yá	牙		4	SC58
*	yān	煙	烟	13	SC23
	yán	言		7	L23
	yán	研		9	L18
	yǎn	眼		11	L20
	yàn	驗	验	23	L23
	yàng	樣	样	15	L8
	yào	要		9	L6
	yào	藥	药	19	L20
	yě	也		3	L5
	yè	夜		8	L19
	yī	衣		6	L12
	yī	醫	医	18	L20
*	yí	宜		8	SC29
	yǐ	已		3	L23
	yǐ	以		5	L7
	yì	易		8	L16
	yì	意		13	L17
	yīn	因		6	L8
	yīn	音		9	L18
*	yīng	英		9	SC14
	yīng	應	应	17	L19
	yíng	贏	赢	20	L19
	yǐng	影		15	L16
	yòng	用		5	L14
	yóu	尤		4	L18
	yóu	油		8	L11
	yóu	郵	邮	12	L21
	yǒu	友		4	L5
	yǒu	有		6	L5
	yòu	又		2	L16
	yòu	右		5	L15
	yú	魚	鱼	11	L10
*	yǔ	雨		8	SC44
	yǔ	語	语	14	L23
	yuán	原		10	L14

	pinyin	字		筆	课
	yuán	員	员	10	L19
	yuán	遠	远	14	L21
*	yuàn	院		10	SC67
	yuē	約	约	9	L20
	yuè	月		4	L4
*	yuè	越		12	SC40
	yuè	樂	乐	15	L18
*	yùn	運	运	13	SC42

Z

	pinyin	字		筆	课
	zá	咱		9	L9
	zài	在		6	L7
	zài	再		6	L7
	zǎo	早		6	L5
	zǎo	澡		16	L17
	zěn	怎		9	L8
	zhàn	站		10	L15
	zhāng	張	张	11	L22
	zhǎng	長	长	8	L12
	zhǎo	找		7	L9
	zhào	照		13	L22
	.zhe	著	着	12	L10
	zhè	這	这	11	L6
	zhèi	這	这	11	L6
	zhēn	眞/真		10	L11
*	zhēn	針	针	10	SC68
	zhèng	正		5	L8
	zhī	知		8	L15
*	zhī	隻	只	10	SC52
	zhí	直		8	L17
	zhǐ	只		5	L13
*	zhǐ	紙	纸	10	SC7
	zhōng	中		4	L5
	zhōng	鐘	钟	20	L13
	zhòng	重		9	L10
	zhōu	週	周	12	L23
	zhù	住		7	L16
	zhuān	專	专	11	L18
	zǐ	子		3	L11
	zì	字		6	L8
	zì	自		6	L11
	zǒng	總	总	17	L22
	zǒu	走		7	L8

Pinyin	Character		L
zuì	最	12	L11
zuó	昨	9	L19

Pinyin	Character		L
zuǒ	左	5	L15
zuò	坐	7	L7
zuò	作	7	L9
zuò	做	11	L5

◎ By Stroke Number

	S No.	Pinyin	Character	L
	2			
	2	.le	了	L6
*	2	rén	人	SC2
	2	yòu	又	L16
	3			
	3	cái	才	L7
	3	gōng	工	L9
	3	jǐ	己	L11
	3	jiǔ	久	L14
	3	kǒu	口	L13
	3	nǚ	女	L11
	3	qiān	千	L22
	3	rì	日	L4
	3	shàng	上	L4
	3	xià	下	L4
	3	xiǎo	小	L4
	3	yě	也	L5
	3	yǐ	已	L23
	3	zǐ	子	L11
	4			
	4	bǐ	比	L10
	4	bù	不	L4
	4	fāng	方	L10
	4	fēn	分	L6
*	4	fù	父	SC78
*	4	gōng	公	SC33
	4	huǒ	火	L13
*	4	jiè	介	SC11
	4	jīn	今	L5
	4	máo	毛	L12
	4	nèi	内	L17
	4	niú	牛	L11
	4	shǎo	少	L6
	4	shén	什	L5

	S No.	Pinyin	Character	L
	4	shǒu	手	L19
	4	shuǐ	水	L10
	4	tài	太	L6
	4	tiān	天	L4
	4	wáng	王	L16
	4	wén	文	L5
	4	wǔ	午	L5
	4	xīn	心	L18
*	4	yá	牙	SC58
	4	yóu	尤	L18
	4	yǒu	友	L5
	4	yuè	月	L4
	4	zhōng	中	L5
	5			
*	5	bái	白	SC70
	5	bàn	半	L9
	5	bāo	包	L11
	5	běi	北	L10
	5	běn	本	L23
	5	bì	必	L19
	5	chū	出	L9
	5	dǎ	打	L9
	5	fù	付	L15
*	5	gōng	功	SC18
	5	jiào	叫	L8
	5	jù	句	L22
	5	kě	可	L7
	5	mò	末	L23
*	5	mǔ	母	SC79
	5	píng	平	L14
	5	qiě	且	L12
	5	qù	去	L6
	5	shēng	生	L4
	5	shì	市	L13

*	5	sī	司	SC34
	5	tā	他	L4
*	5	tā	它	SC4
	5	wài	外	L12
	5	yǐ	以	L7
	5	yòng	用	L14
	5	yòu	右	L15
	5	zhèng	正	L8
	5	zhǐ	只	L13
	5	zuǒ	左	L15

6				
	6	bǎi	百	L15
*	6	bīng	冰	SC19
	6	chī	吃	L7
	6	cì	次	L11
	6	cún	存	L21
	6	duō	多	L6
	6	ér	而	L8
	6	gòng	共	L21
	6	hǎo	好	L6
	6	huí	回	L13
*	6	jiàn	件	SC31
	6	lǎo	老	L8
	6	máng	忙	L6
	6	míng	名	L8
	6	nián	年	L5
	6	quán	全	L14
	6	ròu	肉	L10
	6	rú	如	L14
*	6	sè	色	SC72
*	6	shì	式	SC39
	6	shōu	收	L15
	6	sǐ	死	L15
*	6	tā	她	SC3
	6	tóng	同	L20
	6	xiàng	向	L17
	6	xíng	行	L13
	6	xiū	休	L23
	6	xī	西	L7
	6	yī	衣	L12
	6	yīn	因	L8
	6	yǒu	有	L5

	6	zài	在	L7
	6	zài	再	L7
	6	zǎo	早	L5
	6	zì	自	L11
	6	zì	字	L8

7				
	7	.ba	吧	L7
	7	bǎ	把	L15
	7	bié	别	L11
	7	chǎo	吵	L15
	7	chē	車 车	L10
	7	chuī	吹	L20
	7	dàn	但	L8
	7	dī	低	L19
	7	dì	弟	L14
*	7	dù	肚	SC43
	7	gǎi	改	L22
	7	gào	告	L23
	7	gèng	更	L17
	7	jiàn	見 见	L9
	7	jiū	究	L18
	7	kǎo	考	L18
	7	kuài	快	L6
	7	lěng	冷	L12
	7	méi	没	L5
	7	měi	每	L11
	7	nà	那	L7
	7	nán	男	L11
	7	nǐ	你	L4
*	7	qì	汽	SC26
	7	qiú	求	L22
	7	shēn	身	L14
	7	wán	完	L7
	7	wàng	忘	L18
	7	wèi	位	L22
	7	wǒ	我	L4
	7	yán	言	L23
	7	zhǎo	找	L9
	7	zhù	住	L16
	7	zǒu	走	L8
	7	zuò	坐	L7
	7	zuò	作	L9

	8		长	
	8	bà	爸	L14
*	8	bēi	杯	SC20
	8	cháng	长	L12
	8	cháng	常	L14
*	8	chōu	抽	SC22
	8	dào	到	L6
	8	.de	的	L4
	8	dǐ	底	L23
	8	diàn	店	L6
	8	dìng	定	L17
	8	dōng	东	L7
	8	ér	儿	L6
	8	fǎ	法	L20
	8	fáng	房	L14
	8	fàng	放	L13
	8	fēi	非	L22
	8	fú	服	L20
	8	fù	附	L23
*	8	gǒu	狗	SC54
*	8	guài	怪	SC62
	8	guǒ	果	L14
	8	hé	和	L9
	8	huā	花	L16
	8	jiě	姐	L14
	8	jìn	近	L11
	8	kòng	空	L15
	8	lā	拉	L19
	8	lái	来	L8
	8	liǎng	两	L5
	8	mèi	妹	L23
	8	mén	门	L13
	8	míng	明	L4
	8	.ne	呢	L5
	8	niàn	念	L15
	8	pà	怕	L16
	8	péng	朋	L5
	8	qí	其	L18
*	8	qí	奇	SC61
	8	shè	舍	L13
	8	shì	事	L9
	8	shòu	受	L16

	8	suǒ	所	L11
	8	wán	玩	L13
	8	wǎng	往	L16
	8	xiē	些	L21
	8	xìng	姓	L8
	8	yè	夜	L19
*	8	yí	宜	SC29
	8	yì	易	L16
	8	yóu	油	L11
*	8	yǔ	雨	SC44
	8	zhǎng	长	L12
	8	zhī	知	L15
	8	zhí	直	L17
	9		飞 风	
	9	chóng	重	L10
	9	chuān	穿	L12
	9	fēi	飞	L21
	9	fēng	风	L20
	9	fēng	封	L21
	9	hái	孩	L16
	9	hěn	很	L6
	9	hóng	红	L20
	9	hòu	后	L9
*	9	huó	活	SC50
	9	jí	急	L17
	9	kàn	看	L7
	9	kè	客	L18
	9	liàng	亮	L18
	9	měi	美	L8
	9	nán	南	L10
	9	nǎo	脑	L14
*	9	pián	便	SC28
	9	qián	前	L9
	9	shì	是	L4
*	9	shì	室	SC73
	9	sī	思	L17
*	9	tiáo	条	SC51
	9	wèi	为	L8
	9	wū	屋	L20
	9	xǐ	洗	L17
	9	xìn	信	L14
	9	xīng	星	L13

	9	yán	研		L18
	9	yào	要		L6
	9	yīn	音		L18
*	9	yīng	英		SC14
	9	yuē	約	约	L20
	9	zá	咱		L9
	9	zěn	怎		L8
	9	zhòng	重		L10
	9	zuó	昨		L19

10

	10	bèi	被		L22
	10	bìng	病		L20
*	10	cǎo	草	草	SC55
	10	chá	茶		L10
	10	chú	除		L12
	10	dǎo	倒		L20
	10	fèi	費	费	L23
	10	gāng	剛	刚	L22
	10	gāo	高		L8
	10	.ge	個	个	L5
*	10	gē	哥		SC41
	10	hài	害		L17
	10	hòu	候		L14
	10	jì	記	记	L18
	10	jiā	家		L13
	10	jiè	借		L22
	10	jiǔ	酒		L10
*	10	kū	哭		SC37
	10	liú	留		L23
	10	lǚ	旅		L23
	10	mǎ	馬	马	L21
	10	.men	們	们	L9
	10	ná	拿		L21
	10	nǎ	哪		L4
	10	něi	哪		L4
	10	néng	能		L9
	10	páng	旁		L15
	10	qǐ	起		L9
	10	qì	氣	气	L18
	10	róng	容		L16
	10	shī	師	师	L8
	10	shí	時	时	L9

	10	shū	書	书	L6
	10	sòng	送		L13
	10	téng	疼		L20
	10	xí	息		L23
	10	xiào	笑		L13
*	10	xiào	校		SC36
	10	yuán	原		L14
	10	yuán	員	员	L19
*	10	yuàn	院		SC67
	10	zhàn	站		L15
	10	zhēn	眞/真	真	L11
*	10	zhēn	針	针	SC68
*	10	zhī	只		SC52
*	10	zhǐ	紙	纸	SC7

11

*	11	bù	部		SC25
	11	chàng	唱		L18
	11	cóng	從	从	L8
	11	dài	帶	带	L21
	11	.de	得		L6
	11	dì	第		L14
	11	dòng	動	动	L14
	11	dōu	都		L5
	11	gòu	夠		L16
	11	guà	掛	挂	L21
	11	guó	國	国	L5
	11	jì	寄		L21
	11	jià	假		L13
	11	jiào	教		L19
*	11	jiē	接		SC35
	11	lèi	累		L15
	11	lián	連	连	L18
	11	liáng	涼	凉	L20
*	11	nín	您		SC1
	11	péi	陪		L22
	11	piào	票		L21
	11	qiú	球		L12
	11	shào	紹	绍	SC12
	11	shì	視	视	L19
	11	sù	宿		L13
	11	tíng	停		L19
*	11	tuī	推		SC64

	笔画	pinyin	繁体	简体	Lesson
	11				
	11	wǎn	晚		L17
	11	wèn	問	问	L7
	11	xí	習	习	L16
	11	xiàn	現	现	L15
	11	xǔ	許	许	L22
*	11	xuě	雪		SC45
	11	yǎn	眼		L20
	11	yú	魚	鱼	L10
	11	zhāng	張	张	L22
	11	zhè	這	这	L6
	11	zhèi	這	这	L6
	11	zhuān	專	专	L18
	11	zuò	做		L5
	12				
	12	bào	報	报	L23
*	12	bǐ	筆	笔	SC6
	12	cài	菜		L10
	12	chǎng	場	场	L21
	12	dān	單	单	L22
	12	děng	等		L17
	12	duǎn	短		L12
	12	duì	隊	队	L19
	12	fā	發	发	L19
	12	fàn	飯	饭	L7
	12	gěi	給	给	L7
	12	guì	貴	贵	L12
*	12	hán	寒		SC77
	12	hē	喝		L10
*	12	hēi	黑	黑	SC71
*	12	huà	畫	画	SC5
	12	jǐ	幾	几	L4
	12	jiān	間	间	L9
	12	jiē	街		L16
	12	jiù	就		L7
	12	kāi	開	开	L10
	12	mǎi	買	买	L6
*	12	pǎo	跑		SC16
	12	qī	期		L13
	12	rán	然		L17
	12	shū	舒		L20
*	12	sù	訴	诉	SC76
	12	tāng	湯	汤	L10

	笔画	pinyin	繁体	简体	Lesson
	12	tí	提		L21
	12	tì	替		L21
*	12	tiē	貼	贴	SC74
	12	xǐ	喜		L10
	12	yóu	郵	邮	L21
*	12	yuè	越		SC40
	12	.zhe	著	着	L10
	12	zhōu	週	周	L23
	12	zuì	最		L11
	13				
*	13	ǎi	矮		SC13
*	13	ài	愛	爱	SC21
	13	bān	搬		L15
*	13	bǎo	飽	饱	SC27
	13	dāng	當	当	L17
	13	dào	道		L15
	13	diàn	電	电	L9
*	13	dùn	頓	顿	SC10
	13	gāi	該	该	L19
	13	gēn	跟		L5
	13	guò	過	过	L8
	13	hào	號	号	L12
	13	huà	話	话	L9
	13	huì	會	会	L11
*	13	jiǎo	腳	脚	SC63
	13	jìn	進	进	L15
	13	jīng	睛		L20
	13	jīng	經	经	L23
	13	kuài	塊	块	L12
	13	lǐ	裏	里	L12
	13	lù	路		L16
	13	.ma	嗎	吗	L4
	13	mā	媽	妈	L14
	13	pèng	踫		L21
	13	shǔ	暑		L23
	13	shuì	睡		L17
*	13	tiào	跳		SC17
*	13	wǎn	碗		SC32
	13	wàn	萬	万	L22
	13	xiǎng	想		L8
	13	xīn	新		L18
*	13	yān	煙	烟	SC23

	笔画	拼音	繁体	简体	课
	13	yì	意		L17
*	13	yùn	運	运	SC42
	13	zhào	照		L22
	14				
	14	duì	對	对	L9
*	14	fá	罰	罚	SC75
	14	gē	歌		L18
	14	guǎn	管		L16
	14	guàn	慣	惯	L16
*	14	hàn	漢	汉	SC15
	14	jǐn	緊	紧	L22
*	14	lǜ	綠	绿	SC69
	14	màn	慢		L17
	14	.me	麼	么	L5
	14	piào	漂		L18
	14	qīng	輕	轻	L22
*	14	rèn	認	认	SC47
	14	shí	實	实	L18
	14	shuō	說	说	L7
	14	suàn	算		L23
	14	tuǐ	腿		L22
	14	xiàng	像	象	L11
	14	yǔ	語	语	L23
	14	yuǎn	遠	远	L21
	15				
	15	è	餓	饿	L11
	15	jié	節	节	L13
	15	kè	課	课	L4
	15	liàn	練	练	L19
	15	lóu	樓	楼	L15
*	15	mài	賣	卖	SC9
	15	qǐng	請	请	L7
	15	rè	熱	热	L20
	15	shéi	誰	谁	L6
	15	tán	談	谈	L11
	15	xié	鞋		L14
	15	xiě	寫	写	L12
	15	yàng	樣	样	L8
	15	yǐng	影		L16
	15	yuè	樂	乐	L18
	16				
	16	bàn	辦	办	L22
	16	cuò	錯	错	L10
	16	dān	擔	担	L21
	16	dǒng	懂		L11
	16	guǎn	館	馆	L10
	16	jī	機	机	L21
*	16	jiǎn	撿	捡	SC65
*	16	māo	貓	猫	SC53
	16	qián	錢	钱	L12
*	16	qīn	親	亲	SC80
*	16	shāo	燒	烧	SC66
	16	shū	輸	输	L19
*	16	shù	樹	树	SC56
	16	tóu	頭	头	L12
*	16	xǐng	醒		SC57
	16	xué	學	学	L4
*	16	yā	鴨	鸭	SC38
	16	zǎo	澡		L17
	17				
	17	bāng	幫	帮	L16
	17	diǎn	點	点	L6
	17	hái	還	还	L12
	17	liǎn	臉	脸	L17
*	17	qiáng	牆	墙	SC49
	17	sài	賽	赛	L19
*	17	shēng	聲	声	SC60
	17	suī	雖	虽	L17
	17	xiè	謝	谢	L16
	17	yīng	應	应	L19
	17	zǒng	總	总	L22
	18				
*	18	dài	戴		SC30
	18	jī	雞	鸡	L13
*	18	jiù	舊	旧	SC59
*	18	shuāng	雙	双	SC46
	18	tí	題	题	L20
	18	yī	醫	医	L20
	19				
	19	biān	邊	边	L15
*	19	guān	關	关	SC24
*	19	huài	壞	坏	SC8
	19	lí	離	离	L21
	19	nán	難	难	L19
*	19	shì	識	识	SC48
	19	yào	藥	药	L20

20				
20	jiào	覺	觉	L17
20	miàn	麵	面	L12
20	yíng	贏	赢	L19
20	zhōng	鐘	钟	L13
21				
21	xiǎng	響	响	L16
22				
22	huān	歡	欢	L10
22	tīng	聽	听	L12
23				
23	biàn	變	变	L19
23	yàn	驗	验	L23
24				
24	ràng	讓	让	L20

Index 3. Sentence Patterns

Sentence Pattern	Lesson–Grammar Section
a 啊, the question particle	L8–B5
Action in sequence	L7–A5
	L23–A1
Affirmative and negative sentences	L4–A2.1
Antonym compounds	L12–B4
bǎ 把 construction	L15–A1
【把…給…】	L16–C1
	L22–A1
.ba 吧, the agreement particle	L7–B5
the suggestion particle	L10–B1
the suggestion and command particle	L13–B3
the particle	L15–B2
bāngmáng 幫(忙), the usage of	L16–B3
bèi 被, the passive marker	L22–A3
bǐ 比 (see comparison)	L4–A2.2
bù 不, the adverb	L4–A2.1
bú.shì…jiù.shì 【不是…就是…】	L11–A1
…*bú.shì…, yě bú.shì… ér.shì…* 【不是…也不是…而是…】	L8–A2
búdàn…érqiě/ bìngqiě 【不但…而且/並且】	L21–A3
bù.déliǎo 不得了, the complement	L23–B3
…*bùrú…* 【A 不如 B】	L19–B1
bú.shì…ma? 【不是…嗎？】	L8–A8
cái 才, the adverb	L9–A5
the conditional usage of	L17–A3
more on 才 and 就 *jiù*	L23–A2
Choice-type (A-not-A) questions	L4–A3
chú.le…yǐwài 【除了…以外】	L12–A1
Clauses, Chinese	L10–A3
Chinese clauses/complex sentences	L11–C1
cónglái 從來, the usage of	L22–B1
Coming or going to a place	L6–A2
Comparative constructions/comparisons	L10–A2
more on comparative constructions	L12–C1
of two events	L19–A2
of two performances	L19–A3
of distance	L21–A5
Complements, verbs with descriptive complements	L10–A1
manner or degree complements	L11–A3

verbs with extent complements	L14–A6
verbs with directional complements	L15–A2.1, A2.2
Compounds vs. noun phrases	L7–B1
of antonyms	L12–B4
Conjunctions, correlative	L11–A1
Conveyance, coming/going to a place	L13–A1
emphasis on the conveyance	L13–A2
cóng 從, the preposition	L20–A2
cóng…dào…lái/qù 【從…到…來/去】	L9–A4
cóng…zuò…dào…lái/qù 【從…坐…到…來/去】	L13–A3
cónglái 從來	L22–B1
dǎ jǐ zhé? 打幾折 expression	L12–B3
dǎ pēntì 打噴嚏, the usage of	L20–B7
dài 帶, the co-verb/verb	L21–A6.1, A6.2
dào.shì (bù) 倒是(不) 【Adj 倒是(不) Adj, 可是…】	L8–A3
.de 的 the possessive marker	L4
optional possessive marker	L8–B2
other usage of	L12–B2
the nominalizer	L12–B2.1
the situational	L12–B2.2
…的 N construction	L10–A3, L 11–C1, L13–C1
.de 得 【V 得 Adj】	L10–A1
extent complement marker	L14–A6
manner/degree complement marker	L11–A3
resultative verb complement marker	L7–A6, L9–A6, L15–A2.3, L18–A4
.de, the differences of 的、得、地	L23–C1
–.*dehěn* 得很, the usage of SV	L16–B5
…*de huà* …的話, the particle	L15–B1
…*de shí.hòu* 的時候, expression	L13–B2
děi 得, the auxiliary verb	L5–A6
distance, the expression of	L21–A4
… *duì…guòmǐn* 【A 對 B 過敏】	L20–B4
… *duì…hǎo* 【A 對 B 好】	L10–B2
… *duì… yǒu bāngzhù* 【VO 對 X 有幫助】	L23–B2
… *duì… yǒu xìng.qù* 【A 對 B 有興趣】	L17–A4.2
… *duì… yǒu yì.si* 【A 對 B 有意思】	L17–A4
… *duì… yǒu yǐngxiǎng* 【A 對 B 有影響】	L16–A1.1
… *duì… yǒu yánjiù* 【A 對 X 有研究】	L18–A2
duō/shǎo V *yì.diǎnr* O 【多／少 V 一點兒 O】	L13–B1
duó 多, the interrogative adverb	L20–B3
duō.shǎo qián 多少錢, expression	L7–B3

Durative time expressions	L14–A5
Equational sentences	L4–A2
Frequency expressions	L11–A2, A2.3
gěi 給，the verb	L14–A3
the co-verb	L9–A1
【A 給 B 寄 O 來/去】	L18–A3,
more on the co-verb	L20–B6, L 22–A1
gēn 跟，the conjunction	L5–A2.3
the co-verb	L14–A7, L 19–B2
the difference between *gēn, hé, yě* 跟、和、也	L19–C1
gòu 夠，the usage of	L16–B4
... *guǎn* ... *jiào*... 【...管...叫...】	L16–B1
.*guò* 過，the experiential aspect marker	L10–A4
with frequency expressions	L11–A2.2
with durative expressions	L14–A5
hái.shì 還是，A or B construction	L6–A5
hài 害，the causative marker	L17–B2
hào 號 as "size"	L12–B5
...*hǎo.le* 好了，the particle	L9–B5
hǎo.xiàng...shì.de 【好像...似的】	L11–B4
huì，the auxiliary verb	L9–B3
jǐ 幾，the question word	L5–A5
jǐ yuè jǐ hào 幾月幾號，sentences with question word	L4–A5.2
jiào 叫，the verb	L8–B1
jiào 叫，the co-verb 叫 and *ràng* 讓	L20–A1
jiè 借，the usage of	L22–A1
jiù 就，the adverb	L7–A4
the usage of *jiù* in time expression	L23–A2
kàn 看，as "expressing opinions"	L9–B4
...*kě...*, *yào.bùrán*... 【可...，要不然...】	L17–A2
kě bié...cái hǎo 【可別...才好】	L13–B4
kě.yǐ 可以 *néng* 能，*huì* 會，auxiliary verb	L9–B3
kuài yì.diǎnr 快一點兒，the adverbial phrase	L17–B1
...*lái*， 【V...來】	L6–A2.1, A2.2
【V...來VO】	L6–A3
.*le* 了， the aspect marker	L6–A1
Completed action with .*le*	L6–A1.1
Change status with .*le*	L6–A1.2
Imminent action with .*le*	L6–A1.3
lí 離，expressions of distance	L21–A4, A5
lián ... dōu... 【連...都...】	L18–A1
Location, the Chinese concept of	L23–B1

.ma 嗎, questions	L4–A4
	L6–A2.2
màn yì.diǎnr 慢一點兒, the adverbial phrase	L17–B1
míngmíng 明明, the reduplicated adverb	L22–B3
Movable time adverb	L5–A2.1, L9–A2
nándào 難道, the movable adverb	L22–B2
nánshòu vs. *nánguò* 難受 vs. 難過	L20–B8
nǎr 哪兒, the question word	L6–A2.1
.ne 呢, the question particle	L4–B1
něi yì tiān 哪一天, the question word	L4–A5.3
néng 能, the auxiliary verb	L9–B3
nòng 弄, the causative marker	L17–B2
Notion of "this," "last," and "next"	L6–B2
Notion of "last time, this time, and next time"	L11–B1
Noun phrases	L5–A1
Noun plus noun	L5–A1.1
Noun (time) plus noun (time)	L5–A1.2
Nouns modified by a clause	L13–C1
Noun phrases with measure words	L5–A1.3
piānpiān 偏偏, the reduplicated adverb	L22–B3
Pivotal construction	L13–A4
Place words	L7–A1, L15–A3
Principle	
From Topic to Comment	L8–A3
From Whole to Part	L4–A1, L5–A1, L15–A3, L23–B1
Simultaneous Existence	L5–A2.1, L13–A3
Temporal Sequence	L6–A3.1, L9–A3, A4, L10–A2, L11–A2.1, L12–C1.1, L14–A6, L15–A1, L19–A2, L20–A1, L21–A2
Progressive aspect	L8–A4
Purpose of coming and going to a place	L6–A3
qǐng vs. *wèn* 請 vs. 問	L9–B2
...qù, 【V...去】	L6–A2.1, A2.2
【V...去 VO】	L6–A3
Question-word questions	L4–A5
Question words, 都(不)...construction	L11–A6, L14–A2, L17–A1
question words as indefinites	L14–A2
ràng 讓, the co-verb 叫 and 讓	L20–A1
Relative time expressions	L9–A2
rèn.shì vs. *zhī.dào* 認識 vs. 知道	L15–B3

Resultative verbs	
actual form	L7–A6
potential form	L9–A6
more resultative verbs	L18–A4
shàng 上, in time expressions	L6–B2
shàng yí cì 上一次	L11–B1
shéi 誰, sentences with question word	L4–A5.4
shén.me 什麼, the question word	L5–A4
shén.me dì.fāng 什麼地方, sentences with question word	L6–A2.1
shén.me dōu..., jiù.shì... 【什麼都...，就是...】	L17–A1
shì....de 【是…的】	L8–A1
shì zuò...dào...lái/qù 【是坐…到…來/去】	L13–A2
...shòu ... de yǐngxiǎng 【受…的影響】	L16–A1
Stative verbs/adjectives	L4–A6
Subject omission	L13–B5
suīrán..., kě.shì/búguò/dàn.shì 【雖然…可是/不過/但是…】	L8–A5
Telling the time by the clock	L6–B1
tì 替, the co-verb	L21–A7
Time when expressions	L6–A4
Time when and departure point	L9–A4
Topicalization	L9–A7
V *lái* V *qù* V來V去	L12–B1
Verb–object (VO) compounds	L4–B2
Verb–object construction	L8–B4
Vivid reduplicates	L18–B1
wàng...V 往 …V	L16–B1
wèishén.me 為什麼,	L8–A6
and *yīn.wèi..., suǒ.yǐ...* 【因為 … 所以…】	L17–C1
Winning prizes and awards	L19–B3
xià 下, in time expression	L6–B2
xià yí cì 下一次	L11–B1
.xià.qù 下去, the successive aspect	L23–B5
xiān...zài... 【先...再...】	L7–A5
xiān... ránhòu... 【先...然後 …】	L23–A1
xiǎng 想, the auxiliary verb	L8–A7
xiàng...yíyàng 【像…一樣】	L8–B3
xīngqíjǐ 星期幾, the question word	L4–A5.1
xìng 姓, the verb	L8–B1
yào.shì..., jiù... 【要是 …，就 … 】	L11–A4
yě 也, the adverb	L4–A2.2
yě 也, difference between *yě* and *gēn/hé* 跟、和	L5–A2.3
*...yě.shì...*X 也是, expression	L5–B1

yìbiānr...yìbiānr... 【一邊兒...一邊兒...】	L22–A2
yī...jiù 【一...就】	L14–A4
yì.diǎnr 一點兒, the adverbial phrase	L7–B2, L13–B1, L17–B1
yì.diǎnr yě/dōu bù 【一點兒也/都不】	L11–A5
yíkuàir 一塊兒, the adverbial phrase	L9–B1
yīn.wèi...suǒ.yǐ... 【因為...所以】	L17–C1
....yíxià ...V 一下, expression	L7–B4
...yǐhòu 以後, expression	L9–A2
...yǐqián 以前, expression	L9–A2
yòng 用, the co-verb	L21–A2
yǒu 有, the possessive verb	L5–A1
yǒu 有, the existential verb	L7–A3
yǒu 有, occurs with *yě* and *dōu* 也、都	L5–A2.2
yǒu 有, choice-type questions with transitive verb *yǒu*	L5–A3
yǒu 有, sentences and questions with	L5–A2
yǒu shén.me hǎo V.*de* 有什麼好V的！	L12–B5
yòu 又, again	L13–B5
yòu...yòu 【又...又...】	L16–A2
yuē 約, the usage of	L20–B1
yuè...yuè... 【越...越...】	L12–A2
zài 再 vs. *yòu* 又	L13–B5
zài guò...jiù 【再過...就...】	L19–A1
zài 在, the main verb	L7–A2
the progressive aspect marker	L8–A4
the preposition	L9–A3
zài... shàng 在 ...上, the prepositional phrase	L11–B2
the post-verbal preposition	L14–A1
cóng 從, the preposition	L20–B2
zhè 這, in time expression	L6–B2
zhè yí cì 這一次	L11–B1
–.zhe 著, the progressive aspect marker	L10–A5
zhèng 正, the adverb	L8–A4, L21–A1
zhī.dào vs. *rèn.shì* 知道 vs. 認識	L15–B3
zhǐ.shì 只是, the adverb	L20–B5
zhǐyào... jiù... 【只要 ...就...】	L13–A5
zuì 最, the superlative marker	L11–B3
zuò...dào...lái/qù 【坐...到...來/去】	L13–A1

Index 4. Measure Words

This list includes measure words that are not listed in lesson vocabularies but appear as explanatory notes to new words.

◎ **By Pinyin**

Pinyin	Character		English	Example	L
bǎ	把		bunch	花兒	
bàng	磅		pound	牛肉	13
bāo	包		pack	煙	
bēi	杯		measure word for tea, wine, coffee	茶、啤酒、咖啡、汽水兒	7
běn	本		measure word for books, notebooks	書、本子、小說、字典	6
bù	部		measure word for films, cars, etc.	電影兒、片子、車、公共汽車、公車、小巴	11
chǎng	場	场	measure word for games and performances	比賽、球賽	
cì	次		measure word for frequency	看電影兒	11
dǎ	打		dozen	啤酒	16
dào	道		measure word for dishes	菜	10
dǐng	頂	顶	measure word for hat	帽子	
dòng	棟	栋	measure word for building	宿舍	
duì	隊	队	team		19
duìr	對兒	对儿	pair		17
dùn	頓	顿	measure word for meals	飯	13
duǒ	朵		measure word for flowers	花兒	
fènr	份兒	份儿	measure word for gifts and newspapers	禮物、報紙	14
fēng	封		measure word for letter	信、電子信	
* .ge	個	个	measure word for persons and things	籃球、麵包、電腦、電話、隨身聽、漢字、學分、學期、餃子、漢堡、三明治、圖書館、商場、飛機場、超級市場、女兒、兒子、婦女	5

				、演員、耶誕節、聖誕節、體育館、禮物、雷射唱盤、游泳池、網球場、箱子、書架、孩子、吹風機、頭、球、裁判、球拍、藉口、高爾夫球、噴嚏、法子、問題、包裹、小時、鐘頭、停車位、十字路口、要求、計劃、夏天、典禮、輪胎、獎學金、期末考、大考	
gēn	根		measure word for cigarettes, hair	煙、頭髮	
guàn	罐	罐	can	汽水兒、啤酒	
hé	盒		box	糖	
hú	壺	壶	pot	茶	10
* jiā	家		measure word for stores, restaurants, cinema	書店、公司、百貨公司、百貨大樓、飯館兒、雜貨店、銀行	6
jià	架		measure word for airplane	飛機	
* jiān	間	间	measure word for rooms and building	宿舍、實驗室、大學、公寓、洗衣房、空房、房間、屋子、廚房、洗澡間、客廳、飯廳、廁所	15
jiàn	件		measure word for upper garments and coats, affairs	衣服、大衣、毛衣、外套、襯衫、事	12
jiāo	跤		measure word for falling on the ground	摔	20
* jié	節	节	measure word for classes	課	5
jīn	斤		catty	牛肉	
juǎn	卷		measure word for audio tape	錄音帶、膠帶	
kē	顆	颗	measure word for teeth and candy	牙(齒)、糖	
kǒu	口		measure word for people (in a family)	人	16
kuài	塊	块	measure word for candy	糖	
liàng	輛	辆	measure word for vehicle	車、小巴	

mén	門	门	measure word for courses	課	6
pán	盤	盘	measure word for audio tapes and dishes	磁帶、菜	
piān	篇		measure word for articles and compositions	作文、報告	
piàn	片		slice	麵包	
píng	瓶		bottle	汽水兒	
qún	群		measure word for a group of people or animals	人	12
shǒu	首		measure word for songs	歌曲	18
shuāng	雙	双	pair	靴子、手套、球鞋	8
suǒ	所		measure word for houses	房子	
táng	堂		measure word for classes	課	5
tàng	趟		measure word for trips	玩	21
tào	套		set	衣服	12
tiáo	條	条	measure word for long and soft things	魚、褲子、圍巾兒、圍脖兒、裙子、裙褲、牛仔褲、路、街	
tóu	頭	头	headful	頭髮	
wǎn	碗		bowl	湯	
wèi	位		measure word for people (polite)	老師、司機、師傅、導遊、警察	10
xiē	些		measure word for plural nouns	東西	7
zhāng	張	张	measure word for paper and face	支票、信用卡、畫兒、山水畫、照片、相片、郵票、臉、領單、罰單	
zhī	隻		measure word for birds, dogs, eyes, and one shoe	雞、烤鴨、火雞、貓、狗、兔子、眼睛、球鞋	
zhī	枝		measure word for branches and pens	筆	
zhǒng	種	种	kind	語言	
zuò	座		measure word for mountains	山	